THEGOOD
web site
GUIDE 2007

THEGOOD
web site
GUIDE 2007

graham edmonds

HARPER

Harper
An Imprint of HarperCollins*Publishers*
77–85 Fulham Palace Road,
Hammersmith, London W6 8JB
www.harpercollins.co.uk

A Paperback Original 2006
1

A catalogue record of this book is available from
the British Library

ISBN-13 978 0 00 722515 6
ISBN-10 0 00 722515 6
Set in News Gothic

Typeset by RefineCatch Limited, Bungay, Suffolk
Printed and bound in Great Britain by
Clays Ltd, St Ives plc

Contents

The Good Web Site Guide's Top 10s of the Internet

Introduction

Ten of the Best

The Good Web Site Guide's Top 10s
of the Internet

1. **www.bbc.co.uk** – for TV, news and many free services
2. **www.google.co.uk** – more than just a search engine
3. **www.amazon.co.uk** – not just a book store any more
4. **www.apple.com** – an absolute must for all Apple users
5. **www.24hourmuseum.org.uk** – access to all our galleries and museums
6. **www.ebay.co.uk** – for some a way of life, for others the best online auction site
7. **www.imdb.com** – if anyone has appeared on screen they're listed here on the Internet Movie Database.
8. **www.shockwave.com** – for games and graphics they don't come any better
9. **www.howstuffworks.com** – if you want to find out how something works, start here
10. **www.wikipedia.org** – the people's encyclopaedia

Welcome to the latest edition of *The Good Web Site Guide*. We've now sold over 350,000 copies to date. This edition is fully updated, all the sites have been checked and rechecked, and I've added over 500 more this year. The book now contains well over 5,000 sites in all.

I review the very best sites in each category, and then look for those sites that offer something unique or have features that make them stand out and recommend those too. I also list alternatives, especially in the popular genres such as music, shopping or finance. Essentially I concentrate on what's really useful, and would like to encourage people to see the Internet as a tool like any other and not be intimidated by it.

So what else has changed in a year since the last edition? The number of blogs we're including has increased dramatically;

we've found that they can be a really good source of information, especially when it comes to technology. They are great too for just having your say about something you're passionate about. There are also new sections on emerging technologies such as BitTorrent, RSS and even Widgets.

Quality is still a big issue. The costs and time involved in maintaining a good site are sometimes prohibitive, so that many sites don't seem to be updated as frequently as they should be, while others just die through lack of interest and funding. Still hundreds of sites go live every day, showing that creativity and entrepreneurialism are alive and kicking on the Net.

Lack of time and resources often result in site names (URLs) being turned over to directories, search engines or even adult entertainment sites. Please do let me know if you find any major changes to the sites recommended in this book. I can assure you that all the reviews are accurate at the time of writing. Send comments to: **goodwebsiteguide@hotmail.com**

Keeping Safe

Some people are worried about using their credit card to shop on the Net. In theory it's safer than giving credit card details over the phone, because on most sites the information is encrypted. Before giving out card details, check that you are on a secure line, a small padlock icon will appear on your toolbar, and the http:// prefix will change to https:// Providing you shop from UK sites, you are fully covered by the same fair-trade laws that cover every form of shopping in the UK, but buying from abroad could have some risks attached. If in doubt, shop from reputable firms and known brand names.

There's still a great deal of concern about cookies. A cookie is the popular name of a file which holds some information about your machine and, only if you give out that information, about you. They have a sinister reputation but they enable web site owners to monitor traffic and find out who is visiting their sites. In theory, this means they can tailor their content to their customers or provide a better service. If you're worried about cookies, you can easily delete them or set your computer not to receive them. Be aware, however, that many sites do need cookies to function, especially shopping sites. Check out **www.cookiecentral.com** for more information.

Spyware and Malware is becoming a real issue, especially for Microsoft users, despite their attempts to make Windows more secure, let's hope the new operating system will prove a tougher nut to crack. With many sites use Spyware for sinister purposes such as obtaining credit card details, you should always ensure your system is clean of it, especially if you have an 'always on' broadband connection. Check out our security section on page 423 if you need more information.

Using the Book

Ratings
Standards are now so high that nearly all the sites included in the book follow the key rules on web design; however, some deserve extra recognition.

 Information merit – this is awarded when the site content goes beyond what would normally be considered reasonable and provides a level of information that is exceptional.

 Service merit – awarded to those sites that offer something unique or something that you'd otherwise have to pay for, it's not a reflection of how good the staff are or how quickly they deliver.

 Design merit – given to those sites that ignore the web site sausage-factory approach to design and produce something definitive or use the technology in an original way.

 GWSG **Top Site Award** – reserved for those exceptional sites that offer a combination of quality design, service and content.

In this guide I'm not pretending to be a judge and jury; these ratings are just my opinion, that of a customer and consumer.

Origin – a site's country of origin is not always obvious. This can be important, especially if you are buying from abroad. There may be restrictions or taxes that aren't obvious at the time of purchase. Also, information that is shown as general may apply to one part of the world and not another. For instance, gardening advice on a US site may not be appropriate in the UK. It's also important to know the origin if you're shopping, as import duties and taxes may apply if you're buying something from abroad. Often these are not mentioned and you could end up with a hefty bill which negates the advantage of going there in the first place.

If you have any suggestions as to how I can improve *The Good Web Site Guide* or have a site you think should be included in the 2008 edition, then please e-mail me at **goodwebsiteguide@hotmail.com**

Most Useful

The Good Web Site Guide's Top 10s
of the Internet

1. **www.google.co.uk** – the world's most used search engine
2. **www.kelkoo.co.uk** – for finding the best price for everything
3. **www.yell.com** – the Yellow Pages online
4. **www.met-office.gov.uk** – we all need to know about the weather
5. **www.expedia.co.uk** – for all your travel needs
6. **www.newsnow.co.uk** – create your own news channel
7. **www.which.net** – when you want to know which is best
8. **www.ukonline.gov.uk** – government information
9. **www.nhsdirect.nhs.uk** – help from the NHS
10. **www.pti.org.uk** – transport information, route finding and more

Acknowledgements

I'd just like to end by thanking a few important people:

Firstly, a big thank you to all those people who have written in with suggestions and sites for me to check out, several hundred sites have been included in the book as a result of people e-mailing me. Particular thanks to Margaret Dickinson.

To the excellent team at HarperCollins.

All my many friends and colleagues for their support and suggestions.

Anyone who bought the first books and the booksellers who supported them.

Especially to Deborah Gray for her great patience and excellent advice and ever increasing contributions to the book.

And to Michaela for all else that matters.

Aircraft and Aviation

A

The Internet has proved a great resource for pilots, those with an interest in the history of aviation and those who just like to watch.

www.aeroseek.com   US
AVIATION LINKS
An excellent portal offering over 10,000 aviation-related links in 24 categories – a good place to start for any enthusiast.

See also:
http://luchtvaart.pagina.nl – a comprehensive Dutch site.
www.landings.com – use the directory to navigate this massive but unwieldy site.
www.pilotfriend.com – excellent for information and links.
www.risingup.com – includes performance information on over 500 aircraft.

www.pilotweb.co.uk   UK
PILOT WEB
An excellent overview of the aviation scene with lots of features, help and information. The site is well laid out and easy to navigate with lots of interaction, although you need to subscribe to get the best out of it.

www.aeroflight.co.uk   UK
AVIATION ENTHUSIASTS
This site attempts to offer an 'information stop' for all aviation enthusiasts. It's clearly laid out and has details on international air forces, a section on the media (including specialist books and bookshops), a discussion forum, as well as details of air shows and museums.

www.flyer.co.uk   UK
AVIATION IN THE UK
A good and well-established portal site from *Flyer* magazine devoted to all things aviation in the UK, it offers information on the weather, news, a shop plus chat and forums too. It's excellent for links and there's a slightly pricey ISP facility too.

www.flightinternational.com
UK
AVIATION NEWS

An online version of the best-selling magazine with articles, information and news all laid out in a slick but uninspiring site. Basically it's a taster of what's in the mag and you have to subscribe to get the best out of it; however, there's good information on events, a bookshop and a jobs section.

Other sites from specialist magazines:

www.airlinerworld.com – better than usual magazine spin-off site; you can buy merchandise and chat to other enthusiasts, there's a small gallery too.

www.airpictorial.com – another site plugging the magazine, it's got some news stories, some good historical content and offers aircraft schematic plans to purchase.

www.airsceneuk.co.uk – an e-zine provided by a group of dedicated enthusiasts, this site has lots of information, nostalgia, links to related sites and personal flying accounts. It's also got an air show listing with reports, previews and some good photography.

www.airspacemag.com – the magazine of the Smithsonian Air and Space Museum has a few really interesting articles, but not much else.

Devoted to Aircraft

www.airliners.net
UK

AIRLINERS

With nearly 700,000 photos, this is a huge site. It has a good search facility and should appeal to photographers as well as plane spotters. It also offers a shop, news, chat, links and a huge amount of information.

See also:

www.airchive.com – a labour of love with masses of material posted by someone who is clearly an airline aficionado, possibly without equal.

www.globalaircraft.org – a vast site with information primarily on US aircraft with lots of information and interactivity.

www.zap16.com – excellent site that offers fact sheets and pictures on both military and civil aircraft.

Military and Defence

www.janesonline.com   US
JANES
Janes is the authority on defence forces world-wide and for a
price you can buy books and CD-ROMs that contain all the
information you'll ever need about the world's military might
as well as Jane's Terrorism and Insurgency Centre. You have
to register to get anything out of it, but there are a number of
free newsletter options; anything else you have to pay for. It's
a little stingy really, but I suppose they are protecting their
assets.

www.raf.mod.uk   UK
ROYAL AIR FORCE
This site features lots of information on the RAF – you can
locate a display or fly past, find career advice, check out a
squadron or get technical information. The history section is
particularly good with data covering aircraft from the very first
planes to the latest, illustrated by a gallery of pictures; however,
the time-line section still only reaches 1989.

www.wpafb.af.mil/museum   US

US AIR FORCE MUSEUM
A superbly detailed site with masses of data on the aircraft and
their history from the first planes to space flight. The archive
section is particularly good with features on particular types of
aircraft and weapons, and information about how they were
developed.

See also:
www.fas.org – the Federation of American Scientists has a
fascinating, if somewhat scary site (e.g. nuclear bomb blast
calculator), it contains a listing of the world's military aircraft
too.
www.fighter-planes.com – lots of stats and information about the
world's fighter planes.
www.mar.co.uk – home of the Military Aviation Review with lots
of photos.
www.rafmuseum.org.uk – the RAF museums at Hendon and
Cosford.

A

History

www.century-of-flight.net   US

AVIATION HISTORY

A good overview of the history of flying with background on the
planes and pilots. Excellent for school projects and a good
general browse for anyone interested in the history of flight.

http://theaerodrome.com   UK

FIRST WORLD WAR

Devoted to the aircraft and aces of the First World War, this site
offers lots of background information, personal experiences and
details about the pilots who fought above the trenches. For an
alternative site on Second World War aircraft try
www.compsoc.man.ac.uk/~wingman

See also:
www.battle-of-britain.com – an overview of the battle, the
aircraft and those who fought in it.
www.battleofbritain.net – home of the Battle of Britain Historical
Society.
www.historicaircraftcollection.ltd.uk – home to a collection of
WW2 planes, beautifully restored.
www.spitfiresociety.demon.co.uk – all you need to know about
Spitfires.
www.thunder-and-lightnings.co.uk – a site devoted to British
post war military aircraft, with lots of detail; the site is slowly
being updated.
www.vintageaircraft.org – Vintage Aircraft Association's site with
events, information and photos.

Helicopters, Gliders, Balloons, and Aerobatics

www.gliderpilot.net   UK

GLIDER PILOT NETWORK

Weather, news, links and information on all forms of gliding,
plus chat and classified ads. You need to register to get the best
out of the site.

www.iac.org   US

AEROBATICS

The site of the International Aerobatic Club and the place to go
for information on the sport. See also **www.aerobatics.org.uk**
for the British Aerobatic Association.

Also worth checking out:

http://avia.russian.ee – a not that up-to-date overview of the world's helicopters.

http://exp-aircraft.com – all you need to find out about experimental aircraft and where to buy one.

www.aerostationery.co.uk – maps for aviators.

www.babo.org.uk – the British Association of Balloon Operators.

www.bmaa.org – the British Microlight Aircraft Association.

www.eballoon.org – comprehensive ballooning encyclopaedia including history, clubs, technical information and where to find a ride.

www.globalaircraft.org – a vast site with information primarily on US aircraft with lots of information and interactivity.

www.helicoptermuseum.co.uk – not great but has good links.

www.intotheblue.co.uk/flying-lessons.shtml – flying lessons and aerial experiences.

www.pprune.com – gossip, news and trivia from the Professional Pilot's rumour network.

www.rotor.com – helicopter industry news plus information and links.

www.start-flying.com – here you can get an overview of what it takes to start flying.

www.ulflyingmag.com – oddly designed, but informative site on ultra light flying.

Miscellaneous: Accidents, Maps and Reviews

www.airdisaster.com   US

NO.1 AVIATION SAFETY RESOURCE

A rather macabre site that reviews each major air crash, and looks into the reasons behind what happened. It's not for the squeamish, but the cockpit voice recordings and eyewitness accounts make fascinating, if disturbing, reading. There are some really annoying pop-up adverts on this site, which spoils the visit. See also **www.aaib.gov.uk** for the Air Accident Investigation Branch, which has a monthly bulletin with details of crashes and current investigations.

www.aviationconsumer.com   US

EQUIPMENT RATED

A consumer site dedicated to the aviation world with reviews and tests done on everything from planes to sunglasses. To get the best out of it you need to subscribe. Unfortunately, the dull layout makes it tedious to use in some respects.

See also:
www.aerostationery.co.uk – maps for aviators.
www.airsupply.co.uk – a Yorkshire-based shop supplying equipment and maps; online ordering available.

Antiques and Collectibles

The Internet is a great place to learn about antiques. It's also full of specialist sites run by enthusiastic collectors. If you want to take the risk of buying over the Net, the best prices are found on the big auction sites such as eBay, see page 44.

www.invaluable.com   UK
ART MARKET INTELLIGENCE
The aim of this site is to provide 'impartial electronic information on antiques, fine art and premium collectables to dealers, private buyers, museums and other institutions'. It proves to be a great resource providing contact details and links to hundreds of dealers, catalogues and auction houses worldwide. Use the 'iFind' section to search dealers' stock. The links section is particularly good with access to live auctions (via eBay) that enable you to participate in international sales.

www.atg-online.com   UK
ANTIQUES TRADE GAZETTE
A comprehensive and wide-ranging site covering all aspects of antique buying from auctions to dealers and classified advertising. You need to register to get the best out of it though.

www.antiquesbulletin.co.uk   UK
INTERACTIVE WORLD OF ANTIQUES
A well-laid-out site with good information and links to more specialist sites and dealers. It aims to be comprehensive and does a great job; there are details on auctions, advice on buying and selling, and a bookshop. You can also buy and sell from the site. To access the articles archive, you need to purchase a site licence.

www.antiquesworld.co.uk
UK

AN ALADDIN'S CAVE FOR THE ENTHUSIAST

Catch up on the latest news, obtain details on major and local fairs and events, book a course or indulge your interests by linking to a specialist online retailer or club. You can't buy from this site but the links and information are very good.

www.antiquestall.com
UK

ONLINE ANTIQUES STALL

A no-nonsense site devoted to selling antiques at fixed prices rather than by auction. There's a good search facility and each item has a picture and details of shipping.

www.dmgantiquefairs.com
UK

FOR THE LARGEST ANTIQUES FAIRS

DMG run the largest fairs in the UK. Their attractive site gives details of each fair, including dates, location and local tourist information.

www.portobelloroad.co.uk
UK

THE PORTOBELLO ROAD

The traders from London's well-known antiques market have got together a great site, which not only gives information about Portobello Road itself, but also offers excellent links and a directory.

www.lapada.co.uk
UK

ASSOCIATION OF ART AND ANTIQUE DEALERS

Get information on their fairs, advice on buying and selling antiques and learn how to care for your antiques.

www.bada.org
UK

BRITISH ANTIQUE DEALERS' ASSOCIATION

Attractive and informative listing site for antique dealers in the UK; grouped in 16 categories, it's easy to find a specialist in a particular area of interest. There's also information on their events and lots of advice on buying antiques.

www.bafra.org.uk
UK

THE BRITISH ANTIQUE FURNITURE RESTORERS' ASSOCIATION

If you have an antique that is in need of restoration, then this is a useful place to visit as it helps you find the right restorer. Apart from the usual links page, there's also information and articles

on caring for antiques and how to find a course if you want to
become a restorer.

www.antique-furniture.co.uk   UK
EUROPE'S LARGEST SELECTION
An attractive site from a specialist dealer offering a wide range
of furniture to choose from, good photography and the promise
of a high level of service to match.

Finding more dealers:
www.antiques-atlas.com – an interactive regional listing of
dealers and fairs.
www.antiques-uk.co.uk – a slightly confusing database of
dealers and information with an international section.

www.finds.org.uk   UK
THE PORTABLE ANTIQUITIES SCHEME
An interesting site devoted to volunteered archaeological and
antiquity finds made by individuals who offer to register them so
that they can be researched properly.

Collectibles

www.collectiques.co.uk   UK
COLLECTIBLES
Despite its fairly naff name, Collectiques is a good resource if
you're searching for information or that elusive piece for your
collection. It covers an impressive array of areas of interest from
toys to models, kits and architectural antiques. It's easy to use
and it's great for background info and links.

www.collectorcafe.com   UK
ONLINE COLLECTING COMMUNITY
A portal site which is great for classified ads links, articles and
chat covering most of the major areas of collecting.

www.worldcollectorsnet.com   US
BY COLLECTORS FOR COLLECTORS
Great for discussion groups, collector's message boards and
general chat about collecting. There's also a good online
magazine plus plenty of advice and links.

See also:
www.collectingchannel.com – another good US site.
www.collectingnetwork.com – links to collectors around the world.
www.collectors.com – great for Americana.

Some specialist sites worth a visit:
www.antiqueprintshop.co.uk – a good selection of antique prints.
www.oldbear.co.uk – antique teddy bears . . . ah.
www.sandracronan.com – antique jewellery from Burlington Arcade; upmarket, interesting design, but doesn't give prices!
www.tademagallery.com – to-kill-for art deco and nouveau jewellery, most prices on application.
www.tvtoys.com – links and information for memorabilia from old US TV shows.
www.wwii-collectibles.com – mainly stamps, covers, posters and coins.

Ceramics

www.studiopottery.com   UK
THE POTTERY STUDIO
Divided into three sections (pots, potters and potteries), this site gives information on the history of studio pottery. It's a huge site with over 5,400 pages and it's continually being updated. Everything is cross-referenced with good explanations and photographs.

www.claricecliff.com   UK
THE FIRST LADY OF CERAMIC DESIGN
A must for fans of Clarice Cliff pottery. There is information on auctions, biographical details, patterns, shapes, also a newsletter and forum for related chat. The site offers reproductions and related merchandise for sale.

www.chinasearch.co.uk   UK
REPLACING LOST CHINA
A company specialising in finding china to match services and lost pieces, they also buy unwanted tableware. The site is easy to use and they have items in over 2,500 different designs in stock so they should be able to help.

Antiques on TV

www.bbc.co.uk/antiques   UK

BBC

A typically excellent site from the BBC with links to the major
shows and a very useful price guide covering some 5,000
antiques, plus expert guidance and tips.

See also:
www.david-dickinson.net – all you need to know about the
man . . .
www.pbs.org/wgbh/pages/roadshow/ – home of the US version
of the Antiques Roadshow.

Apple Mac Users

*The following sites specialise in Apple Mac technology and programs.
See also the general sections on Computers, Software and Games
that may also have relevant information.*

www.apple.com/uk   US/UK

HOME OF THE ORIGINAL

Get the latest information and advances in Apple computers at
this beautifully designed site. You can buy from the Applestore,
and they offer finance deals and help for businesses, so
software is surprisingly good value.

Hardware

www.cancomuk.com   UK
APPLE MAC HARDWARE AND SOFTWARE

A messy site offering a wide selection of hardware, peripherals
and software all developed for Apple computers. There are
plenty of deals and free delivery on all orders over £200 before
VAT.

www.macwarehouse.co.uk   UK
GREAT PRICES ON MACS

Part of the Microwarehouse group, they specialise in mail-order
supply with a reputation for excellent service. Good prices and a
wide range make this a good first port of call if you need a new
PC or an upgrade.

See also:
www.macassist.co.uk – buy the Mac that's right for you.
www.macreviewzone.com – more reviews and buying help.
www.mrsystems.co.uk – a London-based specialist store.

Software

www.versiontracker.com   US

 SOFTWARE FOR MACS
A software specialist that's a great place for downloading the latest programs, it has a huge selection and many are free. You have to subscribe to get the best out of it, but it's well worth the effort.

See also:
www.macupdate.com – good for the latest hot software and updates.
www.theapplecollection.com – a huge site with lots of information and downloads but principally a collection of all things sporting the apple logo.

Information and Help

www.macintouch.com   US

 THE ORIGINAL MAC NEWS AND INFORMATION SITE
If you have a Mac then this is the site for you. It has lots of information, bug fixes and software to download, but it is a little overwhelming and it takes a while to get your bearings. Once you've done that, for the Mac user, this site is invaluable.

See also the following:
http://thinksecret.com – the latest information and predictions about what's going on at Apple.
www.applelust.com – a site devoted to forums discussing all things Apple.
www.everymac.com – another good guide to the world of Macintosh.
www.everythingmac.com – great for links.
www.google.com/mac.html – Google's useful Mac-only search engine.
www.macaddict.com – very comprehensive, one for the experts.
www.macfixit.com – fix your problems.
www.macinstein.com – which has a good directory.

A

www.macnn.com – the Mac News network, lots of ratings.
www.macobserver.com – more news, tips and forums.
www.macrumors.com – a great place to find the latest information and ideas about what could be on the way from Apple, good for tips too.

Music for Macs

Here's a selection of sites that offer the Mac owner a place to go to download the latest digital music files. Please be aware that downloading some types of files may be illegal (see page 321).

www.apple.com/itunes – the original.
www.dailytunes.com – linking to iTunes, here you can get recommendations and tips on what to download and buy.
www.limewire.com – a file-sharing program that is suitable for Mac users; more stable than some.
www.macband.com – a well-categorised site covering free music donated by bands.
www.macidol.com – news, discussions, free downloads and even an album.
www.macjams.com – an Apple Garageband community site.
www.macmusic.org – keep up to date with the latest music news, software and hardware. There are over 3,500 music-related links and also forums and advice.
www.mp3-mac.com – lots of downloads and links.

Games for Macs

Here are some great sites to help you if you feel restricted by having an Apple Mac, watch out for spyware though.

www.macgamer.com   US
MAC GAMER MAG
A very good online magazine with all the usual features we've come to expect: news, reviews, links and even a few giveaways. It's all neatly packaged on an attractive website.

www.macgamefiles.com   US
MAC GAME FILE LIBRARY
To quote them 'Macgamefiles.com is the one-stop source for Macintosh game files. The web site features lively libraries of

Macintosh demos, shareware, updaters, tools, add-ons, and more'. And they're right; it's a very useful site with some really good games and software.

See also:
www.apple.com/games – worth checking out Apple's games site.
www.gamedb.com/ssps – a huge number from which to choose.
www.insidemacgames.com – good magazine.

Mac Fans and Miscellaneous Sites . . .

Here are a few sites dedicated to specific Apple products and enthusiasts . . .

www.byodkm.net – the Mac Mini enthusiasts network.
www.cubeowner.com – discussion for users of Apples Cube.
www.macvisionaries.com – for visually impaired Mac users.
www.mdoodle.com – home of the Mac Museum.

Architecture

www.greatbuildings.com   US
ARCHITECTURE ONLINE
This US oriented site shows over 800 buildings and features hundreds of leading architects, with 3-D models, photographic images and architectural drawings, commentaries, bibliographies and web links. It's all well packaged, easy to use and you can search by architect, building or location.

www.emporis.com   US
SKYSCRAPERTASTIC!
An excellent technical and entertaining resource covering high rise and many historical buildings, it has good search facilities and is always being added to. It's run by a company who specialise in the field so the data is pretty authoritative.

www.architecture.com   UK

THE ROYAL INSTITUTE FOR BRITISH ARCHITECTS
A massive site from the RIBA with some 250,000 pages on all aspects of architecture including history, jobs, events and features on great buildings.

A

www.architectstudio3d.org   US
CAN YOU DESIGN LIKE FRANK LLOYD WRIGHT?
Design your own house, make a virtual 3-D model of it inside
and out, then add it to the design gallery. In addition, you
can learn about architecture, in particular, about the architect
Frank Lloyd Wright.

www.buildingconservation.com   UK
CONSERVING ASSETS
They claim to be the online information centre for the
conservation and restoration of historic buildings, churches,
gardens and landscapes; the site seems to live up to its billing
providing plenty of quality information and links.

www.implosionworld.com   US
DEMOLITION
If watching buildings going down instead of up turns you on,
then you should visit this site which offers videos and pictures
of demolitions plus lots of information on explosive demolition.
There's also an educational side to the site and an FAQ section
covering the World Trade Center disaster too.

Also check out the following sites:
http://adam.ac.uk – an arts and design search engine that covers
architecture too.
http://architecture.about.com – some excellent articles and
features at About.com
http://en.wikipedia.org/wiki/Architecture – Wikipedia's well
put together selection of pages about architecture and it's
history.
www.aabc-register.co.uk – the register of architects accredited in
building conservation.
www.archibot.com – a portal and news service devoted to
contemporary architecture.
www.architecturemag.com – *Architecture* magazine.
www.arcspace.com – photos, opinions and features on the most
important architects and their work.
www.bbc.co.uk/history/programmes/restoration – get the low
down on the BBC's architectural salvage projects.
www.english-heritage.org.uk – some of England's finest
buildings.
www.glasssteelandstone.com – a growing architecture
encyclopaedia with details of some 700 buildings.
www.landmarktrust.org.uk – saving national treasures.

www.nationaltrust.org.uk – home to many of our finest buildings.
www.retropolis.net – Art Deco architecture, a labour of love.
www.spab.org.uk – home of the charity The Society for the Protection of Ancient Buildings.

Art and the Arts

One of the best things about the Internet is the ability to showcase things that otherwise would be quite obscure or inaccessible. Now working artists are able to show their wares to excellent effect and we can view their art before we buy. In addition, we can now 'visit' some of the world's great galleries and museums. Here are the best sites for posters, online galleries, museums, cartoons, exhibitions, showcases for new talent and how to get the best clip art for your own use.

Visual Treats

The Good Web Site Guide's Top 10s of the Internet

1. **www.nationalgeographic.com** – beautiful photography and writing too
2. **www.apple.com/uk** – proving that computers need not be dull
3. **http://uk.fmagazine.com** – the gorgeous Flash 8 Forum music magazine
4. **www.scifi.com** – makes the best of all those effects
5. **http://hubblesite.org** – stunning pics from the Hubble Space Telescope
6. **www.musicplasma.com** – information on any artist graphically presented and linked
7. **www.noggin.com** – great for young kids
8. **www.thebanmappingproject.com** – stunning site on the history of Thebes and the pharaohs
9. **www.yoox.com** – make fashion shopping a pleasure
10. **www.edible.com** – unusual food. Not for all, but the site is cool

Resources and Encyclopaedias

www.artlex.com
US

THE VISUAL ARTS DICTIONARY
From abbozzo to zoomorphic, there are over 3,600 definitions of art-related terms with links to related articles on other sites. The cross-referencing is excellent.

www.artcyclopedia.com
CANADA

THE FINE ART SEARCH ENGINE
A popular resource for finding out just about anything to do with art, it's quick, nicely designed and informative. At the time of writing they had indexed 1,800 leading arts sites and offer links to an estimated 150,000 works by 8,000 different artists.

www.accessart.org.uk
UK

MAKING ART ACCESSIBLE
A really good, colourful site dedicated to helping students, children and teachers get to grips with the art world and the meaning behind art. There are good online workshops on topics such as sculpture, use of colour and photography.

http://wwar.com
US

THE WORLD-WIDE ART RESOURCE
This is an effective search vehicle with links to artists, exhibitions, galleries and museums. It now offers over 100,000 works of art from over 22,000 'masters'. New for this edition is an art blogs section, should you feel tempted to have your say.

www.artchive.com
UK

MARK HARDEN'S ARTCHIVE
Incredible, but seemingly the work of one art fanatic, this superb site not only has an excellent art encyclopaedia, but also the latest art news and galleries with special online exhibitions. The quality of the pictures is outstanding. There's also a section on theory, and good links. For more links try
www.chart.ac.uk/vlib

See also:
http://adam.ac.uk – an arts and design search engine and an excellent resource for Arts students.
www.abcgallery.com – Olga's Gallery is hugely informative and well illustrated.
www.askart.com – a massive directory on art and artists, US-oriented.

www.ibiblio.org/wm – the web museum offers background and information on art movements and artists.

A

Art in the UK

www.culture.gov.uk   UK
THE GOVERNMENT'S VIEW
A dense site giving information on how the government is
supporting the arts and museums. There are plenty of facts,
figures and reports to download, as well as links and
information on libraries, the creative industries and even sport.

www.design-council.org.uk   UK
PROMOTING THE EFFECTIVE USE OF DESIGN
This good-looking site effectively promotes the work of The
Design Council through access to their archives of articles on
design and details of their work with government; it also gives
feedback on design issues.

www.artmovements.co.uk   UK
CONTEMPORARY ARTIST'S SHOWCASE
Promoting contemporary arts with portfolios of over 1,300
artists with a magazine, resources and good information on arts
movements.

What's on in the UK

www.artguide.org   UK
THE ART LOVER'S GUIDE TO BRITAIN AND IRELAND
Organised by artist, region, exhibition or museum with more
than 4,500 listings in all. This site is easy to navigate with a
good search engine and cross-referencing making it simple to
find out about events in a particular region, aided by annotated
maps. See also **www.artsfestivals.co.uk** where you can search
for festivals by date or alphabetically.

Art Styles, Periods, Schools, Most Popular Artists and Countries

www.impressionism.org   US
LEARN ABOUT IMPRESSIONISM
An overview of the movement with a tutorial all contained on a
well-illustrated site.

A

www.surrealism.co.uk UK
ONLINE GALLERY
Not as way out as you'd expect, this site gives an overview of
surrealism and features contemporary artists. The online gallery
is OK without being that exciting, but as a showcase it works.

www.graffiti.org UK
THE WRITING ON THE WALL
If you're fascinated by graffiti, then here's the place to go – it's
got a gallery of the best examples, history and links to other
graffiti sites.

www.wga.hu HUNGARY

THE RENNAISANCE
The Web Gallery of Art is a virtual museum dedicated to
European painting and sculpture of the 12th–18th centuries.
It is nice to look at and contains a phenomenal number of
paintings; however, it takes a little time to get the knack of
navigating the site. There is the option to listen to related music
while browsing.

www.the-artists.org UK
20TH CENTURY ART
This site is easy to use, with minimalist design and details of
every major artist of the last century.

www.dlc.fi/~hurmari/preraph.htm UK

PRE-RAPHAELITES
An exhaustive listing of sites and links to pages on the
Pre-Raphaelites, their paintings, lives and even those
who posed for them.

*For biographical information on a huge number of artists see the
entries under Resources and Encyclopaedias. The following have
pages devoted to the particular artists:*
http://arthistory.about.com/od/artistsaz – biographies of over
150 artists plus loads of art history information.
http://csdll.cs.tamu.edu:8080/picasso – Picasso
http://essentialvermeer.20m.com – Vermeer
http://gallery.euroweb.hu/html/h/holbein/hans_y – Holbein
www.chez.com/renoir/indexe.html – Renoir
www.daliuniverse.com – Dali
www.diegorivera.com – Diego Rivera
www.expo-degas.com – Degas

www.expo-klimt.com – Klimt
www.ibiblio.org/wm/paint/auth/rembrandt – Rembrandt
www.lucidcafe.com/library/96jun/gauguin.html – Gauguin
www.mark-rothko.com – Rothko
www.marmottan.com – Monet
www.mos.org/leonardo – Da Vinci
www.musee-matisse-nice.org – Matisse
www.okeeffemuseum.org – Georgia O'Keeffe
www.tamu.edu/mocl/picasso – Picasso
www.vangoghgallery.com – Van Gogh
www.warhol.org – Andy Warhol

World Art

www.asianart.com   US
ART IN ASIA
All you need to know on Asian art. Basically, it covers all the
major cultures in four sections: exhibitions, articles,
associations and galleries. It's not very well cross-referenced
which makes it hard to navigate, although there is a pretty good
search engine.

www.japaneseart.org   France
JAPAN
A virtual tour of the best in Japanese art, with links to antique
dealers, galleries and museums. It's quite information-light so
for more go to **www.kanzaki.com/jinfo/jart.html** where you'll
find well-categorised links on aspects of Japanese culture and
arts. You can also try **http://web-japan.org/museum** although
we found the site unreliable.

http://depts.washington.edu/chinaciv   US
CHINESE CIVILISATION
Essentially an educational resource, this site provides a good
general introduction to the arts and culture of China. Maps and
a good timeline help to make sense of it all. For a snapshot of
contemporary Chinese art visit **www.newchineseart.com**

www.latinart.com   US
THE LATIN AMERICAN ARTS SCENE
A magazine-style site dedicated to emerging and established
artists in Latin America. There is a guide to international
exhibitions showcasing Latin American art and some good
resources available on the site.

A

www.lonker.net/art_african_1.htm   US
> AFRICAN ART
> A good-looking site dedicated to mainly sub-Saharan cave
> and rock paintings. It's well illustrated and authoritative,
> there's also a sister site on Aboriginal Art at
> **www.lonker.net/art_aboriginal_1.htm**

The Major Museums and Galleries

www.museums.co.uk   UK
> MUSEUM SEARCH
> MuseumNet is a simple search engine which allows you to
> search either by subject or location, each entry has a short
> description and a map. There's also industry information and a
> jobs page for those who want to work in a museum, however it
> doesn't list many of the smaller museums.

http://vlmp.museophile.com   UK/US
> MUSEUMS WORLD-WIDE
> Provides links to the world's museums which have an online
> presence and indicates which languages they use. Information
> on galleries, museums and libraries is listed separately.

www.museumstuff.com   US

> MUSEUM GATEWAY
> An outstanding portal devoted to American museums. There's
> information on virtually any topic you can name plus thousands
> of links to specialist sites and museums. They also provide a list
> of museum shops, chat rooms and forums plus links to the fun
> sections on museum sites.

www.coudal.com/moom.php   US

> THE MUSEUM OF ONLINE MUSEUMS
> An excellent place to go if you want to see what the world's
> museums have to offer. The site is very well designed and it's
> easy to get immersed in what's on offer here.

www.24hourmuseum.org.uk   UK

> OPEN ALL HOURS
> Run by the Campaign for Museums, this site aims to give high
> quality access to the UK's galleries, museums and heritage
> sites – and it succeeds. The graphics are clear, it's easy to use
> and really informative. There are a selection of online
> exhibitions, web features, a museum finder, links, news and a

link to **www.show.me.uk** which is the excellent sister site for children.

www.tate.org.uk
UK

THE ARCHETYPAL GALLERY SITE

A real treat with excellent design and quality pictures, the site covers all the Tate galleries and offers information about exhibitions, relevant articles, webcasts and also a good shop.

www.nationalgallery.org.uk
UK

THE NATIONAL COLLECTION

A very comprehensive site, with sections on the permanent collection and exhibitions. There's also a shop with a wide range of books and gifts as well as information for schools and the outreach programme. For access to all the Scottish National Galleries, go to **www.natgalscot.ac.uk** who have a similarly informative and enjoyable site.

www.thebritishmuseum.ac.uk
UK

ILLUMINATING NEW CULTURES

Whether you explore the world's cultures, take a tour, or just browse the collection, this is a beautifully illustrated site. The online shop stocks a selection of gifts and goods based on museum artefacts. Delivery cost depends on weight of purchases. Parents will appreciate the family online tour and children's compass (a museum guide for children). They also arrange museum tours and you can book for special events too.

www.npg.org.uk
UK

THE NATIONAL PORTRAIT GALLERY

With over 64,000 works online and more being added, this is one of the biggest online galleries. It shows the most influential characters in British history portrayed by artists of their time. You can search by sitter or artist, and buy the print. The online shop offers gifts plus pictures with options on print size, framing and delivery, including overseas.

www.royalacademy.org.uk
UK

WHERE ART IS MADE, SEEN AND DEBATED

An interestingly designed and modern gallery site with all the information you need on the Royal Academy as well as ticket information and a shop. There's support for schools, colleges and teachers, plus information and previews of exhibitions.

A

www.vam.ac.uk   UK
VICTORIA & ALBERT MUSEUM
The world's largest museum has a plain functional web site,
with information on visiting, learning and how you can help
support the museum. The online shop offers gifts,
reproductions and books. You can also explore the museum
virtually, visiting most of the galleries plus back-up information
explaining their exhibits with details of what they contain.

www.moma.org   US
THE MUSEUM OF MODERN ART IN NEW YORK
A comprehensive and minimally attractive site that covers the
collection and offers much in the way of information on the
works and artists. There's also an excellent gift shop, although
shipping to the UK is expensive. It can be quite slow at times.

www.metmuseum.org   US
THE METROPOLITAN MUSEUM OF ART IN NEW YORK
A very stylish site, featuring lots of great ideas, with quality
illustrations and photographs, you can view any one of 6,500
exhibits, have a taster by taking the director's tour, become a
member, or visit a special exhibition. The shop offers a great
range of products, many exclusive, and there's a handy
gift-finder service. Delivery costs to the UK depend on
how much you spend.

http://digitalgallery.nypl.org/nypldigital/index.cfm   US
NEW YORK DIGITAL LIBRARY
The library's attempt to make accessible online 'the
accumulated wisdom of the world, without distinction as to
income, religion, nationality, or other human condition', and
with some 450,000 images and a great search facility, it largely
succeeds.

www.si.edu   US
THE SMITHSONIAN
A fairly cluttered site but once you get used to it there's a huge
amount of information on every major aspect of art plus
sections on science and history. The magazine is well worth a
look, especially the journeys section.

www.courtauld.ac.uk   UK
COURTAULD COLLECTION
A minimally illustrated site with details of the collection plus

educational resources and information on the gallery. The gallery's complete collection of 7,000 items is now available to view on their linked site A&A: **www.artandarchitecture.org.uk** What's more, almost all the images on A&A are now available to buy as high quality photographic prints in a range of sizes with prices starting at a very affordable £1.

www.guggenheim.org   US
VANGUARDS OF ARCHITECTURE AND CULTURE
There is the promise of a unique virtual museum, but while we wait, the five branches (Berlin, Bilbao, Venice, New York and Las Vegas) can be visited here. You can find out about exhibitions and collections, projects, tours, events and developmental programmes, while membership entitles you to free entry and a store discount. The store is stocked with a wonderful selection of unusual goods and gifts, and is not bad value, though delivery to the UK is expensive.

www.louvre.fr   FRANCE
FRANCE'S TREASURE HOUSE
Similar to the UK's National Gallery site: there's a virtual tour where you can view the collection and learn about its history, you can also check out the latest exhibitions and buy advance tickets. The shop has some interesting items, but delivery from France ups the cost.

www.hermitagemuseum.org   RUSSIA
THE STATE HERMITAGE MUSEUM
Another beautifully presented museum site with features on the highlights of the collection with a section of superb digital photographs, details of the museum itself, exhibitions and an education centre. There are some pretty extraordinary products for sale in the shop, but delivery begins at £18 and depends on weight, so it could be pretty costly if you place an order for the neo-classical bookcase.

Clip Art

These sites are loaded with pop-ups and advertising which is really irritating; you may just try Google, which has an excellent image search facility. If you know of a site that is ad free please let me know.

A

www.clipart.net   US
THE PLACE TO START IF YOU NEED CLIP ART
With this clip-art search facility you should quickly find the
perfect image. Many linked sites have free art for use, otherwise
cost varies enormously depending on what you want.

See also:
http://classroomclipart.com – a wide selection good for projects.
www.321clipart.com – some 12,000 images.
www.barrysclipart.com – a huge resource with hundreds of
categories.
www.clipartcastle.com – sections on web graphics, photos and
animation as well as clip art. Registration is a right pain though.
www.kidsdomain.com/clip – nice selection by topic.

Cartoons and Drawing

www.cartoonbank.com   US
WORLD'S LARGEST CARTOON DATABASE
Need to find a cartoon for a particular occasion? Then there's a
choice of over 20,000, mostly from *New Yorker* magazine. You
can send e-cards and you can now get some products delivered
to the UK (at reasonable shipping rates). For a massive set of
links to cartoon and humorous sites try the excellent Norwegian
search **www.cartoonstock.com**

www.cartoon-factory.com   US
BUYING CARTOON CELS
Buy cartoon cels, mainly from Disney and Warner cartoons; you
can search by subject or artist. Delivery is expensive, although
they are flexible about payment. See also the Open Directory
Project's section on Animation. It offers nearly 14,000 links at
http://dmoz.org/arts/animation

www.drawingpower.org.uk   UK
THE BIG DRAW
A bid to get us all drawing, the Big Draw happens every October
and here you can get encouragement and details on events and
programmes.

http://drawsketch.about.com/od/cartooning   US
DRAWING AND SKETCHING
An excellent set of links, articles and web pages devoted to all
aspects of drawing from About.com.

Buying Art

www.theartsource.org   UK
BUYING ART THE EASY WAY
A well designed online gallery offering a wide selection of art at
'fair' prices. It's mainly contemporary in style but there's plenty
to choose from and a 14 day money back guarantee.

www.eyestorm.com   UK

BUYING CONTEMPORARY ART
A really attractive and well-designed site which showcases
contemporary art and photography, you can buy online as well.

www.whitecube.com   UK
WHITE CUBE GALLERY
This outstandingly designed site showcases top artists in an
original way and highlights what can be done when web site
development technology is used at its best. Although this
gallery is influential in developing the careers of some of the
best artists working today, you can buy art here at reasonable
prices too.

www.artnet.com   UK
FINE ART ONLINE
Possibly the largest gallery network featuring work from some
18,000 artists, the site is well put together and the information
on offer is extraordinary with an encyclopaedia, price database,
links and a comprehensive directory.

www.commissionaportrait.com   UK
PORTRAITS
If you fancy immortalising yourself in a painting or sculpture,
then this is a good place to go. There are over 100 artists
featured and info on whether they specialise in people or dogs.

Other online art showcase sites and stores worth visiting:
www.artandparcel.com – a messy site that shows the work of
120 artists.
www.artcapitalgroup.com – borrow against your work of art or
borrow funds to buy something for the living room.
www.artlondon.com – a well-designed art store with an
emphasis on the UK, value for money and quality.
www.artprice.com – a subscription service that allows the
subscriber to check on the value of the work from over 300,000

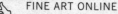

A

artists world-wide. There's also help and a good links section.
www.axisartists.org.uk – a very good showcase site for contemporary artists with lots of content and information as well as links and exhibitions.
www.britart.com – a good-looking, well-stocked site concentrating on the work of British artists.
www.fineart.co.uk – the home of the Fine Art Trade Guild.
www.modernbritishartists.co.uk – a gallery and shop catering for those of us who love and covet the work of modern British artists, including those from early in the last century.
www.newbritishartists.com – good looking gallery, wide variety of artists and paintings.

www.artloss.com   US
THE ART LOSS REGISTER
The register of stolen and lost art. Featured thefts and recoveries makes for interesting, if rather sad reading.

Posters

www.artrepublic.co.uk   UK
BOOKS, POSTERS AND WHAT'S ON WHERE
A nicely designed, easy-to-use site with thousands of art posters and prints to choose from. There is also an option to have posters framed and free shipping world-wide. There is also a glossary of art terms and biographical data on an impressive number of artists. 'What's On World-wide' provides details of the latest exhibitions, competitions and travel information for over 1,250 museums around the world.

www.onlineposters.com   UK
POSTER SHOPS ONLINE
Simply a ranked list of shops that sell posters, from the generalist to the very specialised retailers.

www.barewalls.com   US
INTERNET'S LARGEST ART PRINT AND POSTER STORE
This site backs its claim with a huge range, it's also excellent for gifts and unusual prints and posters but be aware that the shipping costs are high. There's also a gift voucher scheme. See also **www.art.com** which is excellent and does a great line in movie posters as well as art. They've reduced shipping costs making delivery very reasonable.

A

www.postershop.co.uk   UK
FINE ART PRINTS AND POSTERS
There are over 35,000 fine art prints, 8,000 graphics and over 30,000 celebrity photos on offer. There's also a framing service and a good user-friendly search facility where you can search by subject as well as artist. In the museum shop there's a range of art-related gifts to choose from.

www.totalposter.com   UK
GET THE BIG PICTURE
Excellent poster store, specialising in photographic posters with a very wide selection. Extra services include printing up your own photos to poster size, plus pictures of recent key sporting and news events in their 'Stop Press' section. Delivery costs vary.

www.easyart.co.uk   UK
FINE ART PRINTS AND POSTERS
Excellent art shop selling posters, limited editions, photographs, etchings and now, canvas art too. They provide inspiration too with advice on the best place to hang art in your home and a custom art section where you can turn pictures of your friends into pop icons.

Creating Art

www.kurzweilcyberart.com   US
CYBER ART
Once you download the program, watch in fascination as art is created for you as a screen saver. It's free and great fun too. See also **www.storyabout.net/typedrawing** where you can create your own art with an excellent drawing program.

www.saa.co.uk   UK
THE SOCIETY FOR ALL ARTISTS
Help, advice, forums, tuition and a good shop make this a useful site for any artist, amateur or professional. There's also a gallery if you're looking for art to buy. Additional services and discounts are on offer for those who join.

www.watercolor-online.com   US

ALL FORMS OF WATERCOLOUR
Very good site devoted to all aspects of watercolour painting; it has tutorials, advice, links and provides a good place to start when searching for information on the subject.

A

For more watercolour sites try:
http://painting.about.com/cs/watercolours/index.htm – pages of advice from the excellent **www.about.com**
www.wasp-art.skynow.co.uk – a simple online course by Peter Saw.
www.1art.com – online art courses from $120.

www.simplypainting.com   UK
FRANK CLARK
Learn how to paint with leading art teacher Frank Clark, the site has free lessons and tips plus a shop and gallery.

For more inspiration try:
www.codcottage.freeserve.co.uk – an introduction to calligraphy.
www.learn-to-draw.com – text dense, a bit American, but sound. You have to subscribe (about £10) to get the best out of it.
www.talens.com/stepbystep.html – good introduction to colours, learn to paint sunflowers step-by-step.

Arts Councils

Each country in the UK has its own arts body to support artists and their work; you can find them here, along with links to regional and local councils, galleries and museums.

www.artscouncil.org.uk – find out how to get funding in England.
www.artscouncil-ni.org – Northern Ireland has a newsy and informative site.
www.sac.org.uk – excellent and wide ranging site devoted to Scottish art and entertainment.
www.artswales.org – lots of background and support in Wales.

Astrology and Prediction

www.astrology.com   UK
ALL ABOUT ASTROLOGY
A very comprehensive site offering free advice from the stars, you can buy a personalised reading and chart, browse the general horoscopes and now you can get a tarot reading too. You can find celebrity horoscopes, and learn about the history and techniques of astrology. See also **www.horoscope.co.uk** home of *Horoscope Magazine*.

A

www.live–astro.com   UK
RUSSELL GRANT
Now is your chance to buy a horoscope from a real celebrity,
costs range from £1.95 upwards. This site has been expanded
to include dream interpretations, tarot and other astrological
resources as well as the various horoscopes. If your dog appears
a bit blue, you can organise psychic consultations for pets as well.

www.easyscopes.com   US
ASTROLOGY SEARCH ENGINE
Here you can get as many different free horoscopes as you can
handle, the site contains direct links to the daily, weekly,
monthly and yearly horoscopes for each zodiac sign. You just
have to select your zodiac sign and you are presented with a
large list of horoscopes to choose from. It's amazing how
different they all are for the same sign!

www.lovetest.com   US
ARE YOU COMPATIBLE?
It's a bit long winded to use, but enter your birthday and your
partner's and you get a compatibility score based on the star
signs. There are also quizzes, chat, classified ads, links, not
forgetting the love test thermometer.

See also:
www.astro.com – a comprehensive offering with every major
aspect of astrology covered and explained.
www.astroadvice.com – one of the better astrology sites, well, in
terms of design anyway.
www.astro–eclipse.co.uk – a basic site with an overview of the
subject plus links.
www.freewillastrology.com – good-looking site with lots of
predictions about future events, usual star signs and much more
from astrologer Rob Brezsny.
www.tarot.com – tarot, astrology, numerology and the I Ching all
on one site, all problems obviously.
www.thezodiac.com – a fairly amateur site but it's clear and easy
to use with lots of fun astrological things to do.

Auctions and Classified Ads

*Before using these sites be sure that you are aware of the rules and
regulations surrounding the bidding process, and what your rights are*

as a seller or purchaser. If they are not properly explained during the registration process, then use another site. They should also offer a returns policy as well as insurance cover. Whilst there are plenty of bargains available, not all the products on offer are cheaper than the high street or specialist vendor; it's very much a case of buyer beware. Having said that, once you're used to it, it can be fun and you can save a great deal of money.

www.ukauctionhelp.co.uk   UK

HELP WITH USING AUCTIONS

A site dedicated to giving the low down on auctions. It's informative and genuinely helpful – shame about the design, which makes it difficult to use and it's cluttered with lots of adverts. See also **www.auctionseller411.com** which has lots of good advice.

www.bidxs.com   US

AUCTION SEARCH ENGINE

An attempt to allow you to search the auction sites for your wanted items, you can search by category, price or by item. It's quite slow but useful nonetheless.

www.ebay.co.uk   UK

THE WORLDS BIGGEST AUCTION

eBay is one of the Internet's greatest success stories and is one of the most visited sites on the web. With millions of items listed, you are likely to find what you want, from cars to musical instruments. If it's sellable, it's sure to be here. There is a 24-hour support facility, loads of online help and automatic insurance cover on all items up to £250 using PayPal. Previous clients have reviewed many of those who have something to sell, so you can check up on their reliability too. Buying and selling on eBay can be addictive and many businesses now rely on it as a good source of income. It's also easy to fall into the trap of believing that if it's on eBay, then it automatically must be cheap.

Here are some top tips for using eBay (and any auction site for that matter) . . .

1. Don't rely solely on the 'good feedback' reports, they can be bought.
2. Research what you are buying thoroughly. Check out the product you're buying on a price check website such as Froogle, or if it's a specialist product, look it up on the various forums and discussion groups, alternatively, use a search engine.

3.   Be cautious, know your rights. Does the seller actually trade as a trader or is it a private individual? It's a case of buyer beware. If you buy via the 'buy it now' button you should have the same rights as if you buy from any shop as long as they are a UK-based trader, but check!

4.   Only bid on tangible things not schemes or anything you can't physically hold.

5.   Read the small print, especially the descriptions; they may not be all they appear to be.

6.   If anyone asks you to do a deal outside eBay after advertising their products on the site, walk away.

7.   Pay electronically, through PayPal or by credit card, you'll be better protected. Never use a seller's finance or escrow services.

8.   If it seems too good to be true, then it probably is.

9.   Check out **www.scamdex.com** for the latest information on scams.

See also:
www.rummaging.org – an amusing blog run by someone who keeps track of all the unusual stuff that ends up on eBay.
www.startups.co.uk/YemqYqE.html – good advice on how to start a business using eBay.
www.stuffusell.co.uk – a company that will do all the work for you and sell your stuff on eBay – for a commission.
www.vendio.com – provides e-commerce tools for individuals and businesses to automate and maximise your sales on eBay.

www.huntforit.co.uk   UK
FREE SELLING, LOW COMMISSION
A good UK-biased auction site which is cheaper than many of its rivals; it has the added benefit of a system whereby you can bid by text message. The same system can be used to alert potential buyers when something that they have registered an interest in comes up for sale.

www.ebid.co.uk   UK
NO CHARGE TO LIST AN ITEM
Divided into auctions, wanted and swap sections. The auctions can easily be accessed and browsed; its strengths are in computing, electronics and music, although there has been a great increase in the number of collectibles available. There is a special section dedicated to raising money for charity if you want to donate the proceeds of your auction.

A

www.icollector.com US
REDEFINING THE ART OF COLLECTING
An attractive site bringing together the wares of hundreds of auction houses and dealers, icollector is an ambitious project that works well. The emphasis is on art, antiques and collectibles. Be sure that the auction house you're dealing with ships outside the US.

www.qxl.com UK/EUROPE
A PAN-EUROPEAN AUCTION COMMUNITY
This wide-ranging site offers anything from airline tickets and holidays to cars, collectibles and electronics (in several languages). The quality of merchandise seems better than most sites. Another site worth checking out is **www.CQout.co.uk** it had almost 100,000 lots when we visited, a wide selection of categories and a nice design.

www.sothebys.com UK/US
QUALITY ASSURED
Details of their auctions and information on what they do, plus you can buy catalogues and search for items that may be coming up for sale.

www.christies.com UK
FOR THOSE WITH DEEP WALLETS
Christies have a classic site with info on their programme of auctions and on how to buy and sell through them, but you can't carry out transactions from the site. The LotFinder service searches their auctions for that special item – for a fee. There's also a good specialist bookstore and lots of information on how to buy and sell.

www.bid-up.tv UK
BID UP.TV
Linked to the TV channel of the same name, this site shows the auctions they have on TV, you can bid online or call their hotline.

www.ad-mart.co.uk UK
AWARD WINNING
Excellent design and ease of use makes this site stand out; there are fourteen sections, all the usual suspects plus personal ads, boating and pets. See also **www.nettrader.co.uk** which is also really well designed and easy to use.

www.exchangeandmart.co.uk   UK
EXCHANGE & MART
Everything the paper has and more – great bargains on a
massive range of goods found using a good search facility, all
packaged on a bright, easy-to-use site. It is split into four major
sections: home and leisure, motoring, business and, new this
year, money.

www.loot.com   UK
FREE ADS ONLINE
A redesigned site with a clean look and access to thousands of
classified ads in 12 categories, it has an excellent search engine
and many bargains.

www.bumblebeeauctions.co.uk   UK
UK POLICE PROPERTY DISPOSAL
Ever wondered what happened to all those umbrellas, bicycles
and paraphernalia that gets handed in to the Police? Well, if no
one claims them, here's where they get sold off.

Beauty

*Beauty product retailers are popular on the Internet so we've featured a
few of the best ones for advice, help and shopping. New for this edition
is a listing for sites that specialise in organic or natural products.*

http://avonshop.co.uk   UK
AVON CALLING
A very good-looking and easy-to-use site selling a wide range of
cosmetics. They also sell health products and lingerie, a range
for men and kids and an opportunity to support their breast
cancer crusade.

www.lookfantastic.com   UK
ALL A GIRL DESIRES
A well-designed online retailer offering some really good
discounts and a wide range of products, it also offers advice
guides on how to use make-up, shampoo and conditioners, in
fact, virtually everything a girl needs – it's war out there after all.
Oh yes, there's a section for men too.

B

For a Beautiful You

The Good Web Site Guide's Top 10s
of the Internet

1. **www.lookfantastic.com** – more hair and beauty products than you'll ever need
2. **www.beautyconsumer.com** – sort out your skin, nails and body
3. **www.netfit.co.uk** – tone that body
4. **www.allcures.com** – for all those pills and potions
5. **www.yoox.com** – the place to go for the top designers
6. **www.net-a-porter.com** – what's hot from the catwalk
7. **www.asseenonscreen.com** – look like your favourite celebrity
8. **www.figleaves.com** – it's a one stop shop for underwear
9. **www.jewellers.net** – accessorise
10. **www.shoe-shop.com** – what's more important than shoes?

www.osmoz.com   US
MUSICAL PERFUMES
An unusual site with an encyclopaedia devoted to fragrances, reviews and analysis of the latest products. You can use a quiz to find your perfect perfume and there are also links to help you in your search.

www.halfpriceperfumes.co.uk   UK
HALF PRICE?
Well, they are not all half price but there are certainly some fantastic discounts to be had. You have to take the delivery charge into consideration, so you may want to compare prices with **www.supaperfume.com** who also offer great discounts and deliver for free. Also check out **www.fragrancenet.com** who claim to be the world's largest discount fragrance store, but remember to check the international delivery charges.

See also:
www.perfume4u.co.uk – offer a huge choice and some good deals.
www.sendmescent.com – who have some good offers and a no quibble returns policy.

www.mankindonline.co.uk   UK
MALE GROOMING

Innovative and contemporary men's shaving, skincare and hair products. There's lots of help on understanding skin type, good advice and assistance in finding products for specific problems. There's a nice range of gifts both for him and for her, and they'll do the wrapping for you. See also **www.maleorder.co.uk** who offer a wide range of products on a well designed site.

See also:

www.allbeautyproducts.com – excellent site from the Allcures camp.

www.beautybible.com – they claim to have the largest product directory plus good beauty advice, a newsletter and a selection of offers and no adverts.

www.beautyexpert.co.uk – stocking a range of professional beauty products for home use.

www.benefitcosmetics.com – trendy cosmetics from the US, worth it to be different . . .

www.blackbeautyandhair.com – excellent site aimed at black and Asian folk, with a wide selection of products and a good regional directory.

www.buycosmeticsdirect.com – a wide range and lots of excellent offers, jewellery as well as cosmetics.

www.creativenailplace.com – specialist shop covering nail art and beauty.

www.magicmakeup.co.uk – great for special offers.

www.makeupalley.com – reviews, chat and products all on make-up.

www.saveonmakeup.co.uk – certainly good savings to be had here.

www.skinstore.com – good-looking US site selling premium skincare products.

www.spacenk.co.uk – nicely designed store featuring their excellent cosmetics.

www.virgincosmetics.com – delicious products, shop online or arrange to have a party at home.

www.wellbeing.com – strong offering from Boots, easier to shop than at the real store!

Hair

www.ukhairdressers.com   UK
HAIR STYLES DATABASE

Some 1,000 styles illustrated including celebrity styles and virtual makeovers, also with advice and fortune telling.

B

See also:
www.folica.com – great US site on hair care.
www.hqhair.com – magazine-style online store including tips.
www.jazma.com – great advice on black hair care and on the
products the celebrities use. Sells beauty products too.
www.salonproducts-direct.com – products the hairdressers use.
www.salonsales.co.uk – a wide selection of hair products to
choose from.

Natural Beauty

www.thinknatural.com   UK
THINK NATURAL
A good looking site with a wide range of natural health
products, the beauty section has lots of choice, all products
made from natural ingredients.

www.lizearle.com   UK
NATURALLY ACTIVE SKINCARE
They select the best natural ingredients, organic wherever
possible, to create award-winning beauty products. If you've
ever wondered what frankincense is, there is a helpful guide to
ingredients and they've included a few fact sheets too.

www.nealsyardremedies.com   UK
NATURALLY COMITTED
One of the country's most established and respected providers
of natural beauty products. Covers all the body parts, for men,
women and children, while also selling the ingredients for you
to make your own cosmetics.

www.lush.co.uk   UK
SOAP WITHOUT THE SCENT
Lush offer a wide range of soaps and associated products from
their site, it's easy to shop and if you like their soap but find the
smell of the high street shops overpowering, then it's perfect.

See also:
www.bodyshop.co.uk – balancing the rights of the under-
privileged with the demands of a commercial cosmetics
company. There is good product information but you can't buy
online.

www.gentlebodycare.co.uk – for organic hair dyes, baby care and skin products.
www.jerseylavender.co.uk – specialists in lavender based products.
www.luxuriousmoments.co.uk – a wide range of soaps and bath products to choose from as well as a face care range.
www.naturalsoap.co.uk – soap and related products made naturally.
www.whiteginger.co.uk – good range of organic products.

www.acne-advice.com   UK
HELP IS AT HAND
A web site dedicated to advice on treating acne naturally. There is loads of information on acne, its causes and what you can do about it.

Blogging

Keeping a web log or 'blog' is one of the more recent and largest Internet crazes; it allows you to effectively set up your own site cheaply and to a high standard. Its commonest form is that of an online diary covering a specific interest, usually with lots of links to related web sites. Pages are added chronologically and there's usually a facility for visitors to leave comments; some blogs are very informative and entertaining. They are particularly useful for keeping up-to-date with friends and family. The statistics imply blogging is particularly popular with those 15–25 years old. It will be interesting to see how long it is before it catches on with silver surfers.

Here are some sites that can help you on your way and give you all the advice you're likely to need. A good jumping off point is **http://en.wikipedia.org/wiki/Blogging** *– Wikipedia's excellent information pages about blogging and how to get started.*

www.blogger.com   US
THE MOST POPULAR
The original blogger's site, now owned by Google, it's easy to use and free, there are step-by-step instructions and plenty of support.

B

For Sharing

The Good Web Site Guide's Top 10s
of the Internet

1. **www.flickr.com** – great for sharing photos
2. **www.friendster.com** – organise your social life
3. **www.furl.net** – save web pages and share them with your friends
4. **www.wikipedia.org** – share your knowledge
5. **www.dudecheckthisout.com** – put together your own set of favourites and share them with your network
6. **www.friendsreunited.co.uk** – get in touch with old friends
7. **www.feedster.com** – get the latest news, make it relevant to you and your friends
8. **www.kazaa.com** – share your talents with peer-to-peer technology
9. **www.linkedin.com** – create a business network
10. **www.meetup.com** – share your interests with like-minded people

www.bloglines.com   US
ONE STOP BLOG SHOP
A search facility, subscription service and publishing tool all on
one site. It's owned by ask.com so you can be sure it's a quality
offering.

Other sites and software to help you on your way:
http://blogsearchengine.com – search for content on blogs.
http://b2evolution.net – one of the best blog programs.
http://frassle.rura.org – create your own site directory and share
it with others, give your opinions on sites and share them with
your friends.
http://moblg.net – blog services for people with mobiles, camera
phones and PDAs.
http://quacktrack.com – a massive database of blogs, some
135,000 in 1,500 categories. However, many seem to be in
Chinese or languages other than English.
http://radio.userland.com – a respected weblog tool that is easy
to use and with lots of features, including software for those
lacking technical skills.

www.20six.co.uk – here you can even send photos to your blog via a mobile, the site is nicely designed but only the minimum service is free to use.

www.blogarama.com – a directory of almost 21,000 blogs.

www.blojsom.com – a good one for Mac users.

www.blogwise.com – a directory listing in excess of 30,000 blogs.

www.guardian.co.uk/onlineblog (formally **www.onlineblog.com**) – from the *Guardian*, a blog covering the latest in technology and the Internet, news, culture and games.

www.livejournal.com – home of the very flexible *Live Journal* which can be used in a number of creative ways.

www.sixapart.com – offers two beautifully designed blog services: go to 'typepad' for an easy-to-use blog service with lots of options to help you get underway, or for the more advance user, 'moveable type' which, if you take the time to learn how to use it, will offer some features for customising your blog.

www.vidblogs.com – video blogs are said to be the 'latest thing', although, most are just rubbish or plain boring, there are some gems to be found if you search hard enough. Be aware that there's adult content here.

www.technorati.com   US
EXPLORE THE BLOGOSPHERE
Here you can discover over 30 million blogs, explore by topic or just use the search engine.

Books

Books were the first products to be sold in volume over the Internet, and their success has meant that there are many online booksellers, all boasting about the speed of their service and how many titles they can get. In the main, the basic service is the same wherever you go, just pick the bookshop that suits you.

Finding a Book

www.bookbrain.co.uk   UK
BEST PRICES FOR BOOKS
All you do is type in the title of the book and BookBrain will search out the online store that is offering it the cheapest (including postage). You then click again to get taken to the store to buy the book – simple.

See also:

http://amaztype.tha.jp – a book search engine with a difference: type in the title and the results appear in the form of book covers, which you click on to get more results. It's linked to Amazon and it's great fun.

www.bestbookbuys.com – a good US alternative to BookBrain.

www.booktracker.co.uk – UK prices but some book information not always available and some of the information isn't that accurate. Hopefully this will be sorted as the site grows.

www.book-shops.net – a directory of internet bookshops.

Booksellers

*To find a book shop near you go to **www.booksellers.org.uk** or if you're visiting abroad try **www.bookweb.org/bookstores** for virtual booksellers see the list below.*

www.amazon.co.uk   UK

MORE THAN JUST A BOOKSTORE
Amazon is the leading online bookseller and most online stores have followed their formula of combining value with recommendation. Amazon has spent much on providing a wider offering than just books and now has sections for music, gifts, travel, games, software and DVD/video. It also offers an auction service, there's an excellent kids' section aimed at parents, and you can download e-books to read on your PC or handheld computer. It also offers used goods for sale via third party retailers, which can offer great value for money. For books, there are better prices elsewhere, although they have the odd very good offer. See also **www.waterstones.co.uk** who have abandoned their site in favour of Amazon, as has Borders **www.borders.com**

www2.uk.bol.com or www.bol.com   UK

THE EURO-BOOKSELLER
Owned by Bertlesmann, the German media giant, you can get access to books in five European countries and China. Slightly dull, it appeals to the true book lover with lots of recommendations, although it has plenty of offers. Like Amazon it has expanded to include music, video, DVD and games.

www.ottakars.co.uk   UK

E-MAIL A BOOKSTORE
Ottakars' site is clear and easy to use with some nice personal

touches; it offers a mix of store information, recommendation, competitions and they offer free online magazines on a variety of genres that are very entertaining. There's a web page for each store giving information on the locale and events, and while there are no facilities to buy books from the site, you can e-mail your local store to see if they have the book you want.

http://bookshop.blackwell.co.uk UK
NOT JUST FOR ACADEMICS

Blackwells are best known for academic and professional books with 3 million titles to choose from. However, their site offers much more, with the emphasis on recommendation and help finding the right book rather than value for money. For more academic books, a good place to try is
www.studentbookworld.com

www.bookfellas.co.uk UK
GREAT BOOKS DELIVERED FOR LESS

Good, unfussy design, easy to navigate and well categorised too, with the promise of good service including order tracking.

www.swotbooks.co.uk UK
LOW COST BOOKS FOR CLEVER DICKS

A fun bookshop aimed at students and young people that offers DVDs and music too. It also has one of the best e-bookshops around. There are cheaper alternatives though.

www.countrybookshop.co.uk UK
YOUR LOCAL BOOKSHOP

This site is becoming more competitive with offers and discounted magazine subscriptions, but it's easier and more enjoyable to use than many sites.

www.bn.com US
THE WORLD'S BIGGEST BOOKSELLER

Barnes and Noble's site boasts more books than any other online bookseller. In style it follows the other bookshops with an American bias, and looks very similar to Amazon. It has a good out-of-print and used book service; you can also buy software, prints and posters as well as magazines and music. Unusual features include an online university where you can take courses in anything from business to learning a language.

B

www.powells.com   US
MASSIVE
A huge and impressive site which is well designed and relatively
easy to use, Powells seems to occupy most of Portland in
Oregon and for once the cost of shipping isn't prohibitive for UK
customers. A good place to go if you're looking for something
unusual.

www.thebookpeople.co.uk   UK
GREAT VALUE
The online version of this popular mail-order bookseller offers
the expected huge discounts and incentives. The range isn't
huge but enough to satisfy most book lovers.

Specialist Booksellers and Sites

*The following sites specialise in one form or genre of book. For
science fiction and fantasy see page 415.*

www.compman.co.uk – computer manuals.
www.crimetime.co.uk – good overview of what's going on in the
crime fiction world.
www.dancebooks.co.uk – if you need a book on dance, here's
where to start.
www.dymocks.com.au – excellent Australian bookstore.
www.firstbookshop.com – one of the few to offer book tokens.
www.gamblingbooks.co.uk – excellent selection from the High
Stakes bookshop.
www.greenbooks.co.uk – a specialist publisher on environmental
issues.
www.poems.com – home of *Poetry Daily*.
www.poetrybooks.co.uk – the poetry book society.
www.poetrybookshoponline.com – very good specialist poetry
shop.
www.soccer-books.co.uk – features over 1,000 books on
football.
www.stanfords.co.uk – excellent site from the UK's leading travel
and map retailers.

Second-hand Books and Book Finding

www.abebooks.com   UK
ADVANCED BOOK EXCHANGE
A network of some 13,500 independent booksellers from

around the world claiming access to 80 million used, rare and out-of-print books. Just use the excellent search engine to find your book and they'll direct you to the nearest bookseller.

B

www.booklovers.co.uk   UK
QUALITY SECOND-HAND BOOKS
If you can't find the book you want, then this is worth a try. There is an excellent search facility or you can leave them a request. They will then give you a quote if you want to sell a book or arrange a swap. There's also an events listing for book fairs.

www.greenmetropolis.com   UK
GOING GREEN
An interesting take on the bookselling theme, here all (mainly good condition second-hand) books are one price £3.75 with free delivery and there's a donation towards planting a tree. You can sell your books at this site too. Great idea, we hope it catches on.

See also:
www.bibliofind.com – a search engine from Amazon devoted to second-hand and rare books.
www.bookfinder.com – a more detailed search facility than Bibliofind and you can use it in French, German and Italian.
www.hp-bookfinders.co.uk – UK-based book-finding service with an easy-to-use site.
www.shapero.com – a specialist in natural history and travel-related, second-hand books.

Audio Books

www.talkingbooks.co.uk   UK
THE TALKING BOOKSHOP
A talking website for these specialists in books on tape. They have around 6,000 titles in stock and can quickly get another 20,000. They also stock CDs but still no MP3 yet. Search the site by author or reader, as well as by title. There are some offers, but most stock is at full price. See also **www.isis-publishing.co.uk** who have thousands of unabridged audio books and more in the way of CDs.

B

See also:
www.audible.co.uk – many audio books and podcasts to download, the advantage here is that you can listen to them using iTunes; however, it's not cheap and there aren't many offers.
www.audiobooksforfree.com – only free for downloading files which they describe as of 'bearable quality', for anything better there is a charge, but it is still not expensive and files are available in a number of formats.
www.payperlisten.com – a pay-as-you-go service which saves a huge amount on the usual audio book formats.

E-books

These are no longer the preserve of a few classical and out-of-copyright authors. There is a wide range of contemporary literature available, albeit not at the free sites. Many of the sites are online libraries and provide a useful source of information for educational and reference purposes.

www.free-ebooks.net US
E-BOOKS FOR FREE
A straightforward site devoted to making the most of free e-books with recommendations and the encouragement to produce your own e-book. Available in MP3 format for subscribers. See also **http://ebookdirectory.com**

www.sacred-texts.com US

HISTORICAL AND ANCIENT TEXTS
An amazing collection of historic documents and books presented electronically, it covers mythology, religions, folklore and the occult. Many have been translated into English and are well presented with links to related sites and to Amazon.

See also:
http://digitalmediastore.adobe.com – lots available but you have to have the Adobe reader to access them.
http://onlinebooks.library.upenn.edu – over 20,000 books to download with a huge bias towards American titles; it's especially strong on history.
www.bartleby.com/ebook – lots of classics and other free books to choose from. Also provides access to the encyclopaedia as well as American dictionaries and thesauruses.
www.e-book.com.au – a comprehensive source for e-books with a good directory of sites where you can download them for free.

www.fictionwise.com – a massive range of e-books from non-fiction to fiction and they seem to cover all the formats too.

www.manybooks.net – a good selection of free e-books mainly taken from Project Gutenberg.

www.netlibrary.com – awkward to use but a huge selection.

www.questia.com – claiming to be the world's biggest online library with over 60,000 books plus one million journals and other articles, covering thousands of research topics. You have to subscribe, though some content is free.

Literature and Authors

www.gutenberg.org   US
PROJECT GUTENBERG
This is one of the most famous Internet projects ever and one of the first web sites to post free e-books. There are over 17,000 listed. You can't do it justice in a small review, suffice to say it's well worth a visit for any book lover. If you're hooked on it, then there is the chance to become a volunteer proof-reader too.

www.literature-awards.com   US
BOOK AWARDS
A comprehensive listing of the major book awards throughout the world, why they exist and who won them. See also **www.artsfestivals.co.uk** for a literature festival near you.

http://classics.mit.edu   US
THE CLASSICS ONLINE
A superb resource offering over 440 free books to print or download, there's also a search facility and help with studying. If that's not enough, try **http://etext.lib.virginia.edu** with 1,800 publicly-available e-books including classic British and American fiction, major authors, children's literature, American history, Shakespeare, African-American documents, the Bible.

www.wordswithoutborders.org   US
INTERNATIONAL LITERATURE
An attractive e-zine devoted to world literature with reviews, recommendations and articles on books and writers. It's well categorised, interesting and you're bound to find something new.

www.william-shakespeare.info   US
COMPLETE WORKS
This is a straightforward site featuring historical and
biographical details plus a dictionary explaining the language of
the time.

See also:
www.bronte.org.uk – home of the Parsonage Museum in
Haworth with information about the place and an overview of the
Brontes and their lives.
www.ciconline.org/bdp1/ – a new look at Shakespeare, excellent
site design.
www.dickensmuseum.com – home of the Dickens Museum in
London with details about what you can see and links.
www.fantasticsherlockholmes.com – buy illustrations, download
the stories.
www.fidnet.com/~dap1955/dickens – a superb resource
dedicated to Dickens: a real labour of love.
www.janeausten.co.uk – the Jane Austen Centre in Bath with a
good online magazine offering information on everything from
fashion to biographical details.
www.hardysociety.org – the Thomas Hardy Society with good
contextual links.
www.lang.nagoya-u.ac.jp/~matsuoka/Bronte.html – all you
need to know about the Bronte sisters and more.
www.mss.library.nottingham.ac.uk/dhl_home.html –
DH Lawrence resources at the University of Nottingham.
www.pemberley.com – a pretty obsessive site devoted to
everything Jane Austen with discussion groups too.
www.sherlock-holmes.org.uk – home of the Sherlock Holmes
Society of London.
www.yale.edu/hardysoc – award-winning site on Thomas Hardy.

Reading Groups

www.bookgroup.info   UK
READING GROUP GUIDE
An attractive and informative site on how to run a book
group and choose titles, with an archive of titles and how
they've rated them. There's also a forum, and a directory is
promised.

See also:

http://readers.penguin.co.uk – run by Penguin books you can get discounts for your group and use the directory, but you have to register first.

www.complete-review.com – reviews of over 1,600 books plus news, links and a reader's rating too.

www.readinggroupguides.com – an American site offering information and guidance on books and how to run a reading group.

www.readinggroups.co.uk – a neat site run by publisher HarperCollins with news, advice and competitions.

www.thereadinggrouponline.co.uk – a good bookshop and forum aimed at reading groups, run by The Book People.

Children's Books

www.cool-reads.co.uk   UK

CHILDREN'S BOOK REVIEWS
Books for 10- to 15-year-olds, reviewed by 10- to 15-year-olds. An outstanding site both for its design and for its content. The books are well categorised and reviewed using a star rating system. If you're stuck for something to read, then a trip here is well worthwhile. There are also games, quizzes and chat.

www.achuka.co.uk   UK

CHILDREN'S BOOKS
Achuka are specialists in children's books and offer a comprehensive listing of what's available. There's plenty of information on the latest news and awards as well as reviews, author interviews, a chat section and links to booksellers. For shopping you are directed to Amazon.

www.wordpool.co.uk   UK

FOR PARENTS, TEACHERS AND WRITERS
A very useful resource devoted to children's books with lots of advice and recommendations. See also their sister site **www.ukchildrensbooks.co.uk** which is a list of links to sites listed by author, illustrator, publisher and a miscellaneous section.

www.sevenstories.org.uk   UK

SEND A STORY
Newly opened in Newcastle, Sevenstories is a centre for children's books and a museum celebrating the rich and diverse

world of British children's books. There is a facility for children to write and illustrate a story online and send it to a friend or an online gallery. Promises an online bookstore soon.

Other children's book sites:

www.carolhurst.com – good design and great for book reviews.

www.childrensbookshop.com – very traditional site from a shop based in Hay on Wye.

www.myhomelibrary – Anne Fine encouraging children to build a library of their own (with the aid of charity shops), loads of bookplates to download.

www.redhouse.co.uk – a good site devoted to children's books with lots of discounts and recommendations.

www.ucalgary.ca/~dkbrown/ – home of the excellent Children's Literature Web Guide.

www.usbourne.com – good interactive site from this specialist publisher.

www.worldbookday.com – find out about this great event that happens every March.

Resources for Writers

www.writersservices.com   UK
THE WEBSITE FOR WRITERS
A slightly messy site but compensates by having 1,300 pages of help, advice and information for writers updated weekly. It's certainly worth a visit if you are thinking of pouring your heart out in print. See also **www.writewords.org.uk** which is a useful resource for writers.

www.lulu.com   US
SELF PUBLISHING THE EASY WAY
Lulu enables you to take advantage of the latest printing technology to produce books in very small numbers, so dust off that manuscript! They will even host your work and sell it too and you get royalties. It's a relatively cheap and pain-free way to get published. See also **www.lightningsource.com**, **www.selfpublishing.co.uk** and **www.authorhouse.com** who all have their various approaches.

See also:
www.thenewwriter.com – online magazine for writers.

www.theromancereader.com – lots of romantic reviews and links.
www.openinghooks.us – an entertaining site devoted to great opening lines, view the database and get inspired.
www.openwriting.com – an open writing web magazine for writers.

Best Publisher's Websites

www.bloomsbury.com – an attractive site, home of Harry Potter, Scott's Miscellany and more.
www.dk.com – excellent site from one of the leading reference publishers, some good offers too.
www.faber.co.uk – an interesting site from the most literary of publishers.
www.harpercollins.co.uk – now a word from our sponsors – a wide ranging site from the publishers of this book with sections on Tolkein and plenty of celebrities as well as fiction and reference.
www.madaboutbooks.co.uk – a cool site from Hodder Headline.
www.penguin.co.uk – a bright and breezy site from Penguin with plenty to see, information on author events and readers' groups too.
www.randomhouse.co.uk – nice design from one of the biggest publishers, particularly good kids' section.
www.thefridayproject.co.uk – an attempt to turn some of the most creative websites into books.
www.virago.co.uk – an interactive and imaginative site from this publisher of women's literature.

Other book-related sites worth checking out . . .

www.bookaid.org   UK
  BOOKS FOR CHARITY
  A charity dedicated to giving unwanted books to places where books are scarce and needed. Find out about their activities and how you can get involved.

www.bookcrossing.com   UK
  RELEASE A BOOK
1. Read your book.
2. Say what you think about the book on the site with a reference number.
3. Release the book, give it to a friend or leave it somewhere.

You can then get e-mails from anyone who reads the book.
Members have released over 2.6 million books so far, so the
odds on finding one are increasing daily.

Broadband

*As access to ADSL or broadband becomes common, more and more
sites are cropping up to cater for those lucky enough to have it. Here
are some useful sites where you can start your broadband experience.
For information on downloading music, TV or movies go to the
relevant section in the book, where you'll find more information.*

www.broadband-help.com   UK
ALL YOU NEED TO KNOW
A good place to start, here you'll find advice and reviews all
dedicated to help you make the most out of your broadband
experience. See also **www.adslguide.org.uk** which is just as
informative albeit from a less attractive site.

www.broadbandchecker.co.uk   UK

BROADBAND AVAILABILITY
A neat and easy-to-use site; you just type in your postcode and
phone number and the site will tell you whether broadband is
available in your area. You can also compare providers, prices too.

www.jonnybroadband.com   UK
BROADBAND SEARCH
Jonny Broadband says 'I just love scouring the web to dig up the
very finest broadband content around – the really cool stuff that
makes it worth coughing up the cash for a fatter internet pipe in
the first place and most of it is free, if you know where to look.'
Useful and entertaining, although a bit messy. See also
www.razav.com which is cleaner but less fun.

www.broadbandweek.com   UK
ALL THE LATEST DEVELOPMENTS
Keep abreast of all the latest technology and increasing
download speeds at this business-like site.

www.btopenworld.com   UK
BRITISH TELECOM
Here you can establish whether you can get access to
broadband and, if not, they'll tell you more or less when it will

be coming your way. There are details of the various BT packages, other suppliers and also information for business users too.

Other sites worth checking out are:
www.broadband4britain.co.uk – information from this broadband pressure group.
www.ispreview.co.uk/broadband.shtml – informative pages from the excellent ISP review.
www.ntlhome.com/broadband – supplies most of the UK.
www.telewest.co.uk – supplies selected parts of the UK.
www.theregister.co.uk – the latest telecom and broadband news.

Browsers

We're often asked about alternatives to Internet Explorer. Here are the best:
www.mozilla.org – home to Firefox, certainly one of the fastest browsers and it works on all operating systems. It's easy to use and set up too.
www.mozilla.org/products/camino/ – another Mozilla product, here's an alternative to Apple's Safari browser.
www.netscape.com – the earliest real alternative to IE, it offers a huge amount of content and plenty of extra features.
www.opera.com – another claimant for the fastest browser, it's certainly flexible and easy on the eye and has lots of features, there is a mobile version too.

Business

Here are a few essential and helpful business sites; see also the finance section on page 157 for share dealing and other related sites. Be aware that many official-looking sites offering advice are often companies out to make a profit or are part of a larger organisation, so may not be impartial.

www.economist.com
 THE ECONOMIST MAGAZINE
The airports' best-selling magazine goes online with a wide-ranging site that covers business and politics world-wide. You can get access to the archive and also their excellent country surveys. If you're in business, you need this in your favourites box.

See also:
www.better-business.co.uk – a helpful site from this magazine including tips on starting up and even what to do when things get boring.
www.businessweek.com – offering a wide range of business news and information.

www.businesslink.gov.uk   UK

THE NATIONAL BUSINESS ADVICE SERVICE
A government-run site which has a comprehensive set of helpful guides and links, backed up by a hotline. It has to be the first port of call for any small business needing advice or help.

See also:
www.business.com – a US-oriented business search engine.
www.dti.gov.uk – here you'll find a great deal of wide ranging information.
www.sbs.gov.uk – the government's small business service.

www.startinbusiness.co.uk   UK
AN ONLINE BUSINESS STARTER KIT
An excellent portal site on all things to do with business including a good guide to help you start a business. There are plenty of links plus listings of businesses for sale, property, services and potential opportunities.

www.startups.co.uk   UK

BUILD A BETTER BUSINESS
An excellent and comprehensive site designed to help businesses start up and get going. It has basic advice on finances and covers aspects like planning, tax, employment and insurance.

www.businessadviceonline.org.uk   UK

BUSINESS ADVICE
An excellent resource whether you're starting out or want to improve an existing business. There are sections on choosing the right IT systems, contracts, selling techniques and much more.

See also:
www.advertopedia.com – all you need to know about advertising.
www.bawe-uk.org – home of the British Association of Women Entrepreneurs.

www.bized.ac.uk – aimed at students and teachers but a great resource for business people too.

www.business-ethics.com – believe it or not, a magazine devoted to the finer arts of corporate responsibility.

www.bvca.co.uk – the public face of venture capitalism.

www.clearlybusiness.com – offers the same information as above but is a more commercial affair.

www.ecademy.com – a messy business networking and community site.

www.ecourier.co.uk – an excellent online courier management system.

www.fsb.org.uk – home of the Federation of Small Businesses.

www.iba.org.uk – contact a qualified business adviser.

www.linkedin.com – create your own business network.

www.payontime.co.uk – excellent advice on how to manage payment.

www.plaxo.com – a service devised to help you keep your business contacts up to date.

www.uktradeinfo.com – useful if you are going to trade overseas.

www.whichfranchise.com – a slightly messy site that offers the information you need on all the available franchises in the UK, and how to go about getting one.

www.hoovers.com   UK
COMPANY RESEARCH
Get basic information on any UK and US company plus related links and advice; a very useful research tool.

See also:

www.carolworld.com – Company Annual Reports Online; a useful free service.

www.companies-house.gov.uk – a useful site if you want to research companies with access to information and guidance on most aspects of business and the regulations surrounding it. Here you can check-up on whether companies really exist or not.

www.uk.sage.com   UK
BUSINESS SOFTWARE
If you need accounting software to solve virtually any sort of problem or provide a new service, you should find it here. Sage has a good reputation for helping small businesses. See also **www.myob.com** who offer similar products.

Cars

Whether you want to buy a car, check out your insurance or even arrange a service, it can all be done on the Internet. If you want to hire a car see page 557, while for information on road travel go to page 558.

Petrol Heads

The Good Web Site Guide's Top 10s
of the Internet

1. **www.autoindex.org** – home of the highly detailed Global Auto Index
2. **www.autoexpress.co.uk** – excellent online mag
3. **www.autocarmag.com** – that makes two excellent online magazines
4. **www.parkers.co.uk** – find out how much your car is worth
5. **www.conceptcar.co.uk** – the latest in car design
6. **www.speed-trap.co.uk** – the site is a mess but at least you'll know where they are
7. **www.bbc.co.uk/topgear** – the site of the popular TV show
8. **www.modify.co.uk** – bored with your car? Then modify!
9. **www.classicmotor.co.uk** – the first place to go for classic motoring
10. **www.uglycars.co.uk** – laugh at the worst

Motoring Organisations, Campaigning Sites and Government Agencies

www.theaa.co.uk   UK

THE AA
A comprehensive motoring site with a route planner, new and used car info, travel information, insurance quotes, shop and a car data checking facility.

www.rac.co.uk   UK

THE RAC
A much clearer site than the AA's, with a very good route planner and traffic news service. There's also information about

buying a car, getting the best finance and insurance deals, and a small shop.

www.greenflag.co.uk UK

GREEN FLAG

The usual route planner and car buying advice all packaged on a nice-looking and very green site; there's a particularly good section on European travel and motoring advice. See also **www.internationalbreakdown.com** who offer a wide range of cover across the UK and Europe.

www.dvla.gov.uk UK

DRIVER AND VEHICLE LICENSING AGENCY

Excellent for the official line in motoring; the driver's section has details on penalty points, licence changes and medical issues. The vehicles section goes through all related forms and there's also a 'What's New' page. It's clearly and concisely written throughout and information is easy to find but be warned, some pages talk to you.

Just launched is **www.direct.gov.uk/Motoring** Here you can apply for your tax disc online, book theory and practise tests and find out about vehicle recalls. There are also sections on crime, buying and selling cars and information for learner drivers.

www.rmif.co.uk UK

RETAIL MOTOR INDUSTRY FEDERATION

A rich source of information covering all aspects of buying and selling cars for both industry and consumers alike. It's great as a starting place if you want to find out about legislation and the latest news, it also has an excellent links section.

www.smmt.co.uk UK

SOCIETY OF MOTOR MANUFACTURERS & TRADERS

The SMMT support the British motor industry by campaigning and informing the trade and public alike. Here you can get information on topics like the motor show, the tax regime, the latest industry standards, as well as links to other industry sites.

www.abd.org.uk UK

CAMPAIGNING FOR THE DRIVER

The Association of British Drivers aims to be the lobbying voice of beleaguered drivers in the UK. Here you can find out about their campaigns against road user charging, speed limits, the environment and the road infrastructure.

www.rospa.co.uk   UK

ROYAL SOCIETY FOR THE PREVENTION OF ACCIDENTS
An excellent site from ROSPA with loads of information about
road safety with fact sheets available on most issues and
problems that affect every driver and pedestrian. See also
www.cic.cranfield.ac.uk where all the crash testing goes on.

www.roadpeace.org   UK
SUPPORT FOR CRASH VICTIMS
RoadPeace, the UK's national charity dedicated to supporting
bereaved and injured road crash victims and the only national
helpline for road victims. Join a campaign or use the extensive
links section. Salutary.

www.euroncap.com
HOW SAFE IS YOUR CAR
Euroncap is responsible for testing the safety of cars sold in
Europe. Results are posted for each car on its safety
performance in a crash and how 'friendly' it is if you happen to
hit a pedestrian.

www.secureyourmotor.gov.uk   UK
SECURITY TIPS FOR MOTORISTS
Pretty straightforward site detailing the best steps to guard
against your car, bike or truck being stolen. You can take tests to
see how secure your car is or test your security knowledge.

www.carplus.org.uk   UK
RIDE SHARING
Promoting responsible car use; join a car club, help the
environment and aid congestion by sharing your journey with
others; plus info on car sharing and alternative fuels. See also
www.citycarclub.co.uk and also **www.mystreetcar.co.uk**

www.cclondon.com   UK
LONDON CONGESTION CHARGES
All you need to know about the congestion charge and how to
pay it.

www.speed-trap.co.uk   UK
THE SPEED TRAP BIBLE
While not condoning speeding, this site gives the low-down on
speed traps, the law and links to police forces. There's even
data on the types of camera used and advice on dealing with the

courts and police. However, they are sponsored by a speed trap detector company. See also **www.speedcamerasuk.com**

www.parkingticket.co.uk   UK
PARKING PROBLEMS
This site gives details regarding parking and free advice on how to challenge a parking ticket that you feel has been issued unfairly.

Cheaper and Greener Fuels

www.est-powershift.org.uk   UK
CONVERTING TO CLEANER FUELS
A well-put-together and informative site aimed at encouraging drivers to shift to cleaner fuels such as LPG. You can find out how to convert your car, where the fuel stations are and the latest government information such as grants and future proposals.

www.spongecars.com   UK
LPG CONVERSIONS
Excellent overview and information site covering all aspects of converting a car to LPG, an explanation of what it is, how to get a conversion quote and the latest news.

See also:
www.bath.ac.uk/~en2bwp/gaspower.htm – learn about gas-powered cars.
www.evuk.co.uk – not just milk floats and golf carts, it's serious stuff, the electric car business.
www.lpga.co.uk – information from the Liquid Petroleum Gas Association.
www.toyota.co.uk/prius – home of the successful hybrid electrical petrol car.

Car Information and Buying Guides

www.autoindex.org   US
WORLD CAR CATALOGUE
An amazing directory of the world's car makers illustrated using thousands of pictures. There is detailed information on each manufacturer and what they produce. You can search by maker, country, and category or body style.

www.carsurvey.org UK
CAR REVIEWS BY THEIR OWNERS
Don't let the basic design fool you; this is an impressive
collection of reviews on hundreds of cars, by those most
important people – their owners. It's easily searchable and
genuinely useful if you're looking for unbiased opinion.

www.parkers.co.uk UK
REDUCING THE GAMBLE
The premier buying guide with a clear, readable site, this covers
all the information you'll need to select the right car for you.
However, these days you have to register to get the more
detailed information. See also **www.glass.co.uk** which offers
similar information on a minimal site.

www.jdpower.com US
J.D.POWER RELIABILITY
It's only geared to the US market but some models are the same
and you can get a great deal of safety and reliability information
here.

Magazine and E-zine Sites

www.autoexpress.co.uk UK

THE BEST MOTORING NEWS AND INFORMATION
Massive database on cars, with motoring news and features on
the latest models, you can check prices too. It also has
classified ads and a great set of links. You have to register to get
access to most of the information; lots of advertising makes the
site a bit annoying to use.

www.whatcar.co.uk UK
WHAT CAR MAGAZINE
A neatly packaged, one-stop shop for cars with reviews and
data on every car. There's a cars for sale section and an easy-to-
use search facility.

www.autocarmag.com UK

AUTOCAR MAGAZINE
A fine site from this popular weekly with plenty of interactive
features including videos and even a blogging service; there is
news, reviews, advice and shopping too.

www.carnet.co.uk UK
ONLINE CAR MAGAZINE
Car Net is a well-designed and fun site with the latest news and new car reviews as well as feature micro-sites and links to deals on cars and insurance, statistics (on over 6,000 cars) and classifieds. You can also visit the specialist forums and have a go at the trivia quizzes.

C

www.carkeys.co.uk   UK
INFORMATION SERVICE STATION
A wide-ranging magazine-style site with lots of data on current and new models as well as launch reviews and motoring news.

www.womanmotorist.com   US
MOTORING ISN'T JUST FOR MEN
A well-laid-out and interesting American magazine-style site that dispels the myth that motoring is just for men. Lots of advice, buying information, a glossary and car reviews.

TV Tie-in Sites

www.topgear.beeb.com   UK
TOP GEAR
A site to go along with the TV series, it has everything you'd expect along with features on new and used cars, competitions, classifieds and a shop. See also **ww.bbc.co.uk/lifestyle/motoring** which is great for advice on buying and owning.

www.4car.co.uk   UK
DRIVEN
News, sport, reviews, advice, chat and games – it's all here, and you can find out what's been and is being featured on their main motoring programmes.

Traders and Car Finding Services

www.motortrak.com   UK
USED CAR SEARCH
A hi-tech site where, in theory, you can find the right used car. Just follow the search guidelines and up pops your ideal car! It's easy to use and very fast.

www.autobytel.co.uk
US/UK

WORLD'S LEADING CAR BUYING SERVICE

The easy way to buy a car online, just select the model you want then follow the online instructions. They've improved information on used and nearly new cars and will get quotes from local dealers. All cars featured have detailed descriptions and photos. There's also financial information and aftercare service.

www.oneswoop.com
UK

SMART WAY TO BUY

Now owned by Norwich Union, a straightforward and very popular site that concentrates on making the process of buying a car as painless as possible. There are also some good special offers and a finance section. It's very easy to use and faster than most.

www.jamjar.com
UK

DIRECT LINE

Jam Jar is owned by Direct Line Insurance and they want to make it work well. The design is OK, and if you persevere there are some fantastic offers. They are also improving the service by branching into other merchandise related to driving such as personal leasing and insurance.

For more car buying information and cars for sale try:

http://cars.kelkoo.co.uk – the car price checking pages at Kelkoo.

http://uk.cars.yahoo.com – the excellent Yahoo has a used car search engine, car comparison facility and directory.

www.autolocate.co.uk – great for links, good new car guide and review section, also good for used cars.

www.autopoint.ie – Ireland's leading online car retailer and auction house.

www.autoseek.co.uk – thousands of cars for sale, great for links.

www.autotrader.co.uk – claiming to be Britain's biggest car showroom with over 300,000 listed. Nice, clear design.

www.broadspeed.com – car import specialists with a nicely designed and fast site.

www.carseller.co.uk – free advertising if selling and good links.

www.carsource.co.uk – great for data and online quotes, thousands of cars for sale.

www.car-supermarkets.com – a useful list of the UK's car supermarkets with lots of information and how to find them.

www.cartalk.com – a good US magazine site that is something of a cult stateside. It's worth following the links and listening to the radio show.

www.eurekar.com – lots of deals from this specialist importer.

www.fish4cars.co.uk – over 150,000 cars on their database, plus hundreds of other vehicles. Comprehensive.

www.new-car-net.co.uk – informative and well-illustrated car review site.

www.savemoneyoncars.co.uk – bright and breezy site with lots of deals and information on buying a car cheaply.

www.sellyourcarnow.co.uk – sell your car direct to the motor trade using this posting site.

www.showroom4cars.com – bright, brash and fast.

www.topmarques.co.uk – luxury vehicles only, part of Autotrader.

www.vanbuyer.com – vans and more vans of all shapes and sizes.

www.wannavan.com – specialist in supplying vans for business and personal use.

Car Auctions

www.british-car-auctions.co.uk   UK
   CAR REMARKETING
   The leading car auction company uses its site to inform rather than sell online, there are catalogues of upcoming auctions plus information on buying and selling.

Online auction sites

   These seem much the same so find the one that suits you, if you are happy buying a car in this way:
   http://motors.ebay.co.uk – the motor pages from the popular auction site with a vast array of cars, bikes and accessories from which to choose.
   www.autorola.co.uk – a simple way to sell your car to some 1,000 dealers.
   www.autobyauction.co.uk – one of the easier sites to use but it's amazing how few cars are illustrated with photos.
   www.raw2k.co.uk – buy a wreck, do it up or take the parts.

www.hpicheck.com   UK
   DON'T BE RIPPED OFF . . .
   Before you buy a second-hand car it's wise to pay out £39.95

for an HPI check which will tell you about what mileage the car should have, whether it's been in an accident or damaged and also if there's any outstanding finance against it.

www.ukstolencars.co.uk UK

ARE YOU DRIVING A STOLEN CAR?
A simple and free search of the UK stolen cars database offering helpful information and advice.

Disabled Motorists

www.ddmc.org.uk UK
DISABLED DRIVERS MOTOR CLUB
A campaigning site from the DDMC who are devoted to improving the lot of disabled motorists. It has lots of useful information and you can find out about and support their latest campaigns. See also **www.dda.org.uk** home of the Disabled Drivers Association who work along the same lines.

www.motability.co.uk UK

GET MOBILE
A scheme for helping disabled people get mobile by contract hiring a car, the site is very clear and easy to use too.

See also:
www.aixam-cars.co.uk – a leading supplier of quadricycles and adapted cars.
www.dft.gov.uk – the Department for Transport; follow links for disabled people.
www.direct.gov.uk/DisabledPeople/MotoringAndTransport – lots of information on transport schemes and adapting cars.
www.motability.royalsun.co.uk/fullsite/index.html – a motability scheme from an insurance company.

Car Registrations

www.dvla-som.co.uk UK
CHERISHED AND PERSONALISED NUMBERS
Here's the first port of call if you want that special number plate. They sell by auction but there's plenty of help and you search for un-issued, select registrations in both new and old styles. Order over the phone using their hotline.

For more sites offering car registrations try:
www.carreg.co.uk
www.newreg.co.uk
www.northumbrianumbers.com
www.regtransfers.co.uk

Insurance

*Most of the general finance sites (page 157) and motoring
organisations (page 68) will offer links to insurance companies, but
these are worth a try.*

www.easycover.com   UK
CAR INSURANCE
Quotes from a large number of insurance suppliers, you just fill
in the form, and they get back to you with a quote.

See also:
www.diamond.co.uk and **www.girlmotor.co.uk** – specialists in
insurance for women drivers who are statistically a safer bet.
www.cheapest-motor-insurance.co.uk
www.eaglestar.co.uk
www.swinton.co.uk

Looking After and Repairing Your Car

www.ukmot.com   UK

M.O.T.
Find your nearest M.O.T. test centre, get facts about the test and
what's actually supposed to be checked, there's also a reminder
service. You can also run an HPI check from the site and find
out about the foibles of specific models.

www.carcareclinic.com   UK
LOOKING AFTER YOUR CAR
If you need advice on car repairs or faults, then help is at hand
here. There are discussion forums on all sorts of problems
and, if you post a message or ask for advice, there's always
someone to answer. They also provide a databank which is
essentially a glossary of terms and a good set of links. See
also **www.autosite.com/garage/garmenu.asp** which is from
a large American site, here you can find maintenance
encyclopaedias.

www.haynes.co.uk   UK
HAYNES MANUALS
Unfortunately they've stopped the download service, so now
you have to buy the books – there's 2,500 available so there
should be one for you.

www.partsgateway.co.uk   UK

FIND THE PART YOU NEED
An excellent place to go if you want to find a particular part for
your car but don't want to pay dealer prices. If you don't know
what it's called then you can upload a digital photo and they'll
use that to identify exactly what you want. See also
www.eurocarparts.co.uk and **www.247spares.co.uk**

Car Accessories and Kits

www.halfords.com   UK
DRIVING DOWN PRICES
A fairly wide range of products for your car and bike at good
prices and sold from a very good site, there's advice and a store
locator too.

www.autofashion.co.uk   UK
ACCESSORISE YOUR CAR
An entertaining site where you can buy body kits and
accessories for many makes of car, including custom
made.

www.modify.co.uk   UK

COMPREHENSIVE LISTING SERVICE
An outstanding source for information on those companies
that can help you improve your car. There's a directory of
specialists – everything from tuners to insurance, articles on
how to modify your motor and lastly statistics on virtually every
modern car.

See also:
www.autostore.co.uk – specialists in car storage solutions, slow
site though.
www.caralarms.org – every type of car alarm and security
device.
www.gttowing.co.uk – for tow bars, roof racks and trailers, good
site.
www.motech.uk.com – specialists in performance enhancement.

www.roofbox.co.uk – roof boxes and most other storage
solutions.
www.saveanddrive.co.uk – for roof boxes, cycle carriers and
radar detectors.

www.caraudiocentre.com   UK
IN CAR AUDIO SYSTEMS
Here you can get loads of advice and offers on a wide range of
stereos with a price promise and low delivery costs. See also
www.toade.com who have a highly interactive site and can also
supply security, multi-media and navigation equipment on top
of audio.

www.mytyres.co.uk   UK
TYRES
A site where you can save money buying tyres for your car. It
pays to know what you want but the prices appear competitive
and they'll find a fitter for you too.

See also:
www.kwikfit.co.uk – very good site with mobile fitting service,
although you can get cheaper deals by visiting them.
www.tyresafety.co.uk – home of the Tyre Industry Council with
advice on safety.
www.tyres-online.co.uk – basic web site but some good
prices.

Specialist Car Sites

www.classicmotor.co.uk   UK

FOR CLASSIC CARS
By far the best classic car site. Design-wise it's a jumble (it's
better to use the no frames version), but it's comprehensive,
including clubs, classifieds and books; here you can buy
anything from a car to a headlight bulb.

See also:
www.classic-car-directory.com – a well-categorised links
site.
www.hireaclassiccar.com – classic car hire specialist.
www.kit-cars.com – messy American site devoted to kit cars.
www.kitcars.org – an embryonic site developed by an
enthusiast.

motorbase.com – a comprehensive site with plenty of information, links, a forum and a chance to buy everything from cars, tools, books and models.

www.vintage-car-world.com – a German owned site offering news, event information and classifieds.

C

www.pistonheads.com UK
SPEED MATTERS

Pistonheads is a British site dedicated to the faster side of motoring and is great for reviews of the latest cars and chat. It's passionate and very informative.

www.britishmm.co.uk UK
HISTORY OF BRITISH CARS TO 1960

An amateur site with a good make-by-make history of the British car industry, it includes a glossary and information on tax and other historical references. Unfortunately it's not well illustrated.

www.conceptcar.co.uk UK
AUTOMOTIVE DESIGN

A really interesting, comprehensive and well-laid-out site devoted to car design and new concepts, it's great for links and you can tell that it's used by the industry itself.

www.uglycars.co.uk UK
UGLY CARS

There's been a spate of books published about the worst cars sold in the UK and this site goes along with that trend and our fascination with all things that are rubbish. Here you can relish some of the worst excuses for car design and even suggest some candidates to be added.

Learning to Drive

www.learners.co.uk UK
LEARNER'S DIRECTORY

The point of this site is to help you find the right driving school. Just type in your postcode and the schools will be listed along with helpful additional information such as whether they have a female instructor or whether they train for motorway driving. There is plenty of supplementary information on things like theory tests and how to buy a car.

www.2pass.co.uk
UK

THEORY AND PRACTICAL TESTS

 A learner driver's dream, this site helps with your tests in giving advice, mock exams plus other interesting snippets of information such as why the British drive on the left. There are also articles on driving abroad, on motorbikes and driving automatics. There's also help finding insurance, plenty of fun with top stories, quizzes and crash of the month.

www.driving-tests.co.uk
UK

THE DSA

Get the official line from the Driving Standards Agency where you can now book both the theory and practical test online, get advice for learners and instructors and learn about government schemes to promote better driving. For the Highway Code faithfully reproduced as a website and more theory tests go to **www.highwaycode.gov.uk**

See also:
www.bsm.co.uk – one of the UK's biggest driving schools.
www.direct.gov.uk/Motoring/LearnerAndNewDrivers – information on learning to drive from the government.
www.iam.org.uk – home of the Institute of Advanced Motorists.
www.roadcode.co.uk – Highway Code for young people.

Celebrities

Find your favourite celebrities and their web sites using these sites. A word of caution though – there are many celebrity search engines available on the web and while it's easy to find your favourite, it's also very easy to unwittingly access adult-orientated material through them.

www.celebhoo.com
US

FOR EVERYTHING CELEBRITY

A very good fan site directory plus information, birthdays, chat and gossip. See also **www.celebsites.com** for a huge listing of official celeb sites; while at Links for Kids you'll find a selection of sites that have been checked for safety, so hopefully there will be no nasty surprises – **www.links4kids.co.uk/celebrities.htm**

www.thespiannet.com
UK

ACTORS AND ACTRESSES

Lots of actors and actresses listed with links and details

Gossip

The Good Web Site Guide's Top 10s
of the Internet

1. **www.popbitch.com** – the first stop for conjecture
2. **www.salon.com** – excellent and up to the minute e-zine
3. **www.hollywood.com** – over 1 million pages to choose from
4. **www.aintitcoolnews.com** – the latest film gossip and reviews
5. **www.bollywoodworld.com** – all you need on the world's biggest film industry
6. **www.celebhoo.com** – find all the info on your favourite star at this directory
7. **www.debretts.co.uk** – posh celebrity gossip
8. **www.thesmokinggun.com** – if it's sleaze you're looking for, it's probably here
9. **www.mykindaplace.com** – gossip and celebrity news for teenagers
10. **www.teamtalk.com** – sports gossip

including e-mail addresses. It's also a good resource for
aspiring thespians.

www.celebrityemail.com   US
E-MAIL THE STARS
E-mail addresses to over 22,000 of the world's most famous
people. It's quite biased towards Americans but give it a try
anyway, you might get a reply.

www.debretts.co.uk   UK
POSH CELEBRITY GOSSIP
An excellent site from *Debrett* who have been tracking the lives
of celebrities for many years longer than the likes of *OK* and
Hello. There are sections on people in the news plus a good
celebrity search engine. There are also sections on the royal
family, a guide to the season, charities and a fun search section
where you can match birthdays.

www.hellomagazine.com   UK
THE WORLD IN PICTURES
Hello magazine's web site features pictures and articles from

current and previous issues with loads of celebrities. You can't
search by celebrity but you can have fun trawling through the
pictures.

www.eonline.com   US
E!
Entertainment Online features all the latest gossip mainly
oriented towards the US and Hollywood in particular. It's fun
and irreverent and has a reputation for being first with the
news.

www.glamourmagazine.co.uk   UK
LOSE YOURSELF IN GLAMOUR
Gossip, fashion, beauty tips, chat, competitions and, of course,
celebrities are the mainstay of *Glamour* magazine's site. Its
main function though is to plug the real magazine.

www.amiannoyingornot.com   US
VOTE FOR MOST ANNOYING CELEBRITIES
You can spend ages on this site; it's easy to vote and fun to use.
Each celeb gets a page with biographical details and reasons
why they could be annoying or not . . .

www.mugshots.com   US
WHEN IT ALL GOES WRONG
This could only happen in America, mug shots of the rich and
famous when, once in a while, they break the law. There's also
a serious side with sections covering national US events and the
FBI's most wanted list. Ghoulish but fascinating too.

www.thesmokinggun.com   US
FINDING THE SLEAZE – ALLEGEDLY
Devoted to finding skeletons in cupboards, Smoking Gun has
everything from confidential documents and incriminating
evidence to mug shots. If your favourite celeb has done
something wrong, even a small thing, it'll be here.

www.bbc.co.uk/celebdaq   UK
CELEBRITY STOCK EXCHANGE
The BBC's celebrity stock exchange show now lives on in the
form of this web site. It monitors the rise and fall of many
celebrities and allocates a stock price to them – it's fun to see
who's on the up and who's on the slide. See also the Hollywood
Stock Exchange at **www.hsx.com**

www.famousbirthdays.com US
WHO SHARES YOUR BIRTHDAY
A comprehensive listing of celebrity birthdays. Click on any celebrity and you get sent to a Google search page featuring your chosen one.

Charities

The Internet offers a great opportunity to give to your favourite charity or support a cause dear to your heart. There are so many that we're unable to list them all, but here are some top sites with directories to help you find the ones that interest you. For charity cards see page 237 and for health-related charities see page 246.

Charity Information

www.charitychoice.co.uk UK
ENCYCLOPAEDIA OF CHARITIES
A very useful and well-put-together directory of charities with a good search facility and a list in over 30 categories. There's also the excellent 'Goodwill Gallery' where you can post up a service or a donation you're willing to give to charity.

www.caritasdata.co.uk UK
CHARITIES DIRECT
A support site for charities with information on how to raise funds and run a charity, there's also a good directory of UK charities and you can rank them by expenditure, revenue and fund size.

www.charitycommission.gov.uk UK
THE CHARITY COMMISSION
The Charity Commission's mission is to give the public confidence in the integrity of charities in England and Wales, and their site lists over 166,000 charities. There's also lots of advice for charities, a list of their publications and links to related sites.

www.charitynet.org UK
INFORMATION ON THE NON-PROFIT WORLD
A useful database covering charities and non-profit organisations world-wide, it has sections on education, government, IT, legal issues and jobs too.

See also:
www.bcconnections.org.uk – businesses can find out how they can get involved in charity donations and charities can find out how they can get businesses involved in their work.
www.charities.org – information about American charities.
www.helplines.org.uk – the Telephone Helplines Association with useful search facility.

Giving

www.justgiving.com   UK

GIVE EFFECTIVELY
A newsy and informative site devoted to making the process of giving to charity as easy as possible whether you're an individual donor, charity or a company. The site is divided into three sections: Fundraise, Donate and Sponsor so you can go directly to the area that interests you. See also **www.allaboutgiving.org** which is especially informative about unusual ways of donating such as using tax and shares.

www.thehungersite.com   US

CLICK AND GIVE
Just one click and you'll donate a cup of food to the world's hungry via registered sponsors, a brilliant idea and one that works: last year the site funded nearly 44 million cups of food. Sign up and they'll send you a reminder to visit every weekend. There are also sister sites for breast cancer, saving rain forests, animal rescue, child health and a new literacy site. See also **www.freedonation.com** which has similar aims and works along the same lines.

www.careinternational.org.uk   UK
HELPING THE WORLDS POOREST
Care are all about helping the world's most stricken people, here you can learn about their work and donate.

www.missionfish.org.uk   UK
CHARITY AUCTIONS
Make money for charity when you auction your goods through EBay. Various major charities are supported and it's easy to use. See also EBay's pages at **http://pages.ebay.co.uk/community/charity/index.html**

See also:

www.50ways.org – an outstanding American site devoted to ways of giving money to save the world's children from suffering.

www.charitychallenge.com – raise money for your chosen charity by taking an adventure holiday through Charity Challenge.

www.dec.org.uk – donate to emergency appeals and track how the money has been spent.

www.ecpat.net – working to eliminate all forms of child abuse.

www.givewater.org – help get water to where it's most needed.

www.sendacow.org.uk – get livestock to those who really need it in East Africa.

Chat

There are literally thousands of chat sites and rooms on the web covering many different topics. However, this is the area of the Net that people have the most concerns about. There have been loads of cases where people have been tricked into giving out personal information and even arranged unsuitable meetings.

But at its best, a chat program is a great way to keep in contact with friends, especially if they live miles away. So chat wisely by following our top tips for keeping safe.

Chat – Our Top Tips

1. Be wary, just like you would be if you were visiting any new place.
2. Don't give your e-mail address out without making sure that only the person you're sending it to can read it.
3. People often pretend to be someone they're not when they're chatting; unless you know the person, assume that's the case with anyone you chat with online.
4. Don't meet up with anyone you've met online – keep your online life separate. Chances are they'd be a let down anyway, even if they were genuine.
5. If you like the look of a chat room or site but you're not sure about it, get a recommendation first.
6. If you want to meet up with friends online, arrange a time and place beforehand.
7. If you don't like someone, just block 'em.
8. Check out the excellent **www.chatdanger.com** (see below) for more info on how to chat safely.

www.chatdanger.com US

KEEP SAFE IN CHAT ROOMS
A great site devoted to the perils of using chat rooms, full of advice and sensible information, it can be a little slow though, but it's worth persevering. See also **www.thinkuknow.co.uk** who provide advice for young people.

www.aim.com UK

AOL INSTANT MESSENGER
One of the most popular, it's pretty safe and you can easily block people who are a nuisance, or just set it up so that only friends can talk to you.

http://web.icq.com US
ICQ – I SEEK YOU
There are lots of chat rooms here. It's quick and easy to use combined with a mobile phone. There are lots of features such as games, money advice, music and lurve.

www.mirc.com US
IRC – INTERNET RELAY CHAT
A straightforward chat program that is easy to use. Generally it's been overtaken by the likes of AOL but some web sites may opt to use it.

www.trillian.cc US

COMMUNICATE WITH FLEXIBILITY AND STYLE
Trillian enables connections to all the major chat programs through one interface. The reader looks good and you can personalise it too.

www.paltalk.com US
VERSATILITY
A feature-laden system with everything from video conferencing to instant messaging – all free!

www.habbohotel.co.uk UK

FOR UK TEENS
Lots of recommendations from users has meant the inclusion of this site in the book, flexibility, fun graphics and an excellent monitoring policy make it popular. This is the new UK site for **www.habbohotel.com** the basics are free but additional services have to be paid for.

www.there.com   US
  3-D CHAT
  Create your avatar or virtual identity, join in one of the
  conversations or play a game with your new friends, it's
  entertaining and best used in broadband.

C

Children

*You can save pounds on children's clothes and toys by shopping over
the Net; it's easy and the service is often excellent. The Internet is
also a great way to educate and entertain children, they are
fascinated by it and soon become experts, often quickly overtaking
their parents. We've put together a selection of the very best sites
here but for ideas for days out with children see the British travel
listings page 549, for educational sites see page 124 and for parenting
concerns see page 362.*

For Young Children

The Good Web Site Guide's Top 10s
of the Internet

1. **www.mamamedia.com** – great for encouraging communication
    skills
2. **www.bonus.com** – excellent, great looking and fun
3. **www.yucky.com** – learn about science the fun way
4. **www.nickjr.com** – a superb site from Nickelodeon
5. **www.sesamesworkshop.org** – still going strong
6. **www.bbc.co.uk/cbeebies** – great for the very young
7. **www.disney.co.uk** – despite the overt commerciality, it's still
    worth a visit
8. **www.barbie.com** – heaven for 5-year-old girls
9. **www.lego.co.uk** – a little gem featuring the little bricks
10. **www.citv.co.uk** – more games and program links

Shopping for Children

www.toy.co.uk
UK

👍 FIND THAT TOY

A very useful toy search engine, you can search by type,
company or age. Once searched, it lists the toys with details,
price and where you can buy them online.

www.elc.co.uk
UK

EARLY LEARNING CENTRE

A well-designed and user-friendly site that offers a wide range of
toys for the under-fives in particular, it's strong on character
products and traditional toys alike.

www.hamleys.co.uk
UK

FINEST TOY STORE IN THE WORLD

At the Hamley's site you can search for toys by gender, price or
age. There's also an okay selection of character areas within the
store as well as the more traditional range, which is their main
strength. Children can leave a wish list on the site and they do a
birthday reminder service.

www.toysrus.co.uk
UK

NOT JUST TOYS

Good site with all the key brands and 'in' things you'd
expect – you can even buy a mobile phone. Has links to
key toy manufacturer's sites and a sister site called
www.babiesrus.co.uk which covers younger children.

www.theentertainer.com
UK

THE ENTERTAINER

The online spin-off from the Entertainer high street stores; it
offers much in the way of bargains and this bright and breezy
site is easy to navigate. You can search by toy, age, price or
category.

www.newcron.com
UK

CHARACTER PRODUCTS

Newcron has taken over the Character Warehouse site to
produce an online store that offers a wide range of mainstream
and unusual character products. You can search by character,
product or price. See also **www.shop4toys.co.uk** which has a
similar offer.

C

www.woodentoysonline.co.uk
UK

WOODEN TOYS

A wide range of wooden and innovative toys here covering lots of categories and types, all on a well-categorised and easy-to-use site.

www.outdoortoysdirect.co.uk
UK

LOW PRICES ON OUTDOOR TOYS

Excellent value for money with free delivery, a money back guarantee, plus a wide range of goods. The selection consists of everything from trampolines to swings, slides and play houses. Free delivery on most goods. To complete your outdoor experience you can always pay a visit to **www.kiteshop.co.uk** who offer a wide range of kites and advice from an excellent site.

www.krucialkids.com
UK

ALL ABOARD THE KRUCIAL KIDS EXPRESS

This site specialises in developmental toys for children up to eight years old, providing detailed information on the educational value of each of the 200 or so toys. The site itself can be slow, but the prices aren't bad so patience pays off. For educational toys see also **www.mulberrybush.co.uk** who specialise in toys for under 12s.

www.mailorderexpress.com
UK

SHOP IN THE COMFORT OF YOUR HOME

Excellent toy store with games and models too. Shop by brand or by category, with some good prices and special offers. The design is a little old fashioned but effective nonetheless.

Other sites in this very competitive area that are worth a visit:
www.bearcountryuk.com – wide variety at all prices.
www.drtoy.com – a quirky American site run by someone who has reviewed and rated some 2,000 products for children, includes useful and intelligent 100 best toys of the year awards.
www.huggables.co.uk – specialists in teddies and other cute soft toys.
www.imaginarium.com – Amazon's toy store.
www.modelmegastore.co.uk – excellent for models of all types, especially remote control cars; shipping is good value.
www.orchardtoys.co.uk – specialists in fun, educational toys.
www.teddybearsearch.com – find the bear of your dreams . . .
www.theoldtoyshop.com – mainly vintage and collectible toys.

www.totalrobots.com – all sorts of robots, probably one for dads really.

www.toycentre.com – a sparse site with some good prices, most brands represented.

www.toyopia.co.uk – a toy shop which has a fun design and a good range to choose from too.

www.toysdirecttoyourdoor.co.uk – good design, specialists in Brio among other things; accompanied by Thomas' music!

www.toywiz.com – an American site where you can get unusual and new toys, even those that are no longer produced; toys are generally cheaper but shipping is costly.

Products Other Than Toys

www.jojomamanbebe.co.uk   UK
FASHIONABLE MOTHERS AND THEIR CHILDREN
Excellent for everything from maternity wear and designer children's clothes to gifts for newborn babies. Also has sections on toys, maternity products and special offers. All the designs are tested and they aim to be comfortable as well as fashionable.

www.urchin.co.uk   UK
WORTH HAVING A BABY FOR
Urchin has a wide range of products and have won awards for their catalogue business. You'll find: cots and beds, bath-time accessories, bikes, clothes, travel goods, toys and things for the independent child who likes to personalise their own room.
They boast a sense of style and good design, and they succeed. They also have a bargains section.

www.bloomingmarvellous.co.uk   UK
MATERNITY, NURSERY AND BABY WEAR
Excellent online store with a selection of maternity, baby and nurseryware available to buy, or you can order their catalogue.

www.mothercare.com   UK
MOTHERCARE
An attractive site with a good selection of baby and toddler products, also clothing, entertainment and equipment. It's good value and there are some excellent offers. It's not all about shopping though, there are advice sections on baby care, finance, tips on how to keep kids occupied and chat rooms where you can share your experiences.

C

www.gltc.co.uk   UK
THE GREAT LITTLE TRADING COMPANY
A good-looking site offering a wide range of child safety
products, furniture and baby equipment, you can search the
site by age and by product category.

www.greenbabyco.com   UK
FOR GREEN BABIES
A good store where all products are environmentally friendly.
There are clothes, nappies, toiletries, furniture, equipment,
even laundry products amongst its many sections. Delivery is
£3.99 for up to 15kg. For a similar site go to
www.ethosbaby.com and also the attractive
www.gtexpectations.co.uk

See also:
www.babiesisland.co.uk – a good selection of products for
babies, mums and dads.
www.babycare-direct.co.uk – not the most attractive store but a
wide range to choose from and some good offers.
www.babyhut.net – natural products for babies and parents.
www.babyjunction.co.uk – an above average shop with a wide
range of baby and toddler gear in lots of categories.
www.bibsandstuff.co.uk – great for all those hard-to-get things
and equipment generally.
www.cheekyrascals.co.uk – a very good baby equipment store.
www.childhoodinteriors.co.uk – a modern approach to decorating and accessorising your child's room.
www.kiddicare.com – baby accessories and nursery.
www.mamasandpapas.co.uk – good-looking site, you can't buy
online but you can order a catalogue.
www.twinkleontheweb.co.uk – specialists in nappies,
informative and helpful.
www.twinsthings.co.uk – great if you have . . . twins.
www.tyrrellkatz.co.uk – excellent upmarket range of clothes and
stationery on a good-looking site, you have to fax or phone
through orders though.

Things To Do

*It has to be said that many of these sites, while good fun, haven't
changed that much in years. Perhaps after the initial effort they think
that their audience is ever changing, so they don't have to try too
hard. Some are too commercial by half and need to tone down the*

advertising, which in turn would attract more visitors. We have added
quite a few more sites this year in order to provide some variety as
much as anything else.

www.mamamedia.com   UK
THE PLACE FOR KIDS ON THE NET
This versatile site has everything a child and parent could want,
there is an excellent selection of interactive games, puzzles and
quizzes, combined with a great deal of wit and fun. Best of all it
encourages children to communicate by submitting a message
and gets them voting on what's important to them. There's a
superb 'Grown-ups' section with information on getting the best
out of the Net with your children.

www.bonus.com   US
THE SUPER SITE FOR KIDS
Excellent graphics and masses of genuinely good games make a
visit to Bonus a treat for all ages. There are quizzes and puzzles,
with sections offering a photo gallery, art resource and
homework help. Access to the web is limited to a protected
environment. Shame about the pop-ups and advertising.

www.show.me.uk   UK
SHOW ME
A lively site specialising in picking out the best of what's going
on in our museums and galleries and representing it online.
There are games, what's on and special features with
celebrities. It's educational without being overtly so and there
are special sections for teachers and parents too.

www.yucky.com   US
THE YUCKIEST SITE ON THE INTERNET
Find out how to turn milk into slime or how much you know
about worms – Yucky lives up to its name. Essentially this is an
excellent, fun site that helps kids learn science and biology.
There are guides for parents on how to get the best out of the
site and links to recommended sites. See also **www.goobo.com**
– the section on belches is particularly appealing to little
boys.

www.wonka.com   SWITZERLAND
THE WILD WORLD OF WONKA
Ingenious site sponsored by Nestlé with great illustrations and
a fun approach, but it's one for the broadband owners really.

There's lots to see and do, with a store (aimed at parents), lots of games, and other interactive features that change regularly.

www.fffbi.com   US
THE FIN, FUR AND FEATHER BUREAU OF INVESTIGATION
Outstanding activity site with lots of problem-solving crime capers and games to play. The emphasis is on teaching children about other cultures around the world, which it does in a very entertaining and original fashion.

www.switcheroozoo.com   US
MAKE NEW ANIMALS
Over 6,500 combinations of animals can be made at this very entertaining web site, but you need Shockwave and a decent PC for it to work effectively. Deluxe versions now available for sale.

www.bigeyedowl.co.uk   UK
EARLY YEARS EXPERIENCE
One for parents who want ideas for activities to entertain their preschoolers including how to make playdough. Songs and rhymes, kid's recipes, craft ideas and suppliers of craft equipment.

Other activity sites worth checking out:
http://web.ukonline.co.uk/conker – The Kids Ark – join Captain Zeb gathering material on the world, strange animals, myths and facts – before it all disappears.
www.activityvillage.co.uk – a huge array of activities all designed to keep kids busy.
www.alfy.com – excellent with lots of games and plenty of things to do and see.
www.badgeplanet.co.uk – a great site where you can buy and also design your own badges.
www.bbc.co.uk/cbbc – lots to see and do at the BBC's children's TV site.
www.coloring.ws – lots of colouring projects to download and print off, but the site is advert laden.
www.cybersmartkids.com.au – a good Australian site with lots of things to do and see.
www.ex.ac.uk/bugclub – bugs and creepy crawlies for all ages.

www.funschool.com – a bit commercial, but there's plenty to do at this American activity come education site.

www.globalgang.org.uk – a Christian Aid sponsored activity and magazine site mainly covering world issues.

www.headbone.com – part of Bonus with chat and games.

www.hotwheels.com – a good-looking, but slow site from a model car maker that has some good features and games. Needs latest Flash Player to work.

www.kiddonet.com – download the interactive play area for games and surfing in a safe environment. Masses to do and good links. Largely aimed at girls.

www.kids.warnerbros.com – a links page to their children's productions. When you consider what they produce, it's a shame they can't do more.

www.kidscastle.si.edu – a pretty average kids' educational magazine site from the Smithsonian Museum. Useful for homework.

www.kidscom.com – play games, post a message on the message board and write to a pen friend (unfortunately the safe chat lines are still only open during our night-time). A bit dull.

www.kidsdomain.com – masses to download, from colouring books, music demos to homework help games. Split into three age ranges.

www.kidsjokes.co.uk – nearly 13,000 jokes.

www.kidskorner.net – great use of cartoons to introduce and play games – stealthily educational.

www.kidsreads.com – an American site all about kids' books, with games and quizzes. Good for young Harry Potter fans.

www.kidwizard.com – plenty to explore and do from yucky experiments to word games.

www.kzone.com.au – excellent activity site from Australia.

www.lego.co.uk – games, product information, adventures with their leading characters, lots of interactive features make this site something of a gem.

www.lemonadegame.com – how much lemonade can you sell? Learn about market forces in this oddly fascinating game.

www.matmice.com – create your own web site home page and add it to the internet the easy way.

www.missdorothy.com – The good-looking *Dot Comic*, which has loads of activities and is fun to use.

www.netmom.com – a place for mums and kids to hang out.

www.neopets.com – look after a multitude of virtual pets, play games and even trade them.

www.noggin.com – an excellent American activity site for preschool children.
www.puzzlepirates.com – a multi-player role-playing game for children, with excellent graphics and design.
www.roadcode.co.uk – take the road code and traffic light quiz and learn about road safety in the process.

Cookery for Kids

www.stickymitts.co.uk   UK
> JUNIOR CUISINE
> A site devoted to helping children get stuck in to cookery. It offers a series of courses which introduce the basics of cooking and also encourages children to have a go. The site itself is a little dull but the content is great. See also **www.coolmeals.co.uk** which is a brighter affair with the emphasis on nutrition and food groups. Also the BBC's helpful suite of pages by Annabel Karmel **http://www.bbc.co.uk/food/recipes/mostof_cookingwithchildren1.shtml**

Magic

www.magictricks.co.uk   UK
> THE UK'S LEADING ONLINE MAGIC TRICKS STORE
> A magic store chock full of tricks, sets and accompanying equipment. You can send in suggestions for new tricks and even find a magician. There's also a section on TV magicians and a bookstore.

> *See also:*
> **www.magicbypost.com** – magic tricks by mail order.
> **www.magictricks.com** – an American site which has lots of info and links.
> **www.magicweek.co.uk** – well-designed but quite adult.

TV, Book and Character Sites

www.citv.co.uk   UK
> CHILDREN'S ITV
> Keep up to date with your favourite programmes and talk to the stars of the shows. There's lots to occupy children here including chat with fellow fans, play games, find something to do, enter a competition, e-mail a friend and join the club.

www.nickjr.com
US

THE NICKELODEON CHANNEL

Ideal for under-eights, this has a good selection of games and quizzes to play either with an adult or solo. The shop has an excellent selection of merchandise, but beware of shipping costs. For activities aimed at a wider age range check out **www.nick.co.uk** where there is chat, gossip, games and plenty of background info on the shows.

www.sesamestreet.com
UK

THE CHILDREN'S TELEVISION WORKSHOP

Enter Elmo's world which is very colourful, with lots to do. There are games to play, art and music to create and friends to talk to. There's plenty for parents too.

www.bbc.co.uk/cbbc
UK

CHILDREN'S BBC

Lots of activities here, you can catch up on the latest news, play games and find out about the stars of the programmes. There are also web guide links to other recommended children's sites. See also **www.bbc.co.uk/cbeebies** which is for the very young with printable colouring pages, stories and games.

www.bbc.co.uk/newsround
UK

KEEP UP TO SPEED

One of the best bits of CBBC is Newsround, here you can get all the latest news, do quizzes, chat and join their club.

www.disney.com
US

WHERE THE MAGIC LIVES

1. Entertainment – details of films, activities and a Disney A–Z.
2. Kids Island – lots of games and music.
3. Playhouse – games and character sites for younger children.
4. Blast – the online kids' club.
5. Family fun – party planners, recipes and craft ideas.
6. Toontown – multiplayer games.
7. Destinations – Information on the theme parks.
8. Disney Direct – the Disney store, auctions and other sales opportunities.
9. Inside Disney – archives, newsletter and corporate info.

The British version **www.disney.co.uk** is more compact with less about vacations and more emphasis on activity. Both sites

C

are very commercial and really more about selling Disney than having fun.

www.cooltoons.com   UK
RUGRATS, STRESSED ERIC AND MORE
Each character has their own section where you can find lots to do and see. There's also an eight-step guide on how to become an animator. The store has all the related merchandise.

www.jetixeurope.com   UK
FOX TV
All the characters and shows are featured on this bright and futuristic site with added extras like a games section, competitions, a sports page and a magazine. There's also a shopping facility where you earn Brix by using the site, they can then be spent on goodies in the 'Boutik'. The graphics can be a little temperamental.

www.aardman.com   UK
HOME OF WALLACE AND GROMMIT
This brilliant site takes a while to download but it's worth the wait. There's news on what the team are up to, links to their films, e-cards, a shop and an inside story on how it all began.

www.gosh.org   UK
HOME OF PETER PAN
A good site from Great Ormond Street Hospital's charity with a section devoted to Peter Pan – all proceeds from the sale of the books go to hospital. There's also lots to do on the site with competitions, links and information about the hospital itself.

www.guinnessrecords.com   UK
GUINNESS WORLD RECORDS
An outstanding site that offers much in the way of entertainment with footage of favourite records and informative sections on key areas of record breaking such as sport, nature, the material world and human achievements.

Here's where the best children's characters from fiction, cartoon and TV shows hang out:

Favourites for Younger Children

Barbie – **www.barbie.com**
Bill & Ben – **www.bbc.co.uk/cbeebies/characterpages/billandben**
Bob the Builder – **www.bobthebuilder.org**
Boohbahs – **www.boohbah.com**
Fimbles – **www.bbc.co.uk/cbeebies/fimbles**
Ivor the Engine – **www.smallfilms.co.uk/ivor**
Letter Land – **www.letterland.com**
Mr Men – **www.mrmen.com**
Noddy – **www.noddy.com**
Teletubbies – **www.teletubbies.com**
Thomas the Tank Engine – **www.thomasthetankengine.com**
Tweenies – **www.bbc.co.uk/tweenies**

Cartoons and TV

Action Man – **www.actionman.com**
Asterix the Gaul – **www.asterix.tm.fr**
Bagpuss – **www.smallfilms.co.uk/bagpuss**
Batman – **www.batmantas.com** (animated series)
Batman – **www.batmanbeyond.com**
Beyblade – **www.beyblade.com**
Buffy – **www.buffyworld.com** and **www.buffyguide.com** and **www.bbc.co.uk/cult/buffy**
Clangers – **www.clivebanks.co.uk/Clangers%20intro.htm**
Danger Mouse – **www.dangermouse.org**
Dragonball Z – **www.dragonballz.com**
Mary Kate and Ashley – **www.marykateandashley.com**
Pixar – **www.pixar.com**
Pokemon – **www.pokeland.yorks.net** or **www.pokemon.com**
Spiderman – **www.spiderman.sonypictures.com** or **www.spiderman.com**
Thunderbirds – **www.thunderbirdsonline.co.uk**
Toontown – **www.toontown.com**
Yu-Gi-Oh – **www.yugiohkingofgames.com**

Favourite Characters from Children's Books

Alex Rider – **www.alexrider.com**

C

Angelina Ballerina – **www.angelinaballerina.com**
Animal Ark – **www.animalark.co.uk**
Artemis Fowl – **www.artemisfowl.co.uk**
Beano – **www.beano.co.uk**
Goosebumps – **www.scholastic.com/goosebumps**
Lemony Snicket – **www.lemonysnicket.com**
Paddington – **www.paddingtonbear.co.uk**
Roald Dahl – **www.roalddahlclub.com**
Tintin – **www.tintin.be**
Tracey Beaker – **www.bbc.co.uk/cbbc/tracybeaker/**
Winnie the Pooh – **www.just-pooh.com** or
www.winniethepoohbear.net

*More favourite authors can be found at the following publishers
sites:*
www.egmont.co.uk – good for younger kids with lots to
download.
www.harpercollinschildrensbooks.co.uk – home of Narnia.
www.kidsatrandomhouse.co.uk – Jacqueline Wilson, Terry
Pratchett, Roald Dahl and the Edge Chronicles.
www.puffin.co.uk – find out about the latest books from the likes
of Eoin Colfer, Charlie Higson and more.
www.scholastic.co.uk – lots to see and do here for children and
parents.

Harry Potter

*Harry Potter deserves a special mention and with loads of web sites
springing up, here are the official and some of the best unofficial ones.*

www.jkrowling.com   UK
JK ROWLING
The official site from the author of the Harry Potter books is
original in design, cleverly enticing the visitor into exploring the
site while guaranteeing they'll have fun. Catch up on the latest
rumours and get an insight into what it's like to be the world's
best-selling author. You need to switch off your pop-up blocker
to use the site.

See also:
http://harrypotter.warnerbros.co.uk – an outstanding site
offering the latest news on the films plus downloads and lots of
other activities, you can chat, shop for Harry merchandise and
play games.

www.bloomsbury.com/harrypotter – find out all about the books, meet JK Rowling and join the Harry Potter club, send a Howler and more.

www.fictionalley.org – a good fan site that encourages Harry fans to have a go at writing and generally releasing their creativity.

www.mugglenet.com – an excellent fan site put together by some teenage fans, it has features on the books and the films plus links, games and the latest news. The Wall of Shame is particularly entertaining.

www.scholastic.com/harrypotter – here's the US publisher's site with wizard trivia, quizzes, screensavers, information about the books and an interview with JK Rowling, all on a fairly boring web site.

For Older Children

The Good Web Site Guide's Top 10s
of the Internet

1. **www.yahooligans.com** – excellent guide to what's on the web
2. **www.fkbko.co.uk** – safe surfing
3. **www.girland.com** – no boys here
4. **www.mykindaplace.com** – very popular site for young teens
5. **www.dubit.co.uk** – needs patience but the 3-D graphics are great
6. **www.mindbodysoul.gov.uk** – health for teens
7. **www.globalgang.org.uk** – see what children around the world are up to
8. **www.teensites.org** – huge directory of sites for teenagers
9. **www.neopets.com** – virtual pets; better than the real thing!
10. **www.jkrowling.co.uk** – the official Harry Potter site

Search Engines and Site Directories

www.yahooligans.com   US

    THE KIDS' ONLINE WEB GUIDE

    Probably the most popular site for kids, Yahooligans offers
    parents safety and kids hours of fun. There are games, articles

and features on the 'in' characters, education resources and sections on sport, science, computing and TV. It has an American bias.

www.ajkids.com US
ASK JEEVES FOR KIDS
A search engine aimed at children, it's simple, safe and is excellent for homework enquiries and games.

www.fkbko.co.uk UK
FOR KIDS BY KIDS ONLINE
Part of an EU funded project designed to make surfing the net safe for children, it has chat, e-mail, surfing and search facilities and the excellent design makes it easy to use too.

See also:
www.bbc.co.uk/cbbc/search – safe and reliable, as expected from the BBC
www.familyfriendlysearch.com – a simple search engine that searches several of the major directories kids' sections.
www.infoplease.com – good for homework.
www.kidsfreeware.com – freeware for kids.
www.kidtastic.com – safe search for kids.

Help for Children

www.childline.org.uk UK
TELEPHONE 0800 111
Probably the best port of call for almost any kind of help and advice. There's masses of child-friendly information on the site with links, true stories, a problem page, competitions and quizzes. If you need to talk, there's always the confidential phone line.

See also:
www.bbc.co.uk/cbbc/yourlife/noproblem – covers bullying, online bullying, divorce, domestic violence, healthy lifestyle. Other issues such as friendship, confidence, jealousy and running away are also tackled here. There is also the useful 'Ask Arron' section where children can talk about their problems with a psychotherapist.
www.nspcc.org.uk/kidszone – information and help on child abuse.
www.rights4me.org.uk – help for children living in care.
www.talktofrank.com – confidential information about drugs.

Christmas

Sites to give some seasonal cheer and also help you prepare for the big day.

www.happychristmas.com
UK

ONE STOP CHRISTMAS

Choose your gifts here and they'll transfer you to the retail site for you to make your purchase. You can also get the family to write a wish list, send e-cards, have a chat about Christmas, or check the bulletin board for ideas. There are recipes, cocktails and games to play in all the time that you've saved.

www.christmasarchives.com
UK

THE HISTORY OF CHRISTMAS

A curious site written by Christmas historians of noble birth. There is masses of information on Christmas traditions throughout the world, although the site is not easy to navigate. You can buy a traditionally decorated Christmas tree or even one used on a film set, antique decorations and Christmas related books.

www.christmas.com
US

CELEBRATING CHRISTMAS AROUND THE WORLD

A good directory of stores and sites devoted to all aspects of Christmas, it has a strong American bias though.

Other Christmassy sites worth checking out:

www.carols.org.uk – a good database of carols but lots of adverts spoil the site.

www.christmas-carols.net – lyrics for all the best-known carols.

www.christmasrecipe.com – every Christmas recipe you're ever likely to need.

www.emailsanta.com – too lazy to send a letter? Well, now you can e-mail Santa.

www.howstuffworks.com/christmas – all your questions about the advent season answered including the eternal question 'why is Christmas sometimes spelled Xmas?'

www.noradsanta.org – track Santa as he makes his way around the skies.

www.whychristmas.com – explains what Christmas is all about with information on traditions and how it's celebrated in other cultures.

www.northpole.com   US
SANTA'S SECRET VILLAGE
A very good activity site for children and adults too, with
everything from educational activities to shopping.

C

www.christmastimeuk.com   UK
CHRISTMAS SHOP
Selling all you could possibly need during the festive season,
this shop has a wide range and an e-mail service if you want
something specific. Delivery charges vary according to what
you buy and where you are. For another site featuring Christmas
related merchandise go to **www.xmastreesdirect.co.uk**

*For Christmas related merchandise try these sites, see page 366
for sites specialising in parties.*
http://christmas.allrecipes.com – some 1,500 Christmas recipes
and plum puddings.
www.buy-christmas-decorations.co.uk – Christmas decorations
and tree lights too.
www.cardsforgoodcauses.org.uk – charity cards.
www.christmasdinnercompany.co.uk – everything you need
delivered to your door complete with instructions. Not cheap but
high quality and hassle free.
www.fattypuff.com – a good place to go for Christmas cards.
www.lewisandcooper.co.uk – specialists in hampers and plum
puddings.
www.lights4fun.co.uk – for Christmas lights, no matter how
tacky.
www.pinesandneedles.com – buy a tree, get it delivered and, if
you live in London, they'll even decorate it for you.
www.realfooddirect.co.uk – food gifts, hampers, condiments,
soft drinks and Christmas treats.
www.soraiseyourglasses.com – excellent party organising
service.
www.thecarvedangel.com – they make great claims for their
Christmas pudding, also supply foodie gifts.
www.thechristmaslightscompany.co.uk – a lights specialist both
indoor and out.
www.thevanillatree.com – folksy Christmas decorations.
www.xmastreesdirect.co.uk – trees and a wide variety of other
Christmas products.

Competitions

www.loquax.co.uk   UK

 THE UK'S COMPETITION PORTAL
This site doesn't give away prizes but lists the web sites that do.
There are hundreds of competitions featured, and if you own a
web site they'll even run a competition for you. There are daily
updates and special features such as 'Pick of the Prizes' which
features the best the web has to offer, with links to the relevant
sites.

See also:
www.compaholics.co.uk – competitions and gambling too,
heavy on the advertising.
www.myoffers.co.uk – a slow site, with, as the name suggests,
lots of offers.
www.prizemagic.co.uk – humorous site from a person who has
won over £100,000 in competitions.
www.theprizefinder.com – offers a wide range of prizes in lots of
categories; you have to register, though they claim someone
actually won £1 million there.
www.wincompetitionprizes.co.uk – a minimalist approach from
this site, which appears to go for quality rather than quantity.

Computers

*It's no surprise that the number one place to buy a computer is the
Internet. With these sites you won't go far wrong, and it's also worth
checking out the price checker sites on page 378 before going
shopping and checking the software sites on page 439. Mac users
should also check out the section on Apple Macs page 24.*

Information and Reviews

www.itreviews.co.uk   UK
START HERE TO FIND THE BEST
IT Reviews gives unbiased reports, not only on computer
products, but also on software, games and related books. The
site has a good search facility and a quick visit may save you
loads of hassle when you come to buy. See also the
comprehensive **www.technologyowl.com**

PC Essentials

The Good Web Site Guide's Top 10s
of the Internet

1. **www.download.com** – for all your software needs
2. **www.itreviews.co.uk** – read the reviews before you buy
3. **www.kelkoo.co.uk** – for the best prices
4. **www.isr.net** – all you need to know about internet security
5. **www.pcmech.com** – how it all works and how to repair it
6. **www.tucows.com** – software reviews and downloads
7. **www.compman.co.uk** – good offers on computer manuals
8. **www.handango.com** – the best for PDA software
9. **http://grc.com** – get your PC checked for security with Shield's Up
10. **www.vnunet.com** – UK-oriented technology site

www.pcadvisor.co.uk   UK
EXPERT ADVICE IN PLAIN ENGLISH
A derivative from *PC Advisor* magazine, the site offers much
in the way of reviews and information on how to find the best
PC. It also allows you to pick up advice from experts on
technical queries, download programmes and join forum
discussions. You have to register, which is free, to gain access
to the site.

See also:
www.bbcworld.com/clickonline – the technology pages from the
BBC with some entertaining and interesting content.
www.byte.com – one for those who know something about
computer technology.
www.compshopper.co.uk – good for reviews and information.
www.computerweekly.com – fairly dull site but informative on all
aspects of computing.
www.cnet.com – product reviews aplenty, also has downloads
and shopping links.
www.streettech.com – opinions and personal reviews with attitude from several experts.
www.zdnet.co.uk – very good reviews section at this large and
diverse site.

Stores

It's worth checking out price comparison sites such as
www.kelkoo.co.uk *but these stores specialise in PCs and consumables.*

www.pcworld.co.uk   UK

C

    THE COMPUTER SUPERSTORE
    A very strong offering from one of the leading computer stores
    with lots of offers and star buys. They sell a wide range of
    electronics from cameras to the expected PCs and peripherals.

www.misco.co.uk   UK
    ONE STOP SHOP
    Formally Simply.co.uk, this site offers a very wide range of PCs
    and related products.

www.dabs.com   UK
    1,500,000 CUSTOMERS LATER . . .
    One of the most successful online computer product retailers,
    with a very good reputation for service, there are loads of offers
    and a wide range of goods including home entertainment,
    digital photography equipment and mobile phones.

    See also:
    www.ebuyer.com – good design and some excellent offers.
    www.rankhour.com – huge range and competitive.
    www.unbeatable.co.uk – very good prices and a wide range.

www.totalpda.co.uk   UK
    PERSONAL DIGITAL ASSISTANTS
    Good-looking site specialising in PDAs and related products
    with a wide range and some good bargains. See also
    www.expansys.com who have some very good offers.

    PC manufacturers' site addresses:
    Apple – **www.apple.com**
    Dell – **www.dell.co.uk**
    Elonex – **www.elonex.co.uk**
    Evesham – **www.evesham.com**
    Gateway – **www.gateway.com/uk**
    Hewlett Packard – **www.hp.com/uk**
    Mesh – **www.meshcomputers.com**
    Time – **www.timecomputers.com**
    Viglen – **www.viglen.co.uk**

Computer Accessories

www.planetmicro.co.uk UK
ACCESSORISE YOUR PC

Much in the way of add-ons for PCs and essential equipment that can enable you to get more out of your computer, or keep an old PC going. Good design and some good pricing too.

See also:

www.dreamdirect.co.uk – good-looking site mainly selling software but also with an OK range of PC accessories and equipment.

www.inksaver.com – a program that saves money on printing by allowing you to control the amount of ink your printer uses.

www.keytools.com – a great site devoted to providing equipment that is easy to use.

www.powerdesk.com – a desk with built in PC, excellent space saving idea.

www.tonik.co.uk – excellent computer consumables store with free delivery in the UK.

www.cex.co.uk UK
COMPUTER EXCHANGE

Computer Exchange buy and sell used electronics, computers and games. The process is pretty straightforward, so if you have an old PC give them a call.

Information on Repairing and Upgrading Your PC

The following sites are useful if you want to keep up with the latest developments, need help when your PC goes wrong or you just need to learn something.

www.pcmech.com US
PC MECHANIC

Plain English explanations of all the bits that make up a computer, it's easy to follow and use with lots of background information and support. Excellent.

www.modemhelp.org CANADA
MODEM PROBLEMS FIXED

Any problems with your modem? Try here, it's very comprehensive, but then if you have problems with your modem how are you going to access it? Ask a friend . . .

See also:
www.compinfo.co.uk – a bewildering number of computer-related links all set out in a large directory.
www.driverguide.com – advice on finding and installing the right drivers for your PC.
www.help.com – part of the high quality CNET site it has the most up-to-date information on new products and articles and advice. It assumes some knowledge.
www.maximumpc.co.uk – lots of tutorials, useful programs to download and reviews galore.
www.pcpitstop.com – a host of programs to get your PC running on top form. They can even test how well your PC is running and offer advice on how to improve its performance.
www.tomshardware.com – a popular, information-heavy but messy site full of advice and help on the most common problems and issues facing the computer user.
www.warrantyex.co.uk – extended warranties the easy way.
www.wired.com – all the latest news and product information.

Consumer Information and Advice

A new section following requests from readers, these sites help with the latest consumer law and provide answers or give guidance on what to do if you've been wronged.

www.which.net   UK

WHICH? MAGAZINE
Excellent spin off from the magazine with everything from consumer advice to product reviews. You need to be a member to get the best out of it.

www.consumerdirect.gov.uk formerly
www.consumers.gov.uk   UK

THE CONSUMER GATEWAY
A consumer advice site run by the government that offers links and information across all the major areas where issues occur from cars to shopping to home improvements. A good place to start if you have issues you feel strongly about.

See also:
www.adviceguide.org.uk – the Citizens Advice Bureau offers a wide range of tips and advice on the most common problems and how to solve them, plus how to get in touch if you have specific issues.

Services

The Good Web Site Guide's Top 10s
of the Internet

1. **www.businesslink.gov.uk** – if you're in business there's no more helpful site
2. **www.uswitch.co.uk** – find the best household deals
3. **www.flickr.com** – easy to use photo sharing service
4. **www.nhsdirect.nhs.uk** – if you're feeling unwell go here and get help
5. **www.newsnow.co.uk** – outstanding news feed service
6. **www.which.co.uk** – independent consumer advice
7. **www.skype.com** – free internet telephony
8. **www.consumerdirect.gov.uk** – consumer advice
9. **www.theaa.com** – route planning, finances, motoring and more
10. **www.over50.gov.uk** – invaluable resource for oldies

www.bbc.co.uk/watchdog – lots of information on the back of the TV programme with legal FAQs, example letters for complaints and specific features.

www.ciao.co.uk – independent product reviews on a wide range of categories.

www.complaints.com – advice from a good US site.

www.complaint-letter.co.uk – get your letter written by a professional, at a price . . .

www.consumerworld.org – an American site with a huge number of useful links.

www.ethicalconsumer.org – a UK-based site devoted to listing those companies whose environmental and social track records are less than envious.

www.howtocomplain.com – find out how to make a complaint at this easy-to-follow site, which even provides specially designed forms to make your complaint even more effective.

www.oft.gov.uk – home of the Office of Fair Trading.

www.tradingstandards.gov.uk – the Trading Standards site offers a wealth of information on safety and legislation for businesses, education establishments and consumers.

Crime

This section continues to expand. It is intended to be of help to victims of crime or it may even help solve one. Hopefully you won't need it.

www.police.uk   UK

THE POLICE ONLINE

Here you can notify the police of minor crimes and get essential information on the organisation and how it works. There are sections on specific crimes or appeals, recruitment and information on related organisations. The site is easy to navigate and use.

See also:
www.cia.gov – the Central Intelligence Agency.
www.crb.org.uk – Criminal Records Bureau helps employers with criminal records information amongst other services.
www.fbi.gov – the Federal Bureau of Investigation.
www.interpol.com – the fight against international crime.
www.ipcc.gov.uk – Independent Police Complaints Commission formally the Police Complaints Authority.
www.nationalcrimesquad.police.uk – the fight against organised crime.
www.suzylamplugh.org/home/index.shtml – keep yourself safe from crime.

www.cjsonline.org   UK

THE CRIMINAL JUSTICE SYSTEM

A helpful site that tells what happens when someone gets arrested, and provides information about the trial procedure, how a court works and what you need to do if you're a witness. There's a guide to who does what in the legal profession and a section on related links. See also the Crown Prosecution Service at **www.cps.gov.uk**

www.crimestoppers-uk.org   UK

KEEP 'EM PEELED

Information on the Crimestoppers Trust and how you can get involved in their fight against crime with information on the latest campaign and initiatives, links and, of course, their phone number 0800 555 111. See also **www.crimereduction.gov.uk** which has been set up by the government to become the number one resource for the crime prevention practitioner.

www.neighbourhoodwatch.net   UK
NEIGHBOURHOOD WATCH
A directory of neighbourhood watch schemes by county
with advice on preventing crime and how you can set up a
neighbourhood watch scheme in your area. See also
www.crimeconcern.org.uk who give advice on helping
to reduce crime and also the fear of crime in local
communities.

www.iwf.org.uk   UK
INTERNET WATCH FOUNDATION
The IWF works with the police to stamp out the use of
exploitative images of children, obscene and racist content that
is hosted by web sites based in the UK.

www.victimsupport.com   UK
VICTIM SUPPORT
An independent charity that supports the victims of crime
throughout the UK with help and advice. It also advises
witnesses on the justice system and campaigns for equal
opportunities. You can also find out about how you can help or
give funds.

www.virtualbumblebee.co.uk   UK
LOST PROPERTY
The place to go if you have lost something. The police use this
site to post details and pictures of lost property in the hope that
someone will claim them.

www.cifas.org.uk   UK
CREDIT CARD FRAUD
Set up by the credit card industry to provide information about
financial fraud in the UK. It's a dry, text-heavy site but they tell
you what to look out for and there's advice on what to do if you
think that it has happened to you.

www.identity-theft.org.uk   UK
KEEP YOURSELF TO YOURSELF
Information about this fast-growing crime: what happens to
you, who can help, how to protect yourself and what is being
done to stop it. For the equivalent US site see
www.consumer.gov/idetheft

See also:
www.econsumer.gov – the EU's attempt to stop Internet fraud and set up a process to deal with complaints.
www.fraud.org – find out about how you can be defrauded and how to spot fraud on the Internet.
www.fraudbureau.com – a consumer-oriented scam-listing service, you can search for specific complaints and add your experiences too.
www.privacyrights.org – how to protect your privacy.
www.quatloos.com – a listing of all sorts of scams and fraudulent practises; an entertaining and educational read.
www.scambusters.com – more help on scams and annoyances on the Internet.

www.dumbcriminalacts.com   US
THE STUPIDEST CRIMINALS
Here you can find out about the daftest criminal acts in history and have a good laugh at their expense. Some are truly unbelievable and sadly it does lack a bit of credibility as it doesn't always list the source of the stories. See also **www.dumbcrooks.com** which is a bit low tech but the stories are more detailed.

Cycles and Cycling

See page 506 for cycling holidays and tours and page 455 for information on cycling as a sport.

www.cycleweb.co.uk   UK

THE INTERNET CYCLING CLUB
A great attempt to bring together all things cycling. Aimed at a general audience rather than sporting cyclists, it has masses of sections and links on everything from the latest news to clubs, shops and holidays.

See also:
www.bikemagic.com – forums on hot bike topics, reviews of equipment, buying advice, classifieds, the latest news, links and an events calendar.
www.bikeweek.org.uk – find out about Bike Week which is in mid-June.

www.ctc.org.uk – the National Cyclist's Organisation's site offers lots of information on all aspects of the hobby and the benefits associated with getting on your bike.
www.cycling.uk.com – great for cycling links.
www.newtocycling.co.uk – help from Izzy Sez for those who are new to cycling, with advice and links too.
www.procycling.com – a magazine devoted to professional cycling, pretty basic design but it covers all the latest news.
www.tandem-club.org.uk – a pretty basic site devoted to the world of the tandem with discussion groups, classifieds, buying advice, events and a newsletter.

Buying a Bike

www.bicyclenet.co.uk   UK
UK'S NUMBER 1 ONLINE BICYCLE SHOP
Great selection of bikes and accessories, there's also good advice on how to buy the right bike and assembly instructions on all that they sell. Delivery is free for bikes and orders in excess of £50.

See also:
www.cyclestuff.co.uk – a good range of accessories.
www.evanscycles.com – wide range, easy to navigate.
www.wiggle.co.uk – good name and good shop.

Dance

Here are a few sites for those who dance or think they can.

www.danceart.com   US
DANCE!
A slightly messy but enthusiastic site centred on the dance scene, it has lots of links, articles and interviews.

See also:
http://hneeman.oscer.ou.edu/dance_hotlist.html – long ulr but worth it for a good hot list of dance sites.
www.ballet.co.uk – magazine-style site with reviews, interviews, biographies and forums.
www.ballroomdancers.com – excellent and comprehensive offering with video clips.

www.dancebooks.co.uk – where to go for specialist dance titles also CDs, DVDs, videos and sheet music.
www.dancescape.com – a good Canadian dance magazine site.
www.dancesport.uk.com – strictly come dancing, the UK ballroom dancing scene covered.
www.dancescape.com – lots of different styles covered, includes a shop plus chat and lots of adverts.
www.dancetv.com – learn to ballroom dance on Dance TV.
www.dancing-times.co.uk – *Dancing Times* and *Dance Today*.
www.folkdancing.org – home of the Folk Dance Association.
www.irishdancing.com – a cheery site from *International Irish Dancing* magazine.
www.istd.org – home of the Imperial Society of Teachers of Dancing.
www.learntodance.co.uk – buy instructional DVDs.
www.pearldata.co.uk/dance/paul/cool.htm – good for dancing-related links.
www.rad.org.uk – the Royal Academy of Dance.
www.the-ballet.com – a good e-zine all about ballet.
www.young-dancers.org – dedicated to helping teenagers learn to dance.

Dating

Using the Net has become an accepted means to meet people, but be careful about how you go about meeting up; many people aren't exactly honest about their details. If in doubt, err on the side of caution. See also the new section on social networking on page 438.

www.onlinedatingmagazine.com US
AN AUTHORITATIVE INSIGHT
An excellent magazine site devoted to all aspects of dating with site reviews, tips, articles and advice. It is well designed and up to date, there are even some cartoons and it's all written in a chirpy style.

See also:
www.dating-agencies-uk.co.uk/dating-tips.htm – good advice all round.
www.topdatingtips.com – attractive site with lots of articles on dating.
www.wildxangel.com – old site but sage advice.

www.thedatingportal.com   US
>   DATING LINKS
>   A portal devoted to dating sites; they are well categorised but it
>   is geared towards the US market. See also
>   **www.datingbind.com** and for the UK **www.dating-agencies-
>   uk.co.uk**

www.uksingles.co.uk   UK

>   FOR ALL UK SINGLES
>   Not just about dating, this site is devoted to helping you get the
>   most out of life. There are several sections: accommodation,
>   sport and activities, holidays, help for single parents, and
>   listings for matchmaking and dating services. All the companies
>   that advertise in the directories are vetted too.

www.faceparty.com   UK
>   BIGGEST PARTY ON EARTH
>   A combination of dating agency, party organiser and chat site.
>   You download your details and photo to create your own profile,
>   then just join in.
>
>   *Here are some additional sites, there's not much to choose
>   between them, it's all a matter of taste. All are secure and
>   allow you to browse and participate in relative safety:*
>   **www.dateline.co.uk** – 30 years experience at the dating game
>   gives Dateline lots of credibility and it's a good site too, easy to
>   use and reassuring.
>   **www.datingdirect.com** – claims to be the UK's largest agency
>   with over 3 million members, the site is not as sophisticated as
>   some, though they seem to have lots of success stories.
>   **www.dinnerdates.com** – one of the longest established and
>   most respected dining and social events clubs for unattached
>   single people in the UK; find out how you can get involved
>   here.

Disability Help and Information

*In this expanded section you'll find sites that may help if you are
disabled or care for someone with a disability. It's worth checking your
local council's site as they tend to have good local information on the
help that is available in your area.*

Disability Help and Information

The Good Web Site Guide's Top 10s
of the Internet

1. **www.dlf.org.uk** – the Disabled Living Foundation with excellent resources
2. **www.disabilityview.co.uk** – very good magazine site
3. **www.disability.gov.uk** – the Government's site with useful links and information
4. **www.disabilitynow.org.uk** – another excellent magazine and portal
5. **www.jobability.com** – find the right job
6. **www.disabledunited.com** – finding friends, chat and dating
7. **www.disabledholidaydirectory.co.uk** – holidays and travel
8. **www.yourable.com** – forums, discussion and lots of links
9. **www.keytools.com** – tools to make life easier
10. **www.abilitynet.org.uk** – how to get the most from your computer

Information and Advice

www.direct.gov.uk/DisabledPeople formally
www.disability.gov.uk   UK

THE GOVERNMENT'S VIEW
Information and help on rights for the disabled with links to related departments. They have made this site more comprehensive and accessible so you shouldn't need to visit **www.dwp.gov.uk/lifeevent/discare** for an index of benefits and services.

www.bcodp.org.uk   UK

THE BRITISH COUNCIL OF DISABLED PEOPLE
An action-oriented site that has information on how the council works, useful articles and helpful information. It shows how you can get involved whether you are disabled or not, and most importantly, how you can contribute.

www.disabilityview.co.uk   UK

DISABILITY VIEW
Inspired by the magazine of the same name, this site sets out to be the best source of information for all those who have to cope

with a disability, and it largely succeeds. There are loads of links and useful sections such as travel, guides, sports and an events guide.

www.bbc.co.uk/ouch/   UK
OUCH! MAGAZINE
Lively e-zine with lots of features and things to do and see, there are regular columnists, blogs and podcasts, as well as links and the latest news. See also **www.disabilityworld.org** and the more radical **www.raggededgemagazine.com**

For more advice check out the following sites:
www.abilitynet.org.uk – excellent regional database offering help whatever your situation.
www.dialuk.info – the Disability Advice Network.
www.disabilitynow.org.uk – great magazine site dealing with issues and offering advice.
www.disabilityresources.org – an American site devoted to resources available on the Internet.
www.makoa.org – another US site, not a good design, but a huge number of links all the same.
www.scope.org.uk – excellent site devoted to those who have cerebral palsy.
www.youreable.com – great for news, features and jobs.

Independent Living

www.dlf.org.uk   UK
THE DISABLED LIVING FOUNDATION
A charity devoted to helping people who need equipment to live life to the full. This excellent site has information on how to choose the best equipment, masses of links to self-help groups, a bookshop, training information and of course a section on how you can contribute.

See section on motability under cars page 76 as well as:
http://disabledaccessories.com – excellent range and good value make this store stand out.
www.disabledgo.info – a directory of places that have good access and businesses that are sympathetic to disabled people. Pity more towns don't participate.
www.e-accessibility.com – a monthly newsletter largely aimed at people with sight problems, it concentrates on various aspects of technology and computing.

www.inclusive.co.uk – a plethora of gadgets and useful educational tools to help life and learning easier.

www.independentliving.co.uk – equipment and advice on making life easier.

www.keepable.co.uk – formally **motibilitywarehouse.com** excellent selection of products and a well-designed site.

www.keytools.com – an excellent site from a company specialising in providing computer accessories.

www.motability.co.uk – the scheme that helps you contract hire a car or powered wheelchair or scooter.

www.sunrisemedical.co.uk – a wide range of products. Contact them for your nearest dealer.

www.wheelchair-travel.co.uk – self-drive wheelchairs and cars for hire.

Children

www.ncb.org.uk/cdc   UK

COUNCIL FOR DISABLED CHILDREN

From the National Children's Bureau, this site is basically a forum devoted to helping parents and children cope with disability. It's a good starting point if you need information, but it's not an easy site to navigate so patience is required.

See also:

www.cafamily.org.uk – find advice and support on caring for a disabled child.

www.childcarelink.gov.uk – excellent government-run children's information service site.

Students, Education and Sport

www.techdis.ac.uk   UK

HELP FOR STUDENTS WITH A DISABILITY

A site containing masses of help and information designed to enable disabled students to have the opportunity to learn effectively. Most of it is free, so an excellent resource.

www.efds.net   UK

ENGLISH FEDERATION OF DISABILITY SPORT

Covers sport for disabled people. It doesn't miss much and there's an excellent links section which covers many different types of sport, activity and associations.

D

See also:
http://www.abilityinfo.com/index.html – disability information for students and professionals, it has a good news 'ticker' service too.
www.cforat.org – a charity devoted to helping disabled children integrate into the school curriculum.
www.leeds.ac.uk/disability-studies/archiveuk – an archive of articles and writings from activists, scholars and those sympathetic to disability causes.
www.nasen.org.uk – the National Association for Special Educational Needs.
www.skill.org.uk – who help promote opportunities for post-16 year olds in education.

Jobs

www.jobability.com   UK
    LEADING JOB SITE FOR DISABLED PEOPLE
    Now integrated with Totaljobs.com and Leonard Cheshire this is a straightforward site designed to help disabled people find employment; it covers the UK by region plus opportunities in the rest of the world. There's also advice on careers and how to find a job.

    See also:
    www.rehab.ie/uk – training and support to help people with disabilities into the workforce.
    www.remploy.co.uk – provides employment opportunities for disabled people all over the UK and in their own factories.
    www.shaw-trust.org.uk – training and work opportunities for the disadvantaged.

Rights and Having your Say

www.drc-gb.org   UK
    DISABILITY RIGHTS
    A helpful site offering links and views on rights issues for the disabled. The site doesn't always load properly and it's not easy to find your way around, but useful nonetheless – at least there's a search facility.

www.radar.org.uk UK
RADAR
A campaigning organisation devoted to the social inclusion of
disabled people. There's lots of information on the campaigns
and how you can get involved.

www.webequality.org.uk UK
DISABILITY EQUALITY TRAINING
Working with employers to enable disabled people to get
employed and stay employed. There's masses of practical
advice and even a quiz to start you off.

D

www.chooseability.org US
CHOOSE ABILITY
A US-based community site which offers blogging and issues
forums plus news and articles, it has a great feel and attitude
although the site itself is a bit clunky.

See also:
www.csci.org.uk – a charity devoted to ensuring the rights of
those in care. There's also information on what you can do if you
are unhappy with the care you are receiving.
www.dpi.org – Disabled People International, promoting disabled
people's rights around the world.

For Carers

www.carers.gov.uk UK
FOR THOSE WHO CARE
A barely useful resource from the government for carers, there
are links and details of their policies concerning care.

Keeping in Touch

www.disabledunited.com UK

THE MEETING PLACE
A sort of Friends Reunited, but much more as it offers
information on travel, links, chat, forums and, lastly, dating.

Travel

www.disabledholidaydirectory.co.uk UK
HOLIDAY INFORMATION
Very useful directory site devoted to providing holiday

information and contacts for disabled people. They have a wide range of holidays and offer sensible advice on how to get the best out of your holiday.

See also:
www.abletogo.com – a very wide range of holiday options.
www.access-able.com – poorly designed site but lots of useful information.
www.allgohere.com – a directory of hotels that offer facilities for the disabled.
www.disabilitytravel.com – experienced agent and good if you're confined to a wheelchair.
www.tripscope.org.uk – a charity devoted to helping disabled travellers.

Do-it-yourself is under Home and DIY section on page 276.

Dying – Support and Advice

When faced with the death of a loved one, there are a bewildering number of things to be done and decisions to be made at a time of emotional stress and confusion. These sites help you to find your way through this minefield and provide both practical and emotional support.

www.ifishoulddie.co.uk UK

EVERYTHING YOU NEED TO KNOW
Written in response to the confusion felt following a close death, this site takes you through all that you need to know including all the legalities, organ donation, funeral arrangements, wills, inheritance tax and coping with life-threatening illness and bereavement. There is a helpful section on the various funeral arrangements for the major religions although the site itself is careful not to take a religious stand. If you still need help, join in the forum and there are excellent links for more support.

www.funeralsuk.com UK
LOCAL DIRECTORIES
Very good listings for everything you need from funeral directors, to printers, to monumental masons and florists. The 'Topics' section also provides help and links to other related services such as repatriation, wills, an online obituary service and even pet funerals.

Other related sites:

www.argonet.co.uk/body – British Organ Donation Society.

www.dignityindying.org.uk formally **www.ves.org.uk** – dignity in Dying is the new name of the Voluntary Euthanasia Society with guidelines on writing a living will and news about their campaign.

www.gatesofrememberance.com – a site for online tributes.

www.humanism.org.uk – British Humanist Association, providers of non religious funeral ceremonies.

www.naturaldeath.org.uk – helps arrange inexpensive, family-run and environmentally-friendly funerals and provides information on burials on private land.

www.the-bereavement-register.com – to remove the names and addresses of people who have died from databases and mailing files.

Legal and Financial Advice

www.hmcourts-service.gov.uk/index.htm – legal advice and information on probate without recourse to a solicitor.

www.inlandrevenue.gov.uk/leaflets/iht.htm – the Inland Revenue's downloadable leaflets on inheritance tax.

www.lawontheweb.co.uk – jargon-free guide to wills, power of attorney, probate and what happens after a death. Pity about the design.

www.mypersonalfinances.co.uk/life-iht.asp – use the inheritance tax calculator to assess the damage.

www.willaid.org – draw up a will and simultaneously support charity.

Emotional Support

www.befriending.net – volunteers who befriend those facing terminal illness and their carers on a long-term basis.

www.crusebereavementcare.org.uk – the leading charity in the UK specialising in bereavement.

www.samm.org.uk – emotional support to those bereaved through murder and manslaughter.

www.tcf.org.uk – support for bereaved parents and their families with local help groups and literature.

www.winstonswish.org.uk – helps bereaved children and young people rebuild their lives after a family death.

Education

Using the Internet for homework or study has become one of its primary uses; these sites will help enormously, especially alongside the reference and encyclopaedia sites listed on page 396. There is also a section aimed at students on page 478 and search engines for children are on page 101.

Homework and Learning

The Good Web Site Guide's Top 10s of the Internet

1. **www.homeworkelephant.co.uk** – masses of help and info. Top site
2. **www.kevinsplayroom.co.uk** – award winning and popular site
3. **www.learn.co.uk** – sponsored by the *Guardian*, quality assured
4. **www.schoolsnet.com** – an impressive one stop shop for education
5. **www.schoolzone.co.uk** – a superb education search engine
6. **www.samlearning.com** – tips, past papers, even competitions
7. **www.school-portal.co.uk** – create a site for your school
8. **www.s-cool.co.uk** – revision help
9. **www.underfives.co.uk** – a brilliant education site for pre-school kids
10. **www.nc.uk.net** – the home of the National Curriculum

Homework Help

www.bbc.co.uk/learning UK
> GET EQUIPPED FOR LIFE
> Good-looking site covering learning at school, college and adult education. Each section tends to be tied to a particular programme rather than subject, but there is masses here and the quality of content is particularly good. The revision sections are excellent.

www.brainpop.com
US
LEARN BY ANIMATION

A wonderful example of how the Internet should be used. Here you can download animations that cover and explain specific aspects of maths, health, technology, science, English and more. The site is American but very useful for UK students too though only a few topics are available for free; subscription to the whole site is around £50 per year. See also **www.funbrain.com** which is free.

www.cln.org/int_expert.html
US
ASK AN EXPERT

This site lists almost a hundred sites by subject, including somewhere you can ask an expert your homework question – what a doddle! North American bias though. See also the American **www.sparknotes.com** who offer some of their study guides free to use online and a helpful forum if you're stuck.

www.discoveryschool.com
US
ANSWERS TO HOMEWORK, FREE

Go to 'Homework Helper' to access a number of study tools and games including links to over 700 reference sites with the provision to ask questions too. Layout has been improved and you can more easily access the information, it also has an excellent clip art gallery.

www.happychild.org.uk
UK
PROJECT HAPPY CHILD

A mess of a site but one that aims to provide an index of educational resources for schools, parents and children. There's loads to see and do, and it does a good job of highlighting charities, for example, but the poor design gets in the way of its objectives. Well worth a visit, but be patient.

www.homeworkelephant.co.uk
UK
LET THE ELEPHANT HELP

Rightly considered one of the top educational sites with some 5,000 resources and straightforward layout, all aimed at helping children achieve great results. There's help with specific subjects, hints and tips, help for parents and teachers. The agony elephant is great if you get really stuck. It's constantly being updated, so worth checking regularly.

www.homeworkhigh.com   UK
LEARN WITH CHANNEL 4
A slimmed down site but what's left is still well presented and
really useful. It's split into six learning sections: history,
geography, science, maths, English and languages. You can ask
questions, track down lots of information and chat with fellow
homework sufferers. All in all, this is one of the better-looking
homework sites.

E

www.kevinsplayroom.co.uk   UK
AWARD-WINNING PORTAL
An excellent site which is put together with the heavy
involvement of pupils. It's won numerous awards and is a
favourite among teachers and pupils alike. It has over 2,000
approved sites and they are well categorised and reviewed.
There's also a translation service and a links page for
teachers.

www.learningalive.co.uk   UK
FOR PRIMARY AND SECONDARY
From one of the larger software providers, the 'Living Library' is
a useful resource for homework help for both primary and
secondary students; you can either browse by topic or use the
search facility. It can also be accessed directly on
www.livinglibrary.co.uk The 'Pathways' section provides over
4,000 links to a variety of reference sites. There are loads of
resources for teachers too. If you are still short of information,
try the children's section of the Internet Public Library at
www.ipl.org/div/kidspace

www.schoolzone.co.uk   UK
UK'S TOP EDUCATIONAL SEARCH ENGINE
With over 27 million page impressions and bits of resource all
checked by teachers, Schoolzone has masses of information.
Use the search facility under 'resources' to find what you are
looking for, you'll then find the results summarised and graded.
There is free software to download, plus homework help, career
advice, teacher support (they do need it apparently) and much
more. Don't be put off by the confusing layout; it's worth
sticking with. See **www.ukeducationguide.co.uk** who offer
hundreds of links, **www.thelighthouseforeducation.co.uk** and
the American **http://northvalley.net/kids**

www.skool.ie   IRELAND
    INTERACTIVE LEARNING
    An excellent site covering the Irish curriculum but with lots of
    free resources and information, it's well laid out and easy to
    navigate.

www.topmarks.co.uk   UK
    EDUCATIONAL PORTAL
    Developed by a school teacher, this site steers pupils, parents
    and teachers to some of the best educational web sites. Search
    for sites by topic or by age from early years to higher ed.

Pre-school and Infant Education

www.enchantedlearning.com   UK
    FROM APES TO WHALES
    It's messy, uncool and largely aimed at young children, but
    there's loads of good information and activities hidden away,
    especially on nature. You don't have to subscribe to access
    most of the content. Use the search engine to find what you
    need.

www.thebigbus.com   UK

    HOORAY FOR THE BIG BUS!
    Excellent animation and content make this stand out, it can be
    a little slow and you have to subscribe to the CD magazine to
    get the best out of it (you get a free demo one as a trial).
    Excellent for younger children but caters for primary children
    too.

    See also:
    www.pbclibrary.org/mousing – a fun way to develop skills with
    a mouse – the computing kind of course.
    www.pre-school.org.uk – home of the Pre-school Learning
    Alliance.

Primary

www.parentlink.co.uk   UK
    HELPING YOUR CHILD
    A site written by teachers aimed at helping parents to help their
    children by preparing them for the classroom. Very useful
    although it concentrates on numeracy and literacy.

www.dfes.gov.uk/parents/discover   UK
HELP YOUR CHILD DISCOVER

For primary parents who want to be proactive in their child's
education, the Department for Education and Skills has
produced a series of helpful online leaflets on a range of
curricular areas to enable you to support your child at home.

www.primarygames.com   US
GAME-BASED LEARNING

This site is packed full of educational games, some better than
others, but there's loads to do and masses to learn. Check on
'curriculum guide' to find games that match your child's
interests or level. **www.funschool.com** is a similar site.

www.bbc.co.uk/schools/revisewise   UK
REVISE KEY STAGE 2 SATS

The BBC's excellent interactive site to support 10- to 11-year
olds as they prepare for their Key Stage 2 National Curriculum
Tests in English, Maths and Science.

*Here are several subscription-only sites which may be of interest; they
stand out in terms of quality and content, and they may well be used
at your school.*

www.atschool.co.uk   UK
PRIMARY EDUCATION

Specialising in Key Stage 1 and 2, this site is fun as well as
educational and, while the content is strong, you do have to
subscribe. Rates start at £9.99 for a quarterly subscription.
This site does seem quite slow, so probably one for the
broadband users.

www.edontheweb.com   UK
HELP WITH SATS

Written by a teacher, this site is designed to help children pass
their SAT exams. It's lively and well written with lots of activities
too. There is some free material, but subscription to the full site
costs £10 per year.

www.gridclub.com   UK

FOR 7- TO 11-YEAR-OLDS

An excellent site which is backed by the government and
several high-profile contributors including Channel 4. It uses
entertaining educational games to do most of its tutoring but

there are links to the more traditional stuff available too. It's been built with safety in mind and it encourages children proactively. All in all, what an educational site should be; unfortunately, it costs £30 per year for home use.

Secondary

There are so many brilliant educational support sites it is impossible to list them all here. Use extra-curricular or homework help sites to search for the ones that best suit your needs or use the following to get you started. If you can't find what you are looking for here, don't forget our sections on Art, English usage, History, Nature and environment, Reference, Religion, Science and Space all of which are extremely helpful when it comes to homework.

Extra-curricular

www.courseworkbank.co.uk   UK
ESSAY HELP
Claiming to be the UK's largest database of quality essays by students from 14-year olds to those at university, they cover a wide variety of subjects and there's no charge but beware that teachers are familiar with this resource too! Some links don't work and what's available isn't always comprehensive so see also **www.coursework.info** for another 63,000 academic documents, but you have to pay to access these.

www.s-cool.co.uk   UK

FOUR STEPS TO REVISION
Well written and presented, this revision site covers GCSEs, AS and A level exams in four steps: principles, a quick learn guide, trial questions and revision summary. There is an interactive careers guide, discussions, a teacher's page and a great magazine with masses of information and advice aimed at young people.

www.studyzones.com   UK
ONLINE TUTORS
Fabulous resource mainly for GCSE and A level students, you can ask a question related to your studies and they'll get back to you within 24 hours. Submit your essays and they'll grade them and comment on how to improve it. You can search through 7,500 archived answers but to have yours answered you'll have to register, it's free.

www.samlearning.com
UK

EXAM REVISION

SAM stands for self-assessment and marking, and on this brilliant site you can do just that; it has mock exams covering every major subject and key stage plus GCSE and A level. There are top tips on taking exams and the chance to win some great prizes when you register. There is a 14-day free trial then there are various payment options. See also **www.courseshop.co.uk** who offer a wide range of courses from GCSE upwards – again you have to pay.

English

www.englishresources.co.uk
UK

ENGLISH

Hundreds of free resources available here, it's very useful for revision and for teachers too with a good search engine and sections aimed at each secondary school age range. See also our section on English usage on page 137.

History

www.schoolhistory.co.uk
UK

HISTORY REVISION

An excellent site devoted to helping students learn and revise history with quizzes and many free resources. Also has lessons and worksheets for teachers. See also **www.learningcurve.gov.uk** which covers key stages 2 to 5 using information from the National Archives.

Languages See Language section on page 301.

Maths

http://mathworld.wolfram.com
US

MATHS WORLD

An outstanding site devoted to the world of mathematics. It explains the complexities really well and is great for homework. It also has sections on chemistry, physics and astronomy. See also the comprehensive **www.tcaep.co.uk/maths/index.htm** and also **www.mathsisfun.com**

http://nrich.maths.org   UK
MATHS ENRICHMENT
A stimulating offering from Cambridge University that provides
challenging mathematical problems for pupils of all ages.
You'll find a good search facility, interesting graphics,
discussion forums, a mathematics thesaurus and a course
finder service.

Science

www.zephyrus.co.uk   UK
INTERACTIVE EDUCATION
Aimed at children aged between 8 and 14, there is a wealth of
information, simply written with good graphics. For more of the
same try **www.wpbschoolhouse.btinternet.co.uk** with lots of
science materials for all secondary levels; particularly good for
chemistry A level. For a more folksy approach, there's
www.ftexploring.com with more quality information.

http://lgfl.skoool.co.uk   UK
INTERACTIVE SCIENCE AND MATHS
The advent of whiteboards in the classroom is reflected in this
science site that brings complete maths and science to the PC.
Excellent if you've missed a topic in class, haven't understood it
properly, or simply need to revise.

www.exam.net   UK
A LEVEL BIOLOGY
Good site with all you're likely to need to pass this A level, it
has lots of interactive features including video clips, but you have
to pay.

www.biologymad.com   UK
A LEVEL BIOLOGY
An excellent resource for biologists with plenty of information
and support resources. For more of the same and practice
questions see **www.mrothery.co.uk**

Post-16 and Adult Education

www.learndirect.co.uk   UK
ADULT LEARNING
A government backed site which aims to bring education to

everyone whatever their needs. The site explains the background to the initiative plus details of courses and how you can find one that meets your requirements. There's also help for businesses and a jobs advice section. See also **www.lsc.gov.uk** home of the Learning and Skills Council which provides education for over 16-year olds and **www.lifelonglearning.co.uk** aimed at helping people with their further education ambitions.

www.icslearn.co.uk UK
ONLINE COLLEGE
A great alternative to school or college, enrol in an online course in a wide variety of subjects at GCSE or A level. Alternatively, they offer professional qualifications in such subjects as business, beauty, childminding and IT or certificate courses in a range of 'leisure' subjects, such as gardening and art. Courses vary in fees.

See also:
www.city-and-guilds.co.uk – vocational qualifications with over 500 from which to choose.
www.niace.org.uk – a non-governmental organisation formed to 'support an increase in the total numbers of adults engaged in formal and informal learning in England and Wales; and at the same time to take positive action to improve opportunities and widen access to learning opportunities for those communities under-represented in current provision'.
www.support4learning.org.uk – a wide-ranging resource aimed at helping people support their education needs in a more holistic way.
www.wea.org.uk – the Worker's Educational Association helps provide learning opportunities for everyone but especially those who had missed out or been disadvantaged in some way.

National Curriculum, Government Policy and Support

www.nc.uk.net UK
NATIONAL CURRICULUM REVEALED
Very detailed explanation of the National Curriculum and prescribed standards.

www.ngfl.gov.uk   UK
THE NATIONAL GRID FOR LEARNING
The official government education site with sections on every
aspect of learning. There's something for everyone, whatever
your needs. It is particularly good for info on further and adult
education. There are also details on school web sites, a features
section that covers news and events, plus advice on Internet
safety, outstanding for links and some very good content too.

See also:

www.ace-ed.org.uk – help for parents at the Advisory Centre for
Education.
www.becta.org.uk – information on technology and ICT
education.
www.dfes.gov.uk – the Department of Education and Skills' site if
you want a more overall picture on education.
www.he-special.org.uk – support for people who have children
with special educational needs.
www.ofsted.gov.uk – the Office for Standards in Education,
check out the standards of your local schools.
www.parentcentre.gov.uk – more information from the
government on supporting children's learning.
www.qca.org.uk – information on the Qualifications and
Curriculum Authority.
www.sqa.org.uk – for information on the Scottish education
system.

Specialist Education Publishers

*Below are listed some of the key education publishers. They often
have competitions, online help and free books.*

www.activerevision.com – from HarperCollins, at this site you
can test yourself to see how likely you are to pass your exams. It
then recommends which books would help you to get a pass.
www.cgpbooks.co.uk – a basic online shop with details of their
popular study guides, which you can buy online.
www.hoddereducation.co.uk – one of the biggest education publishers offers a fairly staid but useful site. Teachers can order
inspection copies of their books.
www.letts-education.co.uk – excellent site with lots of resources,
news and explanatory notes about their books. Plus the Letts
Challenge for schools, and shop.

www.nelsonthornes.co.uk – a typical publishing site with good background on their titles and how to order them. Some books are available as online resources if you register.

Teacher Resources

www.theteachernet.co.uk   UK

ALL A TEACHER NEEDS
An excellent site that pulls together all the education resources that a teacher is likely to need from advice on how to use the Internet to getting a job and, of course, forums; there's even a certificate generator.

See also:
http://edujourney.net – resources, links and ideas for primary teachers.
www.byteachers.org.uk – a collection of useful web sites created by teachers for teachers.
www.darvill.clara.net – online science resources, lots of quizzes.
www.eteach.com – recruitment for teachers.
www.everythingeducation.org – like an education swap shop this site brings education and business together. A great place to find equipment for schools at a decent price.
www.learninginfo.com – excellent site aimed at helping those with learning disabilities.
www.literacymatters.co.uk – a good resource site for teachers on literacy from pre-school to year 7.
www.primaryresources.co.uk – excellent place to go for free lessons, ideas and worksheets.
www.primaryworksheets.co.uk – a straightforward site listing work sheets for primary school teachers.
www.teachingtables.co.uk – work sheet generation and times table help.
www.tes.co.uk – educational resources and news from *The Times Educational Supplement*.

These sites might also be of interest to anyone interested in schools:
www.fundraising.co.uk – helpful ideas.
www.governornet.co.uk – government advice on school governance.
www.ncpta.org.uk – National Association of Parent Teacher Associations.

www.ngc.org.uk – the National Governors' Council.
www.schoolsdirectory.co.uk – good directory of all 33,000 UK schools showing basic information on each school.
www.schoolswebdirectory.co.uk – directory of school websites, see also **www.school-portal.co.uk**

Home Education

It's becoming more common for children to be fully educated at home. Here are a few sites that offer support.

www.heas.org.uk   UK
    HOME EDUCATION ADVISORY SERVICE
    A good place to start, here you'll find advice and publications covering the topic, subscription costs £12 per annum.

    See also:
    www.choiceineducation.org.uk – a magazine devoted to home education.
    www.education-otherwise.org – a site run by a home education support charity.
    www.schoolhouse.org.uk – home education help in Scotland.

Electrical Goods, Gadgets and Appliances

This section covers stores that sell the usual electrical goods but also offer a bit more in terms of range, offers or service. There's also the odd spy camera and gadget shop.

www.comet.co.uk   UK
    ALWAYS LOW PRICES, GUARANTEED
    A pretty messy site these days with masses of offers on the front page, having said that it's a great place to view the widest range of goods at excellent prices.

www.dixons.co.uk   UK
    OFFERS GALORE
    The Dixons site has plenty of offers and reflects what you'd find in their stores very well. It has a similar but slightly wider product range to Comet, with an additional photographic section. Delivery costs vary.

www.richersounds.com   UK
LOWEST PRICES GUARANTEED
Despite the fact this site wouldn't win design awards, bargain
hunters will want to include this site on their list. It's similar to
the other electrical goods' retailers but with a leaning towards
music and TVs, with plenty of offers and advice. There is a
search facility and they offer a price challenge guarantee.

www.maplin.co.uk   UK
 ELECTRONICS CATALOGUE
Maplin is well established and it's a bit of an event when the new
catalogue is published. Now you can always have access to the
latest innovations and basic equipment at this well-put-together
site. It features the expected massive range with free delivery for
orders over £35.

www.electricshop.co.uk   UK
BETTER PRODUCTS, BETTER PRICES
A good-looking but slightly messy site with a huge range of
electrical goods, with offers too. The site is easy to use and has a
good search facility and it's a combination of all these factors that
make it stand out.

See also:
www.24-7electrical.co.uk – well designed and looks strong on
customer service judging by the number of times they ask you to
contact them.
www.be-direct.co.uk – some very good offers and a wide
range.
www.clearance-comet.co.uk – electrical giant Comet clears
stock through this auction site.
www.discount-appliances.co.uk – excellent range of kitchen
appliances but awful site design. Having said that, product
pictures are good.
www.electricaldiscountuk.co.uk – a pretty straightforward site
with some good offers and a wide range.
www.empiredirect.co.uk – a busy-looking site with lots of offers
and a wide range.
www.hughesdirect.co.uk – a solid offer from this well
established retailer.
www.rtwodesign.ndirect.co.uk – good-looking site from this
kitchen specialist.
www.searchappliance.co.uk – well-illustrated store from
another kitchen appliance specialist.

www.we-sell-it.co.uk – is also worth a visit for good prices on kitchen and other domestic appliances.

www.appliancespares.co.uk   UK
FIX IT YOURSELF
Ezee-Fix has thousands of spare parts for a massive range of products, nearly all illustrated, including fridges, cookers, microwaves, vacuum cleaners, etc. All it needs is online fitting instructions, and more details on the products and it would be perfect.

www.bull-electrical.com   UK
FOR THE SPECIALIST
Fascinating to visit, this mess of a site offers every sort of electronic device, from divining rods to radio kits and spy cameras. There are four basic sections:

1. Surplus electronic – scientific and optical goods, even steam engines.
2. Links to specialist shops – such as spy equipment and hydroponics.
3. Free services.
4. Web services – shopping cart technology, for example.

Other places for technology geeks to get their kicks are **www.gadgetshop.co.uk** who offer free delivery on orders over £50 and a free returns policy, and **www.firebox.com** for a really wide range of gadgets amongst other boy's toys.

www.simplyradios.com   UK
RADIOS SPECIALIST
An excellent site devoted to radios and the first place to go if you want something groovy or the latest thing in digital. For specialists in digital radio go to **www.pure-digital.com**

English Usage

With the success of the book Eats, Shoots and Leaves, *English grammar, punctuation and usage have come under the spotlight and it seems there's even more pressure to get it right. If you're not sure where apostrophes go or what a noun or pronoun is, then these sites can help. If it is a dictionary you're after, those are found on page 400.*

www.learnenglish.org.uk   UK

LEARNING ENGLISH
An excellent site from the British Council primarily aimed at those for whom English is a second language but it has a huge amount of information for students and those who just want to brush up.

See also:

www.apostrophe.fsnet.co.uk – learn how to use and misuse them at the home of the Apostrophe Protection Society.

www.askoxford.com/betterwriting – grammar, spelling, letter writing and effective communication.

www.cogs.susx.ac.uk/local/doc/punctuation/node00.html – a guide to punctuation from Sussex University.

www.dailygrammar.com – grammar lessons and quizzes.

www.englishclub.net – learn and teach English with the help of this comprehensive site; you have to register, but it's free.

www.english-zone.com – an American site and directory devoted to learning English; it's useful, but you have to register, around £20 p/a.

www.gramster.com – a free 'light' programme to help with your grammar; however, the full programme is quite expensive.

www.odps.org/glossword/index.php – the online dictionary of playground slang.

www.phrases.org.uk – look up the meanings and origins of thousands of phrases and sayings.

www.plainenglish.co.uk – the Plain English Campaign and their fight to make everything clear. Check out the free guides, which are most helpful.

www.soundsofenglish.org – English pronunciation.

www.stpt.usf.edu/pms – punctuation made simple.

www.ucl.ac.uk/internet-grammar – a free online course about English grammar aimed at university undergraduates but useful nonetheless.

www.usingenglish.com – a solid English language learning site.

www.vocabulary.co.il – excellent site for building vocabulary using simple word games such as hangman and wordsearch.

www.whoohoo.co.uk – confused by your English dialects? Here's a translation service!

www.wordspy.com – an excellent place to find new words.

www.worldwidewords.org – an interesting and personal look at English and how it's developing abroad.

E-mail

Here's a selection of the best free e-mail providers. There are hundreds to chose from, but hopefully these sites should help you find the one that's right for you, whether you're after efficiency or a trendy @ moniker.

www.fepg.net   US
FREE E-MAIL PROVIDERS GUIDE
Here's the place to start. It lists over 1,400 providers in 85 countries, including over 40 from the UK, so it's pretty comprehensive. It tends to just list them with a few details but there are recommended sites too. There's also a news section and forums.

www.sneakemail.com   US
TOTAL SPAM CONTROL
Sneak E-mail provides an e-mail protection service whereby you can maintain a level of anonymity, stop spam or unsuitable e-mails getting to you, avoid unwanted soliciting or prevent others from selling your e-mail address to marketing companies, for example.

www.twigger.co.uk   UK
ANYWHERE IN THE WORLD
An excellent service that enables you to use your chosen e-mail address wherever you may be. One advantage is that you can see attachments before you download them onto your PC. The service is subscription based; unfortunately not all ISPs covered.

www.emailaddresses.com   US
E-MAIL ADDRESS DIRECTORY
A useful directory of e-mail services and programs to help you manage your e-mail and mail to your site if you own one; there are also tips on how to find an e-mail address and a directory of address directories. See also **www.web-email-addresses.com** a very good directory with site and software reviews.

www.spamcop.com   US
STOP SPAM
Spam is a term used to describe unsolicited commercial e-mail, we all get bombarded by it and at this site you can download a useful little program that will help you minimise it. See also **www.qurb.com** and **http://spamarrest.com** and **www.spaminspector.com**

See also:
http://gmail.google.com – this is Google's e-mail project, it offers lots of memory and flexibility and you can now access via your mobile phone. Make sure you read the small print.
www.cloudmark.com – a highly recommended e-mail security program.
www.didtheyreadit.com – a program that offers an automatic receipt so that you can tell when someone has opened the mail you sent them.
www.havetheyreadityet.com – this program inserts chosen images into your outgoing e-mails and then tells you when and where they have been read.
www.pocomail.com – a well-recommended-flexible and secure e-mail program.

Ethical and Green Topics

Ethics is a difficult subject but if you are concerned about the effect you are having on the environment, want to live a greener lifestyle or are concerned about the origins and manufacture of what you buy, then this listing will help. Some of the sites are already reviewed in other sections of The Good Web Site Guide.

www.alotoforganics.co.uk   UK
LEAN, GREEN SEARCH MACHINE
UK search engine for everything organic including facts, news, events, gifts, food, alternative therapies, finance and shops. For an alternative try **www.greenchoices.org** which is comprehensive.

Animals and Plants

www.forestry.gov.uk – Forestry Commission has details of its work and how you can help sustain Britain's woods and forests.
www.fsc-uk.info – Forest Stewardship Council UK, an international non-governmental organisation promoting the responsible management of the world's forests.
www.ifaw.org – home of the International Fund for Animal Welfare.
www.rspb.org.uk – the Royal Society for the Protection of Birds.
www.rspca.org.uk – the Royal Society for the Prevention of Cruelty to Animals.

Earth

The Good Web Site Guide's Top 10s
of the Internet

1. **http://earth.google.com/** – download the Google Earth program and amaze yourself
2. **www.terraserver.com** – buy satellite imagery
3. **http://visibleearth.nasa.gov/** – download superb images from NASA
4. **www.geographyiq.com** – the online world atlas
5. **www.nationmaster.com** – more planetary statistics than you'll ever need
6. **http://eol.jsc.nasa.gov** – astronaut photography of Earth
7. **www.fourmilab.ch/earthview** – the earth from space
8. **www.earthfromtheair.com** – aerial photographs
9. **www.weatherimages.org** – watching the weather
10. **www.citypopulation.de** – pick a city, learn about it

www.traffic.org – a campaigning site working against the illegal and sometimes appalling trade in animals throughout the world.
www.ufaw.org.uk – improving animal welfare using scientific knowledge.
www.wwf.org.uk – WWF site with detailed information for conservationists on habitats, areas of global importance, endangered wildlife and the latest campaigns.

Energy

www.co2balance.com – information and help on how to lessen your carbon footprint.
www.eaga.co.uk – the Energy Action Grants Agency.
www.energysaving.me.uk – energy saving products.
www.energywatch.org.uk – independent energy watchdog.
www.est.org.uk – home of the Energy Saving Trust.
www.greenelectricity.org – sign up for a greener tariff.
www.nef.org.uk – energy-saving advice from the UK charity for energy efficiency, the National Energy Foundation.
www.ofgem.gov.uk – the UK's electricity and gas regulation body.

www.switchandgive.com – switch suppliers and give the savings to charity.
www.uswitch.com – switch to a green energy supplier.

Environment

www.airquality.co.uk – air quality information across the UK.
www.carbonneutral.com – a UK organisation working to protect the earth's climate. They will calculate your CO_2 emissions and advise on ways to neutralise your carbon debt.
www.cat.org.uk – Centre for Alternative Technology offering practical solutions to environmental problems.
www.defra.gov.uk – the Department for Environment, Food and Rural Affairs.
www.eco-portal.com – massive portal site covering all things green.
www.ecozine.co.uk – a good news site with lots of comment, opinions and links. The design could be more user-friendly though.
www.emagazine.com – the *Environmental Magazine* online.
www.envirolink.org – environmental community site with lots of info and links.
www.environment.about.com – information on environmental issues.
www.environment-agency.gov.uk – the Environment Agency's site offers information on the latest initiatives and news.
www.environmentwebsites.co.uk – a portal for environmental sites.
www.ewg.org – the Environmental Working Group, dedicated to the fight against pollution; US-oriented.
www.foe.co.uk – Friends of the Earth.
www.greenpeace.org – find out about their latest activities and how to get involved.
www.lowimpact.org – Low Impact Living Initiative, a non-profit organisation protecting the global environment.
www.planetdiary.com – monitoring world environmental events.
www.projectearth.com – recognising the damaging effect man has on the environment and pointing the way towards a better future.
www.scorecard.org – the facts on local pollution from this US-oriented but informative site.

www.wen.org.uk – Women's Environmental Network. A campaigning organisation covering environmental and health issues.
www.wri.org – World Resources Institute promoting effective campaigning for a far better world.

Fashion

www.cleanclothes.org – improving conditions for those working in the garment-making industry.
www.ethicalthreads.co.uk – clothing not made in sweatshops.
www.furisdead.com – anti-fur campaigning.
www.iftf.com – the fur trade's organisation for the opposite view.
www.labourbehindthelabel.org – campaigning for worker's rights with a list of good traders and retailers.
www.nosweat.org.uk – join the fight against sweatshop owners.

Finance

www.abcul.coop – Association of British Credit Unions.
www.co-operativebank.co.uk – banking with a conscience; also **www.smile.co.uk** their online bank.
www.ecology.co.uk – The Ecology Building Society which is a mutual society promoting sustainable housing and communities.
www.eiris.org – The Ethical Investment Research Service offers independent research into corporate behaviour.
www.ethicalinvestment.org.uk – ethical savings.
www.invest-trees.com – invest in trees.
www.letslinkuk.net – Local Exchange Trading Schemes.
www.switchwithwhich.co.uk – switch bank accounts.
www.triodos.co.uk – Triodos Bank offers environmentally sound savings accounts.
www.uksif.org – UK Social Investment Forum, the UK network for socially responsible investment.

Food

www.ciwf.org.uk – Compassion in World Farming web site, campaigning for farm animal welfare, includes the Eat Less Meat initiative.
ww.earthsave.org – promotes vegetarianism by helping you choose the right way to eat.

www.farmersmarkets.net – find your nearest Farmers' Market.
www.foodag.com – food additives.
www.freedomfood.co.uk – RSPCA site on farm animal health.
www.goodnessdirect.co.uk – supermarket with over 4,000 items including good range of grocery, fresh and frozen products.
www.organicdelivery.co.uk – a good organic food retailer – delivers to London only.
www.organicfood.co.uk – news and links on all things organic.
www.soilassociation.org – the Soil Association web site with masses of information on organic food, farming and education resources.
www.sustainweb.org – the Alliance for Better Food and Farming site with lots of information and links on sustainable farming, seasonal food and reducing food miles.
www.swaddles.co.uk – a wide range of organic food including meat.
www.vegansociety.com – The Vegan Society web site.
www.vintageroots.co.uk – excellent for organic wines, spirits and beers.
www.whyorganic.org – a Soil Association site covering a variety of issues about organic versus non-organic produce.

Home and Gardening

www.allotments-uk.com – all you need to know about owning an allotment.
www.communityrepaint.org.uk – a UK network to reuse old paint and redistribute to charities, voluntary organisations and local groups.
www.ecosolutions.co.uk – safe water-based paint and varnish removers.
www.greenbuildingstore.co.uk – green building products online.
www.greengardener.co.uk – specialists in biological and organic pest control.
www.hdra.org.uk – The Henry Doubleday Research Association, the leading authority on organic gardening.
www.just-green.com – natural pest control with advice and products.
www.nsalg.org.uk – National Society of Allotment and Leisure Gardeners.
www.organiccatalogue.com – a comprehensive store related to the HDRA.

www.pan-uk.org – the Pesticide Action Network who are working to eliminate the hazards associated with pesticides.
www.salvo.com – reclaim old furniture.

Miscellaneous

www.downsizer.net – a magazine-style site from an online community consisting of those wishing to live more sustainably.
www.idealswork.com – compare and find out about the ethical track records of major companies.
www.naturaldeath.org.uk – The Natural Death Centre's site, covering woodland burials and green funerals.
www.who.int – the World Health Organisation, the UN specialist agency with comprehensive information on every aspect of health.
www.willaid.org – draw up a will and simultaneously support charity.

Recycling

www.cartridges4charity – charity recycling inkjet cartridges, toner cartridges and mobile phones.
www.cleanaway.co.uk – recycling specialists.
www.crn.org.uk – the Community Recycling Network.
www.fonebak.com – mobile phone reuse and recycling.
www.freecycle.org – join a local group and give away unwanted items to other members.
www.letsrecycle.com – waste management company directory.
www.keepwalestidy.org – environmental charity in Wales.
www.oilbankline.org.uk – find your nearest waste oil recycling site.
www.oxfam.org.uk/what_you_can_do/recycle/phones.htm – mobile phone recycling, including school and corporate schemes.
www.paper.org.uk/info/recycling.htm – Confederation of Paper Industries.
www.recoup.org – national charity developing plastics recycling; find a site near your home.
www.vao.org.uk – Vision Aid Overseas, international charity which recycles spectacles.
www.wastewatch.org.uk – nationwide organisation promoting action on waste reduction and improved recycling and reuse.
www.webdirectory.com/recycling – general information on recycling.

E

www.wrap.org.uk – The Waste and Resources Action Programme, creating markets for recycled products.

Shopping

http://shopping.guardian.co.uk/ethicalshopping – useful advice and links.

www.afrigoods.org – quality gifts from Africa with profits going to the artists who made them.

www.cardaid.co.uk – charity Christmas cards.

www.crueltyfreeshop.com – a wide range of products on sale all of which are guaranteed not to have involved any animal cruelty or exploitation in their production.

www.ecozone.co.uk – online shopping for environmentally friendly household products.

www.ethicalconsumer.org – *Ethical Consumer Magazine*, ethical information behind the big brand names.

www.ethiscore.org – identify the best products to support and the ones to avoid by following their ethical score.

www.fairdealtrading.com – Fair Deal Trading Partnership for footballs and trainers.

www.fairtrade.org.uk – home of the Fair Trade Foundation, which exists to enable poor artists and workers to get a better deal.

www.getethical.com – who have a wide range of ethically produced and sourced products plus advice, links and a magazine.

www.goodgifts.org – online charitable alternative gifts catalogue.

www.goodshoppingguide.co.uk – ethical shopping reference book.

www.greatgifts.org – World Vision charity website offering alternative, online gifts catalogue.

www.greenshop.co.uk – online shop selling hundreds of environmentally friendly products including paint and household cleaners.

www.naturalcollection.com – comprehensive range of products from clothing to food and cosmetics.

www.onevillage.org – shop specialising in ethnic products and using the Fair Trade system.

www.surefish.co.uk – Christian Aid web site with information on ethical living including shopping, gifts and energy.

www.traidcraftshop.co.uk – good selection of crafts, foods and other goods from around the world.

Tourism

www.changingworlds.co.uk – worthwhile working holidays.
www.coralcay.org – 'providing resources to help sustain livelihoods and alleviate poverty through the protection, restoration and management of coral reefs and tropical forests'.
www.ecoafrica.com – the wonders of Africa for the ecologically minded.
www.ecoclub.com – a network providing a wealth of information about all aspects of ecotourism.
www.eco-tour.org – Eco Tourism directory.
www.ecotourism.org – the International Ecotourism Society.
www.ecotravel.com – good all-round travel site from US.
www.ecovolunteer.com – if you want to give your services to a specific animal benefit project.
www.responsibletravel.com – eco-friendly and ethically responsible holidays.

Transport

www.carclubs.org.uk – CarPlus charity site looking at responsible car use, car clubs and car sharing.
www.eta.co.uk – The Environmental Transport Association.
www.liftshare.com – car sharing web site.
www.smartmoves.co.uk – the largest UK car club operator.
www.sustrans.org.uk – nation-wide charity encouraging alternative methods of transport.
www.transportenergy.org.uk – a division of the Energy Saving Trust.

Volunteering

www.btcv.org.uk – The British Trust for Conservation Volunteers, including UK and global projects and Green Gyms.
www.csv.org.uk – Community Service Volunteers, the UK's largest volunteering and training organisation.

Water

www.hippo-the-watersaver.co.uk – water-saving device.
www.ofwat.gov.uk – the government regulator for the water industry.

www.wateraid.org.uk – international non-governmental organisation dedicated to the provision of safe water and sanitation.

www.waterconserve.info – general information on water conservation.

E-zines

E-zines are the magazines of the web and there are millions of them, some with great content and quality writing. Here are some of the best reviewed along with a couple of sites that can help you find one that you like. You should be aware that many contain adult or pornographic material.

http://zinos.com   US
E-ZINE DIGEST AND DATABASE
A well-categorised site with information and reviews of some of the world's best e-zines, it's attractive and makes it easy to find what you're looking for but not that comprehensive. See also **www.ezine-dir.com** who offer almost 3,500.

http://ezinearticles.com   US
FOR WRITERS AND PUBLISHERS
Writers are able to post articles on the site, while publishers in need of content can search the database for ready-to-wear content. Free trial membership.

Some of the Best

www.salon.com   US

SALON
An outstanding magazine offering a wide range of articles and topics with quality contributors and excellent writing. It's entertaining and witty covering the latest news and in depth features on current topics.

www.theregister.co.uk   UK

THE REGISTER
An opinionated and newsy e-zine devoted to the technology and computing worlds – it describes itself as 'biting the hand that feeds'. It's not an easy read but it's very authoritative.

www.theonion.com   US
  AMERICA'S FINEST NEWS SOURCE
  A great send-up of American tabloid newspapers, this is one of
  the most visited sites on the Internet and easily one of the funniest.

www.fray.com   US
  STORYTELLING
  A great site offering up true stories which, on the whole, are
  pretty well written. It's well designed, very accessible and
  free.

  See also:
  www.atlasmagazine.com – although moribund, this is still
  worth visiting for its design, which has given the site a place in
  the permanent collection of the San Francisco Museum on
  Modern Art.
  www.120seconds.com – a showcase that gives artists 120
  seconds to entertain us with a piece of multimedia work – some
  quite strange but never dull.
  www.foocha.com – an 'outspoken entertainment review'
  covering movies, games, music, books and the media.
  ww.urban75.com – boasting 500,000 hits per month, provides
  a non-mainstream view of life including news on raves, protest,
  drugs, short stories, photos, analysis and more.

Fashion and Accessories

*The big brands have never been cheaper. Selling fashion and designer
gear is another success story for the internet as customers flock to the
great discounts that are on offer and get access to the latest fashion
trends. Many people still prefer to try clothes on before buying but the
good sites all offer a convenient returns policy.*

Fashion

www.fuk.co.uk   UK
  FASHION UK
  All you ever need to know about the latest in UK and world
  fashion, updated daily. There's a good links library,
  competitions, chat and, of course, shopping. It's all packaged
  into a really attractive site, which initially looks cluttered but is
  OK once you get used to it.

www.vogue.co.uk UK

THE LATEST NEWS FROM BRITISH VOGUE

An absolute must for the serious follower of fashion. There's the latest catwalk news and views, and a handy who's who of fashion. There's also a section on jobs, and you can order a subscription too. For a similar experience try **www.elle.com** or the slightly less fashion-oriented but more fun **www.cosmomag.com**

www.ftv.com FRANCE

FASHION TV

The 24-hour fashion station, so popular in gyms and bars, has a good site offering the latest from around the world. Features include video clips, radio interviews with designers plus links, gossip and horoscopes.

www.net-a-porter.com UK

NET A PORTER

A great-looking site that is easy to use with information on the latest fashions, plus catwalk reports and shopping where you can browse by designer or product type. Delivery costs vary according to what you buy.

www.fashionmall.com US

FASHION STORE DIRECTORY

A huge number of stores listed by category, packed with offers and the latest new designs. The site is well designed and easy to browse. Most stores are American and their ability to deliver outside the US and delivery charges vary considerably.

www.yoox.com UK

TOP DESIGNERS

A great-looking site with top offers from the top designers. It's well laid out and easy to navigate with a good returns policy. You can search by designer or category and the quality of the photos is good. Offers range from a few pounds to massive discounts.

www.haburi.com UK

CUT-PRICE DESIGNER CLOTHES FOR MEN AND WOMEN

Not a big range of clothes but excellent prices. Clear, no-nonsense design makes the site easy to use.

www.apc.fr   FRANCE
FRENCH CHIC FROM APC
Unusual in style and for something a little different, APC's site is
worth a visit. Delivery is expensive in line with the clothes, which
are beautifully designed and well presented. For more of the
French look go to **www.redoute.co.uk**

www.extremepie.com   UK
EXTREME FASHION FOR EXTREME SPORTS
A brand-led selection of clothes from the world of BMX, surf,
skate and other so-called sports. The site is excellent with clear
visuals and delivery costs start at £2.95.

www.pop-boutique.com   UK
BUY SOMETHING THAT'S ALREADY OUT OF DATE!
A fantastic site devoted to fashion chic from the 60s, 70s and
80s, it can be a little slow but worth the wait if you're into the
period. It also sells accessories and offers a good set of related
links.

See also:
www.catwalk-queen.net – entertaining blog that follows the
latest fashions and their victims.
www.closetspy.com – a very good blog site devoted to bringing
you the latest in what's fashionable.
www.fashion.net – a good fashion search engine and directory
with the added advantage that it carries the latest fashion news
too.
www.kitschshop.co.uk – who offer lots beside just clothes.
www.retrorebels.co.uk – quirky and streetwise.

www.badfads.com   US
IT SHOULD NEVER HAVE HAPPENED . . .
An entertaining site featuring the Bad Fad Museum full of
clothes, events and collectibles that maybe we'd be better off not
remembering. The whole is a fun reminiscence of the 70s and
80s.

Other fashion sites worth a peek:
www.colette.fr – an eclectic collection of quirky products and
fashion items, we can't work out if the web site is brilliantly
designed or just plain annoying.
www.fashionangel.com – excellent directory and portal for
fashion-related links.

www.fashionguide.com – US-oriented fashion gossip and tips.

www.fashionplanet.com – New York-oriented fashion magazine and store.

www.firstview.com – be among the first to see the latest from the fashion shows, you have to subscribe though.

www.girlonthestreet.com – home to a New York trend agency with some top tips and a sneak preview on what's coming up.

www.girlprops.com – another New York-based site with masses of accessories to choose from. Delivery is expensive to the UK though.

www.gofugyourself.com – a very amusing blog devoted to the worst fashions worn by the stars. It introduces the word Fugly, meaning 'frightfully ugly' . . . celebrities beware!

www.hintmag.com – a well-designed fashion e-zine with regular features, news and links. The photography is especially good.

www.japanesestreets.com – the latest on Japanese street fashion.

www.lucire.com – another fashion magazine, this one is well thought of and it covers everything from catwalk style to skincare.

www.monsoon.co.uk – good illustrations and online store.

www.ntgi.net/ICCF&D/textile.htm – an encyclopaedia of textiles and materials used in fashion and tailoring.

www.oasis-stores.com – good-looking site with information on the latest trends, also see the vintage collection not available in many stores.

www.toastbypost.co.uk – good mail-order catalogue with the latest designs.

Top Designers

www.armaniexchange.com – cheap Armani
www.bensherman.co.uk – Ben Sherman
www.chanel.com – Chanel
www.christian-lacroix.fr – Christian Lacroix
www.dior.com – Dior
www.gucci.com – Gucci
www.hugo.com – Hugo Boss
www.jpgaultier.fr – Jean Paul Gaultier
www.karenmillen.com – Karen Millen
www.kenzo.com – Kenzo
www.paulsmith.co.uk – Paul Smith

www.tedbaker.co.uk – Ted Baker
www.tommy.com – Tommy Hilfiger

General Clothes Stores

www.arcadia.co.uk   UK
THE UK'S LEADING FASHION RETAILER
The Arcadia Group has over 1,200 stores in the UK and the web
sites are accessible, easy to use and offer good value for money.
Each site has its own personality that reflects the high street
store. Delivery charges vary.

www.burton.co.uk – Burton
www.dorothyperkins.co.uk – Dorothy Perkins
www.evans.ltd.uk – Evans
www.missselfridge.co.uk – Miss Selfridge
www.outfitfashion.com – Outfit
www.topman.co.uk – Topman
www.topshop.co.uk – Topshop
www.wallis-fashion.com – Wallis

www.zoom.co.uk   UK
MORE THAN JUST A SHOP
This is an excellent magazine-style site, with lots of features
other than shopping, such as free Internet access and e-mail.
Shopping consists of links to specialist retailers. You can enter
prize draws and there are a number of exclusive offers as well.
Not always the cheapest, but an entertaining shopping site.

Catalogues

www.kaysnet.com   UK
KAYS CATALOGUE
Massive range combined with value for money is the formula for
success with Kays. While they lead with clothes there are plenty
of other sections outside of that: jewellery, home entertainment,
toys, etc. They offer free 48-hour delivery.

www.freemans.co.uk   UK
FREE DELIVERY IN THE UK AND GOOD PRICES
A similar site to Kays, not the full catalogue but there's a wide
range to choose from, including top brands. They offer free
delivery for UK customers. There are also prizes to be won,

special features on topical themes and information on how to get the full catalogue. For another version of the same web site see **www.grattan.co.uk** for Grattan's catalogue online.

ww.next.co.uk   UK
THE NEXT DIRECTORY
The online version of the Next catalogue is available including clothes for men, women and children as well as products for the home. Prices are the same as the directory, while you can order the full catalogue for £3.50.

See also:
www.aboundonline.com – a catalogue site with a very good choice, which also offers a style guide and outfit finder service.
www.littlewoods-online.com – wide selection from across the range.

Specialist Clothes Stores

www.asseenonscreen.com   UK
BUY WHAT YOU SEE ON FILM OR TV
Now you can buy that bit of jewellery or the cool gear that you've seen your favourite TV or film star wearing, As Seen on Screen specialises in supplying just that. You can search by star or programme, it isn't cheap but you'll get noticed. They also have a handy gift ideas section if you're looking for inspiration. See also **www.celebfashion.co.uk**

www.enokiworld.com   US
VINTAGE CLOTHES FOR MODERN WOMEN
A nicely designed site with a wide range of vintage clothing. Prices and delivery costs vary according to what you buy. See also **www.candysays.co.uk** who offer a wide range of clothes and accessories plus menswear too.

www.bloomingmarvellous.co.uk   UK
MATERNITY WEAR
The UK's leading store in maternity and babywear has an attractive site that features a good selection of clothes and nursery products. There are no discounts on the clothes, but they do have regular sales with some good bargains.

Underwear and Lingerie

www.figleaves.com   UK
MORE THAN JUST A FIG LEAF
Fig Leaves has become a big Internet success with a huge range
of lingerie from most major designers with plenty of offers and on
an easy-to-use site. The site now hosts the upmarket brand
www.rigbyandpeller.com which used to have its own site. There
is free delivery on orders over £25 and a free return option too.

www.amplebosom.com   UK
ITS ALL IN THE NAME
One of the media's favourite Internet success stories, Sally sells
bras for everyone, including large and small sizes, mastectomy,
nursing and maternity bras.

See also:
www.kiniki.com – more men's underwear.
www.lasenza.co.uk – good selection for ladies and reasonable
prices includes glamour, character, nightwear and swimwear.
www.littlewomen.co.uk – solutions for little women.
www.nicolajane.com – good selection of feminine mastectomy
bras and swimwear.
www.victoriassecret.com – for designer style, but beware high
shipping costs.

Shoes

www.shoe-shop.com   UK
EUROPE'S BIGGEST SHOE SHOP
A massive selection of shoes and brands to chose from. The site
is nicely designed with good pictures of the shoes, some of
which can be seen in 3-D, a facility they are expanding. Delivery
is included in the price and there's a good returns policy.

See also:
www.britfoot.com – home of the British Footwear Association
for hard-to-find footwear.
www.cosyfeet.com – a good site devoted to extra roomy
footwear and socks!
www.elephantfeet.com – stylish shoes in larger sizes.
www.faith.co.uk – a well-reviewed and recommended shoe
shop aimed at fashion conscious women. It has a good shoe
comparison feature.

www.immortalsole.co.uk – excellent site devoted to retro trainers!
www.magnusshoes.com – another large size specialist, with a good site.
www.office.co.uk – neat site design from this High Street retailer.
www.shoesdirect.co.uk – straightforward with some good offers.
www.shoetailor.com – a huge range from this popular specialist.
www.shoes.co.uk – a shopping directory devoted to online shoe shops.
www.voodooshoes.com – great name and quite fashion oriented.

www.centuryinshoes.com   UK

SHOE HISTORY
An interesting and very well-designed site devoted to the development of the shoe from 1900 to the present day, each shoe and boot is available to view in three dimensions and you can get into the detail easily.

Accessories and Jewellery

www.jewellers.net   UK

THE BIGGEST RANGE ON THE NET
Excellent range of products, fashion jewellery, gifts, gold and silver; the watch section is particularly strong. There is also information on the history of gems, the manufacturers and brands available. Delivery to the UK is free for orders over £50, and there is a 30-day no quibble returns policy.

www.topbrands.net   UK

WATCH HEAVEN
A large range of watches including Swatch, Casio, G Shock, Baby G and Umbro are available here. The site is fast and easy to use, but a better search facility would save time. Delivery is free for the UK, but prices appear to be similar to the high street.

Also check out:
www.designerdivas.co.uk – good designer jewellery for those who are Delightful-Individual-Vivacious-Attractive-Sexy.
www.funkyaccessories.com – a wide choice with shoes, lingerie and some good offers too.
www.ganesha.co.uk – an excellent store featuring Indian products sold and produced on an ethical basis. Limited amount of clothing, but lots of accessories.
www.geraldonline.com – a wide range of jewellery and watches from Gerald Ratner and associates.

www.jewellerycatalogue.co.uk – guaranteed low prices.
www.madaboutjewellery.com – costume jewellery with
designer style.
www.newurban.co.uk – hats, gloves, scarves all in the latest
styles.
www.timetoindulge.co.uk – a wide range of cheap
jewellery.

www.be-a-fashionista.co.uk UK
DESIGNER BAGS

If you don't want to go to the expense of buying a designer
handbag then you can hire one; however at prices starting at
£29.99 a month you have to be a real fashionista to want this.
For those who just want to buy a bag then chose from any one of
the following **www.blitzbags.co.uk** for designer gear,
www.brandedbags.com for both designer and the more
traditional and **www.ebags.co.uk** for a broad selection.

Finance, Banking and Shares

*The Internet is proving to be a real winner when it comes to personal
finance, product comparison and home share dealing. With these sites
you will get the latest advice and may even make some money.*

General Finance Information Sites, Directories and Mortgages

www.fsa.gov.uk UK

FINANCIAL SERVICES AUTHORITY

The regulating body that you can go to if you need help with your
rights or if you want to find out about financial products; it will
also help you to verify that the financial institution you're dealing
with is legitimate. See also **www.oft.gov.uk** for the Office of Fair
Trading and its informative site.

www.financial-ombudsman.org.uk UK

FINANCIAL OMBUDSMAN SERVICES

When you have a complaint about a financial service this is a
good point of call for sensible advice and help on how to go
about getting a fair hearing.

Money, Money, Money...

The Good Web Site Guide's Top 10s
of the Internet

1. **www.fsa.gov.uk** – the place to start, the Financial Services Authority
2. **www.find.co.uk** – the biggest and best financial portal site
3. **www.fool.co.uk** – for those who want some fun with their finance
4. **www.bankfacts.org.uk** – all the information on internet banking and more
5. **www.uswitch.co.uk** – switch services here and save money
6. **www.inlandrevenue.gov.uk** – home of the tax man
7. **www.unbiased.co.uk** – go here to find a financial adviser
8. **www.pensionguide.gov.uk** – excellent advice on pensions
9. **www.moneysavingexpert.com** – expert Martin Lewis dispenses financial joy
10. **www.paypal.com** – the secure way to pay for stuff online

www.find.co.uk   UK

INTERNET DIRECTORY FOR FINANCIAL SERVICES
Access to thousands of financial sites; split into nine sections: loans, credit cards, insurance, mortgages, investment, banking and savings, life and pensions, advice and information, business services and some hints on best buys. Superb. See also **www.financelink.co.uk**

www.ft.com or www.ftyourmoney.com   UK

FINANCIAL TIMES
FT.com offers up-to-date news and information. The 'Your Money' section is biased towards personal finance. Although it looks daunting, it is easy to use and provides sound, independent advice for everyone.

www.fool.co.uk   US/UK

THE MOTLEY FOOL
Finance with a sense of fun. The Fool is exciting and a real education in shrewdness. It not only takes the mystery out of share dealing but gives great advice on investment and personal finance. You need to register to get the best out of it.

www.thisismoney.com   UK
MONEY NEWS AND ADVICE
Easy-to-use site with reliable 24-hour financial advice from the Daily Mail group. It has loads of information on all aspects of personal finance and is particularly good for comparison tools, especially mortgages, and there's a good 'Ask the Experts' section.

www.iii.co.uk   UK
INTERACTIVE INVESTOR INTERNATIONAL
Now known as Ample, the emphasis is on investment and share dealing with some personal finance thrown in. It retains the interactivity of the original site but with some additional investment information. Also can be reached through **www.ample.com**

www.moneynet.co.uk   UK
IMPARTIAL AND COMPREHENSIVE
Rated as one of the best independent personal finance sites, it covers over 100 mortgage lenders, has a user-friendly search facility plus help with conveyancing and financial calculators. It now also covers banking, refused credit and life insurance.

www.moneychimp.com
THE BASICS
If you're baffled by all things financial, here you'll find really simple explanations on most aspects of finance and the economy. There's a helpful glossary. Be aware that the site is American, so a few of the definitions are slightly different.

For other similar sites go to:
www.advfn.com – a really ugly site but comprehensive, if you can put up with the design.
www.adviceonline.co.uk – independent financial advice on a logically designed site.
www.bbc.co.uk – check out the 'your money' section under 'business and money', great for keeping up to date with the latest financial news.
www.digitallook.com – one of the leading providers of financial information, excellent site.
www.financialplanning.org.uk – help from the Institute of Financial Planning.
www.financial-planning.uk.com – a wide range of advice available but the site could be better organised and accessible.

www.fsa.gov.uk/consumer/compare – one of the best comparison sites with lots of useful tables and excellent common sense advice.

www.marketplace.co.uk – 'independent' advisers from Bradford & Bingley help you make the right financial choices from mortgages to investments and pensions.

www.moneybrain.co.uk – a slick site offering a wide range of financial products and independent advice.

www.moneyfacts.co.uk – a no-nonsense information site which shows the cheapest and best value financial products with lots of authority, it's also a comparatively fast site and less tricky than some. It also covers annuities and offshore banking.

www.moneysupermarket.com – a very good all-rounder with help in most of the important areas of personal finance; good site layout and lots of practical advice add to the package.

www.unbiased.co.uk   UK
FIND AN INDEPENDENT FINANCIAL ADVISER
A good independent financial adviser is hard to come by if you need one. But here's a good place to start. Just type in your postcode and the services you need and up pops a list of specialists in your area. See also **www.sofa.org** for the Society of Financial Planners, both sites give information on how to get a financial adviser and plan your finances. While at the Personal Finance Society, **www.thepfs.org** you can find out how to get the best financial advice and have a financial health check too.

www.quote-engine.com   UK
BEST VALUE CREDIT
A guide to help you find the best deals on credit cards and loans. It's easy enough to use and there are online forms as well as links. It also covers insurance and household bills.

Mortgage Specialists

www.charcoalonline.co.uk   UK
JOIN CHARCOAL
This established mortgage adviser owned by Bradford & Bingley offers mortgages from over 36 lenders. There are also sections on loans, credit cards and insurance.

It's worth shopping around, so check out these sites too:
www.mortgageman.co.uk – aimed at the self-employed or those having difficulty getting a mortgage from the usual lenders, or with CCJs.

www.mortgagepoint.co.uk – geared towards first-time buyers and those with a less than perfect credit history.
www.mortgageshop.com – independent financial advice about which is the best mortgage for you, a somewhat messy site though.
www.mortgages-online.co.uk – good independent source of information.
www.yourmortgage.co.uk – *Your Mortgage* magazine.

Insurance

www.insurancewide.com

UK

HOME OF INSURANCE ON THE WEB
Claim to have a unique system that gives you personalised comparative quotes from most UK insurance providers. They offer a wide range of insurance policies covering life, travel, motor, home, small business as well as sections for students, young people, women and lifestyle.

www.easycover.com

UK

UK'S BIGGEST INDEPENDENT INSURANCE WEB SITE
Here you can get a wide range of quotes just by filling in one form. The emphasis is on convenience and speed.

www.warrantydirect.co.uk

UK

EXTENDED WARRANTIES
Here you can get cover for the important things in life: your car, appliances and your computer.

Other sites worth checking out:
www.eaglestardirect.co.uk – a sparse but useful site from one of the market leaders.
www.elephant.co.uk – instant quotes on a wide selection of policies although they mainly specialise in car insurance.
www.inspop.com – choose the specially selected policy and buy online.
www.insurance.co.uk – another comparison site backed by Lloyds TSB.
www.morethan.com – hyped with the 'Where's Lucky' ads, this site is from Royal Sun Alliance and it's good for quotes in most areas including pets.
www.quotelinedirect.co.uk – quotes on a wide range of insurance areas.
www.soreeyes.co.uk – a wide range of policies and options.

www.theaa.com/insurance – AA Insurance covers travel, cars and home.
www.theidol.com – a wide range of insurance options available here.
www.ukinsuranceguide.co.uk – a good place to find specialist insurers.

For advice on insurance or problems with insurance:
www.abi.org.uk – Association of British Insurers, lots of advice on all aspects of insurance plus industry information.
www.financial-ombudsman.org.uk – help with all aspects of financial services industry.

Investing and Share Dealing

www.investmentguide.co.uk   UK
FOR THOSE WHO GO IT ALONE
An outstanding site that gives you access to three books from Harold Baldwin which are regularly updated and contain high-quality information regarding share dealing and other investments; suitable for beginners or experts. Some information is by subscription.

See also:
www.aitc.co.uk – an excellent guide and advice site to Investment Trusts.
www.citywire.co.uk – advice and analysis from a well-regarded source, some information is subscription only.
www.hargreaveslansdown.co.uk – a wide-ranging site with lots of investment options and advice on where to put your hard-earned cash.
www.investmentuk.org – home of the Investment Management Association where you can find some useful advice and learn how the investment industry is managed and how it works with government.
www.investopedia.com – described as the investment education site, it's packed with information and helps to navigate the investment minefield.
www.londonstockexchange.com – guide to the exchange, how it works plus information on stocks and shares.

Any of the following are worth checking out when it comes to dealing in shares. They are all good sites, each with a slightly different focus, just find the one that suits your needs:

www.apcims.co.uk – home of the Association of Private Client Investment Managers and Stockbrokers and a usefully informative site to boot.

www.barclays-stockbrokers.co.uk – good value for smaller share deals and possibly the best for beginners.

www.cofunds.co.uk – have more control over your investments and savings.

www.deal4free.com – unusual and highly rated dealing site offering spread betting, share dealing and currency trading. You need a good understanding of finance to get the best out of it.

www.earningswhispers.com – the latest hot stock picks and earnings news.

www.ethicalinvestment.org.uk – if you want to invest your money in business that has a moral conscience, then here's the site that will lead you in the right direction.

www.etrade.com – a well-designed share trading site.

www.e-traderuk.com – a directory of investment and related financial sites.

www.freequotes.co.uk – an all singing, all dancing site with the latest share information, tips and links to related and important sites.

www.fundsnetwork.co.uk – an online investment superstore with a huge range of options.

www.gni.co.uk – award-winning trading and investment site, good design.

www.hedgeworld.com – a guide to the seemingly complex world of hedge funds.

www.hemscott.com – one of the more comprehensive offerings with good use of other technologies such as SMS.

www.hoovers.com – good for background information; provides comprehensive company, industry and market intelligence on 42,000 of the world's top businesses.

www.investorschronicle.co.uk – this established magazine offers a useful site for share information and dealing, especially good for data on medium-sized and large companies.

www.invest-trees.com – profits from investing in woodlands.

www.itsonline.co.uk – a well-designed site that concentrates on explaining and campaigning for investment trusts.

www.morningstar.co.uk – a very dense site with huge amounts of information, part of its service is to collate and interpret the output of financial journalists, which must be a job in itself.

www.nsandi.com – National Savings and Investments.

www.sharepeople.com – owned by American Express, it has a nice design and is easy to use with lots of explanation on how it all works. Costs vary depending on the size of trade.

www.sharexpress.co.uk – the award-winning Halifax share dealing service that is a good beginner's site and charges competitively.

www.tdwaterhouse.co.uk – slightly more expensive than Barclays, but still quite good value, well designed with good information to back it all up.

www.trustnet.co.uk – all you need to know about investing in trusts.

Pensions

www.investmentguide.co.uk
UK

FIND A PENSION
Excellent site if you need help around the pensions minefield, with lots of jargon-free and independent information. It tells you how to buy one, how much you should be paying and advice on what you should be saving if you want a golden retirement.

www.pensionguide.gov.uk
UK

KNOW YOUR OPTIONS
A newly designed web site that provides an impartial guide to pensions from the government, which aims to help you choose the right option; there's also information for employers and current pension holders. Also check out **www.thepensionservice.gov.uk** the Department for Work and Pensions which represents the government line on pensions and gives good advice and the latest news. **www.direct.gov.uk/ MoneyTaxAndBenefits/PensionsAndRetirement/ FinancialPlanningForRetirement** also has some useful information and is a good starting point for advice.

For more information on pensions see:
www.dwp.gov.uk – the government's advice site from the Department of Work and Pensions with information on benefits and services.

www.opas.org.uk – the Office of the Pensions Advisory Service helps when things go wrong

www.opra.gov.uk – the Occupational Pensions Regulatory Authority ensures pension schemes are run properly.

www.pensioncalculator.org.uk – a useful and detailed site on calculating your pension.

www.pensionsnetwork.com – good site dedicated to bringing you the best value stakeholder pensions. It's easy to use and comes with a good pensions calculator.

www.sippdeal.co.uk – advice on how to invest your pension in a Self Invested Personal Pension.

www.sipp-provider-group.org.uk – informative site on SIPP.

Banking

Despite various concerns and scandals surrounding the security of some banking sites, internet banking is here to stay and is a very popular and useful way of keeping track of your finances. Common sense is the key to good security. Never e-mail bank information, card, PIN or account numbers under any circumstances; it's also a good idea not to have the information stored on your PC as there are programs capable of obtaining that information without your knowledge. See our security section on page 423 for more on how you can keep safe but also check out **www.banksafeonline.org.uk** *where you'll find a great deal of relevant information and help.*

www.bankfacts.org.uk   UK
BRITISH BANKER'S ASSOCIATION
Answers to the most common questions about banking, advice about Internet banks, the banking code and general information. There's also a facility that helps you resurrect dormant accounts. See also **www.bankingcode.org.uk** where you can find details of the standards of service that all the banks have signed up to. For information on building societies go to the Building Society Association at **www.bsa.org.uk** and also the portal site **www.buildingsocieties.com** which offers a useful regional guide.

www.switchwithwhich.co.uk   UK

SWITCH BANK ACCOUNTS EASILY
Which? magazine's site devoted to a campaign to encourage people to switch to less costly bank accounts. There is advice on the best account for you and how to move your account to the recommended one painlessly.

Tax

www.inlandrevenue.gov.uk   UK
TALK TO THE TAXMAN
The Inland Revenue has a very informative site where you can

get help on all aspects of tax. You can even submit your tax
return over the Internet and there's a good set of links to other
government departments.

www.tax.org.uk   UK
CHARTERED INSTITUTE OF TAXATION
A great resource, they don't provide information on individual
questions but they can put you in touch with a qualified
adviser. It's a good place to start if you have a problem with
your tax.

www.taxbuddies.com   UK

TAX ADVICE
A pretty comprehensive effort with a huge amount of data,
information and advice on aspects of taxation both personal and
business.

http://listen.to/taxman   UK
THE TAX CALCULATOR
Amazingly fast, just input your gross earnings and your tax and
actual earnings are calculated.

See page 65 for our business section.

Credit Checking

www.checkmyfile.com   UK
IS YOUR CREDIT GOOD?
For £6.95 you can get a basic online credit rating on yourself, or
if you pay more, they'll send you a more detailed report. Very
useful and informative, they even keep updating your file on a
quarterly basis. You can also work out your likely credit score
using their online calculator for free. They also offer identity fraud
services and will check out car details. Data protection is
guaranteed too.

See also these sites that offer similar information and services:
www.callcredit.plc.uk – online consumer credit reference
agency with a variety of services.
www.equifax.co.uk – get a full detailed credit report for £9.95
online.
www.experian.co.uk – get a credit report sent for £2.

Debt Management

www.citizensadvice.org.uk   UK

CITIZENS ADVICE BUREAU
Often the first port of call for people with debt issues, the site
offers useful information and the latest campaigns. There's a
search facility to find your nearest office and a link to
www.adviceguide.org.uk which contains basic advice and
information on your rights.

See also:
www.cccs.co.uk – a charity dedicated to helping people get out
of debt.
www.debtcounsellors.co.uk – specialists in advising people on
what to do if they get into financial difficulty and dealing with
creditors.
www.nationaldebtline.com – a free debt help service with
useful links.

Miscellaneous

www.ifs.org.uk   UK
INSTITUTE OF FISCAL STUDIES
Independent analysis of all things financial, especially the tax
system; surprisingly interesting but a pretty dull site.

www.paypal.com   UK

SEND AND RECEIVE MONEY ONLINE
A genuinely useful service, especially for small businesses and
online auction junkies, it's very easy and straightforward to use.
There's a directory of over 42,000 web sites that use PayPal and
details of how your site can get involved. See also
www.worldpay.com

www.moneysavingexpert.com   UK

SAVE ON EVERYTHING
Saving money guides to almost everything we pay out on, from
credit cards to utilities, this is an extremely useful site from TV
and radio pundit Martin Lewis.

Finding Someone

Following the success of Friends Reunited, there's been a massive explosion of sites dedicated to finding old friends and colleagues. Here we've listed all the best sites, and also the place to go to find a phone number, contacts for business and the home.

Directory Sites

www.yell.com   UK

UK BUSINESS DIRECTORY

Basically a search engine and directory devoted to businesses. The online Yellow Pages is a very handy site to have in your favourites list, it's easy to use and you can download the toolbar on to your browser to make it even more convenient. You can even get your search results shown on a map. See also **www.bigyellow.com** for the US.

www.scoot.co.uk   UK

THE SIMPLE WAY TO FIND A BUSINESS

Register, type in the person's name or profession then hit the scoot button and the answer comes back in seconds. Oriented towards finding businesses but useful nonetheless.

www.thomweb.co.uk   UK

THE ANSWER COMES OUT OF THE BLUE

Thomson's offer an impressive site and provide local directories online. It's divided up into the following major categories:

1. A business finder – search using a combination of name, type of business or region.
2. People finder – track down phone numbers and home or e-mail addresses.
3. Comprehensive local information – available on the major cities and regions.

www.bt.com/directory-enquiries   UK

BRITISH TELECOM DIRECTORY

The way to cut those bills to directory enquiries. You're given free access to 10 enquiries per day, but you can have another 200 free searches per month if you register. For a full overview of BT services including checking up and paying your phone bill go to **www.bt.com**

See also:
www.anywho.com – straightforward American-oriented search site with an international section.
www.infospace.com – another good search engine with yellow (business) and white (people) pages sections, it offers much more though including a good web directory.
www.royalmail.co.uk – this site offers a useful address and postcode finder and you can track your recorded deliveries too.
www.ukphonebook.com – simple to use, quick with a no-nonsense design; also has mapping, a business finder and lots of adverts.

www.192.com   UK

THE UK'S LARGEST DIRECTORY SERVICE
The Best Portal site of 2005 has plenty available free of charge such as people and business finders, directories, maps and route planners. In addition, there are various subscription options such as access to the electoral role, historical and current census information and a range of business services. For a fee, they'll even try to track down individuals you've lost contact with.

Finding Old Friends

www.friendsreunited.co.uk   UK

THE ONE STOP SITE TO REUNITE
Once the UK's most visited web site, a phenomenal success story and millions of people have made contact with old friends using the site. The read-only service is free, but access to the full service costs £7.50. For that you get access to the schools and workplace database and the ability to contact people through the site. It's very easy to use and you'll quickly lose yourself. Now offer a genes reunited, dating and a job search.

See also:
www.disabledunited.com – dedicated to uniting disabled people.
www.friend-ships.com – find that person you met on a cruise.
www.gradfinder.com – good site covering many of the world's schools and universities.
www.reunitelostfriends.co.uk – a nicely designed site with some unusual sections such as 'lost sweethearts' and 'mothers groups'.
www.scoutsreunited.co.uk – find your old scouting buddies here.

Some similar sites dedicated to re-uniting old service colleagues:
www.armedforcesfriends.co.uk
www.forcesreunited.org.uk
www.servicepals.com

Try also:
www.arielbruce.com – Ariel Bruce is an ex-social worker with a good track record of finding missing people.
www.find-someone.com – a very commercial US site offering software for sale that may help track someone down.
www.journalismnet.com/people – a tips sheet that contains links and advice on how to find people.
www.missing-you.net – free message posting designed to help find lost friends thought to be in the UK.
www.peopletracer.co.uk – people traced for a fee.
www.reunite.org – helping families who have suffered the trauma of child abduction.

www.andys-penpals.com   UK
FIND A PENPAL
A site devoted to penpals around the world. It's easy to use and free; there are also links to similar sites and a chat room.

Flowers

Sending Flowers

www.interflora.co.uk   UK
TURNING THOUGHTS INTO FLOWERS
Interflora can send flowers to over 140 countries, many on the same day as the order. They'll have a selection to send for virtually every occasion and they offer a reminder service. The service is excellent, although they are not very up front on delivery costs, which can be high. If you can't get what you need here then try **www.teleflorist.co.uk** who offer a similar service.

www.flyingflowers.com   UK
EUROPE'S LEADING FLOWERS BY POST COMPANY
Freshly picked flowers flown from Jersey to the UK from £9.99. All prices include delivery and you save at least £1 on all bouquets against their standard advertised off-line prices. They'll also arrange next day delivery in the UK. The site is simple and

there's a reminder service just to make sure you don't forget anyone.

www.clareflorist.co.uk UK
STYLISH BOUQUETS AND PRETTY PICTURES
Easy-to-use site with good customer services and free delivery to UK with surcharge for same day delivery. Cost reflects the sophistication of the flowers.

Other florists worth checking out are listed below. It has to be said that they are all quite similar, but some sell hampers, chocolates and other gifts too:
wwww.bloomingbritain.com
www.bunches.co.uk
www.florist-england.co.uk
www.flowersxpress.co.uk
www.jwflowers.com
www.longmans.co.uk
www.sayitwith.co.uk
www.serenataflowers.com

Flower Arranging

www.paula-pryke-flowers.com UK
LIVE YOUR LIFE IN COLOURS
A bright and well-laid-out site from one of the UK's premium flower arrangers. There are details of her books and designs, which you can order.

See also:
www.jane-packer.co.uk – another top celebrity with a site offering limited information; however, it does come with a contact e-mail.
www.floralartmall.com – check out the free stuff, including lessons and ideas.
www.nafas.org.uk – informative, if dull, site from the National Association of Flower Arrangement Societies.
www.silkflowerarranging.com – learn how to arrange silk flowers successfully.
www.thegardener.btinternet.co.uk – details on how to achieve the perfect flower arranger's garden and how to arrange them.

Food and Drink

Foodies

The Good Web Site Guide's Top 10s
of the Internet

1. **www.epicurious.com** – more recipes than you'll ever need
2. **www.waitrose.com** – excellent for something special and great articles and feature sections too
3. **www.food.gov.uk** – food news and advice from the Food Standards Agency
4. **www.deliaonline.com** – outstanding site from the queen of cookery
5. **www.tudocs.com** – cookery sites rated and listed in this excellent directory
6. **www.3fatchicks.com** – no nonsense healthy eating and diet advice
7. **www.edible.com** – if it moves, it's edible
8. **www.savoria.co.uk** – 'i veri sapori d'Italia'
9. **www.cheese.com** – the ultimate site on cheese!
10. **www.vegweb.com** – attractive and very useful vegetarian site

Whether you want to order from the comfort of your own home, indulge yourself, find the latest food news or get a recipe, this collection of sites will fulfil all your foodie desires. It features supermarkets, online magazines and information sites, specialist food retailers, vegetarian and organic stockists, drinks information and suppliers, where to go for kitchen equipment and help in finding the best places when eating out.

Supermarkets and General Food Stores

www.waitrose.com   UK

IF YOU ARE REALLY INTO FOOD
Waitrose is offering a very good, comprehensive and well-designed site that oozes quality, so it's a pleasure to do your grocery shopping online. You can buy wine, gifts, organics and some John Lewis products. In addition it also has all the features you'd expect from an ISP: articles and recipes in their *Illustrated*

Food magazine including information on food-related campaigns and organic issues; an excellent gift shop; plus party, flowers and travel sections and even one on competitions and puzzles.

www.ocado.com   UK
AWARD WINNING

In partnership with Waitrose, Ocado offers a supermarket delivery service dispatched from a central warehouse to the south East, Midlands and North West of England but their range is expanding all the time. This site deserves its success as it's easier to use than most of the other supermarket sites.

www.tesco.co.uk   UK
THE LIFESTYLE SUPERSTORE

This functional site has a comprehensive offering, there's a wide range of goods on offer though, including electrical goods, clothes and books. There's also a section on personal finance, other shops, parenting advice and healthy living. Offers now abound with some great savings all aimed at capturing your e-mail address and future custom. As if echoing Tesco's movement away from selling just food, groceries do not seem to be the major function of this site anymore.

www.sainsburys.co.uk   UK
NOT JUST GOOD TASTE

Sainsbury's site has more emphasis on good food, cooking, recommendation and taste, and of course the Nectar loyalty card. The facility to place an advance order at their Calais store, which you can then pick up and pay for in France, will appeal to those who wish to save time on their booze run.

www.asda.co.uk   UK
PERMANENTLY LOW PRICES

There's lots of information about the company and what it stands for plus links to its online shop. There are also sections on financial services, health and offers. Delivery cost alters depending on day and time of delivery.

Supermarkets without internet shopping facilities:
www.iceland.co.uk – the frozen food specialist will deliver from the store but have ceased their online service.
www.morrisons.co.uk – all you can do online is find out about their stores, range and offers.

www.somerfield.co.uk – the emphasis is on offers but there's also a recipe finder, wine guide and essential food facts. Check out whether you're eligible for free delivery.

Alternatives to Supermarkets

www.homefarmfoods.com   UK
DELICIOUS FROZEN FOOD DELIVERED FREE
Good selection of frozen foods and huge range of ready meals with a good use of symbols indicating whether the product is low fat, microwavable, vegetarian etc. With free delivery, it's especially good value, and there is no minimum order. See also www.foodhall.co.uk who have a good selection of specialist stores to choose from.

www.farmersmarkets.net   UK
NATIONAL ASSOCIATION OF FARMERS' MARKETS
A farmers' market sells locally produced goods. Locate your nearest market or get advice on how to set one up.

www.freedomfood.co.uk   UK
RSPCA FARM ASSURANCE
Details of a scheme from the RSPCA to improve conditions for farm animals. The site shows where you can buy these products, lists producers and has some recipes too. You can buy freedom food online at www.farmgatedirect.com

www.goodnessdirect.com   UK
HEALTHY PRODUCTS
A wide ranging health food store that offers advice and information alongside a broad selection of products, it also offers body and haircare products alongside the foods.

www.wholefoodsmarket.com/stores/freshandwild   US
WHOLE FOODS
This delicious American natural foods supermarket has crossed the ocean; find out about their stores and visit the site for their recipes and excellent health information.

The remainder of the Food section is alphabetically arranged by topic.

African Cuisine

www.betumi.com   UK
TRADITIONAL AND CONTEMPORARY
Recipes, information and links on Africa and its food, it also has
some charitable aspects.

See also:
www.afrol.com/Categories/Culture/recipes.htm – West African
recipes.
www.boykie.co.uk/south-african-cuisine.htm – South African
cuisine.
www.congocookbook.com – 150 African recipes and contextual
information as well as an forum.
www.khound.com/topics/africanr.htm – a bit of a mess but a
good overview of African cookery by country and region plus
information on its derivatives too.

Asian and Indian Cookery

www.curryhouse.co.uk   UK
EVERYTHING YOU NEED TO KNOW ABOUT CURRY
Curryholics can get their fill of recipes, recommendations, taste
tests, interviews with famous chefs and a restaurant guide, good
for links too.

See also:
www.curryguidenet.co.uk – a good-looking site with a good
range of recipes and restaurants.
www.currypages.com – an Indian Restaurant guide.
www.currysauce.com – get all the sauces delivered and still win
a year's supply.
www.gcosta.co.uk/curryclub – join Pat Chapman's famous
curry club, access recipes and buy his range of ingredients.
www.redhotcurry.com/food_and_drink/index.htm – excellent
food and drink section from the well-known British Asian portal.
www.simplyspice.co.uk – buy authentic ingredients, including
spices, oils, pulses and package mixes, at very low prices.

www.straitscafe.com   SINGAPORE
RECIPES FROM SINGAPORE
A straightforward site with lots of recipes not only from

Singapore, but from Southeast and East Asia including Japan and China, there's also a good set of links and a useful glossary at the 'pantry'. For Indonesian cooking go to the enjoyable Henks Hot Kitchen, which can be found at **www.indochef.com**

http://japanesefood.about.com   US
JAPANESE FOOD
From the well respected About.com, their section on Japanese food is excellent with recipes and background too.

See also:
www.bento.com – a good-looking site with lots of information on Japanese food and eating out.
www.sushilinks.com – links to all things sushi!
www.yosushi.com – a hi-tech site which features their restaurants and a sushi ordering service to selected areas.

www.thaicuisine.com   US
RECIPES AND RESTAURANTS
This site offers recipes and ingredient information, though the restaurant list is only for the US, see also **http://thai-uk.org/food.html** which has good background information on Thai food, and **www.importfood.com** who supply Thai foods and offer up some 145 recipes.

www.chinavoc.com/cuisine/index.asp   US
CHINESE COOKERY
Lots of tips and background information on Chinese cookery with advice on techniques and recipes. **www.chinavista.com/culture/cuisine/recipes.html** is worth checking out for its list of regional recipes. Also **www.chinatown-online.co.uk** is dedicated to what's going on in London's China Town; it has an excellent food section.

See also:
www.asianonlinerecipes.com – some 2,000 recipes and useful for links too.
www.asiarecipe.com – a messy, but well-intentioned site with a range of recipes and ingredients covering the whole of Asia.

Barbecues

www.barbecuen.com   US
BARBECUES
In the unlikely event that our weather will be good enough to

have a barbecue, then here's a site with all you need to know on
the subject. See also the musically enhanced
www.britishbarbecue.co.uk with 2,000 recipes.

British and Irish Cookery

www.greatbritishkitchen.co.uk   UK
BRITISH FOOD TRUST
The Trust is furthering its mission to promote good British food by
way of an extensive recipe collection with useful sections on
seasonal cooking and information on food traditions, regional
cooking, a glossary and a set of links.

See also:
http://pages.eidosnet.co.uk/cookbook/index.html – a tribute to
British cooking with some fifty recipes, the site is pretty
backward-looking though.
www.godecookery.com/engrec/engrec.html – a curious
collection of transcribed 17th-century recipes.
www.recipes4us.co.uk – have over 2,700 recipes although
some are international.
www.regionalfoodanddrink.co.uk – a regional guide to the UK's
food specialists.

www.rampantscotland.com/recipes   UK
A WEE FEAST
A very simple site listing a good selection of traditional Scottish
recipes, while **www.scottishrecipes.co.uk** also have a small
collection.

www.irishabroad.com/Culture/kitchen   IRELAND
A TASTE OF IRELAND
A good selection of Irish recipes plus a forum and articles. It is
designed for the US ex-pat audience as is
www.foodireland.com/recipes with a similar offering and
www.tasteofireland.com who have more recipes, restaurant
reviews.

www.red4.co.uk/recipes.htm   UK
WELSH RECIPES
Here are over 120 traditional recipes including lava bread,
wines, cawl and Welshcakes. See also
www.hookerycookery.com/welsh-menu.htm where there's a
similar list.

Celebrity Chefs and TV Food Shows

*If you can't find what you're looking for on their dedicated web sites,
checkout www.bbc.co.uk/food where you'll find a list over 40 TV cooks
and presenters. www.channel4.com/life is also worth checking out.
For high quality sites associated with their programmes:*

www.deliaonline.com UK

DELIA SMITH
The queen of British cookery has a clean, well-designed site
stocked with recipes, which can be accessed by the good search
facility. If you join, you get added features such access to the
message-board, competitions and a newsletter. The Cookery
School has a good collection of basic 'how tos' and you can find
our about joining Delia in Norwich. The shop is a pleasure to
browse with sections on gardens, homes and travel as well as
the expected cookware and books.

www.jamieoliver.net UK
WHAT HE'S ABOUT
The official site mainly dedicated to Jamie's diary but there's also
advice on school dinners and links to his restaurant, charity and
kitchenware. In addition you can buy a limited selection of
clothing and other bits and bobs, join in the forums and even see
his moblog. The small recipe collection continues to grow and, of
course, there's an opportunity to buy the books. See also
www.feedmebetter.co.uk for Jamie's campaign for better food
in schools.

www.nigella.com UK
DOMESTIC GODDESS
A disappointing offering that promotes her books, her Living
Kitchen range and herself. There is a forum for discussion and
recipes, although some are from the doyen herself, others are
posted by visitors.

www.rickstein.co.uk UK
PADSTOW, STEIN AND SEAFOOD
Information on Rick, his restaurants and cookery school all
wrapped up in a tidy web site. You can also book a table or a
room as well as order products from the online deli.

www.uktvfood.co.uk   UK
UK FOOD
Very attractive site from this specialist TV channel with lots of
recipes, tips and features based on their programming.

www.foodtv.com   US
FOOD NETWORK
A rather strange but quite appealing site devoted to American TV
cooks. It has some video footage and a search engine that covers
20,000 recipes, plus some good articles.

Cheese

www.cheese.com   US

IT'S ALL ABOUT CHEESE!
A huge resource site with information on over 700 types of
cheese. There's advice about the best way to eat cheese, a
vegetarian section, a cheese bookshop and links to other cheese-
related sites and online stores. You can even find a suitable
cheese searching by texture, country or type of milk. For more
cheese information try the attractive Cheesenet site at
www.cheesenet.info it has an excellent search facility, or the
American Dairy Association's **www.ilovecheese.com** which also
offers a cheese guide and lots of recipes.

www.cheesemongers.co.uk or
www.paxtonandwhitfield.co.uk   UK
OPULENT SITE FROM UK'S OLDEST CHEESEMONGERS
Paxton and Whitfield, the royal cheesemongers, provide a very
clear and easy-to-use online shop but charge £10.00 to ship
goods. A superb selection of cheese and luxury produce, with
hampers, cheese kitchen, accessories and wine. A pleasure to
browse and it's tempting to buy; you can also join the Cheese
Society. See also the British Cheese Board at
www.britishcheese.com where you can learn about our
cheeses, get some recipes and general cheese propaganda.

www.teddingtoncheese.co.uk   UK
BRITISH AND CONTINENTAL CHEESEMONGERS
Much-acclaimed site offering over 130 types of cheese at
competitive prices. The sections are split by country and there's
a good system for showing whether the cheese is suitable for
vegetarians, pregnant women, etc. There is also an
encyclopaedia, a selection of wine and other produce; you can

even design your own hamper. When buying you can stipulate how much cheese you want in grams (150 minimum), shipping from £7.99 for the UK. At **www.butlerscheeses.co.uk** you'll find excellent farmhouse cheeses.

www.fromages.com   FRANCE
TRADITIONAL FRENCH CHEESE
French cheese available to order and delivered within 24 hours along with wine recommendations and express shipping from France. Delivery is included in the price but if you're worried about cost you probably shouldn't be shopping here.

Chocolate, Confectionery and Cakes

www.hotelchocolat.com   UK
DEDICATED TO GOOD CHOCOLATE
An excellent and well-illustrated site from an experienced retailer, they also offer lots of choice and a wide range of chocolate-related gifts and you can even buy in bulk! There's a really good selection facility and the chocolate tasting club. Delivery to UK included in the price and they will guarantee that it's delivered by a specified date.

www.chocaid.com   UK
HELP THE HUNGRY
A great site where you can give to charity when you buy gourmet chocolates. They have a good selection and you can choose which good cause your donation goes to.

www.thorntons.co.uk   UK
WELCOME TO CHOCOLATE HEAVEN
Thorntons offer a comprehensive and easy-to-use site, with an emphasis on gifts. The range is extensive and they supply world-wide, but delivery isn't cheap. There are product sections for continental, premier, gifts and hampers plus flowers and wine. For handmade chocolates try the tempting selections at **www.handmadechocolates.co.uk**

See also:
www.bettysbypost.co.uk – a wide selection of goodies from this well-known Harrogate confectioner.
www.cadbury.co.uk – where you can learn all about chocolate plus lots of recipes and play games.

www.chocolate.co.uk – home of the Chocolate Society.
www.hersheys.com – tour the famous American factory, good for recipes too.
www.lamaisonduchocolat.com – excellent chocolate shop with lots of gift options.
www.prestat.co.uk – hand-made chocolates delivered to your door the next day.
www.virtualchocolate.com – where you can send virtual chocolate, read chocolate-inspired stories and poems.

www.oldsweetshop.com   UK
SWEETS THE WAY THEY USED TO BE . . .
Sweets from an old-fashioned sweet shop, stacked with favourites like Dolly Mixtures, sugared almonds and Parma violets, a visit here is a nostalgia trip as much as anything. Delivery is according to weight. See also **www.sugarboy.co.uk** who offer a wide range of goodies, **www.cybercandy.com** and also **www.aquarterof.com** which is great for old favourites.

www.caketoppers.co.uk   UK
LOOKS GOOD ENOUGH TO EAT
Whether its a sedate cake for Granny, a Bart Simpson cake for the hooligan in your life, or a cake for that diabetic or celiac aunt, there's a cake here for everyone. They'll even transfer your photos into edible images and place them on a cake. You can request just the cake-top decoration to use on your homemade cake.

www.janeasher.co.uk   UK
JANE ASHER CAKES
A pretty workman-like affair, you can order personalised cakes (London orders only delivered or collected by customer), select from a range of mail-order cakes and you can buy equipment too.

See also:
www.botham.co.uk/cakes.htm – offer a traditional range of iced fruit cakes for delivery world-wide.
www.thecakestore.com – great selection but they only deliver to the London area.
www.clickthecookie.co.uk – wide range of cookies and gift options; particularly useful if you want to send themed fortune cookies or a tube of fortune cookie insults.
www.need-a-cake.co.uk – beautiful range of cakes by post, also have a shop for those wanting to do-it-themselves.
www.squires-shop.com – for sugarcraft paraphernalia.

www.pastrywiz.com   US
  PASTRY HEAVEN
  A general food site with the emphasis on cakes and pastry of all
  sorts; there are plenty of recipes and links to keep cake fans
  happy. See also **www.flourbin.co.uk** and get any number of
  different types of flour here.

Cookery Courses and Schools

www.cordonbleu.edu – Classic French cookery with schools in
15 countries.
www.deliaonline.com/cookery-school – Delia Smith offers a
range of one day workshops in Norwich. Also online courses.
www.foodofcourse.co.uk – learn to cook in a farmhouse in
Somerset, good range of courses from foundation to chalet
cookery.
www.leiths.com – Leith's School of Food and Wine has an
excellent reputation; courses for amateurs and professionals.
www.manoir.com – Raymond Blanc offers one-, two- and
four-day courses at his wonderful hotel outside Oxford.
www.rickstein.com – The Padstow Seafood School offers
one-, two- and four-day courses on how to cook fish.
www.travel-quest.co.uk/cooking-holidays.htm – specialist
travel company with listings for holiday cookery courses.
www.vegsoc.org/cordonvert – courses for vegetarian
cookery.

Diet and Nutrition

www.eatwell.gov.uk   UK
  NANNY KNOWS BEST
  A well-meaning and informative attempt by the Food Standards
  Agency to improve the British diet. There are sections on healthy
  diet, ages and stages, health issues, food safety and labelling.

www.3fatchicks.com   US
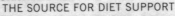
  THE SOURCE FOR DIET SUPPORT
  The awesome Three Fat Chicks have produced one of the best
  food web sites. It's text heavy but entertaining and informative
  about dieting or trying to stay healthy. There are food reviews, a
  breakdown of popular diets, low and low carb recipes, diet tips
  and a 'tool box', which has calorie tables and calculators. There
  are also sections on getting started, losing weight, fitness and a

forum. Check out the fast-food guide to get the nutritional
low-down on your fast-food chain favourites.

www.cookinglight.com

US

THE BEST FROM *COOKING LIGHT* MAGAZINE
One of the world's best-selling food magazines, their slow site
offers a huge selection of healthy recipes and step-by-step
guides to cooking. There are also articles on healthy living.

www.weightwatchers.co.uk

UK

WELCOME TO WEIGHTWATCHERS UK
A much improved site with more information on how to lose
weight, keep motivated, keep fit, chat and, of course, where to
find your local group. There's also a shop where you can buy
specially selected foods and related diet products.

http://atkins-uk.com

UK

DR ATKINS
The world's best-selling dietician offers a site that gives the
background to his low-carbohydrate diet and how you can
lose weight and get healthy on it. You can shop for Atkins
supplements and foods. For another approach try
www.low-carb.com

www.weightlossresources.co.uk

UK

FAD-FREE TOOLS FOR HEALTHY WEIGHT LOSS
Excellent place to go for information on weight loss and diets;
you can keep a weight loss diary, find out about exercise, get
advice on what to eat and catch up on the latest research. You
can also share your experience with others too, but you have to
register to get the best out of it.

www.realslimmers.com

UK

NEVER VISIT THE SUPERMARKET AGAIN
Let someone else do the cooking for you, order a set menu for a
week, or construct your own. The food is relatively inexpensive,
from under £50 per week for everything including breakfast,
snacks, main meals and delivery.

www.hungry-girl.com

US

TIPS & TRICKS FOR HUNGRY CHICKS
A great design combined with useful information all presented in
'bite sized' articles; some is geared towards US readers but it's
still useful and enjoyable to use.

See also:

http://lowfatcooking.about.com – a well-presented and informative section from the About.com web site.

www.caloriecontrol.org – low fat information from the Calorie Control Council.

www.caloriecounter.co.uk – a good site with a diet based on counting calories and exercise.

www.cyberdiet.com – a good all rounder with a wide range of advice, including specialist diets.

www.dailydiettracker.co.uk – a popular and well-put-together site that enables you to track what you eat and monitor your progress.

www.fatfree.com – almost 5,000 vegetarian recipes all fat free or very low fat.

www.fatfreekitchen.com – Indian vegetarian, low fat recipes and healthy eating info.

www.freedieting.com – an excellent site on dieting with the major diets reviewed. It comes with useful advice and tools to help you lose weight.

www.foodsubs.com – a useful food thesaurus with the added benefit that it offers up low fat substitutes to fatty foods.

www.lowcarbiseasy.com – recipes and information on low carb and low GI foods, links and a sugar converter.

www.rosemary-conley.co.uk – all about Rosemary and her healthy lifestyle.

www.weightlossresources.co.uk – a good deal of free information on dieting, diets and exercise; you can sign up to their regime too.

Special Dietary Needs

Also refer to the section on health, page 238.

www.diabeticgourmet.com   UK
DELICIOUS FOR DIABETICS

Lots of recipes and ideas to make food palatable without endangering your blood sugar levels from *Diabetic Gourmet* magazine; see also **www.diabetic.com/cookbook** where there's a great archive of recipes.

www.bdaweightwise.com   UK
BRITISH DIETETIC ASSOCIATION

Excellent health web site from this association who have produced something that looks sensible and easy to follow.

You can follow their tips and get advice from a trained dietician too.

www.nutritionpoint.co.uk   UK
GLUTEN FREE
Their mission is to expand the range of gluten-free products available in Britain. They also provide a helpful checklist indicating which of their products are available on prescription; failing that you can buy goods through a link to an online shop **www.goodnessdirect.co.uk** For more information try **www.coeliac.co.uk** or the US sites **www.gfcfdiet.com** and **www.celiac.com**

www.foodag.com   UK

E-NUMBERS MADE CLEAR
The food additives guide with information on what additives are bad for you and which are derived from animals. The ingredients section provides a list of E-numbers in common food groups indicating the nasties to be avoided.

www.foodallergy.org   US
ALLERGY AND ANAPHYLAXIS
A useful site with information and links on food allergies and their reactions, it's very much oriented to the US so also try **www.anaphylaxis.org.uk** which is also very helpful and UK based.

French Food

http://frenchfood.about.com   US
FRENCH CUISINE
About.com have created a superb resource at this site with a huge amount of data, articles and recipes. Every aspect of French cooking seems to be covered from the ingredients to the shops and presentation.

See also:
www.afrenchkiss.com – make your own gourmet meals with this fun French recipe-creation program.
www.goodfrance.com – a wide range of French food available to buy, with good regional sections and hampers too.
www.hertzmann.com/index.php – French recipes from an obsessive.
www.paniers.com – high-quality French food online, for a price.

Halal

www.halalfoodauthority.co.uk   UK
HALAL FOOD
Information on Halal food and the regulations that surround it; it
explains what Halal means and offers support to suppliers too.

Holland

www.typicaldutchstuff.com   HOLLAND
DUTCH PRODUCE
A wide range of food available here, though mainly oriented
towards confectionary. Delivery costs vary according to how
heavy the order is. For your Dutch cheese fix go to
www.gestam.com

Hygiene and Food Safety

www.foodsafety.gov/~fsg/fsgadvic.html   UK
FOOD SAFETY
A government site with basic advice on handling foods in all
sorts of situations from product-specific advice to helping those
with special needs; there are also good links to related topics.

See also:
www.food.gov.uk – home of the Food Standards Agency who
have lots of information on what is safe to eat.
www.ourfood.com – an overview of food science and hygiene.

Italian Food

www.mangiarebene.net   UK

EAT WELL
An award-winning site that covers everything to do with Italian
cookery. Its aim is to give a grand tour of Italian cuisine – and it
succeeds, including some 600 recipes in the English language
section, but over 1,600 overall. See also **http://italy1.com/
cuisine** which has good regional cooking and food information
as well as lots of recipes and if that's not enough,
www.italianfoodforever.com There is also a small but exquisite
collection of recipes from Marcella Hazan at
www.dolcevita.com/cuisine/recipes/recipes.htm

www.ilovepasta.org US
US NATIONAL PASTA ASSOCIATION
250 recipes, tips, fast meals and healthy options all wrapped up in a clear and easy-to-use site. There's also information on the different types of pasta and advice on the right sauces to go with them.

www.savoria.co.uk UK
TRUE TASTE OF ITALY
There will be no problem fulfilling the minimum order of £50 at this wonderful deli full of culinary indulgences. Delivery is free for orders in excess of £100 (ex-VAT). Alternatively, try **www.esperya.com** which sends produce direct from Italy or **www.dolcevita.com/cuisine** where you'll find produce, recipes and a survival kit for Italian cuisine. At **www.nifeislife.com** you'll find a fast delivery service allied to a wide range of Italian products.

www.getoily.com UK
OLIVE OIL
All you need to know about olive oil, cooking with it, health benefits and history, oh and you can buy it too, along with a good selection of other Mediterranean products.

www.dominos.co.uk UK
PIZZA DELIVERY
Order your pizza online and get it delivered to your home, providing you live near enough to one of their outlets that is. It's a nicely designed site, which also has a few games if you get bored waiting.

Kitchen Equipment

www.lakelandlimited.co.uk UK
EXCELLENT CUSTOMER SERVICE
Lakeland pride themselves on service and it shows, they aim to get all orders dispatched in 24 hours and delivery on orders over £45 is free, otherwise they charge £3.50. The product listing for both kitchen and homeware is comprehensive too.

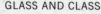

www.urbanbar.com UK
GLASS AND CLASS
A very attractive site from this glass specialist, the range isn't large but it's well presented and there are recipes, links and special offers too.

See also:

www.7day-chef.com – wide range of equipment and kitchen accessories and some excellent offers on top brands too.

www.alessi.com – a tour round the kitchen design powerhouse that is Alessi, the best bit is that you can now buy from this site too.

www.cucinadirect.com – a very wide range of kitchen equipment and related products.

www.divertimenti.co.uk – Divertimenti are also worth a look, they go for quality and they are good for gifts.

www.kingsofhagley.co.uk – excellent cookware shop with lots of choice and a personal service.

www.pots-and-pans.co.uk – Scottish company offering kitchen equipment through a good online store; it's good value but delivery charges vary.

Kosher Cookery

www.koshercooking.com   UK
JEWISH CUISINE
Lots of recipes and links covering all forms of kosher cookery and occasions.

www.totallyjewish.com/food   UK
J-FOOD
Part of the lively Totally Jewish site, which has a magazine-style approach to modern Jewish cookery, including a message board, restaurant guide, chef's questions and features.
For another more personal recipe collection go to
http://screamingmeemies.com/eats

Luxury Food, Deli and Gift Sites

www.allpresent.com   UK
GIFTS FOR THE DISCERNING
An Amazon-style shop offering gifts in the form of chocolates, drinks and bakery items, such as cakes and biscuits, all beautifully boxed. They also sell flowers and cards; delivery costs vary according to what you buy.

www.fortnumandmason.co.uk   UK
EXQUISITE GIFTS
A wide range of gift chocolates, hampers and more from one of the leading luxury stores. There is a whole section devoted to fine

tea including named garden and rare teas plus a wide choice of gourmet ingredients including condiments, wines and spirits.

See also:
www.champershampers.co.uk – family-run hamper business.
www.hamper.com – good design and a wide range of products and you can create your own.
www.harrods.com – not the wide choice that you would expect, but what there is comes with kudos.
www.lewisandcooper.co.uk – they've been producing hampers for many years and here you can create your own or order one of their range.
www.mortimerandbennett.co.uk – London based fine foods retailer with lots of choice and quality too.
www.valvonacrolla-online.co.uk – lots of special food from this Edinburgh retailer.

Meat and Fish

For organic suppliers see Vegetarian and Organic below.

www.traditionalbutcher.co.uk   UK
A TRADITIONAL BUTCHER
John Miles is based in Herefordshire and knows a thing or two about meat. You can buy meats and deli products online. There's a good range and delivery is charged at cost. They seem to take a great deal of care on quality.

See also:
http://highlandgame.com – for fresh venison and partridge plus recipes and information.
www.blackface.co.uk – seasonal, regional and traceable; this Scottish site supplies boxes of lamb, mutton, beef, pork, a good selection of game and haggis.
www.buyostrichmeat.co.uk – for ostrich meat and how to cook it.
www.donaldrussell.co.uk – a butcher who offers a wide range of other produce as well as meats. The site is well illustrated and there are recipes too.
www.swaddles.co.uk – organic butchers, with other produce for sale from a good-looking site.

www.simpsons-seafoods.co.uk
WHEN THE BOAT COMES IN
Supplied from Hull Fish Market, this site offers fresh and smoked

fish as well as fresh and cooked shellfish. The site is nicely designed with small clear pictures of the fish cuts. Under 'special offers' look out for their mixed fish boxes, which change daily. Order by noon for next day delivery. Links to the Sea Fish Industry Authority (**www.seafish.org**) for recipes and more fishy information.

See also:
www.andyrace.co.uk – the peat-smoked salmon comes highly recommended; good for other smoked fish and shellfish as well as other Atlantic fish.
www.kellyoysters.com – for reputedly excellent oysters.
www.martins-seafresh.co.uk – order your fish fresh from this messy site which also has recipes and helpful information.

Mediterranean Food

www.belazu.com   UK
    CAPTURING THE MED
    This attractive site covers the cuisine of Spain, Italy, Greece and Morocco; there's a shop and a list of recipes too.

Middle Eastern Cookery

www.al-bab.com/arab/food.htm   UK
    MIDDLE EASTERN CUISINE
    An excellent overview of Arab cuisine from Arab Gateway with links to key sites covering all the major styles.

www.arabicslice.com   UK
    STEP-BY-STEP ARABIC CUISINE
    A well-designed and well-written cookery site featuring the best of Arabic food with simple step-by-step recipes, lots of explanation and illustrations.

Miscellaneous Food Sites

www.reluctantgourmet.com   US
    GOURMET COOKING FOR BEGINNERS
    Basically a beginner's cookery book, it's well designed and easy to follow with a glossary, guide to techniques, equipment, tips and recipes.

www.cheftalk.com   UK
> THE FOOD LOVER'S LINK TO PROFESSIONAL CHEFS
> Excellent site for articles and discussion about food with tips and
> advice from the top chefs. There's a good links section, recipes
> and a recommended restaurant guide.

www.expatboxes.com   UK
> FOOD PARCELS FOR THOSE LIVING ABROAD
> OK so you miss HP sauce, childhood sweet favourites and
> proper salad cream, relief is at hand here. You can get your
> rations in the form of specially selected hampers or they will
> tailor make and shop the high street for you. Delivery costs are
> high. For the Scottish equivalent try
> **www.scottishfoodoverseas.com**

F

www.hardtofindfoods.co.uk   UK
> FOR SOMETHING SPECIAL
> A great selection of the scarce and unusual from spices to oils to
> beans. You can learn a lot just by browsing, although that turns
> out to be an expensive thing to do.

www.edible.com   UK
> FOR BBQ WORM CHIPS!
> All sorts of insects, unusual meat and bugs you can eat, often
> mixed with something exotic, the food available here is only for
> the culinary brave. The site design is excellent though some
> people might find the intro faintly disturbing . . . See also the
> listings at **www.weird-food.com**
>
> *Other unusual sites to check out:*
> **www.egullet.com** – a messy e-zine devoted to food that has
> some good articles if you can be bothered to wade through the site.
> **www.exploratorium.edu/cooking** – discover the science of
> cookery at this site which makes fascinating reading.
> **www.foodtimeline.org** – a timeline marking the history of
> cookery through the ages, with links and background information.
> **www.topsecretrecipes.com** – discover what really goes into
> America's big brand-name foods.

Organic

www.organicfood.co.uk   UK

> A WORLD OF ORGANIC INFORMATION
> A very informative site which gives the latest news on organic

food. There are sections on why you should shop organic, recommendations on retailers, lifestyle tips, shopping and chat. There are also links to key related sites. See also **www.accessorganic.com** which is great for links and has a search facility.

www.freshfood.co.uk   UK
THE FRESH FOOD COMPANY

Another combined supermarket and information site with a wide range of produce to choose from; this one has a recipe section too. They have a subscription system, which delivers your chosen goods on a regular basis. Delivery is covered by a box scheme, which is like a regular subscription; prices vary according to your commitment.

See also:

www.abel-cole.co.uk – well respected company that offers home delivery, there's advice on the site plus recipes and details on restaurants they supply.

www.crueltyfreeshop.com – the animal-friendly superstore who sell a wide range of products but a limited amount of foodstuffs.

www.farmaround.co.uk – good London-based supplier.

www.festivalwines.co.uk – organic and ethically produced wines.

www.goldenvalleyorganics.co.uk – organic meat, nationwide from Herefordshire.

www.helenbrowningorganics.co.uk – buying advice, recipes and an online shop from this Wiltshire organic farmer.

www.organic-ally.co.uk – no food here but the place to go for your napkins and tableware.

www.organicdelivery.co.uk – a good organic food retailer with some good offers. London delivery only.

www.riverford.co.uk – amazing choice, over 85 types of veg to choose from.

www.sustainweb.org – a farming site with lots of information and links on sustainable farming.

www.swaddles.co.uk – a wide range of organic food including meat.

www.whyorganic.org – a Soil Association site with good background information, nutritional advice and a good organic food directory in the 'organic offers' section.

Recipes, General Food Sites and Magazines

www.kitchenlink.com US

WHAT'S COOKING ON THE NET
A bit clunky to use, but it has so many links to other key foodie sites and food-related sections that it has to be the place to start your online food and drink experience. The design can make it irritating to use and it's got a little slow, but persevere and you'll be rewarded with a resource that is difficult to beat.

www.tudocs.com US

THE ULTIMATE DIRECTORY OF COOKING SITES
The main difference with Tudocs is that it grades each cookery site on its site listing. The listing is divided up into 19 sections, such as meat, beverages, low fat and ethnic. British cookery is in the ethnic section. See also **www.cookingindex.com**

http://epicurious.com US

FOR PEOPLE WHO EAT
Owned by Condé Nast, this massive site combines articles from their magazines with information generated by the Epicurious team, the site has been tidied up but there's still plenty of advice with recipes, cooking tips, TV tie-ins, restaurant reviews, live chat, forums, wine and kitchen equipment. It's fast, easy to navigate and international in feel.

www.allrecipes.com US

THE HOME OF GREAT RECIPES
This site gets its own review because it's not overly cluttered, it's just got loads of recipes which can be found easily and each is rated by people who have cooked them.

http://cookbook.rin.ru RUSSIA

COOKERY ART
Really interesting cookery site with all the usual recipe sections but some unusual ones including exotic and erotic!

www.cookingbynumbers.com UK

COOK WITH WHAT YOU HAVE
It's not a new idea to click on a list of ingredients and for a site to come up with a list of recipes, but here it's done particularly well. There's also help for beginners with some excellent step-by-step guides.

Other sites worth checking out are these, all have loads of recipes and it's just a matter of finding one you like:

www.chef2chef.net – outstanding professional cookery portal site with masses of links.

www.cookeryonline.com – very messy design but pretty comprehensive.

www.cyber-kitchen.com – excellent for links and specialised subjects.

www.goodcooking.com – another excellent food site with some good food writing.

www.ichef.com – good search facility, nice design.

www.meals.com – good for meal planning and recipes.

www.mealsforyou.com – recipes for solutions: healthy, tasty, nutritional and so on.

www.netcooks.com – hundreds of recipes submitted by the public.

www.recipes4us.co.uk – over 2,500 British and international recipes.

www.recipezaar.com – the world's smartest cookbook.

www.ucook.com – the ultimate cookery shop with recipes added.

www.yumyum.com – good fun.

Spanish Food

www.spanish-kitchen.co.uk   UK
SPANISH CUISINE
What looks like a thorough walk through of the cuisine with recipes and explanations of what to expect when you go there.

www.tenstartapas.com   UK
TOP TAPAS
An exercise in the creation of the best ever tapas by several of the UK's top chefs. The whole point of it though is actually to get you interested in Sherry of all things. Still the site looks great.

See also:
www.catacurian.com – enjoy Catalan cuisine here.
www.culinaryweeks.com – Spanish food course in hilariously bad English.
www.delicioso.co.uk – excellent Spanish delicatessen.
www.donquijote.org/culture/recipes – some good recipes from this primarily language-learning site.

www.spanishhampers.co.uk – a great selection of Spanish food for sale, recipes are pretty good too.

Spices

www.apinchof.com
HERBS AND SPICES

US

A bit of a mess but it's very informative about a whole range of herbs and spices with articles from chefs and gardeners. It has recipes and lots of links to help you out.

See also:
www.coolchile.co.uk – the place to get the hottest and widest variety of chilli's.
www.ringoffire.net – a diverse web ring devoted to all that is hot and spicy.
www.seasonedpioneers.co.uk – recipes and spicy foods from all around the globe. Promises new site with more recipes.
www.spiceadvice.com – useful spice encyclopaedia from this American spice retailer who doesn't ship outside the US.
www.thespicebazaar.com – a good-looking and well-laid-out UK-based spice store that also sells dried fruits and herbs.

Vegetarian

www.vegsoc.org

UK

THE VEGETARIAN SOCIETY
An informative and attractive site with advice and help on going vegetarian, a business section and recipes; also covers the Cordon Vert cookery school and there's a good education section for teachers and young people.

www.vegweb.com
VEGGIES UNITE!

US

If you're a vegetarian this is a great place, though not a great design. There are hundreds of recipes, plus features, chat and ideas in the VegWeb newsletter.

www.vegansociety.com
AVOIDING THE USE OF ANIMAL PRODUCTS

UK

The official site of the Vegan Society, promotes veganism by providing information, links to other related sites and books. There is a limited selection of goods in the shop, mostly books

and personal items. For a wider shopping experience go to
www.veganstore.co.uk who offer over 800 suitable products.

See also:
www.ciwf.org.uk – campaigning for farm animal welfare and includes the Eat Less Meat initiative.
www.earthsave.org – a worthy organisation which promotes vegetarianism by helping you choose the right way to eat.
www.living-foods.com – devoted to the subject of eating only raw foods.
www.veggieheaven.com – UK restaurant guide for vegetarians and vegans with nearly 240 listed.

Drink: Non-alcoholic

www.whittard.co.uk   UK
SPECIALITY TEAS DELIVERED WORLD-WIDE
An excellent site dedicated to their selection of teas and coffees; it's easy to use and they will ship throughout the world. Delivery varies according to weight for the UK – free if you spend £50 or more.

See also:
www.anothercoffee.co.uk – coffee making equipment, accessories common and obscure.
www.coffeegeek.com – an American site covering coffee, it's very comprehensive.
www.englishteastore.com – a well-designed site and online shop devoted to all things tea.
www.pgmoment.com – all you need to know about PG tips.
www.realcoffee.co.uk – coffee delivered to your door the day after roasting from the Roast and Post Coffee company.
www.redmonkeycoffee.com – modern online coffee retailer with free UK delivery.
www.tea.co.uk – great-looking site from the Tea Council with lots of facts and reasons given why we should drink more of the stuff.
www.twinings.com – information on tea and their products too.

Drink: Beer

wwww.camra.org.uk   UK
THE CAMPAIGN FOR REAL ALE STARTS HERE
A comprehensive site that has all the news and views on the
campaign for real ale. Sadly, it only advertises its Good Beer
Guide and local versions, with only a small section on the
best beers. Includes sections on beer in Europe, cider and
festivals.

www.realbeer.com   US
THE BEER PORTAL
Over 150,000 pages dedicated to beer, with articles, reviews,
links and shopping all wrapped up in a well-designed site.

See also:

www.beerhunter.com – a very good site, home to expert
Michael Jackson author of the *World Beer Guide*.

www.beersofeurope.co.uk – a beer store who offer a huge range
not just from Europe, but from all over the world.

Booze

The Good Web Site Guide's Top 10s
of the Internet

1. **www.realbeer.com** – 150,000 pages on beer!
2. **www.bbr.co.uk** – the best wine shop
3. **www.winespectator.com** – the most comprehensive wine site
4. **www.superplonk.com** – Malcolm Gluck's great site
5. **www.idrink.com** – recipes for 5,000 cocktails
6. **www.camra.org.uk** – the Campaign for Real Ale
7. **www.whiskeyweb.com** – a whiskey lover's dream
8. **www.sportspubs.co.uk** – guide to pubs where you can watch
   sport
9. **www.wine-searcher.com** – the wine lover's search engine
10. **www.wine-pages.com** – UK wine magazine

Drink: Wine and Spirits

There are many web sites selling wine and spirits, the quality of the information in this section is very high. These are some of the best.

www.bbr.co.uk   UK

THE INTERNET WINE SHOP
This attractive and award-winning site offers over 1,000 different wines and spirits at prices from £4 to over £4,500. There is a great deal of information about each wine and advice on the different varieties. You can also buy related products such as cigars. Delivery for orders over £180 is free; otherwise it's £10 for the UK. They will deliver abroad and even store the wine for you.

www.winecellar.co.uk   UK

NOT JUST WINE AND GOOD VALUE
They also sell spirits as well as wine and, while the choice isn't as good as some online wine retailers, Wine Cellar are good value. Use the search facility to find the whole range which isn't obvious from the home page.

www.wine-lovers-page.com   US

ONE OF THE BEST PLACES TO LEARN ABOUT WINE
Highly informative for novices and experts alike, this site has it all. There are categories on learning about wine, reading and buying books and tasting notes for some 80,000 wines. Also within the site there's a glossary, a label decoder, a list of Internet wine shops, wine writers archive, wine search engine and much more.

www.winespectator.com   UK

THE MOST COMPREHENSIVE WINE WEB SITE
From *Wine Spectator* magazine you get a site packed with information. There's news, features, a wine search facility, forums, weekly features, a library, the best wineries, wine auctions and travel. The dining section has a world restaurant guide, tips on eating out, wine matching and a set of links to gourmet food.

www.wine-pages.com   UK

A GREAT BRITISH NON-COMMERCIAL WINE SITE
Most independently written wine sites are poor; however, wine expert Tom Cannavan has put together a strong offering, which is updated daily. It's well written, informative and links to other good wine sites and online wine merchants.

www.wineanorak.com

 THE WINE ANORAK

For another good British independent wine site, try the Wine Anorak, it's just a great wine zine, with lots of advice, articles, issues of the day and general information on wines and regions.

www.jancisrobinson.com

TV WINE EXPERT

Jancis Robinson has a bright site with wine news, tips, features on the latest wines and information on her books and videos.

www.ozclarke.com

OZ ON OZ

Lots about Oz and what he's up to plus information on how to get his books and his pocket wine e-book. There are also recommended wines and merchants of the month, tips on tasting and information on how to access his mobile wine guide for when you're out and about.

www.superplonk.com

MALCOLM GLUCK

Excellent site from Malcolm Gluck, the author of the Superplonk books, there are offers and tips on where to buy good-value high-quality wines. For full access you have to subscribe.

Other wine sites worth checking out are:

www.booths-wine.co.uk – claims to sell imaginative and distinctive wines. Good for mixed cases of inexpensive wines.

www.cephas.co.uk – superb images of wines and vineyards around the world.

www.internetwineguide.com – a good, if advert laden, all rounder.

www.laithwaites.co.uk – no-nonsense site with lots of offers and a money back guarantee. All wines are illustrated with a picture of the bottle.

www.majestic.co.uk – lots of offers and a well-designed site.

www.vintageroots.co.uk – excellent for organic wines, spirits and beers.

www.wineontheweb.com – good wine magazine with audio features.

www.wine-searcher.com – a wine search engine, type in the wine you want and up pops a selection from various retailers from around the world and UK, all suppliers are vetted for quality and service. Pricey.

www.idrink.com
US

DRINK RECIPES AND COCKTAILS
With over 13,700 drinks recipes you're almost bound to find something to your liking, you have to be a member to get the best out of it though. See also the comprehensive
www.webtender.com

www.barmeister.com
US

THE ONLINE GUIDE TO DRINKING
Packed with information on everything to do with drink, there are over 2,000 drink recipes available and about 630 drinking games. If you have another, then send it to be featured in the site.

www.whiskyweb.com
UK

A WEE DRAM
A comprehensive site for the whisky lover featuring history, information on how whisky is made, links to all the distilleries by region, a list of events and, of course, a shop (phone for delivery rates according to purchase). For information on the Spayside distilleries and details of their whisky festival go to
www.spiritofspeyside.com

Eating Out

www.goodguides.com
UK

HOME OF THE GOOD PUB GUIDE
Once you've registered it has an easy-to-use regional guide to the best pubs, which are rated on food, beer, value, good places to stay and good range of wine. You can also get a listing by award winner. The site hosts the Good Guide to Britain, which is a good resource for what's on where. See also **www.greatbeer.co.uk** one man's passion and guide to over 200 pubs in the UK.

www.dine-online.co.uk
UK

UK-BASED WINING, DINING AND TRAVEL REVIEW
A slightly pretentious, but sincere, attempt at an independent eating out review web site. It has a good and expanding selection of recommended restaurants, covers wine and has some well-written feature articles. It relies heavily on reader recommendation, so there's a good deal of variation in coverage

and review quality and some were written some time ago. Not very user friendly, no search by area.

www.theaa.com

AA RESTAURANT SEARCH
UK

Nestled away in the AA site is a little known gem, an excellent regional restaurant guide to the UK. Simply type in the town name or find the location on an interactive map. Each of the 4,000 listed is graded and there are comments on quality of food, facilities, ambience and, of course, how to get there.

www.viamichelin.co.uk
MICHELIN
UK

A site from Michelin with the emphasis on route finding, but after you register (for free), you get access to a good restaurant finder and hotel guide.

Other restaurant review sites worth looking at before you go out are:

www.conran.com/eat – a guide to Terence Conran's restaurants with online booking and some special offers, nice design too.

www.cuisinenet.co.uk – book online at selected restaurants, nice design.

www.grabameal.co.uk – a pretty comprehensive directory of takeaways and restaurants in the UK, with some 23,500 listed.

www.local-restaurant.com – good restaurant finder for cities, not so good for country areas.

www.squaremeal.co.uk – newsy guide to London's restaurants, it also covers selected ones in the UK.

www.toptable.co.uk – co-ordinates free booking at over thousands of restaurants, bars and party venues in 30 cities in the UK and popular overseas locations; nice design too.

Free Stuff

Free stuff is exactly what the term suggests, and these are sites whose owners have trawled the Net or been offered free services, software, trial products and so on. It's amazing what you can find.

www.freeinuk.co.uk
JUST THE UK
UK

Not just free stuff but also excellent Internet offers from British sites, good design, but not that easy to navigate. The Top Ten section is great.

Other sites worth looking into are these listed below, but most are American so some offers may not apply for the UK.

www.1freestuff.com – one of oldest and probably best categorised.

www.find-a-freebie.co.uk – very well-categorised and extensive selection.

www.freeandfun.com – the usual long list; don't see what's fun about it though.

www.freebielist.com – a well-categorised listing of web-based freebies – easy to use and good links.

www.freestuffpage.com – some really esoteric ones here.

www.thefreesite.com – more web stuff, nice layout.

www.totallyfreestuff.com – massive selection.

Furniture see under Home and DIY page 276.

Gambling and Betting Sites

Gambling sites abound on the Internet and they often use some of the most sophisticated marketing techniques to keep you hooked. For example new screens pop up as you click on the close button tempting you with the chance to win millions. All the gaming sites are monitored by gaming commissions but above all be sensible, it's easy to get carried away. You should be aware that some carry spyware, programs that monitor your online activity.

Gambling and Gaming

www.betgambling.net   US
THE GAMBLER'S PORTAL
A useful gambling directory, which also offers forums and guides to the various games and sites. Its design isn't great but it is quite comprehensive. See also the less cluttered **www.winner.com**

These are the casinos and gambling sites we liked:
www.24ktgoldcasino.com – good graphics and fast response times make this great fun, but you need a decent PC to download the software. There are 40 or so games and you can play either for fun or for money.
www.32red.com – one of the most popular and best British online casinos, with lots of games and ways to bet . . .
www.888.com – claims to be the world's most popular online casino, great design.

www.betasyouclick.com – a directory with links to web sites from around the world, which offer, among other things sports books, casinos, poker rooms, lotteries and competitions.

www.gamble.co.uk – a good directory and review site.

www.gamblehouse.com – reviews online casinos and ranks them according to whether they are licensed, make payments quickly or offer good odds.

www.intercasino.com – easy to use and they've over 80 games to choose from.

www.littlewoodscasino.com – one of the top-rated casino sites.

www.pogo.com – from EA Games, lots to choose from, lots of prizes to play for.

www.slotland.com – for those who love losing their money in slot machines.

www.williamhillcasino.com – consistently highly rated.

Betting

www.settle-a-bet.co.uk   UK

BETS EXPLAINED

If you can't tell the difference between a trixie or a yankee and thought spreadbetting was something that went on toast, then this is the site for you. It has (not always simple) explanations of virtually every conceivable type of bet.

www.oddschecker.co.uk   UK

COMPARE THE ODDS

A great way to ensure you get the best deal from the online bookmakers, you just choose the sport and the event, then you get a read-out of the latest odds given by a selection of bookies – you can click on the bookmaker of your choice to place your bet. It's continually being updated; the site's a must for the committed gambler.

www.ukbetting.com   UK

LIVE INTERACTIVE BETTING

Concentrating on sports betting, this is a clear, easy-to-use site; take a guest tour before applying to join. You need to open an account to take part, using your credit or debit card, minimum deposit £10. See also the popular **www.bluesq.com** also offers a similar but possibly slightly broader service, and special bets on things like soap operas and political elections. Also worth a visit is **www.bet365.co.uk** who cover a wide variety of areas and offer some good deals.

www.mybetting.co.uk
UK

FREE BETTING

My betting works as a collation site for free bets and offers from bookmakers around the Internet. It takes a minute or so to get used to the design but once you're on board it's easy to get yourself a few free bets, albeit at the price of a registration or two.

www.racingpost.co.uk
UK

THE RACING POST

A combination of news, racing and betting on a clear, well-designed site. Also features greyhounds and information on bloodstock.

www.ladbrokes.co.uk
UK

UK'S NUMBER 1 BOOKMAKER

Ladbrokes offer a combination of news, information and sport-related betting with excellent features on racing, golf and the other major sporting events. There's also a casino, lotteries, a specials section where you can bet on politics or big events and, of course, the now ubiquitous poker game.

www.willhill.com
UK

THE MOST RESPECTED NAME IN BOOKMAKING

The best online betting site in terms of speed, layout and design, it has the best event finder, results service and betting calculator. The bet finder service is also very good and quick. All the major sports are featured and there is a specials section for those out-of-the-ordinary flutters. Betting is live as it happens.

See also:

www.bookiealerts.com – a free download, it's essentially a news service geared to betting, useful and you can tailor it to your interests.

www.paddypower.com – a strong site from Ireland's biggest bookmaker with betting on horses, football and other top sports – even politics.

www.sportingindex.com – excellent and wide-ranging spread betting site with offers and competitions.

www.thesportsman.co.uk – high profile betting paper with a virtual version available online.

www.win2win.co.uk – excellent subscription service for serious race-going gamblers.

www.totesport.com   UK
THE TOTE

The Tote has reinvented itself and become a general betting site with casino and instant reward games. It covers a wide range of sports but is especially strong on horse racing where you'll find lots of useful information to back up your betting decisions.

www.thedogs.co.uk   UK

GONE TO THE DOGS

Everything you need to know about greyhounds and greyhound racing. You can adopt or get advice on buying a dog, find the nearest track, get the latest results and learn how to place bets. You can't gamble from the site but they provide links.

Poker

One of the biggest areas of expansion in online gambling, here are the major sites . . .

www.partypoker.com – one of the best and most popular poker sites.

www.pokerroom.com – a good site where you don't necessarily have to download a program to play.

www.pokerstars.com – the one that seems to breed world champions.

www.williamhillpoker.com – one of the most popular UK-based poker games.

Miscellaneous

www.national-lottery.co.uk   UK
IT COULD BE YOU

Find out about Lotto and even play online, there's info on how to play and results of Euromillions and instant win games too. They also tell you about the good causes that the National Lottery supports. If you want to know whether your premium bonds are worth anything try **www.nationalsavings.co.uk** (you need your bondholder number handy).

www.highstakes.co.uk   UK
   HIGH STAKES BOOKSTORE
   Books on virtually every aspect of gambling at this minimalist
   site. It also offers selected links and you can order online too.

www.gamblersanonymous.org.uk   UK
   WHEN THE STAKES GET TOO HIGH . . .
   Where to go when it all gets too much, a straightforward site
   listing crucial phone numbers and information on how to deal
   with the compulsion.

   See also:
   www.gamanon.org.uk – help and advice for addicted gamblers
   and their families.
   www.gamcare.org.uk – an authority on the provision of
   information on gambling, with advice and practical help in
   addressing its social impact.

Games

*There's a massive selection of games on the Internet, here are just
some of the very best ones; from board games to quizzes to your
everyday 'shoot 'em up' type. There are more games for Macs listed on
page 24.*

*It's worth remembering that before downloading a game from a site it's
wise to check for viruses. If you've not got anti-virus software on your
PC, then check out our section on virus management on page 423.
On most sites you'll benefit from the speed of a broadband connection,
which is not the assumed norm for gamers.*

**Parents should be aware that some games are quite violent or contain
sexual references, so it's as well to check them out before letting your
child loose on them.**

Finding Games

http://gamespotter.com   US
   GAMES SEARCH ENGINE
   A really handy site where you can get links to virtually every type
   of game whether it be a puzzle or action. Alternatively, you can
   use the search facility to find something. Each game on the list is
   reviewed as well.

Games Magazines and Information

www.avault.com   US
THE ADRENALINE VAULT
A comprehensive games magazine with demos, reviews and
features on software and hardware – good looking too. There's
also a good cheats and hints section.

www.gamespy.com   US
GAMING'S HOMEPAGE
Lots here as well as the usual reviews and features. There are
chat and help sections and in the resources section, hundreds of
demos plus free games to play. To maximise the fun, you have to
subscribe. See also **www.gamespot.co.uk** which offers lots of
info as well.

www.gamers.com   US
A MOMENT ENJOYED IS NOT WASTED
A great-looking site with all the features you'd expect from a
games magazine but it has more in the way of downloads
and games to play. There is also a chat section and
competitions.

www.happypuppy.com   US
GAMES REVIEWED
Happy Puppy has been around a while now reviewing games in
all the major formats. In addition to hosting game files, they
provide news, reviews, previews and cheats for featured games.
There are also links to related games sites and an active forum.
It's all packaged on a really good web site which is quick and
user-friendly.

www.gamefaqs.com   US
GAMES FREQUENTLY ASKED QUESTIONS
All information is free and donated, there are FAQs and tip
sheets on any number of games, and it seems to be regularly
updated.

http://vgstrategies.about.com   US
ABOUT GAMES
A set of information pages from the excellent About.com with
articles and links covering all the likely strategies needed for
gaming.

See also:
http://games.slashdot.org – described as 'News for Nerds' it looks the part and seems very comprehensive with the latest games news by format.
www.eurogamer.net – another newsy site, this is better laid out than most but there's still a lot to take in.
www.gamestudies.org – an intellectual and scholarly approach to games with articles and emphasis on the cultural, aesthetic and communicative value of gaming.
www.gaming-age.com – more news and reviews.
www.spong.com – the Internet Video Games Archive has a massive amount of information on games. Their intended objective is to archive every game.

Games to Play

www.boxerjam.com   UK
ONLINE GAMESHOW
Excellent site devoted to giving the user access to original and traditional games played online, for cash and prizes.

www.classicgaming.com   US
GAMING THE WAY YOU REMEMBER IT
Probably one for older gamers but there's some good stuff on here so it's at least worth a look and it's amazing how new some of the games are.

www.gamehippo.com   US
OVER 1,000 FREE GAMES
Enough to keep you occupied for hours with games of every type from board to action to puzzles and sports. It's worth checking out **www.freeloader.com** which has a more modern selection available, but you have to register and jump through a few hoops to get them. See also the oddly designed **www.download-game.com** who also offer a large number including old favourites, and Sean O'Connor's site **www.windowsgames.co.uk** where there's a small selection of high-quality games to download.

www.gamebrew.com   US
CHOOSE YOUR GAME
Gamebrew specialises in Java games and there are some brilliant ones to download and play here, you choose from 23 categories from puzzles to casino to arcade.

http://games.yahoo.com
YAHOO!

This popular search engine has its own games section. Here you can play against others or yourself online. The emphasis is on board games, puzzles and quizzes.

US

www.graalonline.com
THE GRAAL KINGDOMS

Set in a mythical realm, this is a good multi-player game with lots of levels and a high degree of interactivity and customisation.

UK

www.worldogl.com
ONLINE GAMING LEAGUE

Join a community of gamers who play in leagues for fun and have a zero tolerance policy for cheaters. You can play all the major online games and compete in the leagues and ladders if you like. To quote them: 'What matters is that people are meeting and interacting with other people on the Internet via our services and their game'.

US

www.planetquake.com
THE EPICENTRE OF QUAKE

Quake remains one of the most popular games played on the Internet; we've now arrived at Quake IV. This site gives you all the background and details on the game for singles and multi-players. It's got loads of links and features as well as reviews and chat.

US

www.scummvm.org
POINT AND CLICK ADVENTURES

Download the program and get access to a number of good games, which were previously unavailable on a PC or Mac.

US

www.shockwave.com

SHOCKWAVE GRAPHICS

Shockwave's fantastic site offers much in the way of high definition games for both action fans and those who prefer to test their minds a bit; the site also offers films and other useful programs. They promise new games every Tuesday.

US

www.lysator.liu.se/tolkien-games   SWEDEN
LORD OF THE RINGS
Get immersed in Tolkien's Middle Earth with some 100 games.
It's got action games, quizzes and puzzles, strategy games and,
of course, role playing games.

www.wireplay.com   US
THE GAMES NETWORK
A good online games resource, the site encourages the players to
interact, it has chat rooms and forums and also organises
competitions.

www.zone.com   US
MICROSOFT GAMES ZONE
With nearly 90 games to choose from you shouldn't be
disappointed. They range from board and card games to multi-
player strategy and simulation games to playing for cash. It's a
shame they've done away with what was a good children's
section.

www.orisinal.com   US
JUST FOR FUN
A selection of high-quality silly and funny games using a very
original and text-free format and design.

www.spaceinvaders.de   GERMANY
SPACE INVADER SHRINE
A fun homage to the original game with history, trivia, tips and of
course you can play the game too.

www.popcap.com   US
100 PERCENT JAVA
An excellent site with very high-quality games to download onto
the PC, Mac, Palm or even your mobile; you can also play on the
web.

www.sodaplay.com   UK
BUILD YOUR OWN . . .
A really interesting and different gaming experience. Here you
can design your models and send them to the 'zoo' for display
and use by others. You can race them and exchange them with
friends too.

www.stickcricket.com   AUSTRALIA
IT'S NOT CRICKET!
Slightly frustrating at first but, once you get the hang of it, it's a lot
of fun.

Game Manufacturers and Console Games

http://cube.ign.com   US
GAME CUBE
Dedicated to the format, there are lots of reviews, previews and
the latest information on what's coming too.

www.hasbro.com/games   US
HASBRO GAMES
A commercial site from one of the biggest manufacturers with a
useful list of what they produce.

www.nintendo.com   US
OFFICIAL NINTENDO
Get the latest news from Nintendo and its spin-offs – N64,
Game Boy and Game Cube. There's also information on the
hardware and details of the games, new and old. For a site
with wider Nintendo info go to the excellent
www.nintendojo.com

http://uk.playstation.com   US
OFFICIAL PLAYSTATION SITE
Looks good with games information, information on the
hardware, previews, new release details and a special features
section with reviews by well-known gamers. There's also a chat
section and a shop.

Also check out:
www.absolute-playstation.com
www.playstation.com
www.psxextreme.com

www.pocketgamer.org   UK
GAMES FOR POCKET PCS
OK so you've bought your handheld PC, you've impressed the
boss, now, what do you really use it for? Oh yes, play games!
There's a great selection here for most different types of operating
systems. If not, then there are links to related sites. Try also
www.handango.com which is not a specialist site, but the

games section has been expanded and the design is much improved.

www.gamespy.com/xbox   US
XBOX
Part of the Gamespy network, this site gives background on Microsoft's toy, with the latest game news, reviews, demos and previews too. See also **www.xboxemea.com/playtogether** and the official site **www.xbox.com** who offer some exclusive previews and information. There's also **www.majornelson.com** which is an unofficial, but well put together, blog devoted to the Xbox.

www.station.sony.com   US
SONY ONLINE GAMES
Sony have put together an exceptional site for online gaming, and with over 6 million members, it's one of the most popular. The site is well designed, easy to use and there are lots of games to choose from. Providing you can put up with the adverts, it's a real treat to use.

www.sega-europe.com   EUROPE
SEGA
Get the latest news on the latest games and buy them at the store. The site is well designed with all the usual features.

Fantasy League and Strategy Games

www.fantasyleague.com   UK
FANTASY FOOTIE
Be a football manager, play for yourself, in a league, or even organise a game for your workplace or school. Get the latest team news on your chosen players and how they're doing against the rest.

www.thedugout.net   UK
CHAMPIONSHIP MANAGER
An excellent site devoted to Football and Championship Manager and soccer gaming. You can discuss the game, get up to speed with the latest tactics, get the low-down on the players and generally join in.

www.primagames.com   US
  PRIMA
  The largest fantasy game publisher offers a site packed with
  reviews, demos and articles. You can also buy a book on virtually
  every strategy game. See also **www.strategy-gaming.com**
  which is pretty comprehensive.

www.gamesworkshop.com   UK
  WAR GAMING
  A comprehensive offering covering war games including
  collecting, painting and gaming itself; there are also forums, chat
  and links to the major games. See also **www.wargames.co.uk**
  which is pretty comprehensive.

Cheats, Hints and Tips

G

www.computerandvideogames.com   US
  THE CHEAT STATION
  Go to the 'tips' section and type in the game or cheat that
  you want. There are cheats for thousands of games so you
  should find what you're looking for. If you can't, check out
  www.xcheater.com who have a smaller selection, but you never
  know your luck.

  See also:
  www.cheatextreme.com – great selection of cheats for most
  platforms.
  www.cheatheaven.com – a one-stop site for cheats in over
  2,000 games covering most consoles. Good search facility, but
  some annoying adverts and pop-ups.
  www.lunabean.com – all you need for video games.
  www.playstation2-cheats.co.uk – cheats for PS2.

Games Shops

*If you know which game you want, then it's probably better to use a
price checker such as Kelkoo (**http://uk.kelkoo.com**) to find the best
price on the game. They will put you through to the store offering the
best all round deal. If you want to browse, then these are considered
the best online stores for a wide range of games:*

http://shop.game.net formerly **www.game.uk.com** – a good comprehensive offering with daily and weekly offers.

www.chipsworld.co.uk – good for Sega and Nintendo.

www.gameplay.com – Gameplay is one of the most visited games sites. Once a magazine site, it's now transformed into a well designed store, browsable by platform and good value.

www.play.com – a good selection of games, many at a reduced price and, with free delivery, it's not surprising that it is such a popular site.

www.streetsonline.co.uk – follow the link to 'gamestreet' for one of the top shops on the Internet. Parents will be sorry that the kids' section has gone. Good value too.

www.telegames.co.uk – around 5,000 types of game in stock, covering all makes. Also has a bargain section.

Miscellaneous

www.etch-a-sketch.com   UK
REMEMBER ETCH-A-SKETCH?
For those of you who don't remember back that far, Etch-a-Sketch is a rather annoying drawing game. It's been faithfully recreated here and it's still just as difficult to do curves. There are also a few other simple games and some links to children's games sites.

www.hangman.no   NORWAY
HANGMAN
A great hangman game, you can play in many categories. Thankfully you can also turn the music off.

www.there.com   US
THE ISLAND GETAWAY
I'm not sure whether this should be categorised under dating, chat or games but it's here, so choose your avatar, give them some personality and play cards!

Card and Board Games

www.tradgames.org.uk   UK
TRADITIONAL GAMES
A history and guide to traditional games, including board games, table games, pub games and lawn games too.

www.chess.co.uk   UK
ULTIMATE CHESS
Massive chess site that's got information on the game, news and
views, reviews and shopping. There are lots of links to other
chess sites and downloads. Also info on backgammon, go, poker
and bridge.

See also:
www.bcf.org.uk – for the British Chess Federation.
www.chessclub.com – for the Internet Chess club who had
over 2,000 players online when we visited, including 19
grandmasters.

www.gammon.com   US
BACKGAMMON
If you like backgammon, here's the place to start. There are links
to live game playing and masses of related information. Also
check out **www.bkgm.com**

www.msoworld.com   US

BOARD GAMES, PUZZLES AND QUIZZES
The ultimate site of its type, there are over 100 board games and
masses of quizzes and tests.

www.monopoly.com   US
MONOPOLY
A pretty boring site, it offers a history plus information on where
you can buy, along with tips on how to play and how you can get
involved in tournaments. See also **http://uk.mymonopoly.com**
where you can create your own personalised game to order.

www.thehouseofcards.com   US
LOADS OF CARD GAMES
Huge number of card games to play and download with sections
on card tricks, history, links and word games – there's not much
missing here. See also **www.pagat.com** for an alternative.

www.solitairegames.com   US
SOLITAIRE
Play online or download a game onto your PC or Mac, there are
plenty to choose from and it's quick. There's also a good set of
links to other online card games.

http://bridge.ecats.co.uk   UK
> BRIDGE RESOURCE
> A good place for information on bridge from a software company
> associated with the game at a high level. See also
> **www.bridgemagazine.co.uk**

Crosswords, Puzzles and Word Games

www.cluemaster.com   UK
> CROSSWORDS AND WORD PUZZLES
> A collection of crosswords and word searches. You have to
> register to get access to the free puzzles, otherwise it costs £1.50
> to download 50 puzzles.

www.crosswordsite.com   UK
> ALL CROSSWORDS
> Hundreds to chose from, with the option either to print off or fill
> in online. There are four levels of difficulty with the hardest being
> quite tough. See also **www.crossword-puzzles.co.uk**

www.fun-with-words.com   US
> THE WORDPLAY WEBSITE
> Dedicated to amusing English, the Fun with Words site offers
> games, puzzles and an insight into the sorts of tricks you can
> play with the language.

www.websudoku.com   ISRAEL
> SUDOKU
> It had to happen, the world couldn't go without an online Sudoku
> site for long. In case you have lived in a cave for the past couple
> of years and don't know what it's about, here's the place to start
> your education with games for players of all levels. It's a great
> site for all fans. See also **www.sudoku.com**

> *Other crossword and puzzle sites worth checking out are listed
> below:*
> **http://crosswords.about.com** – links and tips from this giant
> reference site.
> **www.canopia.com** – odd design but a good choice of puzzles
> and crosswords.
> **www.download.com** – the games section here has masses of
> choice, some free.
> **www.lovatts.com.au** – plenty to chose from at this Australian
> magazine.

Quizzes and General Knowledge

www.thinks.com   UK
  FUN AND GAMES FOR PLAYFUL BRAINS
  Massive collection of games, puzzles and quizzes with
  something for everyone, it's easy to navigate and free.

www.trivialpursuit.com   UK
  TRIVIAL PURSUIT
  A massive disappointment; this is a purely commercial site
  geared to selling the various versions of the official game.

www.playwithyourmind.com   UK
  MIND GAMES AND IQ TESTS
  More than 20 mind-stretching games including word, maths,
  card and logic puzzles; the design isn't great but the games are
  good.

www.mensa.org.uk   UK
  THE HIGH IQ SOCIETY
  Mensa only admit people who pass their high IQ test – see if
  you've got what it takes. The site, which has been upgraded, has
  a few free tests and, if eligible, you can join the club.

www.queendom.com   US
  SERIOUSLY ENTERTAINING
  It's not entirely free but an excellent site for all sorts of brain
  tingling tests, the major difference is that it also offers personality
  profiles and psychometric tests which may help you in getting on
  in your career or just keeping your brain healthy. See also
  www.emode.com

  Check out these sites:
  www.coolquiz.com – several different types of quiz from sports
  to movies and quotes. Nice wacky design.
  www.funtrivia.com – a massive trivia site with over 650,000
  questions.
  www.quiz.co.uk – a couple of hundred questions in
  several unusual categories including kids, nature, food and
  sport.
  www.quizyourfriends.com – a fun quiz creation site.

Gardening

There are lots of high-quality British gardening sites, but some sites are based in America, so bear this in mind for tenderness, soil and climate advice. Due to regulations on the importation of seeds and plants, these can't be imported from outside the UK.

For Garden Lovers

The Good Web Site Guide's Top 10s
of the Internet

1. **www.rhs.org.uk** – home of the Royal Horticultural Society
2. **www.gardenworld.co.uk** – for a garden centre near you
3. **www.crocus.co.uk** – the best gardening shop
4. **www.hdra.org.uk** – the authority on organic gardening
5. **www.carryongardening.org.uk** – gardening chat
6. **www.bbc.co.uk/gardening** – great stuff from the Beeb
7. **www.ngs.org.uk** – home of the excellent National Garden Scheme
8. **www.chilternseeds.co.uk** – masses of seeds, order online
9. **www.nhm.ac.uk/science/projects/fff** – our wild flora and fauna
10. **www.allotments-uk.com** – all you need to know about your allotment

www.gardenworld.co.uk UK

THE UK'S BEST
Described as the UK's best garden centre and horticultural site. It includes a list of over 1,000 garden centres, with addresses, contact numbers and e-mail addresses. Outstanding list of links to other sites on most aspects of gardening; very comprehensive with sections on wildlife, books, holidays, advice, societies and specialists, it now also has the addition of a link to the RHS plant finder service and Latin name converter – excellent.

www.gardenweb.com UK

GARDEN QUESTIONS ANSWERED
Probably the best site for lively gardening debate; it's enjoyable, international, comprehensive and has a nice tone. There are several discussion forums on various gardening topics, garden advice, plant dictionary and competitions. Using the forums is

easy and fun, and you're sure to find the answer to almost any gardening question.

www.kew.org.uk   UK
ROYAL BOTANIC GARDENS
Kew's mission is to increase knowledge about plants and conserve them for future generations. This site gives plenty of information about their work, the collections, features and events. There are also details of the facilities at the gardens, conservation, educational material and lots of links to related sites.

www.rhs.org.uk   UK

ROYAL HORTICULTURAL SOCIETY
An excellent site from the RHS which features a plant-finder service covering some 70,000 plant types, a garden finder and an event finder. There's also advice and information about the RHS, an opportunity to buy advance tickets to their shows and the opportunity to buy from their garden gift collection.

Other gardening advice and information sites well worth trying are:
www.carryongardening.org.uk – award-winning site with all the usual features plus some celebrity input. Good for links and the idea exchange feature.
www.gardenforum.co.uk – outstanding gardening forum site, good if you're a novice to using forums and chat sites.
www.gardenguides.com – a useful American resource site with loads of information on every aspect of gardening. It has lots of tips, handy guides, and a free online newsletter.
www.gardenlinks.co.uk – links to gardening sites in over 40 categories, a good place to start searching for something specific.
www.gonegardening.com – nice design, wide-ranging magazine and shop.
www.plants-magazine.com – very good garden magazine, broad in scope but particularly strong on new plants, a vehicle for selling the magazine itself.

Allotment Gardening

www.allotments-uk.com   UK
ALLOTMENT ADVICE
Lots of links, advice and tips, plus a forum to discuss all your allotment problems. See also **www.nsalg.org.uk** home to the

National Society of Allotment Gardeners, which isn't a great site it has to be said.

Gardening Stores

www.greenfingers.com   UK
COMPREHENSIVE GARDENING

A gardening superstore with many categories and some good offers. There's also plenty in the way of advice and tips, plus an ask the gardener facility.

www.crocus.co.uk   UK
GARDENERS BY NATURE

A good-looking site full of ideas enhanced by excellent photographs, there are some good articles and features, but it's basically a gorgeous shop with thousands of plants and products to choose from and some good offers. Delivery to England and Southern Scotland starts at £5.95 (£1 for seeds). If you live elsewhere you need to contact them to see delivery is possible for a surcharge.

www.blooms-online.com   UK
ONE-STOP GARDENER'S RESOURCE

A beautiful site that will supply all your garden needs and desires. In addition to ordering your seeds and buying your garden furniture, there's a great plant search where you can find plants of specific size and colour for that difficult hole in the border. There are DIY projects, a design service, a gardener's club and advice. Delivery cost depends on your order. Alternatively, you can pick up at their nearest store.

www.gardentrading.co.uk   UK
GARDENING GIFTS

A well-presented site from a company that specialises in gift products associated with gardening from furniture to lighting to small gifts.

Other gardening shops worth checking out are:
www.burncoose.co.uk – nice design, searchable plant catalogue with some good offers.
www.gardentrading.co.uk – less about gardening more about accessorising your patch.
www.glut.co.uk – the Gluttonous Gardener provides unusual presents for every gardener.

www.rkalliston.co.uk – excellent for gardening accessories and gifts.

Garden Design

www.thegardenplanner.co.uk UK
THE GARDENER'S DIRECTORY
Everything you need to plan your perfect garden, this excellent directory is the place to start.

See also:
http://gardendesign-uk.com – a good directory of garden designers.
www.bali.co.uk – the home of the British Association of Landscape Industries, here you can find a company qualified to do the work you want.
www.gardendesigner.com – a serious American site with in-depth advice.
www.sgd.org.uk – Society of Garden Designers to find a landscape gardener.

Organic and Environmentally Friendly Gardening

www.hdra.org.uk UK

HENRY DOUBLEDAY RESEARCH ASSOCIATION
The leading authority on organic gardening. Their site offers a superb resource if you're into gardening the natural way. It's particularly good if you're growing vegetables and includes fact sheets and details on why you should garden organically.

See also:
www.greengardener.co.uk – specialists in biological and organic pest control and wormeries.
www.just-green.com – natural pest control with advice and products.
www.organiccatalogue.com – a comprehensive store related to the HDRA.
www.pan-uk.org – the Pesticide Action Network who are working to eliminate the hazards associated with pesticides.
www.recyclenow.com – the best ways to recycle your rubbish.
www.soilassociation.org – for advice on growing organic food plus the latest news on their campaigns.

British Wildflowers and Plants

www.nhm.ac.uk/science/projects/fff UK
FLORA AND FAUNA

Using the postcode search, find out which plants are native to your area, where to get seeds and then how to look after them once they're in your garden. Sponsored by the Natural History Museum. Visit **www.floralocale.org** for information on sustainable planting as well as a list of approved suppliers.

www.british-trees.com UK
FORESTRY AND CONSERVATION

Comprehensive information on British trees plus a good set of links and a list of books and magazines. For more information on how to care for trees go to **www.trees.org.uk**

www.wildflowers.co.uk UK
BRITISH WILDFLOWERS

An online store specialising in British wildflowers with advice on how to grow them; there's also a search engine where you can find the plants you need using common or Latin names. If you want a wildlife-friendly garden try **www.wildlifegardening.co.uk** which is a basic but informative site.

www.wigglywiggler.com UK
TOUCHY FEELY WILDLIFE

Small business champions Wiggly Wigglers have an online shop specialising in wildlife products for the garden. If you want to attract wildlife, you can find a home for them here, you can stock your pond and buy plants and composters. They also sell seasonal English-grown flowers. Sign up to the podcast or visit the blog for regular updates on what they're up to down there on the farm. For another personal approach visit Jenny's garden at **www.wildlife-gardening.co.uk**

See also:
www.meadowmania.co.uk – another specialist but also offers bulbs and plug plants.
www.wildseeds.co.uk – specialist suppliers of wild seeds and grasses.

Specific Plants, Societies and Specialists

www.alpinegardensociety.org   UK
ALPINES
An informative site on Alpines with articles from the society
magazine, seed exchange, newsletter and shop. You can also
find out about their tours to the best Alpine territories.

www.discoveringannuals.com   UK
ANNUALS GALORE
Based on the successful book, this site offers information on
hardy annuals, half-hardy annuals, biennials and seed-raised
bedding plants of all kinds. There's an A–Z listing on the plants
and it tells you where you can buy them.

www.thecgs.org.uk   UK
COTTAGE GARDEN SOCIETY
The place to go if you want the picture-perfect cottage garden.
The site is quite basic but there's plenty of information to get you
started plus a seed exchange service via their magazine.

www.hardy-plant.org.uk   UK
HARDY PLANT SOCIETY
A society devoted to conserving the older, rare and unusual
garden plants. There's information about how you can get
involved, where their fairs are, plus a seed list and limited plant
information.

www.herbnet.com   US
GROWING AND COOKING HERBS
An American network specialising in herbs, with links to
specialists, and to trade and information sites. It can be hard
work to negotiate, but there's no doubting the quality of the
content – although the quality of the music is up for debate. See
also **www.herbsociety.co.uk** which isn't a great site but does
contain some useful info.

www.nccpg.com   UK
CONSERVING PLANTS AND GARDENS
The National Council for the Conservation of Plants and Gardens
is responsible for maintaining the national plant collections of
which there are over 600. Here you can find out about the
NCCPG's conservation work and plant database and how you
can get involved.

www.rareplants.co.uk
UK

RARE PLANT NURSERY

A site developed by a specialist nursery, which is well illustrated, and pretty comprehensive, it offers information on the plants and can supply plants world-wide.

www.rosarian.com
UK

ROSES

If you love roses or just need information on them, drop in here for a good, long browse. See also **www.davidaustinroses.com** the outstanding rose specialist and also the Royal National Rose Society at **www.rnrs.org**

www.treesbypost.co.uk
UK

MAIL ORDER TREES

A wide variety of trees and shrubs delivered to your door from this specialist grower.

www.vegetable-gardening-club.com
UK

GROWING VEG

Lots of advice and help on growing most types of vegetables, with links and information on what tools to use; for seeds try **www.vegetableseedwarehouse.com** who offer a wide choice.

www.windowbox.com
US

CONTAINER GARDENING

A really good American site which is well worth a look if you're into container gardening in any form. It's well laid out and very well written with great ideas for unusual plant combinations. Worth a long browse.

Other specialists worth checking out:
http://lockyerfuchsias.co.uk – good mail-order service from this Bristol-based company, supplying fuchsias.
www.brogdale.org – basically all you need to know about fruit grown in the UK.
www.citruscentre.co.uk – the place to go for your lemons, limes and more.
www.oaklandnurseries.co.uk – a specialist in showy but tender plants.
www.orchid.org.uk – home of the North of England Orchid Society with a well-illustrated site.
www.orchids.uk.com – attractive site and home of specialist grower Burham Nurseries and you can buy orchids online.

www.topiaryart.com – an online course with background on the subject.

Seed Specialists

www.chilternseeds.co.uk   UK

SEED SPECIALIST
Choose from over 5,000 different types of seeds with many unusual plants including organically grown seeds. Very easy to find the right plant, excellent.

See also:
www.suttons-seeds.co.uk – comprehensive offering with a money back guarantee and an easy-to-use site.
www.thompson-morgan.com – huge range, good advice and good value too.

Gardening Peripherals and Equipment

www.lawnmowersdirect.co.uk   UK
BUY A LAWNMOWER ONLINE
A retailer specialising in mowers and other power tools. You can browse the site by make and it's quick and easy to use, if a little basic.

www.lightingforgardens.co.uk   UK
LIGHT UP YOUR GARDEN
A specialist that offers advice, ideas and a wide range of products to light up your garden, all on a nicely designed site.

www.agriframes.co.uk   UK
GARDEN STRUCTURES
An improved site, from probably the UK's leading supplier, which now shows off their wide range of non-plant garden products to good effect. There's everything here from pergolas, fruit cages, watering cans and lighting, plus information on their made-to-order service too.

www.simplygardeningtools.co.uk   UK
GARDEN TOOLS
A messy, bright site offering a wide range of tools and equipment and free delivery in the UK, plus a money back guarantee. See also **www.fredshed.co.uk** for reviews of the best products.

www.garden-sheds-online.co.uk UK
SHEDS!
A company that is passionate about sheds. There is information
to help you pick the right one and a good selection to choose
from. For the lighter side of life in garden sheds, you should
check out the bizarre but excellent **www.readersheds.co.uk**

www.watergardening-direct.co.uk UK
WATER GARDENING PRODUCTS
Not a great web site, but it all works and there is a good range.
You can order online and ask for advice too.

See also:
www.giantgamesales.co.uk – specialists in giant garden games.

TV Tie-ins and Celebrities

www.bbc.co.uk/gardening UK
GARDENING AT THE BEEB
A set of web pages from the BBC site which offer a great
gardening magazine, featuring celebrities but mixed with helpful
advice and sections such as design inspiration, plant profiles,
ask the expert and today in your garden. You can sign up for their
free newsletter.

www.barnsdalegardens.co.uk UK
GEOFF HAMILTON'S GARDEN
To many people the real home of *Gardener's World*, this site tells
you all about Barnsdale and has features about the garden, Geoff
and his work. There's also an online store selling a limited range
of products and a good set of gardening site links.

www.alantitchmarsh.com UK
ALAN TITCHMARSH
Part of the Expert Gardener site with competitions, biographical
details, sponsored events and some gardening details.

Other important and well-known gardeners:
www.bethchatto.co.uk – find out about her garden and shop for
plants too.
www.gertrudejekyll.co.uk – devoted to the work of this amazing
woman.
www.kimwilde.com – news about what Kim has been up to and
what projects she's working on.

Visiting Gardens and Garden History

www.gardenvisit.com   UK
GARDENS TO VISIT AND ENJOY
With over 2,000 gardens listed world-wide, this site offers
information on all of them and each is rated for design, planting
and scenic interest with Sissinghurst scoring top marks. There's
also information on the history of gardening, tours and hotels
with good gardens. We found some of the information is a little
out of date.

See also:
http://hcs.osu.edu/history – from Ohio State University, the
history of horticulture through biographies of the most famous
gardeners.
www.edenproject.com – for the grandest garden scheme of
them all.
www.gardenhistorysociety.org – an overview of what the
society is about and information on what they're up to, but little
in the way of history bar a few articles.
www.greatbritishgardens.co.uk – good regional reference and
guide that includes biographies of great British garden designers.
www.museumgardenhistory.org – based in Lambeth, this site
offers details of the museum and the famous Tradescant family.
www.nationaltrust.org.uk – offering information on their
gardens and places of interest.

www.ngs.org.uk   UK
NATIONAL GARDEN SCHEME
This is basically the famous yellow book converted into a web
site with details on over 3,300 gardens to visit for charity and the
work they undertake with the money they earn from your
support. See also **www.gardensofscotland.org** which operates a
similar scheme.

Gardeners with Special Needs

www.thrive.org.uk   UK
NATIONAL HORTICULTURAL CHARITY
This charity exists to provide expert advice on gardening for
people with disabilities and older people who want to continue
gardening with restricted mobility. The site gives information on
how the charity works and links to related sites. See also

www.gardenforever.com who offer lots in the way of horticultural therapy.

Gay and Lesbian

www.rainbownetwork.com   UK

LESBIAN & GAY LIFESTYLE
A very well thought out magazine-style web site catering for all aspects of gay and lesbian life. It primarily covers news, fashion, entertainment and health, but there's a travel agency as well. There are also forums and chat sections, classified ads as well as profiles on well-known personalities.

www.gayindex.co.uk   UK

GAY BRITAIN NETWORK
A well-designed and extensive index of gay sites categorised by region, type and orientation. Covers everything from health, chat, adult sites, business, travel and shopping. If you can't find what you are looking for you could also try **www.queery.com** or the American **www.gayscape.com**

For other good gay/lesbian sites try:
www.aegis.com – an excellent site giving the latest information on combating AIDS and HIV.
www.gaybritain.co.uk – excellent graphics, a gay portal site.
www.gaylifeuk.com – well-rounded magazine site with support and advice sections.
www.gaytravel.co.uk – gay travel guide, UK-oriented but with some good world-wide information.
www.glinn.com – the gay gateway to the web.
www.lesbianuk.co.uk – a good information site.
www.outintheuk.com – an excellent gay community site.
www.pinkparents.org.uk – advice site for gay, lesbian and bisexual parents.
www.pinkuk.com – another community site with local information.
www.planetout.com – a good all-round magazine site.
www.stonewall.org.uk – campaigning for justice and equality for gay and lesbian people. Good section on parenting issues.
www.uk.gay.com – British and Irish pages from the big American magazine site.

Genealogy

With more interest generated by the BBC's series Who Do You Think You Are? *and the release of yet more census data, there has been a big upsurge in interest in tracing your family tree. Here are the best sites to help you in your quest. It's a shame that many of the sites are aimed at getting you to part with your money rather than genuinely helping you to find what you want. Others are so poorly designed that, despite their willingness to help, we couldn't put them in the book.*

Family Tree

The Good Web Site Guide's Top 10s
of the Internet

1. **www.ancestry.co.uk** – searching for your ancestors
2. **www.nationalarchives.gov.uk/familyhistory** – UK archives and census data
3. **www.originsnetwork.com** – specialising in UK and Irish research
4. **www.familyhistory.com** – US records
5. **www.bmdindex.co.uk** – birth, marriage and death certificates
6. **www.thegenealogist.co.uk** – good genealogy subscription portal site
7. **www.britishdataarchive.co.uk** – the census on CD
8. **www.spatial-literacy.org** – how surnames spread over time
9. **www.genuki.org.uk** – genealogy first timers start here
10. **www.cyndislist.com** – more genealogy sites than you can shake a stick at

www.sog.org.uk   UK

THE SOCIETY OF GENEALOGISTS
This is the first place to go when you're thinking about researching your family tree. It won't win awards for web design, but it contains basic information and there is an excellent set of links you can use to start you off.

www.cyndislist.com   US

CYNDI'S LIST
A comprehensive listing site where you'll find over 250,000 links in 150 categories to help with your family history research.

www.nationalarchives.gov.uk/familyhistory   UK

NATIONAL ARCHIVES

An excellent site from what used to be the Public Record Office.
The site is easy to use and the information is concisely presented
and easy to access. It has all the census data and lots of advice
on how best to use it. See also **www.familyrecords.gov.uk**
which is a consortium of various libraries and archives. It is
excellent for tracing your family tree and the links selection is
excellent.

www.census.pro.gov.uk   UK

1901 CENSUS

You can search the database for free but for detailed information
you have to pay using a rather odd system. Mapping is also
available from the site to help with place names or boundary
changes. See also the Census related pages at
www.nationalarchives.gov.uk/census

www.bbc.co.uk/history/familyhistory   UK

WHO DO YOU THINK YOU ARE?

Loads of fascinating material on how to find out more about your
family's history, plus articles on other people's journeys of self-
discovery. Based on a radio series, there is also a useful factsheet
on how to trace your ancestors at **www.bbc.co.uk/education/
beyond/factsheets/surnames/surnames_intro.shtml**

www.scotlandspeople.gov.uk   UK

SCOTLAND

Excellent place to start your quest if you're ancestors were Scots.
See also **www.tartans.com** which is a great resource.

www.origins.net   UK

DEFINITIVE DATABASES

This site has information provided from the Society of
Genealogists' records from Scotland going back to 1553 and
from England going back to 1568, and unlike many other sites
in this area, it's also well designed and easy to use. There are
also search tips, access to discussion groups and a new section
devoted to Ireland.

www.genuki.org.uk   UK

VIRTUAL LIBRARY OF GENEALOGICAL INFORMATION

An excellent British-oriented site with a huge range of links to
help you find your ancestors. There is help for those starting out,

news, bulletin boards, FAQs on genealogy and a regional search map of the UK and Ireland.

www.ukfamilyhistory.co.uk UK

ST CATHS

St Catherine's House has been at the forefront of family tree research for some time now and remains a great place to start your search. It offers a full service but without a lot of the hassles that you get through some of the more commercial sites.

www.1837online.com UK
THE KEY TO FAMILY HISTORY

Probably the best of the commercial genealogy sites, it's well designed and relatively free of all the clutter that besets many other pay sites. The resources are excellent although the census data seems limited.

Other useful sites that may help in your family research:
www.achievements.co.uk – a research outfit that have a track record working with TV companies, but who will also give you a quote to research your family tree.
www.ancestral-research.com – one of the better value research companies for those who are unable to do the work themselves.
www.ancestry.co.uk – UK spin-off from the successful US-based site of the same name (see review below). Invaluable resource as it hosts the six British census from 1841–1891.
www.a2a.org.uk – a site that catalogues available archives in the UK; it gives a good description of what each one contains and access details.
www.britishorigins.com – information from an excellent database for people tracking their Welsh and English relatives, some free access, but the full service costs.
www.familysearch.org – The Church of Jesus Christ and the Latter-day Saints' excellent research site with good step-by-step information.
www.genealogypro.com – a very comprehensive genealogists and genealogy services directory.
www.genealogysupplies.com – a shop specialising in genealogy software.
www.genesreunited.co.uk – from the Friends Reunited camp, here you can build your family tree online and share it with your family. There are plenty of resources available to help you too.
www.genfair.com – a bookshop specialising in family history books.

www.historicaldirectories.org – a searchable collection of digitally reproduced directories for England and Wales from 1750 to 1919.

www.ihgs.ac.uk – the Institute of Heraldic and Genealogical Studies offer information on heraldry and help to research your family background.

www.landsearch.me.uk – find out who owned what property . . . for a price.

www.morrigan.com – specialists in Irish genealogy.

www.nla.gov.au/oz/genelist.html – a good starting point for Australians.

www.one-name.org – the place to go if you're only interested in researching one surname.

www.spatial-literacy.org – a really interesting site where you can track over time, the movement and distribution of surnames in the UK.

www.thegenealogist.co.uk – this spin off from the *Genealogist* magazine claims to have the most complete birth, marriage and death records. It's a shame that the site, along with its many spin-off sites, is so poorly designed.

www.ukbmd.org.uk – links to over 400 sites containing local information on births, deaths and marriages.

American Genealogy Sites

Genealogy is a big deal in the US; here are some of the best and most useful.

www.accessgenealogy.com   US
GENEALOGY WEB PORTAL

A massive number of links and access to web rings from a number of different countries give this site 'must check out' status. It is biased towards an American audience but it's very useful nonetheless. See also another portal site **www.genealogyportal.com**

www.ancestry.com   US
NO 1 SOURCE FOR FAMILY HISTORY

This US-oriented site has 1 billion names and access to 3,000 databases. It's especially good if you're searching for someone in the US or Canada. It offers some information for free, but for real detail you have to join. How much you pay to find out about your ancestors depends on what you wish to know. Linked to this is the chat site **www.familyhistory.com** where you can visit surname discussion groups.

www.surnameweb.org   US
ORIGINS OF SURNAMES

A great place to start your search for your family origins. On top of the information about your surname, there are thousands of links and they claim 2 billion searchable records.

See also:
www.ellisislandrecords.org – records of all who entered the US via Ellis Island.
www.genforum.com – a huge number of forums devoted to specific family names.
www.gengateway.com – claims to have the number one family-tree-making software, excellent for links.
www.rootsweb.com – genealogy software.

Google

The world's most visited web site deserves a section to itself, basically because few people use it to its full potential. Here's a run down of the things you can do and find by going beyond the search engine.

Answers – ask any question; get an answer . . . for a price.
Blog search – allows you to find blogs that interest you.
Book search – one of the best and most controversial aspects of Google is the ability to search the text of thousands of books. Google and the book industry are in a heated debate about exactly how much of the book should be available to view.
Directory – a good site directory, categorised by topic.
Froogle – one of the best places to find the cheapest online prices – for everything from toasters to jets . . . well, model ones anyway.
Groups – Google Groups allow people with a shared interest to use the site to host discussions on a myriad of topics. These are all fully searchable too.
Image Search – click on the 'Images' button and type in your request and up pop hundreds of related images. Typing in Good Web Site Guide produced a number of cover images of this book both past and present, thankfully though no images of the author!

Labs – (**http://labs.google.com/**) here you can try out some of the exciting things that Google are developing.

Local – a very fast way to find a local service, check out a location and get route planning too. It includes mapping and satellite images and a hybrid of the two as well if that's what you'd like.

Maps – fairly detailed maps and a lot easier to use than many specialist sites.

Mobile – a version for mobile users who like to browse on the move. There's also an SMS version for those who want information in the form of a text message.

News – allows you to search some 4,500 news sources, while using the 'Alerts' service allows you to keep up to date with the latest news on any topic of your choice.

Scholar – allows you to search 'scholarly' papers, although in practise the term is loosely applied.

Special searches – here there are some topic-related searches which may be helpful, the most popular probably being the Google Apple Mac one. There's also a University search facility.

*Go to **www.google.co.uk/intl/en/help/features.html** where you'll find a number of helpful search tools and services. For example, an excellent calculation tool, a feature that enables you to see a site as it was when it was first indexed by Google, a spell checker and a translation service.*

This review scratches the surface of what Google is about and what it is developing. Some think it's becoming too powerful and all encompassing but often it's hard to see a better alternative.

For Google's rivals see the section on Search Engines on page 419.

Government

www.direct.gov.uk   UK
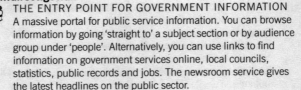
THE ENTRY POINT FOR GOVERNMENT INFORMATION
A massive portal for public service information. You can browse information by going 'straight to' a subject section or by audience group under 'people'. Alternatively, you can use links to find information on government services online, local councils, statistics, public records and jobs. The newsroom service gives the latest headlines on the public sector.

http://parliament.uk

UK

UK PARLIAMENT

A good site giving information on how Parliament works, what's on in the House of Commons, Hansard and a directory of MPs and Peers, should you want to write, as well as links and a glossary.

Other key links:

www.cabinet-office.gov.uk – how the Civil Service supports the government.

www.clicktso.com – The Stationery Office bookstore.

www.electoralcommission.org.uk – managing and modernising the electoral process in the UK.

www.explore.parliament.uk – the UK Parliament's education site aimed at school-age children; it offers lots of information and a tour.

www.localegov.gov.uk – the office of the Deputy Prime Minister and his projects.

www.number–10.gov.uk – send an e-mail to the Prime Minister or learn about the history of No.10 Downing Street.

www.parliamentlive.tv – the workings of Parliament broadcast live. Comes with a calendar of events too.

www.royal.gov.uk – for the monarchy.

www.scottish.parliament.uk – for Scottish issues. To watch live broadcasts of the parliament in action go to **www.holyrood.tv**

www.theyworkforyou.com – find out about your MP's voting history and how often he turns up in Parliament.

www.wales.gov.uk – The National Assembly for Wales.

The Major Political Parties

www.conservatives.com – Conservative party.
www.labour.org.uk – Labour party.
www.libdems.org.uk – Liberal Democrats.

International Government and Political Bodies

http://europa.eu.int – the European Union.
www.commissionforafrica.org – working to make Africa a better place.
www.congress.org – an excellent overview of the US Congress and how it works.
www.europarl.eu.int – how the European Parliament works and

www.europarl.org.uk for info on your MEP.
www.politicsonline.com – a messy and dense site with an overview of US politics.
www.un.org – United Nations.

Activist and Monitoring

For a satirical approach to politics see under Humour, page 288.

www.epolitix.com – an excellent political news site with lots of links and the latest policy announcements.
www.fistfulofeuros.net – a blog site devoted to the goings on in the Eurozone, with lots of contributions and some good writing too.
www.hrc.org – home of the Human Rights Campaign.
www.hrw.org – Human Rights Watch identifies corrupt governments and provides information on where they are going wrong.
www.liberty-human-rights.org.uk – Liberty, protecting human rights and civil liberties.
www.spinwatch.org – an excellent guide to the murky world of spin and corporate garbage.
www.ukpol.co.uk – a good fortnightly political magazine.
www.writetothem.com – the easy way to contact your MP or MEP, there's background information on them too.
www.yougov.com – get involved in polling and take part.

Encouraging the Young

www.explore.parliament.uk – the UK Parliament's education site aimed at school-age children. It offers lots of information and a tour.
www.votesat16.org.uk – a campaigning site aimed at getting 16-year-olds the vote.
www.ukyp.org.uk – home of the Youth Parliament, a campaigning organisation aimed at 11–18-year-olds.

Greetings Cards

What used to be free on the Internet is now largely charged for, and most of the e-card sites now follow the trend, which wouldn't be so bad except that you often have to search through a lot of rubbish to get to the good ones . . .

www.bluemountain.com   US
E-CARDS
Blue Mountain has thousands of cards for every occasion; it's easy to use but you have to subscribe to get the best designs. There are all sorts of extras you can build in like photos, music, cartoons and even voice messages.

See also:
www.bigfoto.com – collection of beautiful photos to customise and send.
www.egreetings.com – big range, busy design that gets on your nerves after a while.
www.greencardcompany.co.uk – Christmas cards on recycled paper, can provide bespoke designs.
www.greeting-cards.com – massive range and geared to the American market, not all free, masses of adverts.
www.jimpix.co.uk – excellent site for unusual and free e-cards, everything from interactive flash cards to ones with an anti-war message.
www.photoecards.com – use your own photos to create a unique e-card.
www.regards.com – nice design and the best bit is that it's free!
www.web-greeting-cards.com – massive selection and well categorised too.

www.fattypuff.com   UK
REAL CARDS
One of the better online card shops, they have a wide range and you can personalise them too.

See also:
http://cards.webshots.com – good for photographic.
www.getcards.co.uk – wide range, personalising service.
www.kisskisscards.com – lots of choice and gifts too.
www.moonpig.com – one of the best and you can upload photos and create your own cards too.
www.sharpcards.info/sk – good design and easy to use.
www.worldwidecards.com – personalised cards.

www.charitycards.co.uk   UK

CONTRIBUTIONS TO CHARITY
Buy your cards here and give money to charity, this is traditionally a Christmas thing but Charitycards have turned it into an all-year round possibility. They will also design and

personalise Christmas cards. There are discounts available and free postage if you buy in quantity, and they also sell stamps. See also **www.cardsforgoodcauses.org.uk** who have a good range and choice.

www.what2write.co.uk   UK
WHAT TO WRITE
A fairly cheesy site that offers suggestions for those situations where you can't think what to write in your card, you can also make suggested entries and send e-cards too.

Health and Fitness

Health

The Good Web Site Guide's Top 10s
of the Internet

1. **www.nhsdirect.nhs.uk** – the first place to go for advice on your ailments
2. **www.embarrassingproblems.com** – for all those difficult issues
3. **www.patient.co.uk** – excellent health portal
4. **www.mayohealth.org** – medical information and health tools
5. **www.dipex.org** – exchange experiences on health issues
6. **www.stjohnsupplies.co.uk** – for everything first aid
7. **www.allcures.com** – excellent online pharmacy
8. **www.netfit.co.uk** – how to get fit
9. **www.self-help.org.uk** – where to help yourself
10. **www.healthfinder.com** – online check up and health library

Here are some of the key sites for getting good health advice featuring online doctors, fitness centres, nutrition and sites that try to combine all three. As with all health sites, there is no substitute for the real thing and if you are ill, your main port of call must be your doctor. Dietary advice sites are listed on page 184, specialist sites aimed at men on page 306 and for women on page 566. The advice for parents, page 362 and teens, page 478 may also be useful. For opticians see page 358.

General Health

www.nhsdirect.nhs.uk UK
NHS ADVICE ONLINE
NHS Direct is a telephone advice service and this is the Internet
spin-off, it comprises of an excellent guide to common ailments
with the emphasis on treating them at home and a superb
selection of NHS-approved links covering specific illnesses or
parts of the body. There's also health information and an A–Z
guide to the NHS.

www.drfoster.co.uk UK
KNOWLEDGE IS POWER
Provides patients with information about health services
including finding a consultant and hospital (HNS and private),
waiting list times and performance data. There's an A–Z of
conditions, a hospital survey and you can fill in your health
profile to find out what conditions people matching your profile
are admitted for. Also gives information on complementary
therapists.

www.nelh.nhs.uk UK
NATIONAL ELECTRONIC LIBRARY FOR HEALTH
This program is working with NHS Libraries to develop a digital
library for NHS staff, patients and the public; it is an outstanding
resource already and can only get better. It should be the first
port of call when researching.

See also:
www.avma.org.uk – an organisation working for better safety for
patients. If something goes wrong then this site is worth a visit.
www.doh.gov.uk – for the Department of Health's informative site.
www.helpthehospices.org.uk – information on how you can
support hospices and where to find one.
www.npsa.nhs.uk – the NHS Patient Safety Agency.
www.patients-association.com – an organisation campaigning
for patients' rights.

www.self-help.org.uk UK
THE SELF-HELP DATABASE
A portal site devoted to providing a searchable database of self-
help and patient organisations in the UK. There are currently
over 1,000 on file. You could also check out
www.ukselfhelp.info for similar information.

www.dipex.org UK

PATIENT EXPERIENCES

An award-winning site devoted to showing you a wide variety of personal experiences of illness, which covers over 100 from cancers to mental health. The idea is to use Internet technology to share information and experiences and to help fellow sufferers get through their illness.

www.healthfinder.com US

A GREAT PLACE TO START FOR HEALTH ADVICE

Run by the US Department of Health, this provides a link to more or less every health organisation, medical and fitness site you can think of. In several sections you can learn about hot medical topics, catch the medical news, make smart health choices, discover what's best for you and your lifestyle and use the medical dictionary in the research section. The site is well designed, fast once it's fully downloaded and very easy to use.

www.patient.co.uk UK

FINDING INFORMATION FROM UK SOURCES

This excellent site has been put together by two GPs. It's essentially a collection of links to other health sites, but from here you can find a web site on health-related topics with a UK bias. You can search alphabetically or browse within the site. All the recommended sites are reviewed by a GP for suitability and quality before being placed on the list.

For a second opinion you could visit **www.surgerydoor.co.uk** which is more magazine-like in style with up-to-the-minute news stories. It's comprehensive and has an online shop. Also try the well-designed **www.netdoctor.co.uk** who describe themselves as the 'UK's independent health web site' and offer a similar service.

www.embarrassingproblems.co.uk UK

FIRST STEP

An award-winning and much-recommended site that works well; it's what the Internet should be about really. The site helps you deal with health problems that are difficult to discuss with anyone; it's easy to use and comprehensive. Younger people and teenagers should also check out **www.coolnurse.com** which is an excellent American site with similar attributes.

www.drkoop.com
US

THE BEST PRESCRIPTION IS KNOWLEDGE
Don't let the silly name put you off, Dr C Everett Koop is a former
US Surgeon General and is acknowledged as one of the best
online doctors. The goal is to empower you to take care of your
own health through better knowledge. The site is very
comprehensive covering every major health topic and is aimed
at all, including both young and old.

www.mayohealth.org
US

RELIABLE INFORMATION FOR A HEALTHY LIFE
The Mayo Clinic has an excellent web site where you can look up
a symptom, condition or what to do in an emergency. You can go
on to learn about your illness and its management, look up the
full fact sheet on prescribed drugs, collect information on healthy
living, or ask a specialist for advice. There are also risk
calculators and self assessments to help you understand your
risk of poor health.

H

www.cellscience.com
UK

MEDICAL DICTIONARY
The dictionary covers Aids, HIV, cancer, cystic fibrosis
and diabetes. It's easy to use and contains listings for
links, hospitals and charities as well as other essential
information.

www.quackwatch.com
US

HEALTH FRAUD, QUACKERY AND INTELLIGENT
DECISIONS
Exposes fraudulent cures and old wives tales, then provides
information on where to get the right treatment. It makes
fascinating reading and includes exposés on everything from
acupuncture to weight loss. Use the search engine or just
browse through the site; many of the articles leave you amazed
at the fraudulent nature of some medical claims. See also the
National Council Against Health Fraud at **www.ncahf.org**
For a very scary experience visit the Museum of Questionable
Medical Devices at **www.mtn.org/quack**

www.kidshealth.org
US

KIDS' HEALTH
An engaging American site with three areas, one for parents, one
for kids and one for teenagers with each having their content
adjusted and focused accordingly. The kids' section is

particularly effective with even quite complex illnesses and
personal issues explained well.

www.stjohnsupplies.co.uk   UK
FIRST AID AND MORE
Here at the St John's Ambulance Brigade shop you can buy
several first aid kits and all the health and safety equipment
you're ever likely to need. For information on the Brigade,
volunteering or taking one of their courses go to **www.sja.org.uk**

For more health information:
http://medlineplus.gov – a health information centre from the
US National Library of Medicine.
www.24dr.com – a site from a UK doctor, lots of help with self
diagnosis and what appears to be a good medical encyclopaedia.
www.bbc.co.uk/health – good all rounder covering lots of
topics, good links.
www.e-med.co.uk – wherever you go your doctor is the strap
line for this site; it costs £20 to join then £15 per consultation.
www.gmc-uk.org – home of the General Medical Council, the
place to go if you have a problem with a doctor.
www.healthcyclopedia.com – a straightforward health portal
with comprehensive coverage.
www.hospitalweb.co.uk – an excellent medical search
engine.
www.medterms.com – a straightforward glossary of medical
terms.
www.nice.org.uk – the National Institute of Clinical Excellence
provides 'robust and reliable guidance on current health best
practice'.
www.studenthealth.co.uk – written by doctors, sensible and
funny with some good competitions.
www.vh.org – lots of information (but no design sense) at the
Virtual Hospital.

Private Health

www.bupa.co.uk   UK
BUPA HOMEPAGE
Health fact-sheets, special offers on health cover, health tips
and competitions are all on offer at this well designed site. You
can also find your nearest BUPA hospital and instructions on
referral. See also **www.ppphealthcare.co.uk** who have over

150 factsheets available on a wide range of health conditions located in the 'Health' section found in 'You and Your Family'. See also **www.privatehealth.co.uk** a portal site devoted to all things related to private health.

Medical Tourism

www.medicaltourist.co.uk   UK
MEDITOURISTS . . .
An interesting twist on the issue of hospital waiting lists, here you can find out how to have your operation abroad and even combine it with a holiday. See also **www.medplex.org**

Medicine and Pharmacy

www.allcures.com   UK
UK'S FIRST ONLINE PHARMACY
After a fairly lengthy but secure registration process you can shop from this site which has all the big brands and a wide range of products. There are also sections on toiletries, beauty, alternative medicine and a photo-shop. There's a good A–Z of both symptoms and conditions plus the facility to ask a pharmacist a question.

See also:
www.boots.com – for prescriptions go to the 'pharmacy' then use the free postal delivery service. There's also an A–Z of common conditions and info on embarrassing problems.
www.drugscope.org.uk – how to get information on drugs.
www.mhra.gov.uk – the government department that deals with safety in medicines.
www.mypharmacy.co.uk – good basic health site from a real pharmacist, with a shop stocking a relatively wide range of products.
www.pharmacy2u.co.uk – who have lots of offers and cover lots of health areas, even a section on embarrassing problems. Prescription service available.
www.rxlist.com – information on drugs and their effects.

Fitness and Exercise

www.netfit.co.uk   UK

DEFINITIVE GUIDE TO HEALTH AND FITNESS
Devoted to promoting the benefits of regular exercise with a
dedicated team who put a great deal of effort into the site. You
can gauge your fitness plus there's information on some 1,500
exercises, tips on eating and dieting, nutrition advice and links to
useful (mainly sport) sites. If you don't like going it alone, they
will even try to link you up with a training partner in your area.
For those hooked on the idea, they've introduced a membership
scheme which promises to sculpt your body into shape – for £52
per year.

www.fitnessonline.com   US
PROVIDING PERSONAL SUPPORT
This good-looking site is from an American magazine group. It
takes a holistic view of health offering advice on exercise,
nutrition and health products. In reality what you get is a
succession of articles from their magazines, all are very
informative but getting the right information can be time-
consuming.

The following sites also offer good advice and information:
www.exercise.co.uk – a good health equipment store
with information on exercise and choosing the right
equipment.
www.fitnesspeak.co.uk – the best prices for gym equipment but
hard on the eyes.
www.thefitmap.com – a portal site for the UK's health and
fitness clubs, find your nearest one.

Alternative Medicine and Therapies

www.altmedicine.com   US

ALTERNATIVE HEALTH NEWS
Keep up to date with the latest therapies and trends with articles
and features from some of the key figures in the world of
alternative medicine. The site is supplemented by an excellent
medical search engine, an overview of the major philosophies
and associated healing techniques plus a good set of related
links.

www.therapy-world.co.uk   UK
THERAPY WORLD MAGAZINE

A well-put-together magazine covering many different types of therapies with a good overview of all of them and some interesting articles.

www.medical-acupuncture.co.uk   UK
ACUPUNCTURE

A good-looking site with information from the British Medical Acupuncture Society on the nature of acupuncture and where to find a practitioner in your area. There are also good links and information on courses. See also **www.acupuncture.org.uk** and also **http://accupuncture.com**

www.drlockie.com   US

HOMEOPATHY MADE EASY

An interesting, clear and simple site that offers sensible advice at all levels. Click on any of the medicine jars to get to the relevant sections on everything from basic information, products and links.

www.armaweb.com   US
AROMATHERAPY

A good information site on aromatherapy with lots of articles, recipes and oil profiles.

www.thinknatural.com   UK
THINK NATURALLY

A nicely designed site with a mass of information on every aspect of natural health including a comprehensive shop with loads of special offers and a very wide range of products.

See also:
http://nccam.nih.gov – home of the US National Centre for Complementary and Alternative Medicine, it's a good place for research.
www.alternativemedicines.co.uk – use the ailment search to find the right alternative products.
www.drweil.com – the vitamin guru has a site that offers much in advice and his own brand of balanced living.
www.eoco.org.uk – the Essential Oil Company for aromatherapy.
www.holisticshop.co.uk – for everything from books to Buddhism.
www.homeopath.co.uk – attractive site but still only partly functional when we visited, good directory of homeopaths though.

www.homeopathyhome.com – slightly confusing but comprehensive.
www.homeopathy-soh.org – home of the Society of Homeopaths.
www.interconnections.co.uk – up-to-date information on living holistically.
www.internethealthlibrary.com – a good directory for alternative health sites.

Yoga

www.yogauk.com   UK
YOGA
Welcome to the yoga village where you can get information on yoga in the UK, subscribe to their magazine, or browse the links section, which has a comprehensive list of stores.

See also:
www.ashtanga.com – ashtanga yoga explained.
www.bwy.org.uk – the British Wheel of Yoga.
www.iyengaryoga.org.uk – all about Iyengar yoga techniques.
www.mydailyyoga.com – simple yoga exercises.
www.yogatherapy.org – using yoga to cure.

Sites Catering for a Specific Condition or Disease

*Here is a list of the key sites relating to specific diseases and ailments. We have not attempted to review them, but if you know of a site we've missed and would like it included in the next edition of this book please e-mail us at **goodwebsiteguide@hotmail.com** There is a separate section on cancer which follows our list. For sites relating to children see the section on parental concern on page 362.*

Acne

www.acne-advice.com
www.acne.org
www.m2w3.com/acne

AIDS and HIV

www.avert.org
www.hivstopswithme.org
www.tht.org.uk

Alcohol and Drug Abuse

www.al-anon-alateen.org
www.alcoholconcern.org.uk
www.alcoholics-anonymous.org
www.streetdrugs.org

Allergies

www.allergy.co.uk
www.allergyuk.org formerly www.allergyfoundation.com

Alzheimer and Dementia

www.alzheimers.org.uk
www.dementia.ion.ucl.ac.uk

Anxiety

www.anxieties.com
www.healthanxiety.com
www.anxietynetwork.com

Arthritis

www.aboutarthritis.com
www.arc.org.uk

Asthma

www.asthma.org.uk

Autism

www.nas.org.uk

Back and Spinal Problems

www.backpain.org
www.chiropractic-uk.co.uk
www.spinalnet.co.uk

Blindness

www.rnib.org.uk
www.sense.org.uk

Bowels and Bladder

www.continence-foundation.org.uk
www.digestivedisorders.org.uk
www.ibsnetwork.org.uk
www.incontact.org

Brain Disease and Injury

www.bbsf.org.uk
www.headway.org.uk

Breast Cancer

See Cancer page 253

Bullying

www.bullying.co.uk

Cancer

See page 253.

Cerebral Palsy

www.scope.org.uk

Chiropody

www.drfoot.co.uk
www.feetforlife.org

Crohns Disease and Colitis

www.crohns.org.uk
www.nacc.org.uk

Deafness

www.britishdeafassociation.org.uk
www.rnid.org.uk
www.thehearingaidcouncil.org.uk

Death and Suicide

www.med.uio.no/iasp
www.naturaldeath.org.uk
www.suicide-helplines.org
www.uk-sobs.org.uk

Dental

www.bda-dentistry.org.uk
www.dentalwisdom.com
www.gdc-uk.org

Depression

http://www.depressionalliance.org

Dermatology

www.dermatology.co.uk
www.skincarecampaign.org

Diabetics

www.diabetes-insight.info
www.diabetes.org.uk

Digestion

www.digestivecare.co.uk

Donation

www.blood.co.uk
www.nibts.org – blood and bone marrow donation
www.scotblood.co.uk
www.uktransplant.org.uk – organ donation
www.welsh-blood.org.uk

Drugs

www.acde.org
www.drugs.gov.uk
www.release.org.uk

Eating Disorders

www.edauk.com

Eczema

www.eczema.org

Epilepsy

www.epilepsynse.org.uk
www.epilepsy.org.uk

Eyes

www.moorfields.org.uk

Fertility

www.infertilitynetworkuk.com
www.ifconline.org

Fibromyalgia

www.ukfibromyalgia.com

Gambling

www.gamblersanonymous.org.uk

Heart

www.bhf.org.uk
www.heartuk.org.uk
www.riskscore.org.uk

High Blood Pressure

www.hbpf.org.uk

Kidney Problems

www.kidney.org.uk

Liver Problems

www.britishlivertrust.org.uk

Lupus

www.lupusuk.com

Meningitis

www.meningitis-trust.org

Mental Health

www.mentalhealth.com
www.mind.org.uk
www.nshn.co.uk
www.rcpsych.ac.uk
www.youngminds.org.uk

Migraine

www.migraine.org.uk
www.migrainetrust.org

Multiple Sclerosis

www.mssociety.org.uk

Older People

www.elderabuse.org.uk
www.helptheaged.org.uk

Osteopathy

www.osteopathy.org.uk

Pain Management

www.pain-talk.co.uk

Plastic Surgery

www.baaps.org.uk

Psoriasis

www.psoriasis-association.org.uk

Repetitive Strain Injury

www.rsi.org.uk

Sexually Transmitted Diseases (STDS)

www.playingsafely.co.uk

Smoking

www.ash.org.uk
www.givingupsmoking.co.uk
www.quit.org.uk

Social, Personal and Emotional Support

www.samaritans.co.uk
www.shyness.com

Spina Bifida

www.asbah.org

Stress

www.isma.org.uk
www.stressrelease.com

Stroke

www.differentstrokes.co.uk
www.stroke.org.uk

Cancer

www.cancerhelp.org.uk   UK
CANCER RESEARCH
An overview of what causes cancer, its treatments and the latest
news. You can also find out how to donate and details of ongoing
clinical trials. See also the sister site at
www.cancerresearchuk.org which has more information.

See also:
www.bowelcancer.org – a good overview with advice on
prevention and what to do if you have the symptoms.
www.bcc-uk.org – the Breast Cancer Campaign.
www.breastcancercare.org.uk – very informative on breast
cancer.
www.breakthroughgenerations.org.uk – details of a major
study on breast cancer.
www.cancerfacts.com – detailed information on most forms of
cancer.
www.cancer.gov – excellent site from the US health
department.
www.goingfora.com – excellent site covering what happens in
oncology and radiology.
www.leukaemiacare.org.uk – useful support for sufferers of the
blood cancers including leukaemias, Hodgkin's and other
lymphomas.

History and Biography

*The Internet is proving to be a great storehouse, not only for the latest
news but also for cataloguing historical events in an entertaining and
informative way, here are some of the best sites.*

History

The Good Web Site Guide's Top 10s
of the Internet

1. **www.ancientcivilisations.co.uk** – stunning site from the British Museum
2. **www.thehistorychannel.com** – great use of interactive features
3. **www.visionofbritain.org.uk** – detailed local information about Britain
4. **www.netserf.org** – excellent resource about mediaeval times
5. **www.biography.com** – 25,000 people listed
6. **www.newsplayer.com** – relive the drama
7. **www.nationalarchives.gov.uk** – tracing history with Britain's national archives
8. **www.thebanmappingproject.com** – outstanding site on ancient Egypt
9. **www.bbc.co.uk/history** – outstanding site from the Beeb
10. **www.besthistorysites.net** – great index of history sites

General History

www.historyworld.net

HISTORY WORLD

An outstanding site containing timelines, articles, quizzes and tours all designed to educate and bring history to life in an engaging and stimulating way, and it's successful. The OCEAN historical index which was once part of this site has gone it alone and now contains more than 35,000 precise links to external sites. It can be found at **www.oceanindex.net**

www.historytoday.com
UK

WORLD'S LEADING HISTORY MAGAZINE

Contains some excellent articles from the magazine, the 'classroom' offers a range of study guides, a timeline and historical dictionary. There are a range of interactive features making it a cut above most magazine-derived sites.

www.bl.uk   UK
THE BRITISH LIBRARY
An overview of who they are and what they provide, on the site
you can get information about the library and see some of their
key treasures such as the Magna Carta. Access the 'Turning the
Pages' project where you can virtually 'turn' the pages of digitised
manuscripts. There is several already available including
Leonardo's notebook, a charming Jane Austin text and the
Lindisfarne Gospels, and more are planned.

www.nationalarchives.gov.uk   UK
DOWNLOAD YOUR HISTORY
From the Public Record Office, the history section has workshops
for students, sections for researching and exhibitions. You can
also pre-order documents for your visit to the centre in Kew. See
also **www.learningcurve.gov.uk** where teachers, parents and
students can see how best to use the resources available.

www.nationsencyclopedia.com   US
THE ENCYCLOPAEDIA OF NATIONS
From the United Nations, this site gives basic information on
190 listed countries plus an overview of their history and culture.

www.pbs.org/commandingheights   US
GLOBAL ECONOMY
An outstanding site devoted to the explanation of how the global
economy works, great for students of politics and history alike.
The broadband version of this site is exceptional but some of the
information is a couple of years old.

www.historyforkids.org   US
HISTORY WRITTEN FOR CHILDREN
A good attempt to explain history to children with the emphasis
on ancient times. There are sections on Islam, India and the
major early European cultures. Unfortunately, the site is laden
with adverts, so keep your pop-up blocker on.

For more general history sites try these:
http://timelines.ws – more history timelines than you can shake
a stick at.
http://en.wikipedia.org/wiki/History – Wikipedia's useful
starting point.
www.about.com/education – a good set of educational history
pages.

www.besthistorysites.net – an attempt to list the best history sites by category; it has a strong US bias.

www.eyewitnesstohistory.com – containing a large catalogue of historical recollections both ancient and modern, takes the 'history through the eyes of those who lived it' approach.

www.fordham.edu/halsall – a messy site presenting copies of history source books that are freely available for use.

www.historyhouse.com – excellent for history trivia and odd facts.

www.historylearningsite.co.uk – great for school, it covers Key Stage 3 and upwards.

www.historymole.com – historical timelines – good, but the number of queries you can run is limited.

www.historyofnations.net – this site offers a potted history on virtually every country in the world.

www.spartacus.schoolnet.co.uk – a useful history encyclopaedia.

www.thehistorynet.com – a good resource from a US magazine site.

Listed here is a selection of specific sites or pages from larger university sites that cover specific periods in time, events or regions. They may not win design awards but the information that they contain is usually comprehensive or sufficient to get you started and direct you to sources of further information.

UK History

www.bbc.co.uk/history   UK

HISTORY INTERACTIVE

Part of the outstanding BBC site, here you can find sections covering all the important bits of British history. The site uses technology well and there are some good articles too. It also shows what's on TV and radio that's history related. **www.uktv.co.uk/uktvHistory** is also useful.

www.visionofbritain.org.uk   UK

BETWEEN 1801 AND 2001

A well designed and truly informative site which, using maps and statistics, tracks the development of Britain through 200 years. Just type in your postcode and you get access to lots of background information on your area such as industry, population, work and poverty. Excellent for schools and for those interested in local history.

See also:

http://hds.essex.ac.uk/gbh.asp – the Great Britain Historical Database has masses of statistics from the 19th and 20th centuries.

http://www.historyofengland.net – a bitty site that covers English history.

www.bbc.co.uk/wales/history – BBC Wales has an excellent section on Welsh history.

www.britannia.com – an American site devoted to travel. It contains a British history section that offers a good overview of the subject.

www.britarch.ac.uk – a portal for British archaeology.

www.british-history.ac.uk – very useful and unfussy site from the Institute of Historical Research.

www.british-history.co.uk – a site offering sections on Roman Britain, 100 Years War, Wars of the Roses, English Civil War, Napoleonic Wars and the Second World War plus access to the British History Webring.

www.britainunlimited.com – biographies of 250 people who shaped Britain.

www.electricscotland.com/history – a good place to start researching Scottish history.

www.enrichuk.net – links to local and regional history projects throughout the UK.

www.history.uk.com – excellent directory and portal featuring some 28,000 sites.

www.iwm.org.uk – home of the Imperial War Museum with an impressive site.

www.lib.byu.edu/~rdh/eurodocs/uk.html – documents important through the history of the UK.

www.livinghistory.co.uk – effectively a portal site for those who love to re-enact history.

www.nidex.com/history.htm – an overview of Northern Ireland's complex history with links.

www.questia.com/library/history/european-history/great-britain/british-history – free books to download on British history from Questia.

www.scottishhistory.com/ – Scottish history portal.

Royalty

www.royal.gov.uk   UK
　　THE BRITISH MONARCHY
　　A comprehensive and entertaining site with a very good

overview of the history of the British monarchy, though for information on other royal families see the rather messy **www.royalty.nu**

Middle Ages and Before

www.netserf.org   US
MEDIAEVAL LIFE
Excellent and well-categorised portal site covering every conceivable aspect of life in the Middle Ages.

See also:
http://the-orb.net – covering European history in mediaeval times.
www.darkagestrust.org.uk – an attempt to recreate England as it was 1,000 years ago.
www.learner.org/exhibits/middleages – a good educational resource.
www.mnh.si.edu/vikings – an exhibition about Viking voyages from the Smithsonian.
www.pbs.org/wgbh/nova/vikings – good interactive overview on Viking life.
www.postroman.info – a good overview of early mediaeval Britain.
www.regia.org – Anglo-Saxons, Vikings and Normans.
www.suttonhoo.org – information on the ship burial.
www.vikingsword.com – a sword expert's view, not only of Viking weaponry but also of swords generally, good links section.

www.essentialnormanconquest.com   UK
THE NORMANS
A good-looking site from Osprey Publishing, which features a 1066 timeline, and blow-by-blow account of the conquest. It's got some good maps and a quiz too.

See also:
http://en.wikipedia.org/wiki/Norman_Conquest – Wikipedia's overview.
www.bayeuxtapestry.org.uk – a scene-by-scene explanation of the Bayeux Tapestry.
www.normanconquest.co.uk – an old site being updated but still useful.

The Tudors to the Georges

www.warsoftheroses.com   UK
WARS OF THE ROSES
Excellent site covering the period 1450 to 1490 with all its
turmoil and politics, it also has a good timeline and links.

www.tudorhistory.org   UK
TUDOR FAMILY TREE
A basic but informative site with a who's who of Tudor times with
background information on what it was like to live then.

See also:
http://tudors.crispen.org – a period-by-period overview, turn the
sound off if you don't like Tudor music.
www.elizabethi.org – a biographical site with a good deal of
background on Elizabethan life as well as biographical
details.
www.renaissance.dm.net – the Renaissance was an amazing
time and, while this site doesn't cover it that well, it does have a
good links section; it's also very oriented towards England.
www.tudorgroup.co.uk – re-enacting Tudor and Elizabethan
times.

www.pepysdiary.com   UK
DIARY OF SAMUEL PEPYS
Put together by an aficionado of Pepys, this is updated daily with
an entry from the diaries on the day he wrote them over 340
years ago. Apart from the fascinating social history, there's lots of
annotation, explanation and cross referencing too, as well as
audio readings, which all help you to picture the scene.

See also:
www.cannylink.com/history17thcentury.htm – a list of articles
on important 17th century events.
www.gunpowder-plot.org – interesting site devoted to the
happenings that surround the Gun Powder Plot of 1605.

www.olivercromwell.org   UK
OLIVER CROMWELL
A detailed biography of the man and his times, there's
background on the civil wars and a guide to places linked with
him that you can visit.

See also:

http://en.wikipedia.org/wiki/Charles_I_of_England –
Wikipedia's excellent section on Charles I.

www.british-civil-wars.co.uk – a detailed review of the wars
and why they happened, backed up with biographies and links.

www.ecwsa.org – the English Civil War Society of America with
a good site with lots of detail, articles and links.

www.open2.net/civilwar – detailed information on the English
Civil War.

www.royal-stuarts.org – the placing of the Stuart monarchy in
history with a strong Scottish bias.

www.georgianindex.net   UK
ALL THINGS GEORGIAN

A scrappy site but one with a wide range of information on
Georgian times, what it was like to live then and what events
took place.

See also:

http://regencygarderobe.com – regency fashion.

www.elizabethpowell.net – a good overview of the Regency
Period via the Regency ring.

The Victorians and Empire

www.victorianweb.org   UK
VICTORIANS EXPLAINED

Background on events, social and political history, biographies
and even entertainment, it's all here.

See also:

http://victorianresearch.org – a scholarly site but with excellent
material.

www.hiddenlives.org.uk – essentially a graphic account of the
lives of the children looked after by the Waifs and Strays Society
but it's also an incredibly interesting insight into Victorian Britain.

www.victorians.org.uk – for information on the daily lives of the
Victorians.

www.victorianstation.com – everything from architecture to
shopping.

www.britishempire.co.uk   UK
THE BRITISH EMPIRE

A thorough walk through the Empire with articles, maps and

sections on science, arts and military power that round everything off. It also has a useful timeline, just to put everything in context.

See also:
http://homepage.ntlworld.com/haywardlad – a slow but pretty comprehensive site on the rise and fall of the Empire.
http://regiments.org – an overview of the land forces who served the Empire and Commonwealth.

The 20th Century

There doesn't seem to be one really good site dedicated to the UK's 20th-century history, although many of the larger history sites do major on this time period. Those listed below do a great job in bringing history to life, whilst informing us about the historical details.

www.1940.co.uk – remembering the 40s, a nice site and shop.
www.backdate.co.uk – an entertainment site devoted to the 60s and 70s.
www.bbc.co.uk/history/historic_figures/thatcher_margaret. shtml – the BBC's pages on Thatcherism.
www.bbhq.com/sixties.htm – a very ugly site but lots of info on the 60s.
www.bergen.org/AAST/Projects/ColdWar/index2.html – a chilling reminder of what it was like to live through the Cold War.
www.britannia.com/history/h90.html – a good index of events in the 20th century.
www.britishpathe.com – Pathe films covered most of the major events of the century and you can buy and see clips here.
www.fiftiesweb.com – entertaining overview of the decade's events and culture.
www.greatwar.co.uk – a well-laid-out site on the 1914–18 war.
www.holnet.org.uk – the history of London.
www.margaretthatcher.org – Margaret Thatcher's official site.
www.movinghere.org.uk – a history of migration to England.
www.number10.gov.uk/output/page123.asp – British prime ministers in history.
www.secondworldwar.co.uk – site devoted to chronicling WW2.
www.sixties.net – a bright and breezy stroll through the 60s.
www.war-experience.org – experiences of those who took part in WW2.

World History

Ancient History

www.ancientsites.com   US
ANCIENT SITES
Seven key times and sites are featured and you must subscribe
to get the best out of it. The whole thing is a little long winded
although worth the faffing around as you get access to lots of
background information and social history. You can also chat to
fellow members.

www.ancientcivilisations.co.uk   UK
INTERACTIVE HISTORY
An outstanding site design from the British Museum. You choose
a theme from the map: cities, religion, buildings, technology,
writing or trade; this provides you with a short overview plus
a timeline which you can stop at any point to get the information
you need. If you want real detail, then go to a specialist site;
however, this site provides sufficient information to start you
off.

www.anthro.net   US
ANTHROPOLOGY
Masses of links in this well-categorised site which covers
everything from Ancient Egypt to Ethnomathmatics!

Other ancient history directories:
http://ancienthistory.about.com – well-categorised links section
with relevant articles from About.com.
www.ancientworlds.net – a directory and overview with lots of
illustrations and graphics, although the site is a bit of a mess.
www.fordham.edu/halsall/ancient/asbook03.html – the
ancient history source book has many links covering all
important areas and regions.

Africa

www.thebanmappingproject.com   US
THEBES AND THE VALLEY OF THE KINGS
A great and genuinely interesting site devoted to life in ancient
Thebes in what is now Egypt, with over 200 interactive maps,
narrative tours and 3-D features. Excellent.

www.homestead.com/wysinger/ancientafrica.html   US
ANCIENT AFRICA'S BLACK KINGDOMS
A thorough overview of the continent's civilisations with links
and pictures. While the design isn't great, it is well worth a visit
by any student wanting to know about Africa's ancient history.

See also:
http://library.stanford.edu/africa/history/hisking.html – links
for loads of articles on African history.
http://royalafricansociety.org – the Royal African Society.
promotes the continent and its many causes, useful for links and
current affairs.
**http://web.cocc.edu/cagatucci/classes/hum211/timelines/
htimeline.htm** – a timeline of African history.
www.africainformation.net – a useful site with plenty of links to
help when researching African history.
www.columbia.edu/cu/lweb/indiv/africa/cuvl – Columbia
University's comprehensive African studies pages.
www.eternalegypt.org – excellent and accessible site covering
5,000 years of Egyptian history with lots of interaction and
information too.
www.fordham.edu/halsall/africa/africasbook.html – excellent
database of sources and links covering African history from the
Ancient Egyptians to Nelson Mandela.
www.newton.cam.ac.uk/egypt – the excellent Egyptology
resource.

Asia

http://coombs.anu.edu.au/WWWVL-AsianStudies.html
                                                        AUSTRALIA
ASIAN STUDIES
Basically a selection of links that cover the whole of Asia by
country, region and centre.

See also:
http://afe.easia.columbia.edu/mongols – a comprehensive site
covering the Mongol empire and its history.
http://depts.washington.edu/chinaciv – lots of information on
China with an excellent timeline.
http://goasia.about.com/library/weekly/blfunan.htm – Asian
history links and articles from About.com.
http://sun.sino.uni-heidelberg.de/igcs – more links on China
than you'll ever need.

http://web.uccs.edu/history/globalhistory/japan.html –
Japanese history covered.

www.1421.tv – interesting site from people who have proved
that the Chinese discovered and mapped the world before the
Europeans.

www.angkor-planet.com/UK-hase.html – an odd site but it
does have a graphic overview of South East Asian history.

www.asianinfo.org/asianinfo/korea/history.htm – an outline of
Korean history.

www.fordham.edu/halsall/india/indiasbook.html – excellent
overview of India's history.

www.gimonca.com/sejarah/sejarah.shtml – a timeline of
Indonesian history.

www.infolanka.com/org/srilanka/hist.html – history of Sri
Lanka.

Australasia and Oceania

www.academicinfo.net/histaus.html   AUSTRALIA
AUSTRALIA

A pretty good directory of sites relating to Australian history
ancient and modern. There's an explanation and review of each
site featured.

See also:
http://en.wikipedia.org/wiki/History_of_Oceania – good as a
starting point for research.

www.awm.gov.au – Australian war memorials.

www.enzed.com/hist.html – useful overview of New Zealand's
past.

www.pvs-hawaii.com/history.htm – A history of Polynesia from
the Polynesian Voyaging Society.

Europe

www.hartford-hwp.com/archives/60   UK
EUROPE AS A WHOLE

A directory of links and articles covering the whole of Europe and
its history; the selection can be a bit disparate, but there is a
search facility on the main site. See also Wikipedia's pages
which are a great starting point at **http://en.wikipedia.org/wiki/
History_of_Europe** It is particularly strong in areas not well
covered by other encyclopaedias such as the Balkans and the
cold war

France

http://chnm.gmu.edu/revolution – the French Revolution explored, this site offers a huge amount of information.
http://en.wikipedia.org/wiki/History_of_France – an alternative overview.
www.napoleonguide.com – an outstanding site on Napoleon and his times, with lots of background information and links to related subjects.
www.napoleonic-literature.com – a very good site about Napoleon and the effect he had on Europe, with background on the battles and his writing.
www.rinfret.com/frhistory.html – a good overview from ancient to modern.

Germany

www.rootsweb.com/~deubadnw/history/maps/maps.htm – maps showing the changing face of Germany and Prussia over the centuries.
www.tau.ac.il/GermanHistory/links.html – a chronological set of links and articles covering German history from ancient times.

Greece

www.ancientgreece.com – an excellent site devoted to all aspects of Ancient Greece.
www.mythweb.com – all the Greek myths illustrated in a fun and entertaining way.

Holland, Belgium and Benelux

http://en.wikipedia.org/wiki/History_of_Belgium – as is so often the case, there's nothing really to beat Wikipedia's section on Belgium, see also **http://en.wikipedia.org/wiki/Benelux**
www.history-netherlands.nl – an excellent chronological site.

Ireland

www.irelandstory.com/today/main.html – from prehistory to the latest Anglo-Irish agreement.
www.ucc.ie/celt – excellent resource on Irish historical events, literature and politics too.

Italy

www.arcaini.com/italy/italyhistory/ItalyHistory.html – a good chronological history of Italy from pre-history to the 20th century.
www.roman-empire.net – excellent site covering all aspects of the Roman Empire with a good kids' section.

Russia

www.barnsdle.demon.co.uk/russ/rusrev.html – an interesting site covering the events surrounding the Russian Revolution.
www.departments.bucknell.edu/russian/history.html – complete overview and chronology of Russian history and they've taken the trouble to make the site look good too.

Scandinavia

http://virtual.finland.fi – virtual Finland with a good overview.
http://woldhagen.org/woldhagen/norway/Nor_hist.htm – Norway's story.
www.lib.byu.edu/estu/wess/scan/hist.html – the Scandinavian studies web for links and documents.
www.pip.dknet.dk/~pip261/denmark.html – Denmark's history.
www.royalty.nu/Europe/Scandinavia – Scandinavian royalty.
www.sweden.se/templates/cs/BasicFactsheet____3116.aspx – a short history of Sweden.

Spain

www.sispain.org/english/history – a chronology of Spanish history with links.
www.users.dircon.co.uk/~warden/scw/scwindex.htm – the Spanish Civil War.

Turkey

http://vlib.iue.it/history/asia/Turkey/index.html – a virtual history of Turkey with links.
www.bbc.co.uk/religion/religions/islam/history/ottoman/index.shtml – the BBC has a strong section on the Ottomans.
www.theottomans.org/english/index.asp – a good site on the Ottomans and their achievements.

Latin America

http://users.snowcrest.net/jmike/latin.html   US
LATIN AMERICAN LINKS
An outstanding collection of links, categorised by country and
region covering Latin and South America and also the Caribbean.

www.ancientmexico.com   US
ANCIENT MEXICO
A beautifully illustrated site covering ancient Mexico and the
Mayan and Aztec empires; there are also similar sister sites on
Chile and Peru.

Middle East

www.albany.edu/history/middle-east   US
HISTORY IN THE NEWS
A very good resource site with lots of documents, articles and
links plus a chronology and social background on the Middle
East and its tormented past.

See also:
http://aina.org/aol – all about the Assyrians.
www.al-bab.com/arab/history.htm – a good overview of Arab
history with links and articles.
www.arab.net – this site offers a short history on most Arab
countries.
www.fordham.edu/halsall/ancient/asbook05.html – all you
need on ancient Persia.
www.mesopotamia.co.uk – excellent site from the British
Museum.
www.prc.org.uk/palestine%2048/history.html – an account of
Palestinian history.

http://www.dinur.org/1.html?rsID=219   US
JEWISH HISTORY RESEARCH CENTRE
This site is a little difficult to navigate and use but it does offer
some 6,000 links which are well categorised; it covers biblical
history too. See also **www.cjh.org** the Center for Jewish History:
well illustrated with a US bias.

http://yadvashem.org   ISRAEL
THE HOLOCAUST
A moving and well-put-together site from the Holocaust Martyrs

and Heroes Remembrance Society. There are thousands of photographs and accounts, all of which make a visit here pretty moving, to say the least.

North America

http://americanhistory.about.com   US
ABOUT AMERICA
Just about all you'll be needing on American history from the ever excellent About.com; it's well categorised with links and related articles too.

See also:
http://americanhistory.si.edu – National Museum of American History.
http://memory.loc.gov/ammem – excellent collection of articles, micro-sites and links from the American Library of Congress.
www.brightmoments.com/blackhistory – excellent African American history site.
www.canadahistory.com – a good place to start.
www.historybuff.com – entertaining site that uses old newspaper coverage to illustrate aspects of US history.
www.historyplace.com – good for articles, features and links.
www.ourdocuments.gov – excellent and advanced site showing the 100 most important documents in US history.
www.lib.washington.edu/subject/History/tm/native.html – Native American history.
www.timearchive.com – *Time* magazine's archive is excellent but you have to subscribe.
www.u-s-history.com – an academic approach.
www.ushistory.org – a history of the US with an amusing touch of bias . . .

Biography

www.biography.com   US
FIND OUT ABOUT ANYONE WHO WAS ANYONE
Over 25,000 biographical references and some 4,000 videos make this site a good option if you need to find out about someone in a hurry, however it is commercial. There are special features such as a book club and a magazine.

See also:

http://almaz.com/nobel/nobel.html – a fascinating site about the people who have won the Nobel prize.

www.britainunlimited.com – biographies of 250 people who shaped Britain.

www.royalty.nu – the world of royalty: historical and recent.

www.rulers.org – an amazing database providing a list of the rulers of every country going back to 1700.

www.s9.com/biography – a biographical dictionary covering the lives of over 28,000 people!

www.sbrowning.com – create your own biographical timelines at this innovative site.

www.who2.com – a good biography portal site that covers celebrities as well as the historically famous.

www.whosaliveandwhosdead.com – basically a list of celebrities cross referenced by what they did. It shows who's alive, who died and when. Morbidly fascinating.

www.whoyoushouldknow.com – in an attempt to educate Americans about the world, this blog features a new world leader every weekday. It's turned out to be an educationally useful and informative site.

Visual History

www.newsplayer.com   UK
RELIVE THE LAST CENTURY
Relive the events of the past hundred years; witness them at first hand as they happened. A truly superb site with real newsreel footage worth the £4 annual subscription fee. See also the BBC's excellent site **www.bbc.co.uk/onthisday** where you can see what happened on a particular day in history. Strongly biased to the 20th century with film clips and eye witness reports.

www.thehistorychannel.com   US

THE BEST SEARCH IN HISTORY
Excellent for history buffs, revision or just a good read, the History Channel provides a site that is packed with information. Search by key word or timeline, by date and by subject, get biographical information or speeches. It's fast and easy to get carried away once you start your search.

www.francisfrith.co.uk   UK
HISTORY IN PHOTOGRAPHS
This remarkable archive was started in 1860 and there are over

365,000 photographs featuring some 7,000 cities, towns and villages. The site is very well designed with a good search facility. You can buy from a growing selection of gifts, photos, maps and now aerial shots too; different sizes are available and it's pretty good value too. See also **www.photolondon.org.uk** where you'll find an excellent photo archive of the capital.

www.old-maps.co.uk UK
OLD MAPS
Access to mapping as it was between 1846 and 1899, just type in your town and you get a view of what it looked like in those times. The quality is variable but it's fun to try and spot the changes. See also **www.alangodfreymaps.co.uk**

www.museumofcostume.co.uk UK
COSTUME THROUGH THE AGES
Excellent site showing how the design of costume has changed through the ages. There's a virtual tour and links to other museums based in Bath. See also **www.siue.edu/COSTUMES/history.html**

Other History-related Sites

www.findagrave.com US
FIND A GRAVE!
Find graves of the rich and famous or a long-lost relative, either way there's a database of over 3 million to search. It really only covers the US.

www.the-reenactor.co.uk UK
TAKE PART IN A BATTLE
OK so you feel the urge to play at being a Viking for the day, well here's where to start. The site lists some 90 societies to join and play a part in. It is divided into sections according to time period and you can find out where re-enactments are taking place, plus the latest news.

www.uchronia.net US
ALTERNATIVE HISTORIES
A bibliography and review site featuring almost 2,500 books that in some way or another scope out alternative histories. It makes interesting reading – the 'what if' scenario fascinates most historians after all.

www.nwhp.org   US
>NATIONAL WOMEN'S HISTORY PROJECT
>An educational site devoted to highlighting and celebrating the
>achievements of women through history.

For a Beautiful Mind

The Good Web Site Guide's Top 10s
of the Internet

1. **www.queendom.com** – test yourself and beat the experts
2. **www.bbc.co.uk** – knowledge, community and TV
3. **www.howstuffworks.com** – so that's how they do it
4. **www.newsnow.co.uk** – keep ahead
5. **www.yahoo.co.uk/recreation/hobbies** – find a hobby
6. **www.thefitmap.com** – get healthy to get brainy
7. **www.wikipedia.org** – look it up, make a contribution
8. **www.24hourmuseum.org.uk** – get cultural
9. **www.bodyandsoulholidays.com** – rest your mind and body
10. **www.readinggroups.co.uk** – join a reading group

Hobbies

www.yahoo.co.uk/recreation/hobbies   UK
>IF YOU CAN'T FIND YOUR HOBBY THEN LOOK HERE
>Hundreds of links for almost every conceivable pastime from
>amateur radio to urban exploration, it's part of the Yahoo service
>(see page 420) and there's a UK section too

>*See also:*
>**http://jobsinart.com/encyclopedia/List_of_hobbies** – a list of
>hobbies and links.
>**www.about.com/hobbies** – a similarly large list but with an
>American bias.
>**www.allcrafts.net** – a wide-ranging directory covering all
>the major crafts and many minor ones. Very good links pages.

Crafts

www.save-on-crafts.com US
SAVINGS EVERYWHERE YOU LOOK
An excellent craft supply and interiors store covering an extensive range of crafts and merchandise. It's well worth a browse and good for the unusual, but shipping is expensive.

www.cass-arts.co.uk UK
ONE STOP SHOP FOR ART MATERIALS
A huge range of art and craft products available to buy online, also hints and tips and step-by-step guides for the novice. There is an online gallery and a section of art trivia and games. The shop has a decent search engine which copes with over 20,000 items, delivery is charged according to what you spend.

See also:
www.artdiscount.co.uk – good value and a wide range on offer.
www.pictureframes.co.uk – show off your masterpiece to best effect.

www.thesunneversets.fsnet.co.uk formerly
www.codcottage.freeserve.co.uk UK
CALLIGRAPHY
A good introduction into calligraphy with lots of advice and help as well as links to related sites. See also **www.calligraphy.co.uk** who also have lots of links.

www.hobbycraft.co.uk UK
ARTS AND CRAFTS SUPERSTORE
A nice retro feel to this site with a wide selection of inspirational ideas and information on what they sell and where their shops are, sadly you can't buy online.

www.sewandso.co.uk UK
SHOP AT THE SPECIALISTS
This site offers a huge range of kits and patterns for cross-stitch, needlepoint and embroidery. In addition, there's an equally large range of needles and threads, some 20,000 products in all. There are some good offers and delivery cost is calculated by weight. It's also worth checking out the specialist pages at About.com **http://knitting.about.com** and **http://sewing.about.com** and if you're a quilter seeking inspiration visit **www.fatquartershop.com**

www.whaleys-bradford.ltd.uk UK
FANTASTIC FABRICS
Whether you're looking for a simple cotton lawn, a shot taffeta, or fabrics for the theatre, Whaley's have it all – and they will send you up to 10 samples free of charge. There is a useful A–Z of fabrics and a good search facility. Also see **www.online-fabrics.co.uk** who also have a wide selection.

www.horology.com UK
THE INDEX
The complete exploration of time, this is essentially a set of links for the committed horologist. It's pretty comprehensive, so if your hobby is tinkering about with clocks and watches, then this is a must.

www.jigboxx.com CANADA
JIGSAWS
Excellent for jigsaw enthusiasts, there's a wide range, a search facility, plus loyalty scheme and you can be kept abreast of the latest designs too. Delivery charges vary.

Coins and Stamps

www.royalmint.com UK

THE VALUE OF MONEY
The Royal Mint's web site is informative, providing a history of the Mint, the coins themselves, plus details on the coins they've issued. You can buy from the site and delivery is free.

See also:
http://coins.to – US coins and much more from the Austin Coin Collecting Society.
www.coinclub.com – good for information and links.
www.coinlink.com – a good directory devoted to all things numismatic.
www.tclayton.demon.co.uk/coins.html – Tony Clayton's informative home page on coins.
www.telesphere.com/ts/coins/faq.html – commonly asked questions about coin collecting.
www.tokenpublishing.com – owners of *Coin News*.

www.stanleygibbons.com UK
STAMPS ETC.
The best prices and a user-friendly site for philatelists. You can

buy a whole collection or sell them your own. Their catalogue is available online and you can take part in auctions.

See also:
www.corbitts.com – auctioneers for stamps, coins, notes and medals.
www.duncannon.co.uk – for accessories and albums.
www.postcard.co.uk – home of the Postcard Traders Association.
www.robinhood-stamp.co.uk – for good prices and range.
www.stamp.co.uk – excellent resource for all stamp collectors.
www.stampsatauction.com – a good auction site devoted to stamps.
www.ukphilately.org.uk/abps – information on exhibitions and events at the Association of British Philatelic Societies.

Model-making

www.themodelmakersresource.co.uk   UK
MODEL-MAKING MATERIALS
A wide range of tools, materials, kits and other modelling essentials here, plus lots of information and links; some good prices too.

www.towerhobbies.com   US
EXCITING WORLD OF RADIO-CONTROLLED MODELLING
An excellent, clearly laid out site offering a vast range of radio-controlled models along with thousands of accessories and parts. The international delivery charge depends on the size of the order.

See also:
www.ehobbies.com – large US retailer with an international division where you'll find a wide range of models, kits and radio-controlled cars.
www.fusionhobbies.com – for cars and tanks.
www.otherlandtoys.co.uk – radio-controlled gifts and gadgets too.

www.brmodelling.com   UK
BRITISH RAILWAY MODELLING
A high-quality magazine site devoted to model railways, it includes a virtual model set for you to play with and articles on

specific types of trains and railways. There's also a forum where you can chat to fellow enthusiasts.

See also:
http://uk.games-workshop.com – for Warhammer and Lord of the Rings models with hints on painting and model-making.
www.corgi.co.uk – home of the leading model car maker.
www.modelboats.co.uk – a model boat magazine.
www.toysoldier.freeuk.com – informative site devoted to toy soldiers.
www.ukmodelshops.co.uk – a directory, mainly railways oriented.
www.wingsandwheels.co.uk – model aircraft specialists.

www.ontracks.co.uk   UK
MODEL AND HOBBY SUPERSTORE
They sell over 35,000 models and hobby items, but it's tricky to find what you want as the site is a bit messy with lots of annoying graphics. Having said that there are some good special offers and delivery prices are reasonable.

www.woodworking.co.uk   UK
WORKING WITH WOOD
A good amateur site offering loads of information about all aspects of woodworking. There's a gallery of work from featured craftsmen plus advice for beginners. The home page contains a link to **www.toolpost.co.uk** where you can get all your tools.

Circus Arts

www.circusfriends.co.uk   UK
CIRCUS IN BRITAIN
The place to go it you want to go to the circus, subscribe to their magazine, or find our about circus education programs. Great for links.

www.oddballs.co.uk   UK
FOR JUGGLERS
For juggling equipment, fire sticks, diabolos, unicycles plus books and videos. The community pages give advice and links to other juggling sites. For a serious approach to the subject and online lessons go to the Internet Juggling database at **www.jugglingdb.com**

Other circus fans and street artists may find these sites helpful:
www.circusnews.com – an American site with loads of
information about the circus scene.
www.contortionhomepage.com – for those that want to get into
the box.
www.streetentertainers.co.uk – for street entertainers.
www.peopleplayuk.org.uk/guided_tours – brilliant on the
history of the circus.
www.trickstutorials.com – a dense site on how to perform
acrobatic tricks. Only the most flexible should try.
www.unicycle.org.uk – how to and info for those into unicycles.

Home and Do-It-Yourself

The web doesn't seem a natural home for do-it-yourself, but there are
some really useful sites, some great offers on tools and equipment and
plenty of sensible advice.

Superstores

www.diy.com   UK
THE DIY SUPERSTORE
B&Q has a bright and busy site with lots of advice, inspiration,
tips and information on projects for the home and garden. It also
has an excellent searchable product database. There are also
plenty of offers and the store has a good selection of products
covering all the major DIY areas. Delivery costs vary according to
how much you buy and how fast you want it. Returns can be
made to the stores. You need to be able to accept cookies before
the site can operate effectively or before you place an order.

www.wickes.co.uk   UK
DIY SPECIALISTS
Good ideas, inspiration and help are the key themes for this site;
it's easy to use and genuinely helpful with well laid out project
details. You can visit their showrooms for product information
and download leaflets on a wide variety of domestic jobs. There's
a handy calculator section where you can work out how many
tiles or rolls of wallpaper you may need.

www.focusdoitall.co.uk   UK
FOCUS DO-IT-ALL
A functional site, which attempts to put over lots of ideas and

inspiration, it also carries a wide range of products at good prices. Delivery is £4.99 on most items and you can return unwanted goods to your nearest store.

www.homebase.co.uk
UK
NEW-LOOK HOMEBASE

The site does not sell paint, wallpaper or small items such as garden trowels, which you might expect in their stores. Instead, they concentrate on an extensive range of household, gardening and DIY equipment, furniture, sheds and conservatories. Other featured items such as kitchens and bathroom ranges are only available in store – which is slightly confusing. There are also a few guides available to help you plan and execute you DIY project.

Other DIY stores worth checking out are:
www.buildbase.co.uk – good site for the professional.
www.decoratingdirect.co.uk – functional and easy-to-use site that concentrates on home décor products at excellent prices.
www.jewson.co.uk – Jewson's site is more corporate than anything but it does have a small section on each part of the house and how they can help.

Buying Tools and Equipment

www.screwfix.com
UK

PRODUCTS FOR ALL DIY NEEDS

Rightly considered to be one of the best online stores, Screwfix offer excellent value for money with wholesale prices on a massive range of DIY products.

www.draper.co.uk
UK
QUALITY SINCE 1919

An attractive site that is easy to use, the only downside being that you have to have the latest downloads for it to work effectively. If you're a regular visitor and know the stock number of the item you want there's a good fast-track service too.

www.diytools.co.uk
UK
MORE TOOLS

Another well-designed and extensive tool store with a huge range of products and a well-categorised search engine. Also check out **www.blackanddecker.co.uk** who have lots of advice on how to use power tools correctly, and also the slow but thorough **www.worldofpower.co.uk** who also supply garden equipment, plus quad bikes and other motorised toys.

Tool Hire

www.hss.co.uk   UK
WHERE YOU CAN HIRE ALMOST ANYTHING
A useful site where you can organise the rental of a huge range of tools and equipment, it's great for those one-off jobs.

Trade Information

www.fmb.org.uk   UK
 THE FEDERATION OF MASTER BUILDERS
Get advice on avoiding cowboys and on getting the best out of a builder. There's information and articles on most aspects of home maintenance, plus hints on finding reputable help.

www.trustmark.org.uk   UK
TRUSTY BUILDERS
A Government-backed initiative to help consumers find reputable firms to do repair, maintenance and improvement work in the home or garden. The site links to approved scheme operators. There is also advice on what to do if things do go wrong.

See also:
www.buildersguild.co.uk – who also offer much in the way of information.
www.findabuilder.co.uk – a trade organisation that will help you find a builder in your area.

Advice and DIY Encyclopaedias

www.hometips.com   US
EXPERT ADVICE FOR YOUR HOME
American the advice may be, but there is plenty here for every homeowner. The site is well laid out and the advice good. Alternatives are **www.naturalhandyman.com** which is fun, or the extensive **www.doityourself.com** which is very detailed.

www.diyfixit.co.uk

ONLINE DIY ENCYCLOPAEDIA

Get help with most DIY jobs using the search engine or browse by room or job type. The information is good especially now they've added more illustrations.

See also:

www.diydata.com – not fully comprehensive but one of the better DIY encyclopaedias.

www.diyfaq.org.uk – practical information from this UK-based forum site.

www.diynot.com – a good all-rounder, encyclopaedia, forums and DIY help.

www.finddiy.co.uk – a list of DIY sites.

www.freddyfixit.co.za – DIY help from South Africa.

www.homedoctor.net – an American site with lots of homey tips.

www.ukdiyguide.co.uk – a useful DIY site listing.

Building and Home Improvements

For further information and advice on finding and using an architect, refer to the section on Architecture, page 27.

www.ebuild.co.uk

BUILD YOUR OWN HOUSE

All the information and contacts you need if you're thinking of buying that plot of land and getting stuck in. There's also a continually updated list of what plots of land are available and where.

The following sites will also prove useful if you're out to build your own:

www.aecb.net – the Association for Environmentally Conscious Building has a helpful site with the relevant information.

www.bricksandbrass.co.uk – the place to go if you have a period home to renovate.

www.builditthisway.co.uk – a good overview from a retired builder on what it takes to build your own house.

www.bwpda.co.uk – home of the British Wood Preserving and Damp Proofing Association, with a 'find a contractor' service.

www.homebuilding.co.uk – a spin off from a magazine, lots of resources and information.

www.planning.odpm.gov.uk – the Office of the Deputy Prime Minister has information on the latest government initiatives on planning.

www.planningportal.gov.uk – a huge and very useful resource about planning regulations, with advice and a guide to the process.

www.plotfinder.net – find a spot to build your dream home, but you have to subscribe.

www.selfbuildit.co.uk – help for first timers.

Salvage

UK

www.salvo.co.uk

SALVAGE AND RECLAMATION

Salvo provides information on where to get salvaged and reclaimed architectural and garden antiques. The site is comprehensive and easy to use with interesting information such as what buildings are due to be demolished and when, so you can be ready and waiting.

Conservatories

UK

www.conservatoriesonline.co.uk

ALL YOU NEED TO KNOW ABOUT CONSERVATORIES

A good portal site which offers links and advice on conservatories, sunrooms, garden rooms and solariums. There's a buyer's guide plus information on materials, styles, even on pools and orangeries.

See also:

www.advisoryservice.co.uk – home of the Conservatory and Windows Advisory Service, a good place to go for getting advice on the right sort of materials to use.

www.conservatories-direct.co.uk – a good, comprehensive site from this specialist.

www.diy-conservatories-uk.co.uk – all you need if you want to erect your own.

Plumbing, Bathroom and Kitchen

UK

www.plumbworld.co.uk

AN ONLINE PLUMBING SHOP

A clean, well organised site catering for all your bathroom and kitchen needs plus a good selection of plumbing tools and

paraphernalia at competitive prices. They have improved the
ordering and delivery information available on the site too.

www.bathroomexpress.co.uk   UK
BETTER BATHROOMS
A wide range of bathrooms and accessories are available at
decent prices, with some interesting luxury items such as
après-shower driers and some unique toilet seats. See also
www.bathroomassociation.org and
www.brighterbathrooms.com

www.alarisavenue.co.uk   UK

KITCHENS AND CANE
A beautifully designed store that offers much in the way of
inspiration and quality products for the kitchen.

See also:
www.bathrooms.com (diverts from **www.plumbers.co.uk**) –
huge portal for bathroom needs and, if you need a plumber, try
the directory of plumbers.
www.fixatoilet.com – could be invaluable!
www.ksa.co.uk – advice on planning kitchens, bathrooms and
bedrooms with a handy facility to find a design specialist.
www.plbg – plumbing forums galore with access to loads of
advice.
www.registeredplumber.com – home of the Institute of
Plumbing with a member directory and their code of practice.
www.tapsshop.co.uk – useful if you need taps.
www.victoriaplumb.com – well designed site with lots of
choice.

www.toppstiles.co.uk   UK
TILES
You can't get tiles delivered but there's a shop-finder service and
details of available ranges including floor tiles.

See also:
www.digitile.co.uk – find out about how to get custom-made
tiles.
www.green-bottle.co.uk – recycling glass into usable products
such as tiles.
www.taylortiles.co.uk – a wide range and sample ordering service.
www.tiles.org.uk – home to the Tile Association and full of good
advice.

Doors

www.handlesdirect.co.uk UK
HANDLES GALORE

A functional site where you can buy, well, handles. It's also got a selection of locks, switches and sockets that match certain handles. The emphasis is on contemporary style, and there's a good advice section which shows you how to fit them. See also **www.diytools.co.uk** who offer a wide range including security products in their 'knobs and knockers' section.

www.doorsdirect.co.uk UK
DOORS AND HANDLES

Features replacement doors for kitchens and bathrooms, you can order made-to-measure or standard and there's a selection of fittings as well.

www.locksmiths.co.uk UK
FINDING A LOCKSMITH

A useful site where you can get help to find a locksmith in your area and some advice on home security.

Paint and Wallpaper

www.decoratingdirect.co.uk UK
DECORATING MATERIALS

A really well-designed store offering a very wide range of decorating products, it's fast, simple to use and it will save a trip to one of those huge DIY stores, or is it just me that hates them? Check out the refund policy before you buy though.

www.dulux.co.uk UK
DULUX

A good-looking, interesting but slow site from Dulux, with a 'mouse painter' that you can use to redecorate a number of pre-selected rooms; there's also product information, and top tips on painting techniques. You can't buy from the site although there is a list of stockists. Crown has a similar but less interactive site that can be found at **www.crownpaint.co.uk**

www.farrow-ball.co.uk UK
TRADITIONAL PAINT AND PAPER

Excellently designed web site featuring details on how their paint and paper is manufactured – something they obviously take pride in. You can also order from the site or request samples. See also **www.firedearth.com** for more traditional high quality paints, tiles and inspiration.

www.paintquality.co.uk UK

PAINT QUALITY INSTITUTE

A very attractive site from a company that specialises in testing paints. There's information on choosing the right type of paint with decorating tips, a calculator and glossary.

www.sanderson-online.co.uk UK

CLASSIC, CONTEMPORARY AND TRADITIONAL STYLE

Find out about the company, its heritage and what designs they have – new and old. You can also order a brochure and visit the Morris & Co pages where they have all the favourite designs. For more information on William Morris try visiting **www.morrissociety.org**

www.wallpaperdirect.co.uk UK

BUY WALLPAPER

A good store offering a wide range of wallpapers, sampling service, advice and free delivery if you order more than £150 worth.

www.communityrepaint.org.uk UK

REUSING OLD PAINT

Not a great web site but a very useful service. The site highlights a number of schemes across the country that take reusable paint and redistribute it to those who can't afford to buy their own.

www.photo-furnishings.com UK

YOUR PHOTOS ON YOUR FURNISHINGS

Outstanding use of web design to sell a novel service, here they will put your photos onto soft furnishings or wallpapers. You have to apply for prices. See also **www.artmeetsmatter.com** who offer all sorts of products.

Lighting

www.lightsaver.co.uk UK

SAVE ON LIGHTING

With lots of savings and a wide range to choose from this site is worth a visit, it's not the epitome of great web design but it's effective nonetheless. You should also check out www.thelightingsuperstore.co.uk and **www.lighting-direct.co.uk** who both offer good alternatives.

Inspiration, Design and Interiors

www.design-gap.co.uk UK

DESIGNER DIRECTORY
A directory of UK-based designers and manufacturers with some 300 pages to browse through. They are arranged alphabetically by first name or company name as well as by category. The illustrations are excellent.

www.design-online.co.uk UK
NEED A DESIGNER?
Design Online's mission is to put buyers and suppliers in touch with each other and to use the Internet to promote the use of well-designed products and services. You just search for the service you want and a list of suitable suppliers with contact details quickly appears. Could do with some illustrations and examples of the work that they are trying to promote. See also **www.designdirectory.co.uk** which is a listing of design consultants.

See also:
http://myinteriordecorator.com – advice from a professional interior designer with good articles. The links are to American stores, unfortunately.
www.bbc.co.uk/homes – loads of inspiration here, the period style guides are particularly helpful.
www.bida.org – home of the British Interior Design Association.
www.tribu-design.com/en – an encyclopaedia of 20th century design and decorative arts.

www.bhglive.com UK
BETTER HOMES AND GARDENS
There's more to this than DIY, but superb graphics and videos give this site the edge. There's lots of help on design and decorating and the encyclopaedia under 'home improvement' is excellent. It's American, so some information isn't applicable to the UK.

www.fengshuitips.co.uk   UK
>   FENG SHUI YOUR HOME
>   Understand the natural forces and apply these tips to enhance
>   and attract good health, wealth and happiness . . . though
>   they don't tell you how to stop the family leaving their
>   shoes by the door! If you want to buy some accessories
>   **www.fengshuiweb.co.uk** has a selection of fountains, crystals
>   and other such items.

Stores for Design

www.habitat.net   UK
>   HABITAT STORES
>   An information-only site with lots of details on their product
>   range. It's all wrapped up in a funky design, which is a little jerky
>   with a normal modem and needs the latest version of Flash to
>   work. You can't order online although you can check store
>   availability. See also the US store **www.crateandbarrel.com**
>   who offer similar products but shipping is very expensive.

www.ikea.com   UK

>   IKEA STYLE
>   You can't buy from the site but you can check whether a store
>   has the item you want to buy in stock before you go (it would be
>   great if more stores did this). Otherwise the site is more the usual
>   store fare with plenty of ideas, articles and product lists.

>   *See also:*
>   **http://sawitfirst.co.uk** – excellent shop featuring contemporary
>   designer furniture and home accessories.
>   **www.afternoah.com** – great for the unusual and the eclectic.
>   **www.bluedeco.com** – a selection of designer products for the
>   home, from furniture to ceramics, with free delivery to the UK.
>   Unfortunately, returns have to go to Luxembourg.
>   **www.interiorinternet.co.uk** – a well-illustrated and unusual
>   selection of designer furniture.
>   **www.maelstrom.co.uk** – a wide selection of contemporary gifts,
>   accessories, gadgets and furniture on a good-looking site.
>   **www.next.co.uk** – a good selection of Next homeware as well as
>   the usual products on a fairly impractical site.
>   **www.oceanuk.com** – a wide range and some good prices too.
>   **www.pier.co.uk** – a very good offering from the Pier. Eclectic and
>   always interesting, there's a wide range to choose from.

www.pussyhomeboutique.co.uk – an eccentric and slightly kitsch range of products, furniture, home accessories and wall panels.

Soft Furnishing

www.simplyfurnishings.com   UK

SOFT FURNISHING
All you need to know about making and buying soft furnishing with plenty of advice for all levels and a good store directory.

See also:
www.clarissahulse.com – gorgeous leafy designs on soft furnishings, and wall paper too.
www.crowsonfabrics.com – nice products but no online ordering.
www.monkwell.com – beautiful ranges but you can't buy online.

Furniture

www.mfi.co.uk   UK
MFI HOMEWORKS
MFI offer a nicely designed site with all the best aspects of online shopping and a wide range of surprisingly good furniture for home and office available for order online or via a hotline. Delivery is included in the price.

www.furniture123.co.uk   UK
SMART PLACE TO BUY FURNITURE
This company has a well laid out web site offering a good range of furniture, many offers, tips and free delivery.

www.heals.co.uk   UK
STYLISH CONTEMPORARY DESIGN
Heals has a beautifully designed web site which gives information about the store and inspiration for the home. There's an online store which stocks primarily gifts and home accessories, but there's a special services section where you can get information on furniture and interior design.

www.conran.com   UK
TERENCE CONRAN STYLE
As well as information on all his restaurants, this site has an online shopping facility that allows you to buy Conran-designed

accessories as well as stuff for the home including a good range of furniture and kitchen products.

www.ancestralcollections.co.uk UK
REPRODUCTIONS FROM THE BEST HOMES
A web site that has developed well with a wide range of high quality beds and furniture on an attractive site with good pictures and descriptions of the products. They've expanded into gifts too and offer good value for money.

Other furniture retailers and sites that may be worth a virtual visit are:
www.bfm.org.uk – a useful directory of British furniture makers.
www.connectedlines.com/styleguide – a basic guide to furniture styles.
www.davidlinley.com – posh contemporary classics.
www.furniturebusters.com – a wide range and masses of offers too.
www.mufti.co.uk – more posh, beautifully designed furniture.
www.new-heights.co.uk – simple, stylish solid wood.
www.pinesolutions.co.uk – a very well-designed furniture store, they also sell sofas and oak furniture.
www.sofaweb.co.uk – good value sofa and sofa bed shop.
www.sofaworkshopdirect.co.uk – well designed with quality photos of the sofas and what looks like a good online service.
www.thebedshed.net – the jaw-droppingly bad jingle has now gone, leaving a decent product range and store directory.
www.twelvelimited.com – beautiful recycled furniture and home accessories.

TV and Celebrity Designers

www.llb.co.uk UK
LAURENCE LLEWELYN-BOWEN
Join the fan club, view Laurence's designs from greeting cards to cutlery to wallpaper, then find out how to buy them. There's lots here, even competitions. See also **www.bbc.co.uk/homes** with lots of ideas and helpful hints, in particular, go to 'Changing Rooms' which has top tips, articles and biographies.

www.ukstyle.tv/homesandproperty UK
UK STYLE TV
A bright and breezy site packed with ideas from the TV shows and features on the various projects and aspects of the home.

There's an 'ask the expert' section and a guide full of practical ideas and tips too.

www.channel4.com/4homes   UK
GRAND DESIGNERS
Nicely designed site from Channel 4, with helpful guides and an excellent style section. Help and advice is on hand from their resident guru.

Miscellaneous

www.howtocleananything.com   CANADA
STAIN REMOVAL PAR EXCELLENCE
A group of cleaners have got together to produce a site that contains over 1,000 cleaning tips for outside or inside the house or the car – except for curry!

www.thistothat.com   US
GLUE
A site that helps you work out which is the right glue to use. Just input the two things you want to glue together and the site makes a recommendation . . . what could be easier! For more sticky info see **www.diystickit.co.uk** produced by a glue manufacturer, with advice on which glues to use to solve problems.

Humour

The Internet has become home to an amazing array of funny sites. Here's just a few of the best. You should be aware that most aren't suitable for children.

Jokes, Links and Directories

www.comedy-zone.net   UK

COMPLETE COMEDY GUIDE
Excellent and wide-ranging comedy site with lots of links and competitions, alongside quotes, jokes and chat.

For other comedy portals and loads of jokes go to:
http://uk.dir.yahoo.com/entertainment/humour – Yahoo's excellent listing devoted to humour and bizarre sites.

Funny, Adult and Entertaining

The Good Web Site Guide's Top 10s
of the Internet

1. **www.snopes2.com** – urban legends, all true of course
2. **www.comedy-zone.net** – the place to start, loadsalinks
3. **www.b3ta.com** – great for the gross
4. **www.joecartoon.com** – freaky entertainment
5. **www.emotioneric.com** – pick an emotion and Eric will act it for you
6. **www.theonion.com** – irony from the USA
7. **www.funnymail.com** – more jokes than you can shake a stick at
8. **www.boreme.com** – viral and adult entertainment
9. **www.davesdaily.com** – unusual stories from around the world
10. **www.engrish.com** – excellent selection of Asian English

www.bored.com – a great directory of humour sites.
www.funnybone.com – huge database with lots of rude jokes.
www.funnymail.com – lots of jokes and well categorised with good features such as tests, top 10 jokes of all time, newest jokes and so on.
www.humorlinks.com – massive portal for all things funny.
www.humournet.co.uk – categorised jokes, links and funny pictures.
www.jokecenter.com – hundreds of jokes, vote for your favourites.
www.jokepost.com – hundreds, all well categorised.
www.jokes2000.com – e-mail you the latest jokes.
www.jokes.com – typical jokes directory but these are rated, tame, racy etc . . .
www.kidsjokes.co.uk – 12,000+ jokes, great for the family.
www.weirdwebbed.com – a directory of the weirdest web sites.

www.uebersetzung.at/twister   AUSTRIA
TONGUE TWISTERS
An international collection of tongue twisters, over 2,000 in 107 languages when we last visited, nearly 400 in English – 'Can you can a can as a canner can can a can?' as they say.

Multi-media

www.funny-downloads.com
US

THE BEST IN MULTI-MEDIA HUMOUR
What used to be Olley's Place has transformed into a subscription-only site costing $15 for lifetime membership. For that you get access to a superb selection of funny video clips and comedy downloads, there is some free content though and you should be aware that most of it is adult oriented.

Other sites offering video clips, viral e-mails and generally daft adult-oriented entertainment:
http://uk.news.yahoo.com/promo/office/index.html – Yahoo's excellent Office Attachments page.
www.b3ta.com – a particularly silly and very popular e-zine.
www.boreme.com – excellent collection of video clips.
www.britpod.com – alternative talk radio, available as podcasts.
www.cyberparodies.com – a mixed bag of song parodies.
www.ebaumsworld.com – good but a pain to use.
www.gagreport.com – a messy site with a huge collection of humorous videos and jokes.
www.jengajam.com – a daily listing of photos, games, trivia and videos.
www.sofunnyjoke.com – more funny videos and pictures.

Stand-up Comedy

www.chortle.co.uk
UK

GUIDE TO LIVE COMEDY IN THE UK
Chortle provides a complete service, listing who's on, where and when – also whether they're any good or not. There's also a comic's A–Z so that you can find your favourites and get reviews on how they're performing, or not, as the case may be. See also **www.jongleurs.co.uk** whose entertaining site has audio clips and details of what's on and when at their clubs.

Comedy Magazine and Satirical Sites

www.theonion.com
US

AMERICA'S FINEST NEWS SOURCE
A great send-up of American tabloid newspapers, this is one of the most visited sites on the Internet and easily one of the funniest. See also **www.thespoof.com** a great spoof news site.

www.private-eye.co.uk   UK
PRIVATE EYE

A pretty average effort really considering the wealth of material that must be available, there are a few of the best cartoons and features, but it's only updated every couple of weeks or so.

www.freakingnews.com   US
PHOTOSHOP CONTESTS

Playing with Photoshop to make new pictures is the hobby of many, but here you can enter your masterpiece of deception in competitions.

www.whitehouse.org   US
THE WHITE HOUSE

A great micky-take on the US presidency, very clever and vicious too. **www.deadbrain.co.uk** has a similar feel and approach but is mocking British politicians and celebs.

www.punch.co.uk   UK
PUNCH MAGAZINE

A new look and more commercial approach from *Punch* with plenty of cartoons and some of the best of *Punch* available to browse and buy.

www.viz.co.uk   UK
NOT FOR CHILDREN

A very good reflection of what you get in the real thing with lots of games and downloads, you can even contribute to Roger's Profanisaurus.

http://community.sparknotes.com/sparktests/index.epl   US
TAKE THE SPARK TESTS

The Spark is actually a spin-off from the Spark notes revision guides. Its best feature, and the reason why millions visit, is the tests. From the popular personality test, through bitch and bastard tests to the wealth test, all are good for a laugh and, of course, very accurate. Dare you take the 'death test' or the 'unintelligence test' though?

www.bizarremag.com   US
BIZARRE MAGAZINE

The magazine is devoted to 'life in the extreme' and the site reflects this with a selection of pictures and stories. It's all geared to getting you to subscribe. Be aware that the content is adult oriented.

www.nicecupofteaandasitdown.com UK
TAKE A BREAK
Put your feet up and while away some time here, review your
favourite biscuit or not . . . take your time . . . make tea. . . . lovely.

TV Comedy

www.bbc.co.uk/comedy UK
BBC COMEDY
An outstanding site with a comedy guide and lots to see and do.
There are features on each major programme and even a
comedy blog, also links to associated sites, clips to watch and
radio features to download.

www.comedycentral.com US
THE HOME OF SOUTH PARK AND MORE
Great for South Park and selected American TV shows, but also
with clips and background information and stand-up comedy too.

www.thesimpsons.com US
HOME OF THE SIMPSONS
The official site with biographies, background, quizzes and
more, plus the ever-present merchandise store. If you are a real
fan then go to the Simpsons archive at **www.snpp.com**

See also:
www.britishcomedy.org.uk – a poor site but good background
on some classic radio comedy.
www.britishcomedyhelpdesk.moonfruit.com – any questions
about British and TV comedy, ask the helpdesk . . .
www.guardian.co.uk/rickygervais – download all the highly
successful podcasts.
www.phill.co.uk – a comprehensive directory of TV comedy.
www.rickygervais.com – home site of the popular comedian.

Urban Legends, the Unlikely and the Unloved

www.snopes2.com US
URBAN LEGENDS
An outstanding collection of all those stories and myths that have
that edge of unlikely truth about them. Well categorised and with
a good search facility, it's easy to find your favourites. See also
www.thisistrue.com which is full of unlikely but true stories.

www.darwinawards.com   US
FATAL MISADVENTURES
The Darwin Awards have been going several years now and their
site is packed with stories, urban legends and personal accounts
of those who have 'improved our gene pool by removing
themselves from it in really stupid ways'.

www.halfbakery.com   US
INVENTIONS OR NOT
A fun catalogue of useless inventions and ideas, some real, most
not; it's very silly really and it's a shame that there are not more
illustrations.

www.craptowns.com   UK
OUR CRAP TOWNS
The site that spawned a best-selling book. Here's an eclectic
collection of towns in the UK and US that have been awarded the
status of being crap, most for no apparent reason. Irreverent and
pretty funny, there are some very angry people out there.

www.iusedtobelieve.com   US
CHILDHOOD BELIEFS
A catalogue of childhood misconceptions and beliefs, you can
rate them and even add your own. It's the sort of site that makes
you smile and you can't help joining in.

www.museumofhoaxes.com   UK
HOAXES
The world's greatest hoaxes and April Fools are catalogued here.
It makes entertaining browsing and is sometimes unbelievable.

Cartoons

www.bcdb.com   US
THE BIG CARTOON DATABASE
A catalogue covering all the major producers of cartoons, the
main characters and of course the cartoon series themselves. It
has an American bias but it's pretty comprehensive and you can
rate your favourites too.

www.weebls-stuff.com   UK
WEEBLS
An award-winning site and one of our favourites. It's home to the
Weebl and Bob cartoons as well as many other cartoons and

includes the unforgettable tune that is 'Everyone loves Magical Trevor'.

www.joecartoon.com   US
FREAKY CARTOONS
Follow the gruesome, messy adventures of Joe, download the cartoons and send them to your friends and buy the T-shirt – he's a legend after all. Superb animation and very funny, but you need patience for the downloads.

www.emilystrange.com   US
ENTER THE WORLD OF EMILY STRANGE
Another animated site with outstanding illustrations that's worth a visit just to look at the design, if nothing else. Emily is a popular icon with teenagers and here you can participate in her freaky adventures.

See also:
www.cartoonbank.com – outstanding New Yorker cartoons for sale in various formats and guises.
www.cartoonstock.com – a database of over 70,000 cartoons.
www.howstrange.com – the wonders of what can be done with Photoshop.
www.marsdencartoons.com/directory.htm – a comprehensive directory of cartoonists with links.
www.nonstick.com – home of Warner Brothers cartoons with some available to download, plus links and background information on those involved.
www.tomandjerryonline.com – all you need to know about the awesome Tom & Jerry.
www.unitedmedia.com/comics/peanuts – home of Charlie Brown and Peanuts.

www.super-jam.com   UK
YOU BE THE DANCING QUEEN . . .
Pick a digital photo of yourself or your friend, crop and download, pick a body and start dancin' . . .

Miscellaneous and Just Weird

www.strangereports.com   US
PRANKS ONLINE
Play pranks on your friends using the service available here, with trick web sites and fake news reports it's almost irresistible, but

beware their revenge . . . See also **www.computerpranks.com**
and also **www.prank.org** both of which contain classics.

http://officeolympics.net   US
THE OFFICE OLYMPICS
OK so it's a slow day at the office, you've got nothing to do, well
you could follow the example set here and set up your own Office
Olympics . . . with events such as cubicle hurdles and chair hop,
you can't go wrong. See also **www.bullshitbingo.co.uk** where
you can create your own bingo cards featuring the latest office
slang and buzzwords.

www.freakydreams.com   US
DREAM INTERPRETED
You just type in the description of your dream and an 'accurate'
interpretation pops up in seconds.

www.staregame.com   US
HE WHO BLINKS . . .
Pick your character, press play and the first to blink loses . . .

www.20q.net   US
TWENTY QUESTIONS
Pick something and the site will guess what it is within twenty
questions, it's amazingly accurate and very time consuming as
you try to beat it without cheating.

www.user-error.co.uk   UK
EXCUSE GENERATOR
Apart from the excellent excuse generator which is very handy,
there's also a virtual makeover section, articles on the unusual
universe we live in and, if you're in a disagreement with
someone over some fact or other, they'll help you settle your bet.

www.smalltime.com/dictator   UK
GUESS THE DICTATOR
You think of a dictator or TV sit-com character, answer the
questions put to you and the site will guess who you are thinking
of . . . it's spookily accurate.

www.optillusions.com   US
OPTICAL ILLUSIONS
A good selection of optical illusions to download, plus links to
other similar and funny sites. The visit is completely spoiled by

the large amount of adverts both pop-ups and banners. See also
www.grand-illusions.com

www.emotioneric.com   US
EMOTIONAL ERIC
A cult site in the US. Eric will act out any emotion in any
situation, you just have to place your request.

www.snapbubbles.com   US
VIRTUAL BUBBLE WRAP
How comforting, when you have the urge to pop and there's
no bubble wrap to hand, just come here for the nearest
substitute.

www.engrish.com   US
MISTAKEN ENGLISH
This site started off as a list of humorous mistakes that the
Japanese made with English; it's now expanded slightly to take
in other cultures and it's very funny. See also **www.rahoi.com/
2006/03/may-i-take-your-order.php**

www.thetoastshop.co.uk   UK
IT'S ALL ABOUT TOAST
One of the best fake commercial web sites lovingly put together.
See also **http://isolatr.com/** and **www.petroldirect.com**

www.pickthehottie.com   US
PICK THE HOTTIE!
Probably the best of many sites where people post photos of
themselves and their friends (or enemies) the idea being that you
vote for the hottest-looking people and the ugliest too.

*While we're on the subject of the unattractive, check out these
sites listed below . . .*
www.badfads.com – home of the Bad Fads Museum, fashion
victims galore.
www.mulletmadness.com – in celebration of the haircut and
culture.
www.mulletsgalore.com – more mullets!
www.uglydress.com – Bridesmaids' dresses from hell, dare you
to look at this without putting your hand over your mouth.
www.uglyfootballers.com – yes we well remember them . . .

Internet Service Provision

There are so many Internet Service Providers (ISPs) that it would be impossible to review them all and it's moving so fast that any information soon becomes outdated. However, help is at hand and here are some sites that will help you chose the right one for you.

www.net4nowt.com   UK

THE PLACE TO START LOOKING FOR THE BEST ISP
This is a directory of Internet service providers offering news and advice on the best ones. There is an up-to-date critique on each ISP with comments on costs and reliability. There is also a good summary table featuring all the ISPs, which proves useful for comparisons.

www.ispreview.co.uk   UK

INTERNET NEWS
Find out what's really going on at this impressive site – they are especially good at exposing the worst performers. There's plenty in the way of news, offers and a top 10 ISP list.

See also:
www.cisas.org.uk – home of the Communications and Internet Services Adjudication Scheme, which aims to solve disputes between ISPs and customers.
www.ispa.org.uk – Internet Service Providers Association with an informative site.
www.thelist.com – the ISP providers guide from the US.

Jobs and Careers

There are several hundred sites offering jobs or careers advice but it's largely a matter of luck if you come across a job you like. Still, it enables you to cover plenty of ground in a short space of time without trawling the newspapers. These sites offer the most options and best advice.

Career Guidance

www.careers-portal.co.uk   UK
AWARD-WINNING CAREERS SERVICE
An excellent portal site that is part of the National Grid for Learning, with lots of advice on universities, jobs and how to

apply. There's a very useful careers directory and it's all geared to helping you choose the right career. However, it also involves buying their guides.

www.careers-gateway.co.uk   UK
THE CAREERS GATEWAY

Great advice and lots of information, for example, how to launch a proper career, evaluate your options and read articles to help you decide what you can do with your life. There's a virtual career show, quizzes designed to help and advice for HR professionals too.

www.reachforthesky.co.uk   UK
CAREERS ADVICE FROM SKY TV

Sky has put together a great web site that doesn't just look good. However, it's developed into more of a teen magazine, but there is a good deal of advice here plus some fun too.
www.connexions-direct.com is another useful resource for young people.

www.careersolutions.co.uk   UK
HELP TO GO FORWARD

A good place to start if you're not sure what you want to do next with your career, don't know where to start or you've been made redundant. Using the site enables you to narrow your options and clarify things. The list of links is logically laid out and very helpful.

Job Finders

www.transdata-inter.co.uk/jobs-agencies   UK
DIRECTORY OF JOB SITES

Don't let the long URL put you off, this is an excellent place to start on your search. The Directory lists all the major online employment agencies and ranks them by the average number of vacancies, the regions they cover, whether they help create and store CVs and what industries they represent. Clicking on the name takes you right to the site you need.

www.jobs.co.uk   UK
JOB SEARCH ENGINE

With this facility you can search all the major job sites in one go, it's easy to use and quite accurate providing you have a defined job title. They also offer all the usual features such as CV help and advice. See also **www.jobsearch.co.uk** with over 30,000 jobs on offer.

www.gisajob.co.uk
UK

SEARCH FOR YOUR NEXT JOB HERE

The largest of the UK online job sites with over 28,000 vacancies. You can search by description or sector or get advice on your career. It's good for non-senior executive types.

www.workthing.com
UK

IT'S A WORK THING

One of the best-looking job sites with a reputation to match, this site must be one of the first to visit when job hunting across a wide range of industries. Registered users can set up an e-mail alert when a job matching their search criteria appears. There is also help for businesses trying to improve their people skills and recruitment. There is also advice on training and personal development too.

www.monster.co.uk
UK

GLOBAL JOBS

With thousands of jobs available in 26 countries, there are plenty to choose from. The site is well designed and easy to use with the usual help features. At the time of writing there were over 44,000 UK jobs listed in over 20 categories.

www.stepstone.co.uk
UK

EUROPEAN INTERNET RECRUITMENT

Regarded as one of the best, Stepstone has a huge number of European and international vacancies. It's quick, easy to use and offers lots of time-saving cross-referencing features. You can also register your CV. For other overseas jobs see **www.overseasjobs.com**

Other job finder and career sites worth checking out:
www.deskdemon.com – jobs and resources for secretarial and support staff.
www.doctorjob.com – graduates only need apply.
www.fish4.co.uk/iad/jobs – part of the excellent Fish4 suite of sites, here you'll find plenty of jobs from several major agencies and big recruiters.
www.jobserve.co.uk – a well-categorised job search engine covering the major industries, good design.

www.jobsite.co.uk – award winning site listing some 40,000 jobs; offers some good career advice too.

www.reed.co.uk – some 260,000 vacancies from a wide range of categories.

www.thegumtree.com – jobs in London.

www.totaljobs.co.uk – 96,000 jobs listed in a wide range of sectors.

These government-run sites might also be useful:

http://jobseekers.direct.gov.uk formally **www.worktrain.gov.uk** – it's all here – jobs, training and voluntary work.

www.aimhigher.gov.uk – how to get the qualifications to get the job you really want.

www.apprenticeships.org.uk – find out about how to start off with an apprenticeship.

www.dfes.gov.uk – the Dept of Education has lots of helpful advice.

www.jobcentreplus.gov.uk – information about job centres and how to go about finding a job.

www.tiger.gov.uk – the government's guide to employment law.

www.volunteering.org.uk – volunteer for something, it looks good on the CV.

Other Careers and Related Sites

www.i-resign.com/uk   UK
THE INS AND OUTS OF RESIGNATION

Pay a visit before you send the letter, it offers a great deal of advice both legal and sensible. The best section contains the funniest selection of resignation letters anywhere. There are also jobs on offer, links to job finder sites and a career guide service. For a helpful site on employment law go to **www.emplaw.co.uk** which does a thorough job.

www.homeworking.com   UK
WORKING FROM HOME

A site full of advice and information for anyone considering or actually working from home. There are links and directories as well as forum pages where you can share experiences with other home workers. For more advice on home working try **www.startups.co.uk/aERh62A.html**

www.eoc.org.uk   UK
　　EQUAL OPPORTUNITIES COMMISSION
　　A very informative site and it's where to go if you think you are
　　being discriminated against.

www.adastra-cm.com   UK
　　CAREERS ADVICE
　　An excellent site from a career management consultancy with
　　some really sound careers advice within their newsletters, which
　　is written in a very accessible style.

www.alec.co.uk   UK
　　CV WRITING
　　A site that charges for advice on how to prepare yourself for
　　interviews and how to write and use your CV, see also
　　www.cvspecial.co.uk, **www.cvtips.com**,
　　www.bradleycvs.co.uk and **www.ineedacv.co.uk**

Online Practise Tests

www.queendom.com   UK
　　SERIOUSLY ENTERTAINING
　　Apart from the fun tests there's a serious side to this site that
　　allows you to take the sort of tests you're likely to face when
　　applying for a job. See also **www.emode.com**

Language: Learning and Translation

*In this new section you'll find a selection of sites that will help you learn
a language, whether it's in depth or for a short trip. There's also help if
you just want some text translated.*

www.ilovelanguages.com   US
　　LANGUAGE LINKS
　　A directory of language-learning sites; it's US oriented but a good
　　place to start. The list is pretty comprehensive, featuring some
　　2,000 sites.

www.bbc.co.uk/languages   UK
　　LEARN WITH THE BBC
　　Featuring the BBC's extensive list of language courses, it covers
　　all the major European languages plus Chinese and Japanese.

There are lots of features and the site is well integrated with the books and TV programmes.

See also:
www.csulb.edu/~txie/online.htm – the place to start if you want to learn Chinese.
www.elanguage.com – language-learning software to buy.
www.ethnologue.com – excellent resource regarding the history of the 6,900 known languages of the world.
www.eurocosm.com – excellent free resources for the major European languages and cultures.
www.ielanguages.com – basic tutorials for nine European languages.
www.indianlanguages.com – a good introduction to Indian languages.
www.languageguide.org – tries to pull together language resources using volunteers; it is a bit of a mess but you may find something useful.
www.learn-japanese.info – basic course in Japanese for English speakers.
www.linguascope.com – interactive language-learning resources, unfortunately not free.
www.nationalarchives.gov.uk/latin/beginners – a guide to Latin for beginners.
www.parlo.com – learn about the culture as well as the language; again fee-paying courses.
www.usingenglish.com – excellent range of resources for English as a second language for students and teachers.

Translation Services

Listed below are a few sites that are helpful if you just want to translate a short piece of text.

http://babelfish.altavista.com/tr – one of the originals, easy to use and good for the major European and Far Eastern languages.
http://dictionaries.travlang.com – some 35 language dictionaries to choose from.
www.foreignword.com – lots of links and dictionaries, good for the less widely used languages.
www.freetranslation.com – very good for short phrases, also offers professional services.

www.langtolang.com – more links, services, e-books and software to download.

www.smartphrase.com – a helpful online phrase book.

Sign Language

Not all language can be heard . . .

www.british-sign.co.uk – a sign dictionary, help and discussion forums.

www.britishsignlanguage.com – a visual dictionary.

www.handspeak.com – good site on international sign language.

www.learnbsl.org – excellent and well-designed virtual guide to British Sign Language.

Legal Advice and the Law

We all need help with certain key events in life: marriages, moving house, making a will or getting a divorce. Maybe you need advice on lesser issues like boundary disputes or problems with services or property? Here are several good sites that could really make a difference. There's more on divorce and separation in the section on problem relationships, page 384.

www.advicenow.org.uk   UK

INDEPENDENT LAW AND RIGHTS ADVICE
A great site designed to keep up with and explain the law in layman's terms. It's well designed and information is easy to find; it also offers links to the relevant site if required. Excellent.

www.compactlaw.co.uk   UK

LEGAL INFORMATION FOR ENGLAND AND WALES
An extremely informative and useful site that covers many aspects of the law in a clear and concise style, there are usable documents – you can download some free, others to buy, case histories, news, tips and plenty of fact-sheets.

www.uklegal.com   UK

LEGAL RESOURCES AT YOUR FINGERTIPS
This site offers a superb selection of links to everything from private investigators to barristers to legal equipment suppliers.

www.family-solicitors.co.uk   UK

FAMILY LAW REFERENCE

Excellent resource for everyday legal issues covering everything
from wills to neighbourhood disputes. Great for links too with an
excellent search facility for finding a family law solicitor near you.
See also **www.solicitors-online.com** for the Law Society's advice
on lawyers. Another site that will help you find a lawyer is the
well-put-together **www.lawyerlocator.co.uk**

www.desktoplawyer.net   UK

THE UK'S FIRST ONLINE LAWYER

This site is quite straightforward if you know what you need and
have read through the instructions carefully. First you register,
then download the software (Rapidocs) enabling you to compile
the document you need. The legal documents you create will
cost from £2.99 upwards depending on complexity. The range of
documents available is huge and there are more being added.

www.legalservices.gov.uk   UK

GOVERNMENT ADVICE

The replacement for legal aid, this is the official line on legal
matters with guidance on how to access legal assistance, where
to get information and news on latest changes to the Community
Legal Service and Criminal Defence Service. It could be a lot
more user friendly. For Scottish legal aid go to **www.slab.org.uk**

See also:

http://library.kent.ac.uk/library/lawlinks/gateways.htm – a
useful portal containing categorised links.

http://nchacti01.uuhost.uk.uu.net/carelaw – an explanatory
law site aimed at young people.

www.childrenslegalcentre.com – accessible site on how the
law works for young people and how to protect their rights.

www.clsdirect.org.uk – free legal advice from the Community
Legal Service.

www.courtservice.gov.uk – information on how the court
service works.

www.divorce-online.co.uk – fast-track divorces and good advice.

www.eisil.org – an amazing resource covering aspects of
international law, everything from the charter of the UN to laws
governing the recovery of astronauts from international waters!

www.emplaw.co.uk – the low-down on British employment law.

www.findlaw.com – an American law portal.

www.freelawyer.co.uk – a London-based legal services shop.

www.infolaw.co.uk – a legal document search engine.
www.lawassure.co.uk – subscribe to excellent personal legal advice and related services.
www.lawpack.co.uk – legal book specialist.
www.lawscot.org.uk – the Law Society of Scotland.
www.lawsociety.org.uk – the Law Society of England and Wales.
www.lawsoc-ni.org – the Law Society of Northern Ireland.
www.legalpulse.com – well-designed site along the lines of Desktop Lawyer although not as comprehensive.
www.legalshop.co.uk – affordable solutions to your legal problems; a good site, with a business section too.
www.multikulti.org.uk – legal documents and other helpful information for new citizens and minorities available in many languages.
www.officer.com – site for American law enforcement officers; some interesting reading.
www.oldbaileyonline.org – interesting site offering up the proceedings of the Old Bailey from 1674 to 1834.
www.sweetandmaxwell.co.uk – specialist legal publisher.

www.dumblaws.com

US

THE DAFTEST, STUPIDEST LAWS

Did you realise that in England placing a postage stamp that bears the Queen's head upside down is considered treasonable, or that in Kentucky it's illegal to fish with a bow and arrow? These are just a couple of the many dumb laws that you can find on this very entertaining site. It's now been expanded to include dumbest criminals, dumbest warnings and place names.

Linux

Linux is a free operating system that competes with Windows; it has a reputation for stability and is gaining popularity. Here are some informative sites to help you.

www.linuxlinks.com

US

LINUX DIRECTORY

A Yahoo style directory with over 32,000 links, forums and articles. It's well categorised and a good place to start.

See also:
http://beginnerslinux.org – a personal guide for beginners.
www.linux.com – authoritative site with good tutorials.

www.linux.org – a Linux community site, good once you've learnt a bit.

www.redhat.com – a company with its own version of Linux, lots of support.

Magazines and Subscriptions

Where to buy and subscribe to your favourite magazines, see also our News section, page 353.

www.newsstand.co.uk   UK

A GIFT THAT LASTS ALL YEAR

A wide range of titles that are available by subscription, on a well categorised site. It has a strong British bias, a pity there are not more overseas and foreign language magazines available.

www.zinio.com   US

DIGITAL MAGAZINES

You have to download the bespoke viewer and subscribe, but here are a large selection of magazines for you to read on your PC – UK editions of some magazines now available. The quality is good and it allows you to turn the pages realistically; however, it's best viewed on a wide-screen PC.

See also:

www.actualidad.com – newspapers of the world and links to their sites.

www.magazinecity.com – large selection of subscriptions, you pay in dollars.

www.magazinesubscriptions.com – subscriptions from one of the biggest magazine publishers IPC.

www.subscription.co.uk – a good range of UK magazine subscriptions.

www.whsmith.co.uk – some good offers on subscriptions which are available to UK addresses only.

Men

Here are a few sites especially for blokes, lads and real men. For more information on fatherhood, check out the section on Parenting, page 362.

Aimed at Men

The Good Web Site Guide's Top 10s
of the Internet

1. **www.sharpman.com** – odd but essential advice on staying sharp
2. **www.menshealth.co.uk** – excellent magazine site
3. **www.firebox.com** – the place to find 'boys toys'
4. **www.fathersdirect.com** – advice and support
5. **www.kiniki.com** – the best underwear
6. **www.clareflorist.co.uk** – because you're bound to need a florist at some stage
7. **www.realbeer.com** – 150,000 pages devoted to beer...perfect
8. **www.hard2buy4.co.uk** – when you need help buying a gift
9. **www.askmen.com** – a great e-zine full of information
10. **www.blokesonly.co.uk** – a shopping sanctuary

Magazine Sites

www.fhm.co.uk
UK

FHM MAGAZINE

A good reflection of the real thing, with sections on everything from serious news to the lighter side, with the usual blokey features, it suffers from lots of advertising though.

www.gqmagazine.co.uk
UK

GENTLEMEN'S QUARTERLY

A stylish site, which gives a flavour of the real magazine, it contains a few stories, competitions, fashion tips and the odd feature.

www.sharpman.com
UK

SHARP!

While a little odd, it's good fun and there's some useful advice. Split into seven key sections: dating, with tips on conversation and repartee; toys, from fitness gadgets to snowboards; work, getting the best out of the Internet; travel, staying sharp abroad; grooming, looking the part; toys – the best advice on windsurfing; tips (a new section), a motley selection of articles on how to make yourself even sharper.

See also:
http://theladsmag.co.uk – reviews from all the best men's magazines; slow site.
www.askmen.com – a very good American men's magazine covering almost every topic you're likely to need.
www.dullmen.com – the dullest web site from the National Council for Dull Men, very funny too.
www.modernman.com – nicely designed men's magazine site from the US with loads of interesting articles and features.
www.nutz.co.uk – a portal site featuring men's interests; some adult content.

Health

www.menshealth.co.uk   UK

MEN'S HEALTH MAGAZINE
Lots of advice on keeping fit, healthy and fashionable too. There's also an excellent section on the number one topic – sex, plus others on wealth, health, sport and a shop that sells subscriptions and recommends the latest gear.

www.menshealthforum.org.uk   UK
STOP MOANING!
An excellent all-rounder revealing the truth behind the state of men's health and lots of discussion about specific and general health issues facing men today – good for links too.

Other men's health sites:
www.dipex.org – excellent cancer help site.
www.orchid-cancer.org.uk – promotes the awareness of testicular and prostate cancer.
www.sda.uk.net – The Sexual Dysfunction Association.
www.vasectomy-clinic.co.uk – no-scalpel vasectomy – honest!

Fatherhood

www.fathersdirect.com   UK
A MAGAZINE FOR FATHERS
Once an e-zine written by fathers for fathers, this domain has been taken over by the National Information Centre on Fatherhood. It's loaded with advice and support for dads trying to fit in both work and kids. There's information on policy and practice as well as on issues such as parenting, domestic

violence, child protection, young offenders and separated families, with special sections for African Caribbean and Muslim fathers.

www.fathers-4-justice.org UK
FIGHTING FOR ABSENT FATHERS' RIGHTS
Learn more about their well-publicised campaign for truth, justice and equality in family law. Here you can join the movement, find out about forthcoming events and buy the T-shirt.

See also:
www.coeffic.demon.co.uk – father's rights and other male discrimination issues on a word-heavy but consequently informative site.
www.fathers.com – an American magazine-style approach to fatherhood.
www.fnf.org.uk – Families Need Fathers campaigning for the child's right to access two parents.
www.parents4protest.co.uk – ugly but useful with lots of sad stories, anger and frustration. Great links.

Shopping

www.firebox.com UK
WHERE MEN BUY STUFF
An online shop aimed totally at boy's toys, with its own bachelor pad containing all you need for the lifestyle. There are masses of games, videos, toys and, of course, the latest gadgets. Delivery costs vary. See also **www.big-boys-toys.net** and **www.boysstuff.co.uk** both of which are worth a visit if you can't find what you want at Firebox. If you want to be the first and the one with the most talked about gadgets then go to **www.coolest-gadgets.com**

www.mankindonline.co.uk UK
MALE GROOMING
An above-average shop devoted to male grooming products and gifts, it also offers advice on things like skincare and has a newsletter you can subscribe to. Delivery is free on orders over £60 but otherwise it's £3.50 for the UK. See also **www.maleorder.co.uk**

www.condomsdirect.co.uk   UK
> CONDOMS UK
> Many different types of condoms are available to buy, and you
> get free delivery if you spend more than £10 – there's even a
> price promise and the assurance of a fast and discreet service.
> It's also worth checking out **www.condomania.com**

Motorcycles

www.bmf.co.uk   UK
> BRITISH MOTORCYCLISTS FEDERATION
> At this site you can join the BMF, get involved with their activities
> or just use the site for information. You can also get club
> information and e-mail them on any issues. For the international
> governing body go to **www.fim.ch/en**

www.motorcycle.co.uk   UK
> THE UK'S MOTORCYCLE DIRECTORY
> Essentially a list of links by brand, dealer, importer, classics,
> gear, books and auctions. **www.moto-directory.com** is a similar
> American site with listings in 24 categories.

www.motorworld.com   US
> ALL YOU NEED TO KNOW ABOUT MOTORCYCLES
> Good coverage of both machines and events with multimedia
> features. Although the site is American there's good British
> coverage.

www.fowlers.co.uk   UK
> WHERE TO GET YOUR GEAR
> A smart looking site housing a good shop and information
> dedicated to motorcycles, clothing and accessories – they
> seem intent on providing good customer service too. Also worth
> a visit is **www.customlids.co.uk** who offer a wide range of
> clothing.

> *See also:*
> **www.autotrader.co.uk/BIKES/bikes.jsp** – a section of *Auto
> Trader* magazine, Bike Trader has a huge number of bikes for
> sale and is a good place to put your bike up for sale too.
> **www.bikenet.com** – parts, gear and accessories.
> **www.classic-motorbikes.com** – great if you want to purchase a
> classic bike.

www.hondahornet.co.uk – a good-looking specialist site.

www.mag-uk.org – home of the Motorcycle Action Group dedicated to campaigning on behalf of motorcyclists in the UK.

www.mcia.co.uk – home of the Motorcycle Industry Association, this site offers a fair amount of information for all levels.

www.motorbikes.be/en – a Belgian site which offers the technical specs of over 5,000 motorbikes.

www.motorcycleshow.co.uk – details of the motorcycle show.

www.scootering.com – home of *Scootering* magazine.

www.twistngo.com – *TAG Magazine* for scooter fans. See 'What Scooter' section to help make your choice.

www.umgweb.com – owned by the auctioneer e-Bay, here you can find used motorcycles for sale.

Movies

All you need to know about films and film stars including where to go to get the best deals on DVDs and videos. For information on the stars also check out the celebrities section on page 81.

News and Information

http://uk.imdb.com   US

INTERNET MOVIE DATABASE

The best and most organised movie database on the Internet. It's very easy to use and every film buff's dream with lots of features and recommendations, plus games, quizzes, chat and movie news. Another good database site is **www.allmovie.com** which has a really good search engine.

www.aintitcoolnews.com   US

AIN'T IT JUST COOL

A renowned review site that can make or break a movie in the US. It's very entertaining and likeable, albeit a bit messy. Harry Knowles's movie reviews are by far the best bit of the site, although they can go on a bit. You can search the archive for a particular review or contribute a bit of juicy gossip by e-mailing Harry direct.

See also:

www.metacritic.com – a site that compiles reviews from around the world, and gives the reviewed movies a score based on them. Also covers games, music and books.

www.mrqe.com – the Movie Review Query Engine. Just enter the film title, and reviews from magazines from all round the world pop up.

www.mymovies.net – a portal, shop, news and e-zine all wrapped up in a fairly poorly designed site. Having said that there's a lot here so patience is rewarded, but you have to subscribe to get the best out of it.

www.rottentomatoes.com – a comprehensive review site and store.

Film Magazine Sites

www.empireonline.co.uk   UK

THE UK'S NUMBER ONE
An epic of a site with masses of information and background on the latest movies and the stars. There are two main review sections, one dedicated to the cinema and one entitled, 'At home' for DVD and soundtrack and book reviews. You can also see trailers of new films, see pictures of the stars and production stills in the gallery and subscribe to the magazine.

www.insidefilm.com   US

FILM FESTIVAL DIRECTORY
Comprehensive news on the film festival with a calendar and features on awards.

www.eonline.com   US

E IS FOR ENTERTAINMENT
This is one of the most visited entertainment news sites and it has a reputation for being first with the latest gossip and movie news. It's vibrant, well designed and has a tongue-in-cheek style which is endearing; some of the reporters do prattle on though.

www.variety.com   US

VARIETY MAGAZINE
The online version of the show business stalwart magazine has an excellent and entertaining site with all the hot topics, news and background information you'd expect plus biographies and international film news. You have to subscribe to get access to many of the sections.

www.brightlightsfilm.com   US
FILM JOURNAL
A diverse and well written e-zine devoted to film that covers a
wide variety of topics and film styles. It can be quite eccentric,
which adds to the appeal, and some of the content is pretty odd,
but it's essential reading for film buffs.

For more gossip see:
www.boxofficemojo.com – excellent US film news and box
office information site.
www.ew.com – *Entertainments Weekly* has a really attractive
site with lots of features.
www.hollywood.com – over one million pages of gossip, news,
trailers and multi-media library.
www.hollywoodreporter.com – all the latest gossip and you can
subscribe to the magazine.
www.teenhollywood.com – aimed at teenagers, following the
top teens in Hollywood.

Bollywood

www.bollywoodworld.com   INDIA
THE BOLLYWOOD PORTAL
If it's Bollywood, then it's covered on this site. There are the
movie reviews you'd expect plus lots of news, what's hot and
what's not, pictures of the stars and much more. There is a
music channel, radio, blogs and chat.

See also:
www.bollywhat.com – here you can find a good beginner's
guide.
www.planetbollywood.com – odd design but loads of
information, gossip and awards.

Awards and Industry

www.oscars.com   US
THE ACADEMY AWARDS
Stylish and as tastelessly glitzy as you'd imagine it should be,
this is the official tie-in site for the Oscars. There's an archive and
even some games to play. For the Golden Globes go to
www.thegoldenglobes.com and for a celebration of the worst
Hollywood has to offer, the Razzies, go to **www.razzies.com**

www.bafta.org   UK

BRITISH ACADEMY OF FILM & TELEVISION ARTS
A site giving all the information you need on the BAFTAs, their
history and how it all works.

www.bfi.org.uk   UK

BRITISH FILM INSTITUTE
A top site from the BFI packed with information on how the film
industry works with archive material, links and how to make
movies. Refreshing that there's not much mention of Hollywood!
For the American Film Institute go to **www.afi.com** where you'll
find an excellent site.

British Movie Industry

www.britmovie.co.uk   UK

DEDICATED TO BRITISH CINEMA
A site devoted to the history of British cinema and its wider
contribution to film-making in general. There's a great deal
of information, links and background and it's all well
cross-referenced. There is now a search facility on the site,
which we called for in previous editions, and the site seems
to be more regularly updated than of old.

See also:
www.britishfilm.org.uk – excellent set of articles on the history
of British cinema.
www.britishhorrorfilms.co.uk – a very entertaining
romp through the history of British Horror films, with lots of
detail!
www.britshorts.com – short British and European films.

Independent Film-making

www.indiewire.com   UK

INDEPENDENT CINEMA
An enthralling site covering independent cinema, the films,
people and gossip. It stands out as a site that genuinely feels
like it's contributing positively to an industry. See also
www.exposure.co.uk who cover the low budget end of
film-making.

www.kamera.co.uk   UK
ART HOUSE & INDEPENDENT REVIEWS
A well-written review site covering the world of art house and
independent cinema. It also has a good book review section and
interviews with important actors and directors. There's also a
directory and forums where you can put your views.

See also:
http://shootingpeople.org – a community site aimed at the
independent film maker, with lots of advice and help.
www.bifa.org.uk – British Independent Film awards.
www.raindancefilmfestival.org – a high profile sponsor of
independent films, with a useful site and e-zine.

Specialist Film Sites

www.bmonster.com   US
COOLEST CULT MOVIES
A highly entertaining site devoted to B movies, oddities and
actors that aren't quite top drawer. It's well categorised and
obviously a labour of love for its contributors. See also
www.badmovieplanet.com

M

See also:
www.americanwest.com/films/films.htm – good for links to all
things Western.
www.classichorrorfilms.com – not a great site but it's got all you
need on the subject.
www.classicmoviemusicals.com – a well-categorised but
slightly dull site covering musicals.
www.earlycinema.com – excellent site on the first decade of
cinema with timeline, biographical details and information on
the technology they used.
www.horror.net – a database of some 3,200 horror-related sites.
www.ianfleming.org – the place to go for all Bond fans.
www.movie-locations.com – a guide to the world's movie
locations.
www.movie-trailers.com – masses of movie trailers going back
many years, it's quite nostalgic.
www.mysterynet.com/movies – the top movies reviewed with
links to other related genres.
www.paulkerensa.com/movietimeline – an historical timeline
of everything that happened in the Movies and when.

www.scifispace.com – excellent fan site with lots of detail and links.

www.sciflicks.com – a comprehensive site covering the Sci Fi genre.

www.scriptfly.com – buy movie scripts, thousands to choose from.

www.silentsaregolden.com – a great place to start if you want to find out about silent movies.

www.surfnetinc.com/chuck/trio.htm – The Old Corral, a directory devoted mainly to Westerns.

Cinemas

Listed below are the major cinema companies and their sites – although it is hard to keep up with their mergers:

www.cinemas-online.co.uk – a portal site with links to all the country's cinemas.

www.cineworld.co.uk – straightforward and easy-to-use guide. You can't book on line but promise a new site soon.

www.odeon.co.uk – book online at this attractive site.

www.showcasecinemas.co.uk – lots here to see and do.

www.uci-cinemas.co.uk – good-looking site with all the usual information and previews. Now owned by Odeon and will soon be merged with their site.

www.ugccinemas.co.uk – standard features including online booking. Now owned by Cineworld, also about to be subsumed.

www.myvue.com – Vue, the company formed from the amalgamation of Warner Village Cinemas and SBC International Cinemas, has a cleanly designed site with hidden extras.

Movie Humour

www.moderntimes.com   US

LISTEN TO YOUR FAVOURITE MOVIES

Download extracts from over 50 movies, it's a little confusing at first but once you've got the technology sorted out it's good fun.

http://rinkworks.com/movieaminute   US

DON'T HAVE TIME TO WATCH IT ALL?

Summaries of the top movies for those who either can't be bothered to watch them or just want to pretend they did, either way it's really funny.

www.moviecliches.com   US
THE MOVIE CLICHÉ LIST
Clichés listed by topic from aeroplanes to wood, there's
something for everyone here . . .

See also:
www.badmovieplanet.com – a collection of the worst films ever
made.
www.continuitycorner.com – the place to go if you're a born
nitpicker, it has hundreds of movie mistakes and believe it not
one person has submitted over 120 of them.
www.nitpickers.com – more pettiness.
www.razzies.com – awards for the worst movies.
www.thestinkers.com – more awards for bad films.

Film Companies

*Some of the best web sites are those that promote a particular film.
Here is a list of the major film producers and their web sites, all of which
are good and have links to the latest releases. Most have clips,
downloads, screensavers and lots of advertising.*

        http://spielbergfilms.com
        www.disney.com
        www.dreamworks.com
        www.foxmovies.com
        www.miramax.com
        www.paramount.com
        www.spe.sony.com
        www.uip.com
        www.universalpictures.com
        www.warnerbros.com

Downloading Movies

*There's no doubt that downloading films and TV shows is likely to be the
next big thing in digital. As technology moves on, the facility to carry
large movie files such as MP4 will get ever easier – just check out Tivo's
TivotoGo concept (**www.tivo.com**) to see the potential. Once
downloaded you can burn your own DVDs too.*

M

BitTorrent

This is a relatively new technology that allows for the downloading of large amounts of data using a speedier, more user-friendly technology than has previously been available. Staggering to believe, but BitTorrent has been taken up at such a rate that it's apparently been responsible for around a third of all internet traffic in the past year. This is changing the way that ISP's allocate their data flow and makes possible the transfer of extremely large files by taking small bits of the required file, not from just one computer, but all the other computers that have downloaded the relevant BitTorrent program and have the file that you have requested. This group of computers is called a 'swarm' and the transfer of data using this method is called a 'torrent' and it means download speeds can be some twenty times faster than normal.

Check out the following . . .
http://en.wikipedia.org/wiki/Bittorrent – from the ever helpful Wikipedia a guide to BitTorrent and the terminology.
http://jabberwalker.com.ar – a torrent search engine.
www.bittorrent.com – the original site and program.

Interestingly, the film industry has embraced the technology and unlike the music industry seems to welcome peer-to-peer (P2P) file sharing. The BBC has started to make available some programs as downloads and it's just a matter of time before other channels follow suit. With the latest technology you'll need a broadband connection. Here are a few sites that are leading the way (be warned that some carry adult-oriented content).

http://filmdownloads.aol.co.uk – AOL with some of the first proper blockbusters available.
www.cinemanow.com – the world's largest legal video download store, apparently; whatever, the quality is great.
www.ezmovies.net – a good subscription service specialising in movies.
www.freemovienow.com – not much free but one of the better designs.
www.lightspeedmovies.com – a wide variety of content including games, fast download times.
www.moviedownloadworld.com – a selection of some 15,000 movies.
www.sharedmovies.com – possibly the one with the most content.

www.ultimatemoviedownload.com – a popular file-sharing program with lots of content; costs vary according to what you buy.
www.xvidmovies.com – a well-used service using the MP4 format.

Buying and Renting Movies

*It's probably best to start with visiting a price checker site first such as **www.kelkoo.com** (see page 378) but these are the best of the movie online stores.*

www.sendit.com formerly **www.blackstar.co.uk**   UK
THE UK'S BIGGEST VIDEO STORE
The biggest online video and DVD retailer, it is very good value, boasts free delivery and has a reputation for excellent customer service. If you want to shop around try **www.blockbuster.com** who have a less packed site and offers on a wide variety of films.

www.dvdstreet.infront.co.uk   UK
FOR DVD ONLY
Part of the Streets Online group, this is a great-value and easy-to-use site that only sells DVDs. There are lots of other movie related features too, such as the latest news and gossip or reviews.

www.screenselect.co.uk   UK
RENT A DVD MOVIE
Rent as many DVDs as you want with packages from £9.99 per month. Pick the title of your choice and it's dispatched the same day, you then return it seven days later in the pre-paid envelope and they immediately dispatch the next DVD on your list. The range offered is excellent covering 48,000 titles in twenty genres plus new releases, coming soon and a good search facility too. For alternative contractual arrangements based on £1.99 per DVD hired, go to **https://dvd.easycinema.com**

See also:
http://svp.co.uk – internet retailers of blank CS/DVD media. Sells computer accessories too.
http://uk-dvd-rentals.co.uk – reviews the DVD online rental services helping you to select the best for your needs.
www.dvdoptions.com – rent your favourite DVDs from £9.95 for seven nights.
www.dvdpopcorn.com – a good-looking UK-based DVD shop with some good offers, and prices include postage and packing.

M

www.dvdreview.com – great for news and reviews.
www.dvdtimes.co.uk – DVD and cinema news and reviews.
www.lovefilm.com – a very good subscription DVD store with over 50,000 DVD titles and some downloads.
www.mymovies.net – a good review and film store with a movie club.
www.play.com – a very strong selection of DVDs and CDs too with some good offers.

www.xiddi.com   UK
DVD SHARE AND SWAP

A good alternative to DVD rental, here you build up credits (Xids) that enable you to select from a good range of films and popular titles, you only really pay for the postage.

Memorabilia

www.vinmag.com   UK
POSTERS, CARDS AND T-SHIRTS

Vintage magazines, stand-up cut-outs, posters, T-shirts and magazine covers complete the picture from this established dealer.

www.asseenonscreen.com   UK
AS SEEN ON SCREEN

At this site you can buy what you see on the screen, your favourite star's shirt or dress can be replicated just for you. You can also search by star, film and TV show.

www.propstore.co.uk   UK
PROPS FOR SALE

An extensive selection of props and replicas await you here with everything from snow globes to clothing. Each piece is unique and has been bought from the relevant film company and the provenance is provided.

See also:
www.efilmposters.com – who sell posters from a good British site.
www.memomine.com – for Hollywood memorabilia.
www.moviemarket.co.uk – posters, framed prints and memorabilia delivered to your door.
www.ricksmovie.com – some 14,000 posters and related items.
www.vinylandfilmposters.co.uk – film and music related posters.

Music

Most people with a computer know about downloading music and much has been written about the effect that downloading free music has had on the music industry, mainly at the expense of musicians losing income. Some suggest that it's damaging to the industry by taking away their livelihoods, while others say it stimulates sales by enabling potential customers to sample music they wouldn't have heard otherwise. Whatever the stance, some of the sites listed are really different file sharing programs that allow users to exchange files easily whether it is music or not. It's best to read up on the subject (see the section on BitTorrent on page 318) before downloading any of the programs, but once you're up to speed it couldn't be easier.

Some of these sites are also prone to change, as regulations are introduced to block their activities, it's also quite difficult to establish their origin in some cases. The legal constraints that surround music file sharing are unclear but it's fair to say that in many cases copyright laws are broken. If you're not sure about using them, then I suggest you go to the pay sites. Personally, I think it's only fair that musicians should earn something if we enjoy their creativity and talent.

In America, some of the big music companies have prosecuted people who have downloaded music without paying, so be cautious. Having said all that, there are high-quality sites that allow you to sample music, offer legitimate free tracks and charge reasonable prices for the music – it's often still cheaper than buying a CD.

Please be aware that some may contain adult material including pornography (music files aren't the only things traded) and many carry some sort of spyware so that they can adapt to your tastes and advertise accordingly. See our security section on page 423 if you want to get rid of spyware. There are compatibility issues too, for example a track downloaded from Napster won't work on an iPod, as they use different software. There are two reasons for this, the first is about securing the track so that the artist gets paid and copyright is maintained, the second is about keeping you loyal to the product. Again it's best to read up on the subject before you buy.

M

iPod, Audio Players and Download Sites

These are the most popular digital audio players, all offer a basic free version with a full featured version to buy and download. With these you can download music, rip and burn CDs and get access to radio stations. Some offer movies and video playback too.

We'll start with the gadget that has dominated music downloading over the past few years, the iPod. If you own a digital player that is not an iPod, then it probably comes with its own software or is affiliated with one of these programs. For information on Podcasting, see page 378.

Podcasting

The Good Web Site Guide's Top 10s of the Internet

1. **www.podcastalley.com** – the podcast portal
2. **www.podcast.net/** – the podcast directory
3. **http://en.wikipedia.org/wiki/Podcast** – Wikipedia explains it all
4. **www.podcastingnews.com/** – all the latest and best podcasts
5. **www.ipodhacks.com** – for the technically minded
6. **www.bbc.co.uk/radio** – listen again, download your favourite radio programme
7. **http://encyclopodia.sourceforge.net/en/index.html** – get Wikipedia on your iPod
8. **www.guardian.co.uk/rickygervais/** – the world's most popular podcast
9. **www.podcastbunker.com** – quality not quantity. An excellent selection
10. **www.podcastpickle.com** – podcasts and vidcasts too

www.apple.com/uk/itunes   UK
  UK IPOD
  If you have an iPod here's where to start, the iTunes program can be used with a PC or Mac and it's very easy to select, buy and download your music choice. They offer possibly the largest quality selection of music and audio products including over 1,000 music videos available to download.

See also:
www.dailytunes.com – linked to iTunes, it gives recommendations and rediscovers long-lost songs.
www.ipodhacks.com – all the iPod tips and tricks.
www.ipodlounge.com – excellent site devoted to all things iPod.

http://sonique.lycos.com   US
THE SONIQUE PLAYER
A good-looking and versatile audio player with lots of options, it plays all the major formats and with its link to the Lycos search engine it's easy to find music.

www.musicmatch.com   US
MUSIC MATCH PLAYER
A good-looking and popular audio player with lots of functions and access to a catalogue of some 800,000 songs, competitively priced.

www.real.com   US
REAL PLAYER
A popular and versatile audio and video player; the free version is probably good enough for most users, the radio features are great too.

www.winamp.com   US
WINAMP PLAYER
The Winamp player is better looking than most and easy to use, but the free version isn't as good as some of the other free players. Having said that, the Pro version, which costs $20, is excellent. There's also plenty of stuff to download on the site.

Here's a list of sites that enable you to download a wide variety of music and audio files, although I suggest you start your search at **www.100topmp3sites.com** *Some of these sites come with their own downloading formats and players, which may mean they can't play some formats except their own.*

http://magnatune.com – from record label Magnatune, you can get a decent sample of their artists' tracks before you buy.
www.bleep.com – good selection of the usual artists and tracks with the addition of 'some obscure gems that have passed under the radar'.
www.dmusic.com – independent digital music site, but the good stuff is hard to find.

www.eclassical.com – many free classical greats (seem to be mainly Polish recordings) and many more to buy.

www.emusic.com – offers exclusive DJ mixes, live performances and prides itself on quality alternative music, over one million MP3s to choose from.

www.launch.com – high-quality offering from Yahoo with lots of features, the emphasis is on popular music and the latest releases.

www.listen.com – a subscription service, where for $12.99 a month you get the Rhapsody player and access to some 1.5 million songs.

www.mp3-mac.com – MP3 directory for Mac users, some don't have iPods after all.

www.mperia.com – downloads using the BitPass system, which means you don't need to be at your own computer to buy them. A wide range of music styles covered, but mainly it's for independent labels and musicians to sell their work.

www.napster.co.uk – another re-launch of Napster, it's attractive and easy to use, it also claims to have one million tracks available. Prices start at 79p per track or £9.95 per album. Doesn't support Mac.

www.peoplesound.com – an attempt to sell the work of unsigned artists by promoting them alongside established artists, some surprisingly good stuff here and much of it is free.

www.pro-music.org – a useful information site on the music industry and legitimate music downloading.

www.wippit.com – good looking, wide range of downloads and pretty good value with prices starting at only £4.99 a month.

File-sharing Programs and Free Downloading

With the advent of BitTorrent (see page 318) it will be interesting to see how many of these survive.

www.zeropaid.com   US
FILE-SHARING PORTAL

A site that lists all the many file-sharing sites, it seems very comprehensive but is not that easy to navigate as the text is quite dense.

http://opennap.sourceforge.net   US
CONNECTING PEOPLE

A variant of the original Napster program, this is freeware and you can select some of the many specialist and general servers which hold music, then use the program to search them for the music you like.

www.imesh.com   ISRAEL
SHARE THE PASSION
No central servers here, you join the network and as a member you can use the search facility to find music or files available from other members. Supposed to be spyware free.

www.kazaa.com   US
NUMBER 1
Kazaa rapidly became probably the most popular music download site in 2003. It has lots of features, it's easy to use and, unlike some of its competitors, attractive to look at. It comes with virus protection too, although some files we downloaded came with spyware attached. It works in a similar way to iMesh. Note, this program was illegal in Australia at the time of writing.

www.xolox.nl   HOLLAND
SHARE AND DISCOVER
An excellent program which allows you to search for files and music across many of the established networks featured above. It's very easy to use and there's a parental control option.

M

See also:
www.emule-project.net – an unexceptional peer to peer network, but one that guarantees that it's free of adware and spyware.
www.morpheus.com (redirects from **www.musiccity.com**) – use the FastTrack file sharing system, their version is called Morpheus. It's quite secure, but has lots of ads. Good design, lots of unsigned bands and legal.

www.riaa.org   US
RECORDING INDUSTRY ASSOCIATION OF AMERICA
Get the latest information on their attempts to stop music piracy, the legal issues plus their awards and industry statistics. See also the site for Electronic Frontier Foundation **www.eff.org** who campaign on legal issues surrounding digital media.

www.goaudio.co.uk   UK
DIGITAL PLAYERS
A specialist retailer devoted to digital players with some competitive prices on iPods and other makes such as Creative and Rio.

Buying CDs and Other Audio Products

It's as well to start by checking prices of CDs through price comparison sites such as those listed on page 378. These will take you to the store offering the best combination of price and postage. All the stores listed below offer good value plus a bit extra.

www.hmv.co.uk   UK
    HIS MASTER'S VOICE ONLINE
    Excellent features and offers on the latest CDs and videos. There are sections on most aspects of music as well as video, DVD and games with a good search facility. You can listen to selections from albums before buying if you have RealPlayer. Sign up to a monthly contract to access unlimited downloads selecting from a choice of one million tracks. Spoken word or books on tape are available as well. Free UK delivery.

www.cd-wow.com   UK
    OUTSTANDING VALUE
    A very easy site to use with some great offers on CDs and there's free delivery too. Probably still the best site for value at the time of writing.

www.cduniverse.com   US
    WIDE RANGE AND GREAT OFFERS
    There is a massive range to choose from and some good discounts; delivery normally takes only five days. You can also buy games, DVDs and videos. Excellent, but can be quite slow, and delivery is very expensive.

www.minidisco.com   US
    HOME OF THE MINIDISC
    The minidisc is alive and well here with some good offers on the players and information on the latest developments. Delivery to Europe takes about a week, costs vary. See also **www.minidisc.org** which is a messy site but contains everything you need to know about minidiscs.

    For more great offers on music try these sites:
    www.101cd.com – renowned for offering good value.
    www.amazon.co.uk – as good as you'd expect from Amazon.
    www.andante.com – excellent classical e-zine and online store.

www.recordstore.co.uk – choose from thousands of vinyl records, CDs, T-shirts, record bags and assorted DJ gear.
www.timelesstracks.com – devoted to the music of the 50s, 60s, 70s and 80s with some excellent prices on CDs.
www.towerrecords.co.uk – wide variety and some good offers – better service than you get from the real store. US-based site so beware of delivery charges.
www.virgin.net/music – average music store with reviews, digital downloads from 79p per track, unlimited downloads for a tenner a month.

www.secondsounds.com   UK
THE USED CD STORE
With a huge range to choose from, prices from as low as £1.99 and free delivery, you can't really go wrong; they guarantee mint condition or your money back. You can browse by artist or through the bargain bins, and of course they are interested in buying from you too.

www.htfr.co.uk   UK

HARD TO FIND RECORDS
Although they specialise in new and deleted house, garage, techno, electro, disco, funk, soul and hip-hop vinyl, they will try and find any record previously released. They also offer a complete service to all budding and serious DJs.

See also:
www.eil.com – who specialise in rare and collectible CDs and vinyl.
www.funkishere.com – rare funk and jazz funk.
www.recordfinders.com – a US-based vinyl specialist.

Bands, Groups and Stars

http://ubl.artistdirect.com   US
THE ULTIMATE BAND LIST
It is the place for mountains of information on groups or singers. It has a totally brilliant search facility, and you can buy and download from the site as well, although the prices are not as good as elsewhere. For a similar, but better organised site try **www.allmusic.com** where you can also get excellent information and videos.

www.onehitwondercentral.com
US

A CATALOGUE OF ONE HIT WONDERS

US-oriented information site on those who only triumphed once, never to be seen again. It's arranged by decade and you get some interesting titbits in the artist profiles.

www.musicbrigade.com
US

WATCH YOUR FAVOURITE ARTIST

An excellent site where you can download your favourite music videos; when we visited they had nearly 10,000. In the UK subscription starts at £4.99 a month or £49.99 per annum.

For Aspiring Bands

www.taxi.com
US

FOR UNSIGNED BANDS

Looking to get a music contract for your band? You should start here, there's loads of information, contacts and links that will help you on the rocky road to success and stardom – well that's the theory anyway!

For more places to find something new and get help if you're in a band, see also:

www.audiogalaxy.com – for sampling new and some existing bands.

www.bpi.co.uk – the British Phonographic Industry and what they do.

www.burbs.co.uk – British Underground Rock Bands, home of the UK's real music scene.

www.totalband.com – an excellent web resource for bands and musicians who want to set up their own web site.

www.tunetribe.com – provides bands and musicians with a showcase for their work and they get paid for it too.

www.joescafe.com/bands
UK

BAND NAMES

So you can't think of a name for your band? Here is the 'Bando-matic' which will offer all sorts of never before used band names in seconds. This time we got 'Pubescent Wheelhouse'. They've branched into song titles too, but can't imagine 'Cycles of Grass' making the top 20!

Music TV, Awards and Magazine Sites

www.bbc.co.uk/totp   UK
TOP OF THE POPS
The Top of the Pops sites are different, but the principle site is a
great magazine featuring the current charts with loads of good
features and articles as well as competitions, trivia and lots of
information. For those with longer memories try
www.bbc.co.uk/totp2 for golden oldies, 23,000 artists'
biographies, and 1 million sound clips and loads of general
interest content.

http://uk.fmagazine.com   UK
 F MAGAZINE
This one is for broadband users only. The look is stunning and
it's a pleasure to use. The site is presented as an on-screen
magazine and you turn the pages by clicking on the corner of
the page almost like you would a real magazine. The content
is pretty good too; it's aimed at the UK market and covers the
new bands and artists with interviews and videos as well as
articles.

www.grammy.com   US
THE GRAMMY AWARDS
An overview of the awards, who won what and when, and then
where to buy their music. For the Brit awards go to
www.brits.co.uk where you'll find a similar site. The MOBO
awards are celebrated at **www.mobo.net**

www.mtv.co.uk   UK
MUSIC TELEVISION
MTV offers loads of info on events, shows and the artists as well
as background on the presenters and creative bits like movie and
music video clips. Great design.

www.nme.com   UK
NEW MUSICAL EXPRESS
If you're a rock fan then this is where it's at. There's all the usual
information, it's well laid out and easy to access. The archived
articles are its greatest asset, featuring 150,000 artists and
every article, feature and review they've ever published plus full
UK discographies, pictures, e-cards, ring tones and links to the
best web sites.

M

www.q4music.com   UK
  Q MAGAZINE
  A music magazine site that reflects its parent magazine
  extremely well, with many of the features and all the authority
  that goes with it.

www.popworld.com   UK
  WHERE POP COMES FIRST
  Brilliant site that concentrates on pop, it's fun and has great
  graphics. You have to register to join but once you're in you get
  access to their new shop, competitions, features on your
  favourite bands, clips from Popworld TV, fashion tips and much
  more. You need the latest Flash download from Macromedia to
  get the best out of it.

www.rollingstone.com   UK
  ROLLING STONE MAGAZINE
  The archetypal music magazine has an excellent site with all the
  features you'd expect to see including reviews, photos, articles
  on the bands, downloads, links and games.

www.thebox.co.uk   UK
  SMASH HITS YOU CONTROL
  Similar to Q but with added features such as the ability for you to
  select a tune to be played on their TV channel and you can
  influence their overall selection by voting for your favourite
  songs. You need to be a member to get the most out of it.

www.vh1.com   UK
  MUSIC CHANNEL
  VH1 is a music channel and here's the associated web site
  which is packed with information, interactive features, preview
  videos and downloads.

Sites for Specific Types of Music

Blues

www.bluesworld.com   US
  HOMAGE TO THE BLUES
  If you're into the blues then this is your kind of site. There are
  interviews, memorabilia, 78 auctions, bibliographies,
  discographies and lists of links to other blues sites. You can order
  CDs via affiliated retailers and if the mood takes you, order a
  guitar too.

Music

The Good Web Site Guide's Top 10s
of the Internet

1. **www.apple.com/itunes** – great design, songs from 79p
2. **www.kazaa.com** – possibly illegal but for free downloads there's none better
3. **www.cd-wow.com** – for those who still buy CDs here's the best for value
4. **www.htfr.co.uk** – Hard to Find Records has been a saviour to many
5. **http://ubl.artistdirect.com** – info on virtually anyone who has ever recorded a song
6. **www.clickmusic.co.uk** – all you need to know on the subject
7. **www.lyrics.com** – stop the arguments, this provides the lyrics to hundreds of songs
8. **www.ticketmaster.co.uk** – for your concert tickets
9. **www.sunhawk.com** – the place to download sheet music
10. **www.mediauk.com/directory** – more radio stations than you'll ever need

M

Classical and Opera

www.gramophone.co.uk   UK

GRAMOPHONE MAGAZINE
An outstanding site with features, reviews, competitions, shop and concert listings; there's also an awards section plus the editor's choice with the top recommendations.

www.operabase.com/en   US
OPERA BASE
This site offers opera listings, information on festivals and provides background to the history of opera. For the *Opera* magazine site go to **www.opera.co.uk** which offers articles and links.

Other key classical music sites:
www.aria-database.com – information on over 1,000 arias.
www.branarecords.com – restores and publishes recordings from neglected artists.
www.choralnet.org – excellent site devoted to choral music.
www.classical.net – great for information and links.
www.classicallink.com – a very good portal site.
www.eclassical.com – download MP3s, many are free.
www.eno.org – the English National Opera.
www.mdcmusic.co.uk – good offers on CDs.
www.royaloperahouse.org – book online, see where your seat is and get the latest news.
www.wno.org.uk – Welsh National Opera.

Country

www.thatscountry.com   CANADA
COUNTRY MUSIC SCENE
A good overview of country music with offers and links as well as information on the artists and bands.

See also:
www.cmdn.net – country music dance.
www.countrymusic.org.uk – still a very naff site that covers the UK scene.
www.countrystarsonline.com – find the link to your favourite country stars.
www.roughstock.com – all-round magazine site, live radio and recommended for its excellent history of country.

Dance and Beat

www.anthems.com   UK

DANCE, HOUSE AND GARAGE
Great design combined with brilliant content, there's everything here for dance fans – news, information and samples of the latest mixes or, if you're feeling rich, you can buy them too, although you'll probably find cheaper elsewhere.

See also:
www.artofthemix.org – playlists, create your own or use someone else's.
www.beatport.com – digital download dance and beat specialist, great design.

www.garagemusic.co.uk – reviews and samples plus the latest on the UK scene, annoying adverts though.
www.juno.co.uk – good dance music store with a wide range.

Disco

www.disco-disco.com   US
DISCO FEVER
A great site devoted to all things Disco. It's quite comprehensive but it's also worth checking out **www.discomusic.com** which has lots of downloads and also **www.radiowdrc.com** for the World Disco Community.

Folk

www.folkmusic.net   UK
FOLK ON THE WEB
A straightforward site from *Living Traditions* magazine, a collection of articles, features, reviews and news.

See also:
www.folking.com – a good all-round site with news, downloads and shopping.
www.thetraditionbearers.com – a project aimed at keeping alive our traditional songs.

Hip Hop and Rap

www.sohh.com   US
SITE OF HIP HOP
Voted the best of its kind by *Rolling Stone*, this site offers all you'd expect in terms of news, reviews, forums, interviews and samples. It also has links to shops and other related sites.

See also:
www.britishhiphop.co.uk – the story of British hip hop and artist listing and discography.
www.contrabandit.com – apparently hip hop's last hope . . .
www.hiphopville.com – where to go for all the gear.
www.rapdict.org – the Rap Dictionary helping you through hip hop slang.
www.rapstation.com – a temperamental site but one that really delivers in terms of information and news.

Indie

www.playlouder.com   UK
INDIE MUSIC
Great graphics and excellent design make Playlouder stand out
from the crowd; it covers the indie music scene in depth with
all the usual features, but with a bit more style. See also
www.drownedinsound.com which is a very good e-zine
devoted to the scene and **www.pennyblackmusic.com** for more
articles.

Jazz

www.jazzonln.com   US
JAZZ ONLINE
Reviews, links, artist interviews and a guide to the different types
of jazz are all features here. You can download videos too,
although you need 'Quicktime' to view them.

See also:
www.allaboutjazz.com – well organised, slightly dull but very
comprehensive.
www.jazzcorner.com – a beautifully designed jazz magazine
site and directory.
www.jazzimprov.com – an e-zine about jazz improvisation.
www.jazzreview.com – lots of reviews and discussion plus a
photography section and downloads.

Karaoke

www.streamkaraoke.com   US
SING ALONG
Over 20,000 tunes to download but you have to subscribe,
which costs from $4 a month depending on which package you
take. See also the British **www.singtotheworld.com**

Pop

www.popjustice.com   UK
POP MUSIC
Opinionated, a bit pompous but very well informed, Pop
Justice gives you the insider's guide to pop music. See also
www.pop-music.com and **www.bbc.co.uk/music/pop**

Reggae

www.reggaetrain.com   US
REGGAE TRAIN A COME
An excellent and comprehensive portal site devoted to all things
reggae, with several hundred links.

See also:
www.niceup.com – comprehensive reggae archive site with a
massive database and links.
www.reggaefusion.com – a huge site devoted to Jamaican
music.
www.reggaereview.com – a monthly web magazine from
California.
www.reggaetimes.com – a good site connected with *Reggae
Times*, lots of reviews and links.

Rock and Heavy Metal

www.rocksite.com   US
INFORMATION THAT ROCKS
Devoted to rock music, there are band listings, tour news,
reviews plus links and a musicians directory. All this wrapped up
in an appropriately designed site.

M

For more try:
www.heavy-metalinks.com – horrible-looking site but it does
have all the links you'll need.
www.history-of-rock.com – a good overview of the roots of rock
and roll.
www.live4metal.com – good e-zine with reviews, interviews
and tour news amongst other things.
www.rockhall.com – the Rock and Roll Hall of Fame has an
outstanding site dedicated to celebrating only the best.
www.rockhaven.co.uk – a UK-oriented rock portal site.
www.rocklist.net – a compilation of lists from the major music
magazines categorised by year, from the 50s to date, with links
to the relevant sites.
www.rocknrollzone.com – a good, colourful portal and news
site.

World Music

www.fly.co.uk   UK
> GLOBAL MUSIC CULTURE
> An excellent e-zine devoted to world music, with sections by
> continent including features and links and a search facilty.
>
> *See also:*
> **www.africanmusic.org** – the African Music Encyclopaedia.
> **www.frootsmag.com** – a highly rated e-zine.

Music Information

www.clickmusic.co.uk   UK

> EVERYTHING YOU NEED TO KNOW ABOUT MUSIC
> This is great for all music fans. It has quick access to details on
> any particular band, with tickets, downloads, gigs and gossip.
> Shopping is straightforward: just click on the store or use the
> search engine to find something specific. See also
> **www.musites.com** where you can find a rather variable but
> improving music search engine.

www.musicsearch.com   US
> THE INTERNET'S MUSIC SEARCH ENGINE
> Musicsearch is a directory site with over 20,000 links to
> reviewed music sites, the search facility has improved and you
> can offer up sites to be included.

www.bl.uk/collections/sound-archive/cat.html   UK
> BRITISH LIBRARY SOUND ARCHIVE
> This catalogue contains over 3.5 million entries; there are only a
> few sounds you can listen to online, but more are being put on
> the site. You can find out how to get a listening appointment and
> order copies of the sounds, music or oral recordings. For more
> sound effects check out **www.sounddogs.com**

www.musicplasma.com   US
> IF YOU LIKE MUSIC, YOU'LL LOVE . . .
> At this site you type in the name of the band or artist you like,
> and up pops a graphic depiction of all related performers in the
> same genre. It's a great way to extend your music tastes and the
> site design is really innovative.

M

See also:

www.eartothesound.com – a very good music information portal.

www.gracenote.com – what looks like a corporate site also holds the CD database. Click on the CDDC tab and you get access to an excellent search facility which also offers relevant links to bands and labels.

www.hitsquad.com – a well-categorised portal site aimed primarily at musicians.

www.thisdayinmusic.com – what happened on a particular day plus quizzes and information on music history, although you have to join to make the most of it.

www.useyourears.co.uk – unusual site providing an extensive music portal, everything from instrumental help to recording studios.

www.vitaminic.co.uk – a music club, excellent portal and host to many specialist music sites. You have to join to get the best out of it, including downloads.

Learning Music

Long-winded though the site URL is, it's worth paying a visit to **www.si.umich.edu/chico/mhn/enclpdia.html** *where you can find a music encyclopaedia in which you can sample the sound of many instruments.*

M

www.youthmusic.org.uk   UK
MUSIC SUPPORT

Youth Music is a charity that aims to provide music learning and opportunities to hear live, high quality music to those who may not have the means to hear it or see it performed. They have several interesting projects and you can learn about how to get involved here.

See also:

www.abachamusic.com.au – who offer a fun approach to music theory.

www.playmusic.org – great for kids to learn about the orchestra with audio clips to hear the sounds produced by the different instruments.

www.musictheory.net – good, free music theory lessons.

Sites for Specific Instruments

General

www.backstreet.co.uk – equipment hire and shop from this London-based studio.

www.electricbluesclub.co.uk – hours of fun digging around on this site, with links and online lessons for a range of instruments plus masses of info on a variety of styles not just blues.

www.harmony-central.com – all sorts of instruments reviewed and rated.

www.music4worship.co.uk – a music store covering a wide range of musical instruments.

www.musicianshop.com – another musical instrument store, especially good for guitarists.

www.starland.co.uk – musical instruments by mail order, some good offers too.

www.yamaha-europe.com – information on their full range of instruments, including digital pianos and a range of music technology gear plus info on their music schools and teaching system.

Electronic

http://nmc.uoregon.edu/emi – great introduction to electronic music and instruments.

www.etcetera.co.uk – download all the latest sampling and music creation software here.

www.kvr-vst.com – technical site with downloads and reviews of the latest hardware and software.

www.synthzone.com – excellent source for articles, links and reviews for all things to do with electronic music making.

Guitar

www.accessrock.com – free interactive web site for aspiring rock guitarists, great range of lessons.

www.guitar.com – good all-rounder, all you need to know.

www.guitarsite.com – masses of information.

www.guitarstrings.co.uk – a guitar specialist shop.

www.ultimate-guitar.com – brilliant guitar site with news, reviews, lessons (including complex effects) but maybe best of all, over one thousand tabs.

Keyboard

www.pianonanny.com – complete piano course.
www.pianoshop.co.uk – masses of links, pianos for sale and information on learning.

Percussion

www.drummersweb.com – drummer's delight.
www.giggear.co.uk – a well-stocked shop for all the band's needs.
www.rhythmweb.com – the place to go for all things percussive.

Strings

www.violin-world.com – complete resource for all string instruments.

Wind and Brass

www.saxophone.org – great for info and links.
www.wfg.sneezy.org – woodwind.

Sheet Music

M

www.sunhawk.com   US
DOWNLOAD SHEET MUSIC
Well-designed site where you can download music from a wide variety of styles including pop, Christian, country, Broadway, jazz and classical; you have to pay but there are some freebies.

See also:
www.musicroom.com – a huge range and free postage in the UK.
www.sheetmusicarchive.net – specialising in classical music.
www.sheetmusicplus.com – US-oriented but a wide range and some new stuff.

Lyrics and Songs

www.lyrics.com   US
THE WORDS TO HUNDREDS OF SONGS
There are songs from hundreds of bands and artists including Oasis, Madonna, Britney Spears and Queen. You'll have to ignore the directory section that makes up most of the page,

there's an A–Z listing at the bottom. Hopefully they'll redesign soon.

Other good lyric sites:
http://home.iae.nl/users/kdv/en/ring.htm – a web ring for lyrics.
www.azlyrics.com – over 50,000 lyrics.
www.britishacademy.com – support and advice for songwriters.
www.letssingit.com – big archive plus karaoke!
www.songfacts.com – information, background and trivia about thousands of songs.

www.kissthisguy.com   US
MISHEARD LYRICS
Mr Misheard lists all those lyrics that you thought were being sung but in reality you were just not quite listening properly. This time we liked the Red Hot Chili Peppers' lyric 'Can't stop the spirits when they need you' misheard as 'Can't stop the ferrets when they need food', but there are hundreds more.

Concerts, Clubs and Tickets

www.bigmouth.co.uk   UK
UK'S MOST COMPREHENSIVE GIG GUIDE
UK based, with lots of links to band sites, news, events listing and information on what's up and coming. Great search facilities and the ability to buy tickets make this a really useful site for gig lovers everywhere. It's geared to rock and pop though.

www.ticketmaster.co.uk   UK
TICKETS FOR EVERYTHING
Book tickets for just about anything and you can run searches by venue, city or date. The site is split into five key sections:

Theatre – theatre, drama and musical
Performing arts – comedy, classical and opera
Music – gigs, jazz, clubs, rock and pop
Attraction – shows, anything from Disney on Ice to air shows to museums
Sports – tickets for virtually every sporting occasion.

See also **www.seetickets.com**

www.efestivals.co.uk   UK
FESTIVALS
Excellent place to review and preview festivals, there are photo galleries and you can buy online too.

www.uk-clubbing-directory.co.uk   UK

Find out about your local hot spots, link through to their site and buy tickets. You'll also get the low-down on events, holidays and international music festivals. See also **www.niteclubbers.net** which is more edgy and **www.uk-cl.co.uk** which is great for links.

Nature and the Environment

The Internet offers charities and organisations a chance to highlight their work in a way that is much more creative than ever before, it also offers the chance for us to get in-depth information on those species and issues that interest us.

Wildlife and Environmental Organisations

www.panda.org   UK
WWF

The official site for WWF with information on projects designed to save the world's endangered species by protecting their environment. You can find out about how to support their work, how to get involved, the latest news, information on the key projects and some great photos. There is also some good kids' and educational material embedded in the news section. An American organisation called the National Wildlife Fund has a similar excellent site at **www.nwf.org**

www.foe.co.uk   UK
FRIENDS OF THE EARTH
Not as worthy as you might imagine, this site offers a stack of information on food, pollution, green power, protecting wildlife in your area and the latest campaign news.

www.envirolink.org   US
THE ONLINE ENVIRONMENTAL COMMUNITY
A huge site focused on personal involvement in environment issues. There are several well-categorised sections including:

organisations, educational resources, jobs, governmental resources, actions you can take to help and environment links. There is also a good search facility on environment-related topics.

www.environment-agency.gov.uk   UK
THE GOVERNMENT'S RESPONSE
The Environment Agency's site offers information on the latest initiatives and research. It also has sections on air quality, conservation, flooding, waste and navigation. There is help on how to improve the environment plus contact details regarding any issues you have.

www.planetdiary.com   US
WHAT'S REALLY HAPPENING ON THE PLANET
Every week Planetdiary monitors and records world events in geological, astronomical, meteorological, biological and environmental terms and relays them back via this web site. It's done by showing an icon on a map of the world, which you then click on to find out more. Although very informative, a visit can leave you a little depressed.

www.biodiversityhotspots.org   US

CONSERVATION INTERNATIONAL
A pleasure to visit, this site is a great example of how the Internet can be used to inform us about what is going on in the world. It highlights 34 places in the world where wildlife and the environment are in a particularly perilous state. Click on the interactive map and you get taken to a beautifully produced micro site with as much information as you need on each place. It shows how you can help and you can sign up for the newsletter too.

http://earthobservatory.nasa.gov   US
THE EARTH FROM ABOVE
Really outstanding photography and detailed information on the environment presented in an interesting and thought-provoking way. Owned by NASA, the site offers sections on the atmosphere, land and air as well as the latest news stories.

www.projectearth.com   US
NAVIGATING TOWARDS A BETTER ENVIRONMENT
Outstanding site devoted to recognising the damaging effect man has on the environment and pointing the way towards a better future.

http://earth.google.com   US
GOOGLE EARTH

Download the program and you get access to an amazing array
of geographical and mapping tools. It's addictive stuff with
incredible detail and in 3-D too. The Mac version is now available
and there are more sophisticated versions for those who want
to pay

*For more or specialised information on ecology, nature and the
environment try these sites:*

http://wcs.org – home of New York's Wildlife Conservation
Society who have a very informative site.

www.ace.mmu.ac.uk/eae – most of your questions answered
here at the excellent Encyclopaedia of Atmospheric
Environment.

www.airquality.co.uk – a site devoted to monitoring the air
quality around the UK.

www.cat.org.uk – a messy site from the Centre for Alternative
Technology, but contains good information.

www.defra.gov.uk – the Department for Environment, Food and
Rural Affairs has a newsy site that offers lots of information and
does it pretty well when you consider the size of their brief.

www.environmentwebsites.co.uk – a portal for environmental
sites.

www.ewg.org – an excellent and detailed site from the
Environmental Working Group, dedicated to the fight against
pollution – warning, contains some scary information.

www.genewatch.org – an organisation devoted to monitoring
the development and effect of GM plants and other uses of gene
modification and testing.

www.greenpeace.org – find out about their latest activities and
how to get involved.

www.grist.org – an e-zine devoted to nature and the
environment. It's well written and in places pretty funny. You can
have your say in the forums and catch up with the latest news.

www.ifaw.org – home of the excellent International Fund for
Animal Welfare.

www.jncc.gov.uk – find out what advice the government is
receiving from the Joint Nature Conservation Committee. Very
detailed and technical reports available, which may be of use to
campaigners.

www.nhpa.co.uk – staggeringly beautiful nature photography
from a commercial site; although you have to pay for images it at
least reminds us what it's all about.

www.nationalgeographic.com/animals – excellent site with details of their travels and photos, it's a shame that the '.co.uk' site is no more than an advert for their TV channel as there are many aspects of the US site that could be replicated in the UK one.

www.scorecard.org – the facts on local pollution; US-orientated, but an informative site.

www.traffic.org – a campaigning site working against the illegal and sometimes appalling trade in animals throughout the world.

www.ufaw.org.uk – improving animal welfare using scientific knowledge.

www.wri.org – World Resources Institute promoting effective campaigning for a far better world.

Eco Help

www.coralcay.org   UK
HOW YOU CAN JOIN IN
In Coral Cay's words its aim is 'providing resources to help sustain livelihoods and alleviate poverty through the protection, restoration and management of coral reefs and tropical forests'. Sign up for an expedition or a science project in Malaysia or the Philippines.

See also:
www.ecoclub.com – a network providing a wealth of information about all aspects of ecotourism.

www.eco-portal.com – a messy but huge database and links site.

www.ecotourism.org – American site with useful links.

www.ecovolunteer.com – if you want to give your services to a specific animal benefit project.

www.environmentjob.co.uk – jobs and volunteer work in the environment industry.

Natural Phenomena and Geology

http://library.thinkquest.org/C003603/   US
FORCES OF NATURE
An amazing site that covers all the known natural disasters, giving background information, simulations and multimedia explanations with experiments for you to try at home.

www.em-dat.net US
EMERGENCY DISASTERS DATABASE
Browse through the dispassionate facts covering disasters both man-made and natural, you can search by country, region and type of disaster. Fascinating and disturbing, believe it or not, there's a running commentary called 'disasters of the week'.

See also:
http://gldss7.cr.usgs.gov – the Earthquake Hazards Program has plenty of information on earthquakes. In fact it's amazing how many there are.
http://serc.carleton.edu/NAGTWorkshops/visualization/ collections/tsunami.html – an amazing site devoted to tsunami of December 2004 with excellent animation.
http://volcano.und.nodak.edu – all you need to know about volcanoes, the site is poor but the photos are spectacular.
www.discoveringfossils.co.uk – excellent guide to the UK's geology and where to go fossil hunting.
www.exploratorium.edu – Museum of Science, Art and Human Perception has an excellent site particularly on seismic science.
www.fema.gov/kids – Federal Emergency Management Association site aimed at young kids.
www.geographyiq.com – comprehensive geography site.
www.geology.com – an American site covering the whole subject.
www.naturalhazards.org – interesting site with basic information on natural phenomena and links.
www.phenomena.org.uk – a very British view of natural phenomena and the more enjoyable for it.
www.rockwatch.org.uk – an ebullient site aimed at bringing geology to life for young people.
www.tsunami.org – the Pacific Tsunami Museum with stories, photos and links.

Dinosaurs

www.jpinstitute.com US
JURASSIC PARK
Excellent offering from the Jurassic Park Institute, particularly for kids, with loads of games and activities, well organised information on hundreds of dinosaurs, timelines and details about the different geologic era. The 'dinolab' is best for broadband users.

See also:
www.bbc.co.uk/dinosaurs – excellent site with lots of features.
www.dinodata.net – easy to use and information-packed.
www.dinosauria.com – masses of information and articles for the serious-minded adult and child.
www.jpinstitute.com – entertaining and educational site, home of the Jurassic Park Institute.
www.prehistoricplanet.com – good but out-of-date.
www.strangescience.net – an interesting site showing how scientists have developed the latest theories about dinosaurs and made mistakes along the way.
www.ucmp.berkeley.edu/diapsids/dinolinks.html – horrid URL but phenomenal list of dino-related web links.
www.ukfossils.co.uk – excellent and informative site on where to find fossils in the UK, includes information on geology too.

Nature Information and Media

www.nhm.ac.uk   UK

THE NATURAL HISTORY MUSEUM
A superb user-friendly web site that covers everything from ants to eclipses. You can get the latest news, check out exhibitions, take a tour, browse the Dinosaur database or explore the wildlife garden. There are details on the collections, galleries, educational resources and contacts for answers to specific questions. See also the Smithsonian National Museum of Natural History, which also has a great site at **www.mnh.si.edu**

www.bbc.co.uk/nature   UK

WILDLIFE EXPOSED
A brilliant nature offering from the BBC with sections on key wildlife programmes and animal groups. The information is good and enhanced by video clips.

Other nature sites worth checking out are . . .
www.enature.com – an American magazine site with a huge amount of information and features on all aspects of nature.
www.naturephotographers.net – a magazine devoted to wildlife photography with a great selection of shots and advice.
www.virtualparks.org – just stunning photography from the parks of Canada and the US.

Rainforest and Plant Conservation

www.rainforest-alliance.org   UK
RAINFOREST INFORMATION
Excellent for information and links to related sites, with lots of
news and background on major rainforest projects. A good place
to start any research.

See also:
http://ths.sps.lane.edu/biomes/rain3/rain3.html – a long URL
but worth a visit for the information it contains. It also offers
possibly the worst combination of background and text colours
we've seen so be prepared!
www.greenpeace.org.uk/forests formerly
www.saveordelete.com – a campaigning site from Greenpeace
aimed at exposing the tragic loss of rain forests throughout the
globe.
www.plantlife.org.uk – devoted to saving wild habitats and
conserving botanically important sites.
www.rainforest.org – home of the Tropical Rainforest Coalition
with up-to-date information on rainforest destruction and how
you can help.
www.rainforestconcern.org – home of a charity which aims to
protect the world's rainforests. The site gives an overview of the
problems faced and details on how you can help.
www.rainforestlive.org.uk – a UK education site, it could do
with an update, but there is some good stuff here.
www.rainforestweb.org – a comprehensive portal devoted to all
things to do with rain forests.
www.ran.org – Rainforest Action Network, another group
devoted to saving the rainforest, this one is American. You can't
help asking why these charities don't get together?
www.rbgkew.org.uk/conservation – the conservation schemes
from the Royal Botanical Gardens at Kew.

British Nature

www.naturenet.net   UK

UK COUNTRYSIDE, NATURE AND CONSERVATION
Ignore the rather twee graphics and you'll find a great deal of
information about nature in the UK. Their interests include:
countryside law, upkeep of nature reserves, voluntary work,
education and environmental news. There is also a useful guide

to planning regulations. You can also search the site for specifics and there is a good set of links to related sites.

www.uksafari.com   UK
BRITAIN'S WILDLIFE
A good overview of the UK's wild animals with a section on each and tips on wildlife gardening, a photo gallery and lots of additional stuff like film clips, facts and figures and information on nature sites.

www.phenology.org.uk   UK
NATURE'S CALENDAR
Phenology is the study of nature through recurring natural phenomena; this site aims to catalogue all that's relevant to the UK. It has several excellent sections, in particular the children's and the one devoted to mapping, where you can create your own records.

See also:
www.bbc.co.uk/nature/animals/wildbritain/springwatch – join Bill Oddie's Springwatch initiative, which involves recording the advent of spring in your locality.
www.british-trees.com – information on native trees with good links.
www.englishnature.org.uk – supply maps, photos and information on all our nature reserves and explains why reserves are so important – all on an excellent site.
www.forestry.gov.uk – Forestry Commission has details of its work and how you can help sustain our woods and forests.
www.snh.org.uk – excellent site on Scotland's nature and heritage.
www.treecouncil.org.uk – inspiring a love of trees, it comes with a section on some of our favourite trees.
www.wildlifetrusts.org – one of our most wide-ranging nature charities, highlighting the work of the 47 Wildlife Trusts and 2,500 nature reserves around the UK.
www.woodland-trust.org.uk – dedicated to protecting our woodland heritage.

General and Endangered Animals

www.arkive.org   UK
RAISING AWARENESS OF ENDANGERED SPECIES
Sponsored by the Wildscreen Trust this site's aim is to catalogue

and picture all the world's endangered species and has a separate section for the UK. Each animal and plant has a page devoted to it giving details on how and where it lives, including pictures and movie clips. You can help by donating pictures and film.

See also:
http://digimorph.org – a collection of x-ray and computer generated photos of many animals including dinosaurs, fascinating stuff.
http://netvet.wustl.edu/e-zoo.htm – a fun portal site devoted to the animal kingdom, good for research and homework.
www.wildlifesearch.com – links to sites on almost every animal.

For further ecological sites devoted to endangered species try:
www.animalaid.org.uk – join a campaign to stop exploitation of animals.
www.endangeredspecie.com – American site with lots of good photography and background on the causes of species decline.
www.rarespecies.org – an organisation that devises conservation strategies, very interesting to find out how it's done.
www.redlist.org – the Red List of critically endangered and threatened species.

Apes and Early Humans

www.becominghuman.org   US
HUMAN ORIGINS
A superb site detailing the progress of human evolution, showing our development in an interactive and enthralling way. Beautifully illustrated throughout; however, it can be a little slow, so best seen by broadband users.

For other sites that feature our evolution and our nearest relatives try:
www.archaeologyinfo.com/evolution.htm – good site on human evolution, the Hall of Skulls is great for showing our development through time.
www.chimps-inc.org – a non-profit organisation devoted to chimpanzees.
www.gorilla.org – home of the Gorilla Foundation and Koko.
www.greatapeproject.org – campaigning on rights for apes.

www.janegoodall.org – very well-put-together site featuring the work of this pioneer with biographical details and information on chimpanzees and how you can help preserve them.
www.unep.org/grasp – the Great Apes Survival Project aims to help preserve the species, specifically orangutans, bonobos, gorillas and chimpanzees.

African Wildlife and the Big Cats

www.africam.com   SOUTH AFRICA

ALWAYS LIVE, ALWAYS WILD
Web cameras have come a long way and this is one of the best uses of them. There are strategically placed cameras at water holes and parks around Africa and other of the world's wildlife areas, and you can tap in for a look at any time. You have to register to get the best out of it, but even a quick visit is rewarding.

See also:
http://elephant.elehost.com – an excellent elephant-only portal site.
www.5tigers.org – excellent site on tigers and how we can help to save the remaining five species.
www.cheetahspot.com – all you need to know about the cheetah.
www.greatcatsoftheworld.com – an overview of the big cats from a US nature centre.
www.lioncrusher.com – all large carnivores and a good picture archive.
www.wildnetafrica.com – this wildlife portal provides information on African animals and how to see them.

Bears

www.bears.org   US
BEAR BELIEFS
An overview of the major species of bears with lots of background, photos, myths and also detailed information on their habits and lifestyles.

See also:
http://nationalzoo.si.edu/Animals/GiantPandas – excellent site on pandas from the Smithsonian.
www.polarbearsalive.org – the web's largest polar bear site! Lots of info and photos too.

Birds

www.birds.com   US
ALL ABOUT BIRDS
An online directory and guide to birds covering both wild and
pets. It's biased towards America but otherwise excellent, except
that it's a bit too commercial.

See also:
www.birdguides.com – informative site with free videos and a
specialist store.
www.birdlinks.co.uk – some 500 bird-related links.
www.birdsofbritain.co.uk – a strong monthly web magazine for
British bird watchers.
www.bto.org – tracking birds and their behaviour.
www.ornithology.com – a good, if serious, site dedicated to wild
birds.
www.rspb.org.uk – the Royal Society for the Protection of Birds
have a nice site detailing what they do, and how you can help.

Insects

www.bugbios.com   US

BUGS AND INSECTS
A beautifully designed site exposing insects as miracles of
nature, with amazing macro-photography, information and links.
See also **www.virtualinsectary.com** which contains some great
photography. Home of the Invertebrate Conservation Trust a visit
to **www.buglife.org.uk** is also very informative.

http://butterflywebsite.com   US

BUTTERFLYING
Not that great design-wise but an interesting site on butterflies.
Although it's biased towards the US, it does have sections that
cover Britain and it also has a very good links section. For
another excellent site devoted to British butterflies go to
www.butterfly-conservation.org who hold information on all
resident and migrating butterflies and moths found in the UK.

Marine

www.wdcs.org   UK
WHALE AND DOLPHIN SOCIETY
All the latest news and developments in the fight to save whales

N

and dolphins. There's also information on them, how and where
they live, a 'Sightings and Strandings' section and details of how
to book a whale-watching holiday.

See also:
www.flmnh.ufl.edu/fish – the University of Florida's Department
of Ichthyology has a good site where you can find an overview
of all things fishy plus links and a good selection of
photographs.
www.seasky.org – one man's love affair with the sea and space.
In the sea half you'll find some excellent sections on such things
as coral reef and ocean exploration.
www.seawatchfoundation.org.uk – here you can learn more
about cetaceans, and their sightings around the UK.

Zoos and Safari Parks

www.safaripark.co.uk   UK
   SAFARI ONLINE
   A detailed site on the UK's safari parks including opening times,
   animal information and facts on endangered species.

www.sandiegozoo.org   US
   SAN DIEGO ZOO
   Probably the best zoo site. You can get conservation information,
   check out the latest arrivals and browse their excellent photo
   gallery. The highlights are definitely the zoo cams featuring
   pandas, elephants, apes and polar bears (remember the 8-hour
   time difference).

Other good zoo sites:
www.bristolzoo.co.uk – good looking and fun for kids.
www.dublinzoo.ie – slow but good content.
www.londonzoo.co.uk – excellent and comprehensive zoo site,
also covers Whipsnade Wildlife Park.
www.marwell.org.uk – masses to see and do.
www.mbayaq.org – beautiful site from Monterey Bay Aquarium
with web cams, online field guide and info on ocean research
projects.
www.seaworld.com – information on holidays and the
attractions at their three zoos.

www.bornfree.co.uk   UK
  ZOO CHECK
  Zoo Check is a charity whose mission is to promote Born Free's
  core belief that wildlife belongs in the wild. They expose the
  suffering of captive wild animals and investigate neglect and
  cruelty. They want tighter legislation and the phasing out of all
  traditional zoos. If you want to know more then this is where
  to go.

News and the Media

*The standard of web sites in this sector is usually very high making it
difficult to pick out one or two winners, just find one which appeals to
you and you won't go far wrong. Nowadays it's easy to create your own
news feeds, in this section we show you how.*

World News

www.sky.com/skynews   UK
  WITNESS THE EVENT
  Sky News has fast developed a reputation for excellence and that
  is reflected in their web site. It has a well-rounded news service
  with good coverage across the world as well as the UK. You can
  view news clips, listen to news items or just browse the site.
  There are special sections on sport, business, technology and
  even a few games.

www.bbc.co.uk/news   UK
  FROM THE BBC
  As you'd expect, the BBC site is excellent – similar to Sky but
  without the adverts. You can also get the news in several
  languages and tune into the World Service or any of their radio
  stations.

www.channel4.com/news   UK
  AWARD-WINNING NEWS
  High quality journalism reflects the independent and serious
  nature of their news coverage. There are some interesting links
  and a forum – you can even register to receive 'Snowmail' from
  Jon Snow himself.

www.itn.co.uk
UK

INDEPENDENT TELEVISION NEWS
As well as links to independent TV and radio news sites, ITN houses the world's largest TV-based video archive and is also home to the ITN stills collection. It's not cheap (video starts at £100 and stills at £25 for a one-off use) and is aimed at the professional market, but there is some amazing stuff here.

www.cnn.com
US

THE AMERICAN VIEW
CNN is superb on detail and breaking news with masses of background information on each story. It has plenty of feature pieces too. However, it is biased towards the American audience, for a similar service try **www.abcnews.com**

www.newsnow.co.uk
UK

NEWS NOW!
A superb news-gathering and information service that you can tailor to your needs and interests. The layout is confusing at first but it allows you to flick between latest headlines from 3,000 leading news sources without visiting each site separately, you can then read their choice of stories in full on the publishers' web sites. It's updated every five minutes!

www.ananova.co.uk
UK

NEWS ON THE MOVE
Ananova has been changed a few times and in the latest guise you get a well-put-together site that is much clearer than some. They've also teamed up with Orange to produce a mobile text messaging news service.

www.moreover.com
US

DYNAMIC CONTENT
With real-time news and rumour reporting, Moreover has become the news site of choice for many business people and journalists as it enables them to target the type of news and information they are looking for, saving time and effort all round. You need to subscribe to gain access.

http://english.aljazeera.net
UAE

AL JAZEERA
The English version of the well-known Arab news agency. It's very good for world events and as you'd expect outstanding when it comes to gaining an insight into the Arab world. See also **www.arabnews.com** the Arab English language daily.

Other news sites worth a visit are:

www.anorak.co.uk – humorous newspaper reviews.

www.copydesk.co.uk – a very good blog site devoted to news and popular culture, it's great for news links too.

www.economist.co.uk – business, world events and in-depth reports.

www.findarticles.com – an article search engine from LookSmart with access to some 900 publications.

www.irishnews.com – a competent site from *Irish News*.

www.newseum.org – an attempt to archive US newspapers.

www.nuzgeeks.com – excellent links.

www.positivenews.org.uk – for a positive spin on the news.

www.private-eye.co.uk – some of the best features from the mag, but not much news if truth be told.

www.publist.com – a news search engine covering over 150,000 titles world-wide.

www.reuters.co.uk – strong site from this world-renowned news agency. Those with broadband can benefit from their excellent TV news feeds.

www.theregister.co.uk – for technology news.

www.time.com – an excellent site from *Time* magazine.

www.topix.net – a news collation site which is exceptional for American news.

www.worldflash.com – download a news ticker and get the latest news as it happens.

N

Events and Future News

www.drudgereport.com   US
NOW FOR THE REAL NEWS
One of the most visited sites on the web. It's a pain to use, but the gossip and tips about upcoming features in the papers make it worthwhile. One of its best features is its superb set of links to other news sources.

www.foreignreport.com   UK
PREDICT THE FUTURE
Owned by Janes, the Foreign Report team attempt to pick out trends and happenings that might lead to bigger international news events. Browsing through their track record shows they're pretty good at it too.

Newspapers Online

www.telegraph.co.uk   UK
THE *TELEGRAPH*
The *Telegraph* has the best site for news and layout with all its
sections mirrored very effectively on the site.

Other major newspapers with sites worth a visit include:
www.dailymail.co.uk – not so much the paper as a portal for
Associated Newspapers, which is disappointing, but there are
some good articles and features.
www.guardian.co.uk – clean site with lots of added features and
guides.
www.independent.co.uk – good online debate as well as
news.
www.thesun.co.uk – very good representation of the paper with
all you'd expect.
www.timesonline.co.uk – no surprises here.

www.fish4news.co.uk   UK

LOCAL NEWS MADE EASY
An outstanding web site, just type in your postcode and back will
come a collated local 'newspaper' with regional news headlines,
sport and links to the source paper sites and small ads. Also see
www.newspapersoc.org.uk and go to the 'newspaper' to find
your local paper.

www.whatthepaperssay.co.uk   UK

WHEN YOU'VE NOT GOT TIME
Can't be bothered to sift through the papers? At this site you can
quickly take in the key stories and be linked through to the
relevant newspaper site too. You can also sign up to its daily
e-mail bulletin so you need never buy a paper again. See also
www.thepaperboy.com which is a bit more colourful and has a
good search facility.

RSS – Creating your Own News Feed

*RSS or Really Simple Syndication is one of the latest Internet toys and it
enables you to create your own news feeds or newspaper, tailoring
them to your tastes. You can even share them with friends and family.
First you download your 'aggregator' program (see below for the list)
then look out for sites that offer a feed; they usually have an RSS or*

XML sign at the bottom of the page or an orange button. Most major sites have them, while some programs and sites allow you to set up your own.

http://uk.my.yahoo.com
UK

MY YAHOO

Probably the simplest way to construct your own news feed, sign up then follow the well-written instructions. It's pretty easy to maintain; however, you are limited in terms of look and design.

www.feeddemon.com
US

FEED DEMON

Considered to be one of the best RSS newsreader programs, it's certainly very straightforward and easy to set up. It costs $29.95, although you can download a trial version. Everything is explained and for those new to this technology, it's probably the best on the market.

See also:

www.bloglines.com – excellent for creating your own news blog.
www.completeRSS.com – a useful directory of news feed links.
www.crayon.net – nice design and easy to use but geared solely to the US market.
www.feedster.com – free and it's relatively easy to set up, although you'll ideally need to know your news feed URLs first.
www.jetbrains.com – home of the Omega Reader, which is highly rated for its ability to find things fast.
www.newsgator.com – synchronise your news gathering with Outlook.
www.newzcrawler.com – hot on Feed Demon's tail as one of the best RSS services. It has the advantage of looking like a familiar e-mail program.
www.sharpreader.net – excellent if you want your news organised by topic.
www.syndic8.com – another news feed and directory site.
www.pluck.com – a good basic, free reader.

www.daypop.com
US

THE NEWS SEARCH ENGINE

Day Pop searches the latest news events using as its source news sites and weblogs. It's continually updating, taking news from the top sites every three hours. We found it variable but it's a lot more selective than Google, for example. It's at its best when a hot new story appears and doubtless it will improve over time.

Opticians

Buying glasses and contact lenses online isn't as daft as you'd think, there are great savings to be had . . .

www.glassesdirect.co.uk   UK
FROM £15
A well-designed site with sections on standard, rimless, semi-rimless and bendable glasses. There's also advice on how to interpret your prescription and what sort of frame would suit. You can order trial glasses to see if the frames fit comfortably too.

See also:
www.allaboutvision.com – US site providing all you need to know about eyes and vision.
www.antiquespectacles.co.uk – maybe you'd rather go for an antique pair?
www.boots.co.uk/bootsopticians – advice-laden section, you can book an appointment for an eye test.
www.glassesonspec.co.uk – upload a photo and try on virtual glasses until you find a pair that suits you.
www.optical.org – home of the regulatory body for opticians in the UK.
www.postoptics.co.uk – eye-care products and contact lenses by post.
www.specs2go.co.uk – good range and money back guarantee.
www.specsavers.co.uk – see their whole range of frames and contact lenses.
www.thecontactlensshop.com – aim to supply the cheapest contact lenses in the UK. Free delivery.

Organiser and Diary

www.opendiary.com   UK
THE ONLINE DIARY FOR THE WORLD
Your own personal organiser and diary, easy to use, genuinely helpful and totally anonymous. Simply register and away you go but follow the rules faithfully or you get deleted. Use it as you would any diary, go public or just browse other entries.

See also:
http://pim.kde.org – a free suite of programs including an address book and organiser, good for Linux users in particular.

http://uk.calendar.yahoo.com – Yahoo has an excellent, free and easy-to-use calendar facility.

www.calendars.net – create your own calendar here, especially good for web masters.

www.calendarzone.com – information on calendars, categorised by subject from astrology to the religious.

www.datereminder.co.uk – never forget a birthday or anniversary again, just load them in here and you'll get reminded near the time.

www.filofax.co.uk – if you can't live without the real thing.

www.livejournal.com – download your own journal and customise it to suit.

www.supercalendar.com – good for groups and businesses as well as individuals but it costs around £15 per annum.

www.yourorganiser.com.au – good-looking site, easy to use with a personal or group organiser facility.

Over 50s

If you're over 50 then you're part of the fastest growing group of Internet users, and some sites have cottoned on to the fact with specific content just for you.

Links

www.50connect.co.uk   UK

 LIVE LIFE TO THE FULL
A very strong portal site with masses of information and links covering a wide range of topics. It's incredibly useful; however, there are plenty of annoying adverts to go with it.

See also:
www.age-net.co.uk – another portal site but one that takes a magazine-style approach.

www.laterlife.com – a comprehensive site with lots of links and advice in many categories.

www.lifes4living.co.uk – an upbeat site dedicated to chat and links, some good offers too.

www.seniority.co.uk – a very comprehensive offering covering all you are likely to need with advice and links. Not exactly the most inspiring design though.

www.silversurfers.net – not the easiest site to get to grips with but it has a huge number of links in over 50 categories.

Magazines, Fun and Advice

www.saga.co.uk UK

THE SAGA GROUP

While this is a commercial organisation aimed at the over 50s, it offers much in the way of advice, help and information in key areas such as health, travel and money; plus the magazine is excellent.

See also:

http://bigjohn.blog-city.com – an entertaining blog from ex salesman Big John.

www.theoldie.co.uk – *The Oldie* magazine, which is great fun.

www.togs.org – where devoted fans of Terry Wogan meet.

www.over50s.com – a well-designed magazine-style site, good information and financial advice.

Information and Help

www.over50.gov.uk UK

ARE YOU OVER 50?

A useful and informative site from the government devoted to helping older people by offering practical help. You'll find many links to government departments and voluntary organisations, plus help guides to download. There's a separate section devoted to Scotland.

www.helptheaged.org.uk UK

HELP THE AGED

Find out how you can get involved in their work, what they do plus the latest news. You can also go to 'home shopping' and buy all sorts of useful gadgets to make life easier.

www.grandparents-association.org.uk UK

THE GRANDPARENTS' ASSOCIATION

Offers a newsletter, factsheets, advice and support for grandparents who are caring for their grandchildren as well as those who have lost touch with theirs.

See also:

www.csv-rsvp.org.uk – home of the Retired and Senior Volunteer Program.

www.experiencecorps.co.uk – voluntary work and a positive use of your experience.
www.hmrc.gov.uk/pdfs/ir121.htm – income tax details for pensioners.
www.housingcare.org – information on housing options for older people, their relatives and carers.
www.info4pensioners.gov.uk – the government's guide to pensioners' entitlements.

www.age-exchange.org.uk   UK
MAKE YOUR MEMORIES MATTER
Share your experiences and pass them on. Age Exchange aims to 'improve the quality of life for older people by emphasising the value of their memories to old and young, through pioneering artistic, educational, and welfare activities', they are also active in improving care for older people. This site gives details of how you can join in.

Activism

www.ageconcern.co.uk   UK
WORKING FOR ALL OLDER PEOPLE
Learn how to get involved with helping older people, get information and practical advice on all aspects of getting old. You can also make a donation and join one of the many campaigns they are running.

See also
www.agepositive.gov.uk – a government site with information on the latest anti-ageism legislation.
www.caredirections.co.uk – excellent site devoted to rights with the emphasis on care.
www.cspa.co.uk – a campaigning group devoted to getting better pensions, improved NHS facilities, care for the elderly and an end to age discrimination.
www.entitledto.co.uk/over60.asp – work out which benefits you are entitled to claim.
www.natpencon.org.uk – home of the National Pensioners Convention.
www.wiseowls.co.uk – dedicated to tackling ageism, while providing a good community site.

Lifelong Learning

www.hairnet.org   UK
TECHNOLOGY EXPLAINED
So you've bought the PC and now you need to know how to work
it properly? Hairnet, which in 2006 changed its name to Digital
Unite, explains all through a series of forums and specific
courses designed to help you get the most from technology. See
also **www.seniornet.org** which is a pretty boring but
comprehensive guide.

www.u3a.org.uk   UK
LIFELONG LEARNING
An organisation working to improve the lives of older people
through the concept of life-long learning and learning for the
pleasure of it. The site offers details of the subjects covered and
how to contact the relevant groups.

Travel

www.saga.co.uk/travel   UK
HOLIDAYS FOR THE OVER 50S
A superbly illustrated and rich site from Saga who've been
specialising in holidays for older people for many years. Here
you'll find everything from top-quality cruises to weekend breaks.

See also:
www.classicski.co.uk – a skiing operator specialising in mature
skiers whether they be beginners or experienced.
www.eldertreks.com – a good site from a specialist in adventure
travel for the over 50s.
www.responsibletravel.com – have an excellent range of
environmentally sensitive holidays for over 50s in their
'activities' listing.
www.travel55.co.uk – a great database of travel sites
specialising in travel for older people.

Parenting

*As a source of advice, the Internet has proved its worth, and especially
so for parents. As well as information, there are useful sites that filter
out the worst of the web and give advice on specific problems. Some of*

the education web sites, page 124, also have useful resources for parents as do the health sites, page 238. For shopping, see the children's section on page 89 and the general shopping section, starting on page 429. In addition, there is loads of useful stuff for parents in the travel section on pages 499 and 549 about taking children on holiday and activities to do with the children in the UK.

For Parents

The Good Web Site Guide's Top 10s
of the Internet

1. **www.raisingkids.co.uk** – detailed encyclopaedia on bringing up kids
2. **www.babyworld.co.uk** – information and community services
3. **www.babycentre.co.uk** – all the top topics covered
4. **www.parentalk.co.uk** – excellent magazine site
5. **www.nctpregnancyandbabycare.com/** – National Childbirth Trust
6. **www.kidshealth.org** – health advice for kids and parents
7. **www.bestbear.co.uk** – childcare help and advice
8. **www.babygoes2.com** – travelling with kids
9. **www.nhsdirect.nhs.uk** – help with ailments
10. **www.miriamstoppard.com** – advice from the leading guru

Advice and Information

www.babyworld.co.uk   UK
        BE PART OF IT
        Babyworld is an online magazine that covers all aspects of
        parenthood. There's excellent advice on how to choose the right
        products for your baby and for the pregnancy itself. The layout is
        much improved and it's easier to find information.

www.babycentre.co.uk   UK
        A HANDS-ON GUIDE
        A superb site with a massive amount of information and links to
        all aspects of pregnancy, childbirth and early parenthood. The
        content is provided by experts and you can tailor-make your
        profile so that you get the right information for you. There's also a

series of buying guides to help you make the right decision on baby shopping.

www.babyzone.com
US

THE NORTH AMERICAN WAY

From the massive American site on parenting, here you get a week-by-week account of pregnancy, information on birth and early childhood. The links are very good and there's plenty of information on offer to parents. See also the similarly well-constructed **www.parentsoup.com**

www.raisingkids.co.uk
UK

FROM BIRTH TO . . .

An information-laden site devoted to helping parents get through the minefield of child raising with sections on every life stage, it's particularly good on parenting teens. You can also ask an expert, and, amongst many sections, there's advice on travel, education and safety.

www.netmums.com
UK

LOCAL INFORMATION

A very useful support site for mums that provides localised information about what's going on and what help is available.

www.ukparents.co.uk
UK

YOUR PARENTING LIFELINE

Chat, experiences, stories and straightforward advice make this site worth a visit – there are competitions, links and plenty of opportunities for interaction.

www.all4kidsuk.com
UK

IF YOU'RE LOOKING FOR SOMETHING TO DO

This aims to be a comprehensive directory covering all your parental needs from activities to schools. It's got an easy-to-use search engine, where you can search by county if you need to.

www.miriamstoppard.com
UK

MIRIAM STOPPARD LIFETIME

An excellent web site from the best-selling author with lots of advice on being a parent, how to cope with pregnancy and keeping yourself and your family healthy. New information is continually being added, so it's very up to date and will become a great resource for parents.

www.parentalk.co.uk   UK
THE SENSIBLE APPROACH
Interesting articles and sensible advice characterise this site.
There is a helpful section for working parents and one for
employers plus a good links section for expert advice on a wide
range of topics. If the advice here isn't enough, you can buy their
books or take the course. For another good site with the same
aims try **www.parentlineplus.org.uk**

www.parentcentre.gov.uk   UK
THE LOW-DOWN ON EDUCATION
The Parent Centre is for all parents and carers who want to help
their child or children to learn. It really covers everything from
choosing a school or nursery to detailed information on what
a child should learn. It also provides information about the
rights and responsibilities of parents in a wider sense, advice
and links.

www.babydirectory.com   UK
A–Z OF BEING A PARENT
The Baby Directory catalogue is relevant to most parts of the UK.
It lists local facilities plus amenities that care for and occupy your
child. The quality of information varies by area though.

www.tommys.org   UK
PREMATURITY, MISCARRIAGE AND STILLBIRTH
Information on getting through some of the tragedies that occur
in pregnancy plus details on how you can help.

Other useful sites:
www.allkids.co.uk – a well-categorised portal site covering all
things for children including good shopping directory.
www.arc-uk.org – a charity that helps with antenatal results
and the choices that surround them when an abnormality is
found.
www.babyandkids.co.uk – an American-style advice site aimed
at the UK.
www.babynames.com – over 6,500 names to choose from plus
other services and lots of adverts!
www.ncb.org.uk – home of the National Children's Bureau who
provide support for children's charities and organisations.
www.nctpregnancyandbabycare.com – a well-designed and
informative site from the NCT covering the first year or so.
www.parenthood.com – lots of advice from this US-oriented site.

www.pinkparents.org.uk – support site for lesbian, gay and bisexual parents and parents-to-be and their children. You need to subscribe to get access to all areas.

www.surestart.gov.uk – the government's guide to help in getting your child the best possible start in life

Party Organising

In this section you'll find all you need to organise the perfect party.

www.partydomain.co.uk   UK
PARTY PARTY!!
Probably the best of the party shop sites with a wide range of fancy dress gear, lots of themed party ideas and options plus a party calendar. Shopping is secure with lots of delivery options.

See also:
www.charliecrow.co.uk – a wide range of fancy dress costumes primarily for kids' parties.
www.evite.com – where you can create your own invitations.
www.fancydress.com – masses of fancy dress costumes.
www.justforfun.co.uk – a good selection of party products here.
www.kids-party.com – a great resource, find out all you need to hold a kid's party in your area.
www.partypieces.co.uk – very experienced party suppliers with a wide range of products.
www.printed4u.co.uk – party invitations printed.

Pets

Here's a selection of web sites devoted to pets: shop and information sites, and specialists too.

www.mypetstop.com   UK
MULTINATIONAL PETS
Apparently the only multilingual web site about pets. It's superb for information and health advice as well as links too. It has sections devoted to each type of pet and animal, and each is pretty comprehensive.

For other good online pet information, services and stores visit:
www.allaboutpets.org.uk – excellent advice and care site from the Blue Cross charity.

www.bluepet.co.uk – specialists in organic food for pets.

www.lostpets.co.uk – an informative site on what to do if you lose your pet includes a lost pet finder service.

www.newpet.com – advice and help for those who are thinking about getting a pet for the first time.

www.petpack.co.uk – an attractive store, advice and care site with a wide range of products.

www.petpals.com – at-home pet-care services.

www.petplanet.co.uk – good for the shop and up-to-the-minute news.

www.petsathome.com – a fairly basic site from this pet retailer.

www.petsmiles.com – a good directory site featuring some 55,000 companies.

www.ukpets.co.uk – a directory of pet shops and suppliers, plus advice and a magazine devoted to pets.

Pet Insurance

www.pethealthcare.co.uk   UK
PET INSURANCE
This is a good place to start looking for insurance to cover your vet's bill. It also has lots of good advice on how to look after pets and what to do when you first get a pet.

See also:
www.animalfriends.co.uk – an insurance company that devotes all profits to animal charities.
www.petplan.co.uk – one of the largest pet insurers.

P

Travel

www.pethealthcare.co.uk   UK
UK HOLIDAYS WITH PETS
This site is devoted to finding holiday accommodation where your pets are always welcome – simply arranged by region, easy. There's also a bookshop and a good set of links.

See also:
www.defra.gov.uk/animalh/quarantine/index.htm – animal quarantine and advice on overseas travel.

www.preferredplaces.co.uk – a holiday specialist with a good 'pets welcome' section.

Animal Charities

www.rspca.org.uk   UK
THE RSPCA
News (some of which can be quite disturbing) and information on the work of the charity plus animal facts and details on how you can help. There's also a good kids' section. It's a good site but a bit tightly packed.

Other charity sites:
www.aht.org.uk – applying clinical and research techniques to help animals.
www.animalrescue.org.uk – fight animal pain and suffering.
www.animalrescuers.co.uk – a directory of centres and people who will help distressed animals.
www.animalsanctuaries.co.uk – index of charities and animal rescue centres.
www.bluecross.org.uk – excellent site with information, help and advice.
www.pdsa.org.uk – People's Dispensary for Sick Animals has a good-looking site with details on how to look after pets and how you can help.

www.giveusahome.co.uk   UK
RE-HOMING A PET
A nice idea, a web site devoted to helping you save animals that need to be re-homed; it's got a large amount of information by region on shelters, vets and the animals themselves as well as entertainment for kids.

TV-related

www.channel4.com/petrescue   UK
PET RESCUE
Details of the programme plus information and links on animal charities and sites, there are also stories, games and chat. See also the excellent BBC web pages on pets which can be found at **www.bbc.co.uk/nature/animals/pets**

Sites for Different Species

Birds

www.avianweb.com   US
FOR BIRD ENTHUSIASTS

A massive site devoted to birds, it's especially good for information on parrots. There are sections on species, health and equipment as well as advice on looking after birds.

See also:

www.birdcare.co.uk – lots of articles and advice on avian health.

www.boglinmarsh.com – racing pigeons.

www.parrot-rescue.co.uk – excellent site devoted to rescuing and looking after birds that have out-grown their owners or need help.

www.rspb.org.uk – mainly wild birds but some good advice.

www.theaviary.com – oddly designed American site but one with lots of information and links.

Cats

www.cats.org.uk   UK
HOME OF CAT PROTECTION

A well-designed and informative site, with advice on caring, re-homing, news and general advice, and an archive of cat photos with competitions for the best. The online shop offers delivery in the UK but charges vary.

See also:

www.catoutofthebag.com – a wide range of cat-related products from a good-looking site. It also includes things like homewares and gifts.

www.crazyforkitties.com – nice site devoted to all things cat and kitty.

www.fabcats.org – a charity devoted to cat care.

www.freddie-street.com – fantastic and funny: the story of the Freddie Street cats. There's some good information in there too.

www.i-love-cats.com – a directory of cat sites.

www.moggies.co.uk – home of the Online Cat Guide, not an easy site to use, but it has exceptional links to pet sites.

P

Dogs

www.the-kennel-club.org.uk   UK
DOGS OFFICIAL

The place to go for the official line on dogs and breeding with information on Crufts and links to related web sites, plus shop and tips on looking after your pooch.

www.dogs.co.uk   UK
COMPLETE DOGS

A comprehensive if slightly unattractive site that seems to have all bases covered when it comes to dogs – although it's mainly a good shop. There are also forums and links.

See also:
www.bugsie.co.uk – yes, it's a mobile dog washing service!
www.canismajor.com/dog – an American magazine site.
www.chazhound.com – for information, fun and games.
www.doglost.co.uk – the place to go if your dog is missing; if you still need help, try **www.lost-doggies.com**
www.dogmadshop.com – good-looking doggie-oriented shop with lots of interesting products for you and your pooch.
www.dogpatch.org – a directory and search engine devoted to dogs.
www.dogs-and-diets.com – comprehensive nutritional information for dogs and you can buy a bow-lingual bark translator!
www.dogster.com – yes, you can set up a web site devoted to your dog alone . . .
www.i-love-dogs.com – a directory of web sites devoted to dogs.
www.loveyourdog.com – a children's guide to caring for dogs.
www.woofwoofdirect.com – daft-sounding title but a very good dog-related gift and accessory shop.

www.ncdl.org.uk   UK
THE DOG'S TRUST

Excellent web site featuring the charitable works of the Dog's Trust (formerly the National Canine Defence League) the largest charity of its type. Get advice on how to adopt a dog, tips on looking after one and download doggie wallpaper. For Battersea Dogs Home go to **www.dogshome.org** who have a well-designed site.

Fish

www.ornamentalfish.org   UK
  ORNAMENTAL AQUATIC TRADE ASSOCIATION
  An excellent site beautifully designed and well executed.
  Although much of it is aimed at the trade and commercial side,
  there is a great deal of information for the hobbyist about looking
  after and buying fish.

  See also:
  www.aquariacentral.com – a huge site with masses of
  information on every aspect of looking after fish.
  www.fishdoc.co.uk – excellent site of fish illnesses and ailments.
  www.fishlinkcentral.com – a good directory site for information
  on fish.

Horses

www.equiworld.net   UK
  GLOBAL EQUINE INFORMATION
  Not the most helpful design but a directory, magazine and advice
  centre in one, with incredible detail plus some fun stuff too
  including video and audio interviews and footage, holidays and
  the latest news. The shop consists of links to specialist traders.

  See also:
  www.equine-world.co.uk – lots here too, including classified
  ads, shopping and links.
  www.horseadvice.com – a health-oriented site that supplies a
  huge amount of information.
  www.horses-and-horse-information.com/horsehealth.shtml –
  health information from a large American site.

Rabbits and Rodents

http://www.rabbit.org   US
  HOUSE RABBIT SOCIETY
  It's all here, from feeding, breeding, behaviour, health advice and
  even info on house-training your rabbit. Has a nice kid's section
  and plenty of cute pictures.

  See also:
  www.rabbitwelfare.co.uk – lots of chat, advice and links from
  the Rabbit Welfare Association.

www.caviesgalore.com – information, forums, games and names.

www.cavycapers.com – a guinea pig haven on the web! A nice site too.

www.gerbils.co.uk – home of the National Gerbil Society.

www.webcom.com/lstead/rodents/rodents.html – good information on caring for rodents and some interesting material on genetics. Shame there are no pictures.

Other Pets

http://exoticpets.about.com – comprehensive information and news stories.

www.ameyzoo.co.uk – a specialist exotic pet shop with fact sheets on how to look after them properly.

www.easyexotics.co.uk – attractive site covering exotic plants as well as pets, it aims to take the mystery out of looking after them; sections on tarantulas and arrow frogs.

www.exoticpetvet.net – advice from specialist vets.

www.kingsnake.com – an American community site devoted to snakes.

www.petreptiles.com – comprehensive pet reptile information.

www.ukreptiles.com – an OK directory site for reptile enthusiasts, good for links.

Photography

www.photographyworld.co.uk   UK

COMMUNITY OF PHOTOGRAPHERS

A good portal site with links to all aspects of photography, there's information on everything from models to lessons. For more links and research try **www.photolinks.net** which is pretty comprehensive.

www.rps.org   UK

THE ROYAL PHOTOGRAPHIC SOCIETY

An improved site dedicated to the works of the RPS. There are details on the latest exhibitions and the collection, you can become a member and get the latest news about the world of photography.

www.nmpft.org.uk   UK
> NATIONAL MUSEUM OF PHOTOGRAPHY, FILM AND
> TELEVISION
> Details of this Bradford museum via a high-tech web site:
> opening times and directions, what's on, education resources
> and a very good museum guide.

www.eastman.org   US
> THE INTERNATIONAL MUSEUM OF PHOTOGRAPHY
> George Eastman founded Kodak and this New York-based
> museum too. This site is comprehensive and amongst
> other things, you can learn about the history of photography,
> visit the photographic and film galleries, or obtain technical
> information. Become a member and you're entitled to
> benefits such as free admission and copies of their *Image*
> magazine.

www.nationalgeographic.com/photography   US
> NATIONAL GEOGRAPHIC MAGAZINE
> Synonymous with great photography, this excellent site offers
> much more. There are sections on travel, history, maps, news,
> education, and for kids. In the photography guide pick up tips
> and techniques, follow their photographers' various locations,
> read superb articles and accompanying shots in the 'Visions
> Galleries'. Good links to other photographic sites.

www.life.com/Life   US
> *LIFE* MAGAZINE
> *Life* magazine is wonderfully nostalgic and still going strong.
> There are several sections, features with great photos, excellent
> articles, and an option to subscribe; however, they could do
> much more and it's a little frustrating to use.

> *See also:*
> **www.iphotocentral.com** – a dealer in old photographs.
> **www.photographymuseum.com** – odd site from the American
> Museum of Photography.
> **www.photolinks.com** – a comprehensive but slightly messy
> links directory.
> **www.photonet.org.uk** – home of London's Photographers'
> Gallery, find out what's on and buy prints.
> **www.rleggat.com/photohistory** – the history of early
> photography.

P

www.bipp.com   UK
> BRITISH INSTITUTE OF PROFESSIONAL PHOTOGRAPHY
> The place to go if you want to hire a professional photographer,
> there are some 3,500 on its books. It also offers advice to
> students and others interested in a career in photography.

Great Photographers

www.masters-of-photography.com   US

> ONLINE GALLERIES
> A simple site with a superb array of galleries devoted to the real
> masters of the art of photography – you can spend hours
> browsing here.

> *See also:*
> **www.anseladams.com** – a great place to buy Ansel Adams
> photos.
> **www.davidbaileyphotography.com** – the official site with some
> great shots to view.
> **www.npg.org.uk** – National Portrait Gallery offer up interviews,
> biographies and the work of some of the great photographers.
> **www.photography-museum.com** – American Museum of
> Photography.
> **www.r-cube.co.uk/fox-talbot** – the Fox Talbot museum.
> **www.staleywise.com** – excellent gallery, very strong on Norman
> Parkinson.
> **www.temple.edu/photo/photographers** – excellent site with
> essays on all the great photographers and their work.

Photo Libraries

www.bapla.org   UK
> PICTURE LIBRARIES
> Home of the British Association of Picture Libraries and although
> it's basically an industry site it has lots of information and links to
> all the major libraries in the UK.

> *See also:*
> **www.corbis.com** – one of the biggest libraries, much of which is
> free.
> **www.freefoto.com** – who say they offer the largest free image
> database.
> **www.freeimages.co.uk** – 2,500 free quality pictures.

www.gettyimages.com – the leading commercial library with lots of royalty-free images to download.

www.webshots.com – which is great for wallpaper and screensavers.

Photographic Advice

www.bjphoto.co.uk   UK
THE *BRITISH JOURNAL OF PHOTOGRAPHY*
An online magazine with loads of material on photography. Access their archive or visit picture galleries that contain work from contemporary photographers, find out about careers in photography and where to buy the best photographic gear.

www.betterphoto.com   UK
TAKE BETTER PICTURES
A very well-laid-out and comprehensive advice site for new and experienced photographers with a buyer's guide plus introductions to and overviews of traditional and digital photography.

See also:
www.88.com/exposure – a temperamental site but one that offers up a great deal of information both for beginners and the well versed.

www.photo.net – an American site with lots of advice and reviews.

www.photographyblog.com – a lively and personal blog created by a professional photographer.

www.photozone.de – a brave attempt at providing a rounded community site covering most aspects of photography with reviews and technical help.

www.shortcourses.com – all you need to know about digital photography.

Photography Stores and Equipment Reviews

www.jessops.com   UK
TAKE ADVICE, TAKE GREAT PICTURES
Jessops are the largest photographic retailer in the UK and they offer advice on most aspects of photography plus courses and free software for their digital printing service. They do give you an opportunity to go shopping for your camera and accessories.

P

See also:

http://photography.ebay.co.uk – eBay's comprehensive photo equipment auction section.

www.bestcameras.co.uk – good range and a clutter-free site. Recommended.

www.cameras2u.com – this store has a wide range, good prices and you can download their helpful guides too.

www.dcresource.com – information and reviews on digital cameras.

www.digitaltruth.com – unusual design, but very comprehensive equipment shop and portal site.

www.dpreview.com – digital photography cameras and equipment reviewed.

www.ffordes.com – a good site offering used equipment alongside the new.

www.photoglossy.com – specialists in paper, material and printing accessories.

Photo Storage, Development and Sharing

http://photos.fotango.com   UK
ONLINE DEVELOPERS

Fotango will take your film and digitise it, then place your pictures on a secure site for you to view and select for printing the ones you like. The service is quick and easy to use; costs don't seem much different from the high street although single prints can be expensive.

www.flickr.com   CANADA

PHOTO COMMUNITY

A fast-growing membership and an indication of what will be the way forward for sharing photos with friends, family and colleagues. It's very easy to set up with the best feature being the facility to tag your photos with key words making it easier to search and share your collection. It's also got good security should you only want to share your album with a few people.

www.fotopages.com   US
PHOTO BLOG

Here you can set up your own photo blog, which you can share with friends and family. It's pretty easy to get going and it's really effective, you can archive material, add captions, text and even links.

http://picasa.google.com
US
ORGANISE YOUR PHOTOS
Picasa is one of Google's many projects, download it and you
can organise your photos and, more to the point, quickly find
them when you need to. See also **www.hello.com** which is
another program that works a little like an instant messenger
service but for photos. If you discuss photos with friends or as
part of your business, it's a good way to see them at the same
time. Mac users should check out **www.apple.com/dotmac/**

See also
www.beanpix.com – aside from offering the usual storage and
online album facilities, Beanpix also enables you to market and
sell your own photos.
www.bootsdigitalphotocentre.com – photo sharing and an
online developing service from Boots.
www.my-expressions.com – expose yourself with this photo-
blogging service.
www.ofoto.com – excellent site from Kodak.
www.photobox.co.uk – great design, probably the best for
digital photo storage.
www.ringo.com – simple to use, has the popular vote.
www.snapfish.co.uk – a site that offers good value prints from
digital shots as well as a sharing facility.

Miscellaneous Photography Sites

www.getmapping.com
UK
AERIAL PHOTOGRAPHS
Just type in your postcode and get a picture of your home taken
from above on a sunny day last year. There are lots of cost
options and you can also get a map to go with it.

www.panoramas.dk
DENMARK
PANORAMIC PHOTOGRAPHY
A great use of the Quicktime program, thousands of sites and
movies all devoted to or celebrating panoramic photography.

www.playingwithtime.org
US
TIME-LAPSE PHOTOGRAPHY
This site is part of a larger photographic project, here you can
see incredible movies filmed with time-lapse photography.
Excellent.

See also:
www.darknessandlight.co.uk – atmospheric prints from this Cambridge-based photographer.
www.francisfrith.co.uk – historical photos to buy.
www.pimpampum.net/bubblr – a fun site where you can create comic strips from photos uploaded from Flickr and your own Mac or PC.

Podcasting

Driven by the popularity of the iPod, creating downloadable broadcasts is one of the fastest growing and most popular pastimes on the Internet. Here are the major sites where you can get help, download for free or just learn how it's done. See also Radio on page 392

www.podcast.net is the best podcast directory, while a good podcast portal is to be found at www.podcastalley.com Both are useful starting points. A good audio/video search engine can be found at the Singing Fish http://search.singingfish.com

If you're new to podcasting visit http://en.wikipedia.org/wiki/Podcast where Wikipedia explains it all; however, if you want to get Wikipedia on your iPod, then go to http://encyclopodia.sourceforge.net/en/index.html

For podcast content try . . .
www.bbc.co.uk/radio – listen again, download your favourite radio programme.
www.guardian.co.uk/rickygervais – the world's most popular podcast.
www.podcastbunker.com – quality not quantity, excellent selection.
www.podcastingnews.com – all the latest and best podcasts.
www.podcastpickle.com – podcasts and vidcasts too.

For the technically minded try www.ipodhacks.com, while if you want to create your own podcast site start at http://podsites.com

Price Checkers

Here's a good place to start any online shopping trip – a price comparison site. There are many price checker sites; however, the sites listed here allow you to check the prices for online stores across a much wider range of merchandise than the usual books, music and film.

It should be said that some fail to take into account the cost of sending the products. For example, the last edition of this book was listed by one supplier at a sale price of £1, but they charged over £4 to send it! However, it was listed by the price checker as the cheapest option.

To Pick Up a Bargain

The Good Web Site Guide's Top 10s
of the Internet

1. **www.ebay.co.uk** – bid for a bargain
2. **www.kelkoo.co.uk** – compare prices
3. **http://froogle.google.co.uk** – search for the product, find the best price
4. **www.pricechecker.co.uk** – get a great deal on thousands of products
5. **www.freeinuk.co.uk** – your guide to everything free
6. **www.which.co.uk** – it may be cheap but is it reliable?
7. **www.thesimplesaver.com** – the simple way to save money
8. **www.gooddealdirectory.co.uk** – the best brand names for the best prices
9. **www.abebooks.com** – the cheapest place to buy a book
10. **www.unbiased.co.uk** – sort your finances out, then shop!

P

www.kelkoo.co.uk   UK

COMPARE PRICES BEFORE YOU BUY
Kelkoo is probably the best price-checking site with 20 categories in their shop directory including books, wine, white goods, even cars and utility bills – they have links with eBay. There are plenty of bargains to be had, in fact they keep popping up on every page.

www.checkaprice.com   UK
CONSTANTLY CHECKING PRICES
Compare prices across a huge range of products, from the usual books to cars, holidays, mortgages and electrical goods. If it can't do it for you, it patches you through to a site that can.

Other good sites:
www.buy.co.uk – excellent for the utilities – gas, water and electrical as well as credit cards and mobile phones.
www.dealtime.co.uk – easy-to-use directory and price checker covering a wide range of goods.
www.froogle.co.uk – Google's price checker service.
www.pricechecker.co.uk – a straightforward site which also covers flights and telephone tariffs.
www.priceguideuk.com – a good UK-oriented service.
www.pricerunner.com – a good all-rounder with a news section giving the latest information on deals and technology updates.
www.pricescan.com – all the usual, plus watches, jewellery, sports goods and office equipment – good store finder.
www.price-search.net – mainly computers and gadgets.
www.pricewatch.co.uk – good for computers and finance.
www.unravelit.com – unravel your troubles and get the best deal here. Good for utilities and finances.

Problems and Relationships

Sites of particular interest to fathers are found on page 306 and mothers on page 568.

www.ondivorce.co.uk   UK

MANAGING DIVORCE AND SEPARATION
The first place to go when faced with divorce or separation.
There is sound financial, legal, practical and emotional support and excellent links. See also **www.family-solicitors.co.uk**

www.gingerbread.org.uk   UK
SUPPORT FOR LONE-PARENT FAMILIES
Gingerbread is an established charity run by lone parents with the aim of providing support to lone parents. The site is fun to use and well designed, and is one of the few web sites that is available in several languages. For more advice on being a single parent see **www.oneparentfamilies.org.uk** who have a useful 'helpline' information search facility.

See also:
http://britishdna.co.uk – paternity testing.
www.baaf.org.uk – British Association for Adoption and Fostering work with children separated from their birth families and their carers.

www.blendedfamilybliss.com – offers US-style practical and sympathetic advice.

www.homestart.org.uk – the leading family support charity.

www.napac.org.uk – National Association for People Abused in Childhood.

www.ncds.org.uk – National Council for the Divorced and Separated, information on their network of local clubs.

www.nfm.u-net.com – offers mediation services for those facing separation and divorce. Aims to help find solutions to problems before resorting to court.

www.relate.org.uk – relationship counselling for couples or families, face-to-face, online or by phone.

www.reunite.org – a charity specialising in international child abduction provides an impressive site with loads of information.

www.stepfamilies.co.uk – chat with other step-parents, read articles, submit poetry all on an informal, upbeat site.

Childcare

www.bestbear.co.uk   UK
MARY POPPINS ONLINE

Select your postcode and they will provide you with a list of reputable childcare agencies or nurseries in your area. There are also homepages for parents, carers and agencies all with information and ideas. There is also a parents' forum. See also **www.sitters.co.uk**

www.childcarelink.gov.uk   UK
SURESTART

Surestart is part of the government's childcare programme and the web site is designed to provide information about childcare options in a given locality. Search by postcode or town name. It also has a good links section.

www.daycaretrust.org.uk   UK
CHILDCARE ADVICE

Daycare Trust is a national childcare charity which works to promote high-quality, affordable childcare for all. This site is designed to give you all the information you need on arranging care for your child; there are sections on finance and news, and you can become a member.

Dealing With Areas of Parental Concern

General

www.childline.org.uk   UK
A CHILD'S-EYE VIEW
There's a huge amount of advice on a wide range of issues from
bullying, domestic violence, dealing with death, racism and
exam stress. The advice is aimed at youngsters, but it is worth
parents looking at that advice too.

www.nchafc.org.uk   UK
NATIONAL CHILD HELP
A charity aimed at helping children and parents across a wide
range of subjects, issues and problems. A good place to start
getting help.

Alcohol

See the section on drugs and alcohol on page 384.

Allergies

www.anaphylaxis.org.uk   UK
ALLERGY AND ANAPHYLAXIS
A useful site with information on food allergies and their
reactions with good alerts and advice for schools and young
adults. Also try the helpful American site **www.anaphylaxis.com**
For info on E-numbers go to **www.foodag.com**

Bereavement

www.childbereavement.org.uk   UK
CHILD BEREAVEMENT TRUST
Support for those who have suffered the loss of a loved one.
There is a section dedicated to families and one for young
people. The Cruse Bereavement Centre also has a site aimed at
young people at **www.rd4u.org.uk**

Bullying

www.bullying.co.uk   UK
HOW TO COPE WITH BULLYING
Advice for everyone on how to deal with a bully; there are

sections on tips for dealing with them, school projects, problem pages and links to related sites. See also **www.successunlimited.co.uk.** Another good site to try is **www.kidscape.org.uk**

Child Protection

www.teachernet.gov.uk/wholeschool/familyandcommunity/ childprotection   UK
>KEEP THEM SAFE
>Although primarily aimed at teachers, this site gives the low-down on child protection law and policy. For the Government's integrated agenda for the well-being of every child go to **www.everychildmatters.gov.uk**

Computers and the Internet

www.cyberpatrol.com   US
>INTERNET FILTERING SOFTWARE
>The best for filtering out unwanted web sites, images and words. As with all similar programs, it quickly becomes outdated but will continue to weed out the worst. You can download the very commercial free trial from the site. See also **www.netnanny.com** whose site offers more advice and seems to be updated more regularly.

www.pin.org.uk   US
>PARENTS' INFORMATION NETWORK
>Provides good advice for parents worried about children using computers. It has links to support sites, guidance on how to surf the Net, evaluations of software and buyer's guides to PCs.

>*See also:*
>**http://tcs.cybertipline.com** – home of the 'Don't believe the type' campaign with advice on how to spot dodgy characters online.
>**www.iwf.org.uk** – the Internet Watch Foundation who combat child online abuse.
>**www.kidsmart.org.uk** – aimed at schools, this is a good course on how to stay safe on the net.
>**www.missingkids.com/adcouncil** – advice to parents on how to spot internet exploitation.
>**www.netsmartz.org** – good advice for staying safe online.

www.parentscentre.gov.uk/usingcomputersandtheinternet – a government site used to promote the benefits of the Internet as an educational tool to parents. Excellent for links.

www.safekids.com – a basic site that is a useful place to go for links and resources if you're worried about your children coming across something unsuitable on the Net.

Disability and Rare Disorders

www.cafamily.org.uk   UK
SUPPORT FOR FAMILIES
A charity that provides support and advice to parents of children with a medical problem or disability. They have information on over 1,000 rare syndromes and can often put families in touch with others facing similar problems: See also the Council for Disabled Children at **www.ncb.org.uk/cdc**

Divorce

www.itsnotyourfault.org   UK
DIVORCE AND SEPARATION
A useful site with sections for parents, teens and children that attempts to take some of the anguish and guilt out of divorce and separation. See also page 380 and for legal advice, page 303.

Drugs and Alcohol

www.theantidrug.com   US

TRUTH: THE ANTIDRUG
An outstanding site devoted to the fight against drugs with help for parents and children alike. There's plenty of advice, articles and general information and it's all written in an accessible style, and in several languages.

www.talktofrank.com   UK
TALK TO FRANK
The NHS's drug site has non-judgemental, factual information on all the major recreational drugs with useful information on what to do in an emergency – or call The National Drugs Helpline 0800 776600. **www.hit.org.uk** or **www.drugscope.org.uk** are good alternatives.

Dyslexia/Dyspraxia

www.bda-dyslexia.org.uk   UK
> BRITISH DYSLEXIA ASSOCIATION
> A good starting point for anyone who thinks that their child
> might be dyslexic. There is masses of information on dyslexia,
> choosing a school, a list of local Dyslexia Associations where
> you can get assessment and teaching, articles on the latest
> research and educational materials for sale. There is also
> information on adult dyslexia. For similar material visit
> **www.dyslexia-inst.org.uk** who also offer testing and teaching
> through their centres. If you're thinking of opting out and taking
> the home education route go to **www.dyslexics.org.uk**

www.dyspraxiafoundation.org.uk   UK
> DYSPRAXIA EXPLAINED
> Information and practical help aimed at anyone who is coping
> with a dyspraxic child including how to find your local support
> group and up-to-date research news.

Eating Disorders

www.edauk.com   UK
> EATING DISORDERS ASSOCIATION
> If you think you have a problem with eating then at this site you
> can get advice and information. It doesn't replace going to the
> doctor but it's a place to start. There are helplines – youth is
> 01603 765 050, others 01603 621 414.

Health

*See the section on Health Advice, page 238, and Women's Health on
page 571.*

www.kidshealth.org/teen   US
> IT'S GOT IT COVERED
> An excellent American site divided into three sections: parents,
> kids and teens. It is really comprehensive and a good place to
> go if you want information about an illness, developmental
> concern of just some advice. The teen section is particularly
> good, especially on food and its relationship to health. Two more
> excellent sites can be found at **www.healthykids.org.uk** and
> **www.childrenfirst.nhs.uk**

Law

www.childrenslegalcentre.com UK
FREE LEGAL HELP
A charity that provides free and confidential legal advice and an information service, which covers all aspects of the law affecting children and young people. They can help provide advocates in disputes with the Local Education Authority and campaigns for children's rights in the UK and overseas. To keep in touch with policy changes relating to children and young people go to **www.childpolicy.org.uk**

Missing Children

www.missingkids.co.uk UK
UK'S MISSING CHILDREN
This site is dedicated to reuniting children with their families. The details of those missing are based on police and home office data. You can search by town or date and there's also a section on those who've got back together.

Also try:
www.fredi.org/anglais/indexen.htm – a French charity devoted to helping and preventing child abuse and abduction.
www.missingpersons.org – the missing persons helpline 0500 700700.
www.ncmec.org – the National Center for Missing Children, an American site with a great deal of information.
www.salvationarmy.org.uk – look under 'quick links' for their family tracing service.

Racism

www.britkid.org UK
DEALING WITH RACISM
A game that shows how different ethnic groups live in the Britain of today, full of interesting facts and information. There's a serious side, which has background information on dealing with racism, information on different races and their religious beliefs. See also the football-related **www.kickitout.co.uk** which is also very useful.

Safety

www.childalert.co.uk   UK
CHILD SAFETY
This is about bringing up children in a safe environment; there
are tips, product reviews and a shop, stories, links and masses of
advice and information. Except for the shop, the site is well
designed and it's easy to find things. See also
www.yoursafechild.com

www.childcarseats.org.uk   UK
CAR SAFETY
All you need to know about buying, fitting and using child car
seats.

Sex

*The following sites provide accessible, factual information. The sections
on health, page 238, men, page 306, teens, page 481, and women,
page 566, may also provide relevant information.*

www.playingsafely.co.uk   UK
HERE TO ANSWER YOUR QUESTIONS
Great site that has lots of information on sex as well as games
and links to related sites. The emphasis is on safe sex and AIDS
prevention. See also the Terence Higgins Trust at
www.tht.org.uk this is the leading AIDS charity.

www.likeitis.org.uk   UK
TELLING IT LIKE IT IS
A really outstanding site from the Marie Stopes Institute giving
good, straight information on all the major issues around sex and
puberty that face teenagers today. The 'Cool or Fool' quiz is
excellent and there's a 'Dear Doctor . . .' facility too.

www.fpa.org.uk   UK
FAMILY PLANNING ASSOCIATION
Straightforward and informative, you can find out where to get
help and there's a good list of web links too. See also the British
Pregnancy Advisory service at **www.bpas.org**

Speech

www.speechteach.co.uk   UK
SPEECH THERAPY
Information, help and advice on what to do if your child has
speech problems or communication difficulties. The site
aims to provide a learning resource for parents and teachers
alike.

Stress and Mental Health

www.rethink.org/at-ease   UK
YOUR MENTAL HEALTH
At-ease offers loads of good advice on how to deal with stress
and is aimed specifically at young people. Go to the A–Z section,
which covers a large range of subjects from dealing with
aggression to exam stress to how to become a volunteer helping
others. See also **www.youngminds.org.uk**

www.isma.org.uk/exams.htm   UK
EXAM STRESS
Top tips on coping with exams from the International Stress
Management Association.

Property

*Every estate agent worth their salt has got a web site, and in theory
finding the house of your dreams has never been easier. These sites
have been designed to help you through the minefield. For advice on
building your own house go to page 279 in the home section.*

www.upmystreet.com   UK

FIND OUT ABOUT WHERE YOU WANT TO GO
Type in the postcode and up pops almost every statistic you need
to know about the area in question. Spooky, but fascinating,
it's a good guide featuring not only house prices, but also
schools, the local MP, local authority information, crime and
links to local services and trades people. It also has a classified
section and puts you in touch with the nearest items to your
area. See also **www.hometrack.co.uk** which is a subscription
service but offers a huge amount of data about house prices
and the area.

www.landreg.gov.uk   UK
LAND REGISTRY
A new look for this site which provides information on house and land prices by region, details on how to register land and your rights. You can also make inquiries about a property's history.

www.conveyancing-cms.co.uk   UK
CONVEYANCING MARKETING SERVICE
Conveyancing is a bit of a minefield if you're new to it, but this site aims to help with advice and competitive quotes. **www.theclc.gov.uk** is the home to the Council for Licensed Conveyancers, which lists them and offers advice on how to choose one. See also **www.easier2move.com** which is nicely designed and very informative.

www.checkmymove.com   UK
PROPERTY SALE TRACKER
Check on the progress of your house move by using this handy tracking service. The only downside is that it depends on your solicitor and estate agent signing up to the service, which they are charged for. It will be interesting to see how this idea progresses.

www.home-repo.org   UK
HOME REPOSSESSION
A very useful and informative site that blows the lid off the goings on behind what happens when a house is repossessed and what you should do if you find yourself in arrears. It's assertive and entertaining too.

For more properties and help with moving home try these sites. Some are just for buyers, but many have homes to rent too.

www.beach-huts.co.uk – great site, providing you want to buy or rent a beach hut.

www.cityscope.co.uk – flashy website from this London specialist.

www.easier.co.uk – free, no-hassle advertising also has a finance section.

www.findaproperty.com – 184,000 properties listed, biased to the South East.

www.heritage.co.uk – covers listed buildings only for sale plus information on their upkeep.

www.hol365.com – really good site design and a massive range of services and properties from thousands of estate agents nationwide.

www.houseweb.co.uk – highly rated with comprehensive advice and thousands of properties for sale.

www.itlhomesearch.com – independent home search and advice site that also covers Spain and Ireland – rent or buy.

www.knightfrank.com – world-wide service, easy-to-use site.

www.land-property-grab.com – track down and nab yourself some unclaimed property . . . legally!

www.naea.co.uk – National Association of Estate Agents with their code of conduct, links and the latest property news.

www.primelocation.co.uk – one of the biggest property search engines.

www.propertyfinder.com – Britain's biggest house database, excellent site with lots of advice, information, houses and associated services

www.property-platform.com – home of the Guild of Professional Estate Agents with a property search facility.

www.rightmove.com – very clear information site with a good property search engine.

www.smartnewhomes.com – search engine dedicated to new homes.

www.themovechannel.co.uk – an OK portal site. Each agent or property site gets a review and a link. Better than it looks at first glance.

www.ukpad.com – details of property auctions in the UK.

www.ukpropertyshop.com – claims to be the most comprehensive estate agent directory covering 3,000 towns in the UK.

www.vebra.com – above-average property search engine, much faster than most.

Renting

www.landlordzone.co.uk   UK

RENTAL PROPERTY KNOWLEDGE

Very useful for landlords and tenants alike with the latest news available and lots of advice too. It's great for links and easy to navigate though a bit advert heavy.

See also:

www.arla.co.uk – home of the Association of Residential Letting Agents with lots of useful information.

www.homelet.co.uk – claim to take the risk out of renting by offering sound advice and insurance for both tenants and landlords – good design.

http://uk.easyroommate.com   UK

FIND A FLATMATE

This service is available in 18 countries, including the UK. Simply select your town from the pull down list, enter your details and preferences and they'll search for available matches – simple.

See also:

www.flatshare.com – great for London.

www.shareflatmates.com – also US, Canada and Australia.

Property Abroad

www.french-property.com   UK

NO.1 FOR FRANCE

If you are fed up with the UK and want to move to France this is the first port of call. They offer properties for rent or for sale in all regions and can link you with other estate agents.

www.overseaspropertyonline.com   UK

MOVING ABROAD

This site was formerly **www.spanish-property-online.com** and remains a good starting point if you want to find property and advice on buying in Spain. However, it has extended its range to cover Europe, the Caribbean, North America, Australia and New Zealand.

See also:

www.adhspain.com – excellent site from this Spanish property specialist.

www.bulgariandreams.com – it's the place to be, apparently.

www.buy-property-dubai.com – Dubai property.

www.fopdac.com – home to the Federation of Overseas Property Developers, a trade association site that has some useful advice and contact information.

www.french-property-news.com – a poorly designed site, but good advice and links.

www.islandsforsale.com – yes, buy yourself a whole island!

www.latitudes.co.uk – French property specialists.

www.prestigeproperty.co.uk – links with estate agents in nine countries.
www.property-abroad.com – a site covering Spain, Italy, Greece and Florida.
www.realestateslovakia.net – beautiful chateaux in Eastern Europe.
www.worldclasshomes.co.uk – properties in Spain, Portugal, France and Bahamas . . .

Storage and Removal

www.reallymoving.com   UK

MAKING MOVING EASIER
A directory of sites and help for home buyers including mortgages, removal firms, surveyors, solicitors, van hire and home improvements. You can get online quotes on some services and there's good regional information. The property search is fast and has plenty of choice. For a helpful directory of removal and storage companies with information and advice try **www.helpiammoving.com** and also the British Association of Removers has an informative site at **www.barmovers.com**

www.removal-companies.co.uk   UK

FIND THE BEST REMOVAL FIRM
An easy way of getting quotes from several removal companies in one go, just follow the simple instructions.

www.packnmove.co.uk   UK

ALL BOXED UP
Here you're offered a wide range of packaging options each designed to help you move your stuff in the most efficient way, whether you have a one room flat or a mansion. It includes calculators too, so you order the right quantity. See also **www.a1box.co.uk**, **www.removalboxes.co.uk** and **www.removal-boxes.com**

Radio

You need a decent downloadable player such as RealPlayer or Windows Media Player before you start listening. The downside is that quality is sometimes affected by Net congestion although that's becoming less of a problem these days as broadband becomes more common. See page 378 for information on Podcasts and page 356 for RSS. It will be interesting to see how this area of the Internet develops as people are increasingly able to tailor their listening according to their tastes.

www.mediauk.com/directory   UK

DIRECTORY OF RADIO STATIONS
Excellent site. You can search by station, presenter or by type, there's also background on the history of radio and articles on topics such as digital radio. The site also offers similar information on television and magazines.

See also:
http://dir.yahoo.com/News_and_Media/Radio – Yahoo's list of nearly 7,000 stations and related sites.
http://windowsmedia.com/Mediaguide/Radio – home to Microsoft's media listings, which is very comprehensive.
www.comfm.com/live/radio – a French site with access to thousands of stations.
www.icecast.org – download the player and get access to radio stations and video streams.
www.live365.com – good-looking site with thousands of radio stations to choose from and it's easy to customise to your tastes too. The basic service is free, but for CD-quality sound and to broadcast your own radio station, you have to pay.
www.publicradiofan.com – ugly site with thousands of stations listed but they are listed by time-zone so you should be able to find something you like playing at any one time.
www.radio-locator.com – a huge directory of radio, US-oriented.
www.radio-now.co.uk – radios to buy, listen live, plus lots of links.
www.shoutcast.com – another huge selection using the Winamp player. If you fancy yourself as a DJ, it's free to join in and broadcast here.
www.virtualtuner.com – tune in to a vast number of stations at this good-looking site, the top 500 is interesting in itself.

www.radioacademy.org   UK

UK'S GATEWAY TO RADIO
Radio Academy is a charity that covers all things to do with radio including news, events and its advancement in education and information. It has a list of all UK stations including those that offer web casts. You get more from the site if you become a member.

www.bbc.co.uk/radio UK
THE BEST OF THE BBC
Listen to the news and the latest hits while you work, just select
the station you want. There's also information on each major
station, as well as a comprehensive listing service. Some
features such as football commentary on certain matches will be
missing due to rights issues. Most of the stations have some level
of interactivity, with Radio 1 being the best and most lively, you
can also tap into their local stations and of course the World
Service.

www.virginradio.co.uk UK
VIRGIN ON AIR
Excellent, if slightly messy with lots of ads plus plenty of stuff
about the station, its schedule and stars. There's also a good
magazine with the latest music news. You can listen if you have
Windows Media Player, RealPlayer, iTunes, WinAmp or Ogg
media players.

Other independent radio stations online are:
www.capitalfm.com – Capital Radio.
www.classicfm.com – classical music and background
information.
www.coolfm.co.uk – Northern Ireland's number one.
www.galaxyfm.co.uk – good range of dance music.
www.heart1062.co.uk – London's heart.
www.jazzfm.com – live broadcasts, cool site too.
www.lbc.co.uk – two stations providing the voice of London.
www.resonancefm.com – London-oriented arts station.

www.mercora.com US

CREATE YOUR OWN STATION
This is the site that is revolutionising the way we listen to radio
and download/share music. The idea is to download the
program and effectively create a radio station that matches your
tastes and those of your friends. As it's still in beta mode (i.e.
testing), it's still free, at time of writing anyway.

Railways

*These are sites aimed at the railway enthusiast. For information
on trains and timetables see page 554 while for railway modelling
go to page 274.*

www.nrm.org.uk   UK
NATIONAL RAILWAY MUSEUM
An excellent museum site packed with information and details
on their collection, you can even take a virtual tour. See also
Great Western's very informative museum site at
www.steam-museum.org.uk

www.heritagerailways.com   UK
HERITAGE RAILWAY ASSOCIATION
This site offers an online guide to the entire heritage railway
scene in the UK, including details of special events and
operating days for all heritage railways with lots of links
world-wide.

www.narrow-gauge.co.uk   UK
NARROW GAUGE
The new and improved Narrow Gauge Heaven (formerly Narrow
Gauge on the Web) steams in with latest news and a better photo
gallery plus all the narrow gauge information you'll need. You
can also contribute your own articles or just browse.

See also:
www.drcm.org.uk – good site on the Darlington Railway
Museum.
www.gensheet.co.uk – keep up to date with timetable changes
and diversions.
www.heritagerailway.co.uk – geared to selling the mag but
plenty of links and some archive material.
www.icrs.org.uk – home of the Inter-City Railway Society with
an informative, highly comprehensive and useful site.
www.mylinkspage.com/rail.html – the brain resource centre.
www.pcrail.co.uk – a rail enthusiast's dream: simulations of
railway operations and journeys. The site is well designed and
simulations cost around £35.
www.railcentre.co.uk – the Stockton and Darlington railway.
www.railfaneurope.net – information on European trains.
www.railpictures.net – lots of pictures of mainly American trains.
www.railway-technology.com – the latest industry news.
www.rpsi-online.org – Ireland's Railway Preservation Society.
www.steamlocomotive.com – steam trains in the US.
www.steamtrain.info – a spectacular Scottish railway.
www.trackbed.com – in excess of 2,500 pages on Britain's
railway heritage, a labour of love.
www.trainorders.com – a US rail community site, there's a lot

R

here with particularly lively discussion forums.

www.trainspotters.de – a good site from a German rail fan.

www.trainweb.org – an ugly directory of train- and railway-related sites.

www.uksteam.info – a well-organised site covering steam train preservation.

www.vintagetrains.co.uk – home of the Birmingham Railway Museum.

Reference and Encyclopaedia

If you are stuck with your homework or want an answer to any question, then this is where the Internet really comes into its own. With these sites you are bound to find what you are looking for. For schoolwork, also refer to the education section, page 124. You should also check out your County/Borough library site, which gives you access to a huge amount of free online reference material. This includes sites such as Oxford Reference Online (including the entire OED), The Britannica Online, The Times Digital archive, the Naxos Music Library and more. Most of these sites are not available for free public use, but the library services have come to an agreement with the publishers and they are accessible to anyone with a library card. You may have to call into your local library to get an access number.

www.refdesk.com   US

THE BEST SINGLE SOURCE FOR FACTS

Singled out for its sheer size and scope, this site offers information and links to just about anything. Its mission is 'only about indexing quality Internet sites and assisting visitors in navigating these sites'. It has won numerous awards and it never fails to impress. Users outside the US may find it too biased towards that country.

www.about.com   US

IT'S ABOUT INFORMATION

A superb resource, easy to navigate and great for beginners learning to search for information. Experts help you to find what you need every step of the way. It offers information on a wide range of topics from the arts and sciences to shopping.

www.ipl.org   US

THE INTERNET PUBLIC LIBRARY

Another excellent resource, there are articles on a vast range of subjects, its particularly good on literary criticism. Almost every country and its literature is covered. If there isn't anything at the library, there is invariably a link to take you to an alternative web site. Check out their children's section 'kidspace' for first-class children's reference materials and 'teenspace' for teenagers.

See also:
www.archive.org – an excellent resource in the making. The 'Wayback Machine' is fun, though it has a serious side; it catalogues old sites so that they may never be lost.
www.factbites.com – a Google-style search engine that offers up results based on facts that match whole topic, rather than just spotting words that happen to appear on random, less relevant web pages. It is good for general searches and it is better than Google in some ways, although it comes with a big US bias.
www.plymouth.gov.uk/cyberlibrary – librarians have compiled a really useful set of reference links, organised alphabetically, of course.
www.ibiblio.org – holds a huge collection of textual, audio and software resources.
www.libraryspot.com – is similar in scope to IPL, but has a more literary emphasis and an entertaining trivia section for those obsessed by top 10s and useless facts.
www.questia.com – claims to be the biggest online library with over 65,000 books and one million articles. You can preview the books for free but have to join for full access (£75 per year). Excellent search facility.

www.theanswerbank.co.uk   UK
QUESTIONS ANSWERED
Just go to any one of the listed categories and type in your question, and you'll get a list of articles and links relating to your query. Some results returned are quite odd so you have to be quite specific. It may be better to use a search engine such as **www.ask.co.uk**

www.homeworkelephant.co.uk   UK
LET THE ELEPHANT HELP WITH HOMEWORK
A resource with some 5,000 links and resources aimed at helping students achieve great results. There's help with specific subjects, hints and tips, and help for parents and teachers. It's constantly being updated, so worth checking regularly.

R

See also:
www.homeworkhigh.co.uk – Channel 4's excellent homework help site.
www.kidsclick.org – more than 600 topics and subjects covered.

Encyclopaedias

www.wikipedia.org US

THE FREE ENCYCLOPAEDIA
In an amazingly short time Wikipedia has become something of an Internet phenomenon. Basically, it's an encyclopaedia created by anyone who wants to contribute. The English version has almost 500,000 entries and although the quality varies, it's a great place to go for researching, though it's wise to double check your facts.

http://encarta.msn.com US

THE ENCARTA ENCYCLOPAEDIA
Even though the complete thing is only available to buy, there is access to thousands of articles, maps and reference notes via the concise version. It's fast and easy to use, though navigating it is a bit of a pain.

Other useful encyclopaedias:
http://encyclozine.com – wide range of topics covered plus good use of games, quizzes and trivia.
http://i-cias.com/e.o/index.htm – Encyclopaedia of the Orient – for North Africa and the Middle East.
www.babloo.com – interactive encyclopaedia aimed at kids.
www.bartleby.com – one of the best. It offers access to a huge amount of reference work, but also fiction, verse and narrative non-fiction, largely with an American bias.
www.eb.com – *Encyclopaedia Britannica* – they are really cagey about the cost, though. Remember, you can access this via you local library website.
www.encyclopedia.com – possibly the most comprehensive free encyclopaedia on the net, nice design too.
www.everything2.com – similar in concept to Wikipedia with masses of information but they can't be bothered to organise it, so unless you have plenty of time, try something else.
www.highbeam.com – outstanding site with access to huge amounts of data, from newswires to books, maps and images. You have to subscribe to get full access, although there are some free articles and you can preview texts for free.

www.infoplease.com – the biggest collection of almanacs, plus an encyclopaedia and an atlas.

www.seop.leeds.ac.uk – UK mirror site for Stanford Encyclopedia of Philosophy.

www.si.edu/resource – encyclopaedia and links to the massive resources of the Smithsonian.

www.spartacus.schoolnet.co.uk – Spartacus Encyclopedia is excellent for history homework.

www.utm.edu/research/iep – the Internet Encyclopedia of Philosophy.

www.wsu.edu/DrUniverse – ask Dr Universe a question, any question . . .

Specialist Reference Sites

Classics and Literature

www.eserver.org   US

THE ENGLISH SERVER

A much-improved humanities site, which provides a vast amount of resource data about almost every cultural topic. There are some 34,000 texts, articles and essays available on subjects from the arts and fiction through to web design.

http://classics.mit.edu   US

THE INTERNET CLASSICS ARCHIVE

An excellent site for researching into the classics, it's easy to use and fast, with more than enough information for homework whatever the level. See also the excellent

www.bibliomania.com for a wider range of resource materials.

www.perseus.tufts.edu   US

PERSEUS DIGITAL LIBRARY

An excellent source of data for ancient classics and mythology, history and early science. It also offers most of Shakespeare and Marlowe and, although it concentrates largely on pre-1600, it's ever expanding.

See also:

www.mythweb.com – an enjoyable and informative site devoted to Greek mythology.

www.pantheon.org – which contains over 6,000 definitions covering mythology, legends and folklore.

Dictionaries and Words

For information on grammar, pronunciation, plain English and learning English see the English usage section on page 137. For language and translation go to page 301.

www.askoxford.com UK
ASK OXFORD UNIVERSITY
A pretty decent effort at making a dry subject interesting. You can ask an expert, get advice on how to improve your writing and, of course, use the famous dictionary and thesaurus. See also **www.oed.com** where you subscribe to the Oxford English Dictionary at a cost of £50 for 3 months or access via your local library website (see introductory notes). At **www.bbc.co.uk/balderdash** you can actually participate in writing the OED.

http://dictionary.cambridge.org UK
CAMBRIDGE UNIVERSITY
This site has seven dictionaries: English, American English, idioms, phrasal verbs, a learner's dictionary, French/English and Spanish/English – all free.

www.onelook.com US
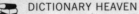
DICTIONARY HEAVEN
Onelook claim to offer access to 1001 dictionaries and over 7½ million words, at a fast, user-friendly site. It also offers a translation facility and reverse dictionary facility, where you describe a concept and it gets back to you with related words.

See also:
www.allwords.com – a well-categorised portal site on everything to do with words, including help with crosswords and translation.
www.collins.co.uk/wordexchange – Collins dictionary with several useful word tools including a Scrabble dictionary.
www.crossword-dictionary.com – here you can type in the word you're looking for, with the gaps, and the dictionary will come up with a list of suggestions; while at **www.oneacross.com** you can type in the pattern and the clue to get your answer.
www.dictionary.com – here you can play word games as an added feature.
www.wordorigins.org – the origins of some 400 words and phrases explained.

www.wordspy.com – the latest on how words are being used and new words.

www.worldwidewords.org – International English from a British point of view, new words and phrases analysed.

www.yourdictionary.com – very comprehensive, the last word in words, apparently.

www.thesaurus.com   US
IF YOU CAN'T FIND THE WORD
Based on Roget's Thesaurus, this site will enable you to find alternative words – useful but not worth turning your PC on for in place of the book. The site is related to **www.dictionary.com** and has several other facilities including translation into 11 languages.

www.visualthesaurus.com   US
THE VISUAL THESAURUS
If you get bored looking up words or looking for alternative meanings for words in the usual way, then check out the Visual Thesaurus. It's fun to use, if a bit weird. Unfortunately, it now requires a subscription after the free trial.

www.peevish.co.uk/slang   UK
DICTIONARY OF SLANG
A comprehensive dictionary of English slang as used in the UK, with good articles and search facility. See also **www.urbandictionary.com** for a listing of the words allegedly used by today's yoof.

www.acronymfinder.com   US
WHAT DO THOSE INITIALS STAND FOR?
If you don't know your MP from your MP3, here's where to go. With over 475,000 acronyms it should help you find what you're looking for.

www.symbols.com   US
WHAT DOES THAT SYMBOL MEAN?
Here you can find the meaning of over 2,500 symbols, with articles on their history.

www.techweb.com   US
THE TECHNOLOGY DICTIONARY
Get the latest business and technology news plus an excellent technology encyclopaedia. For a dictionary that specialises in

jargon and Internet terms only go to either **www.jargon.net** or
www.netdictionary.com for enlightenment.

Other word-related sites:
www.ag.wastholm.net – if you need an aphorism, it's probably
here.
www.identifont.com – identify any font and find one that you
like, also has information on the many different types available.
www.rhymezone.com – type in a word, up pop all those that
rhyme with it.
www.word-detective.com – a magazine devoted to words and
wordplay.

Maths and Numbers

www.mathsisfun.com   UK
MATHS RESOURCES
A good site devoted to the basics of maths, it covers all the
bases and was started by a British maths teacher. All is
well explained with lots of diagrams. See also the
helpful **www.amathsdictionaryforkids.com** which provides
a useful visual dictionary of mathematical terms.

www.onlineconversion.com   UK
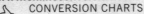
CONVERSION CHARTS
Converts just about anything that can be converted. From the
usual length, weight and currency to international clothing sizes,
cooking volumes, astronomical light – it will even calculate your
retirement date.

See also:
www.easymaths.com – Key Stage maths help.
www.google.com/help/features.html@lculator – this link takes
you to Google's very useful calculator function.
www.math.com – a very comprehensive US maths site.
www.mathguide.de – a German maths portal and search
engine.
www.math-net.de/links – maths links.
www.megaconverter.com/mega2 – annoying design but some
useful converters.
www.scenta.co.uk/tcaep – if you need details on a particular
equation, it's almost certain to be here.
www.univie.ac.at/future.media/moe – a useful collection of
advice, tools and information.

Geography, Atlases and International Statistical Data

See also the section on geology on page 344.

www.nationmaster.com   US
WORLD STATS
A well-designed site, which is excellent for comparative statistics on countries and people. The great benefit to this one is that it also includes access to a good encyclopaedia.

www.ntu.edu.sg/Library/Collections/Databases   SINGAPORE
STATISTICS AND MORE STATISTICS
Free information and statistics about national economies – not that easy to use at first, but it's all there.

www.internetgeographer.com   UK
GEOGRAPHY WEB RING
A good source of information on geography for all ages with quizzes and a population clock which enables you to see the population grow before your eyes. An alternative portal on physical geography can be found at **www.geog.le.ac.uk/cti/phys.html** which includes climatology, geomorphology, hydrology, oceanography and volcanology.

www.atlapedia.com   US
THE WORLD IN BOTH PICTURES AND NUMBERS
Contains full colour political and physical maps of the world with statistics and very detailed information on each country. It can be very slow, so you need patience, but the end results are worth it.

www.geographyiq.com   US
THE WORLD LISTED
A great site covering all the information you'd expect. List freaks will love the rankings pages: they cover everything from largest to oldest to richest. Great for homework.

See also:
http://earth.google.com – Google's excellent resource.
http://plasma.nationalgeographic.com/mapmachine – home of the National Geographic's Map Machine where you can zoom in to any part of the world.

R

www.cia.gov/cia/publications/factbook – the CIA's famous fact book.

www.citypopulation.de – a really impressive site with a world population database including maps and flags.

www.geohive.com/index.html – population statistics combined with information on other key economic factors.

www.geosense.net – a good geography quiz game.

www.plcmc.org/forkids/mow – where you can find depicted all the flags of the world.

www.population.com – has a huge amount of data and information.

www.prb.org – the Population Reference Bureau holds masses of data on the world as well as on the US.

www.statistics.gov.uk – great for statistics on the UK.

www.worldatlas.com – a pretty comprehensive world atlas and gazetteer.

Practical Skills

www.ehow.com   US
HOW TO DO THINGS
A directory and search site that provides information on how to do a mass of jobs and everyday tasks – categorised by subject.

Religion

In this section we've attempted to list sites that are of general interest and try to explain the philosophy of the religions, rather than those sites that simply reflect the opinions of those who preach.

www.omsakthi.org/religions.html   US
RELIGION WORLD-WIDE
This site provides a clear description of each world religion including values and basic beliefs with links to books on each one. For links see also the World Religion Gateway at **www.academicinfo.net/religindex.html** and the extensive **www.adherents.com** who offer statistics on some 4,200 religions and religious bodies.

More general information sites about religion:
http://about.com/religion – About has an excellent overview of the major religions and some minor ones. It also offers a newsletter and covers areas such as spirituality too. Rutgers

University has made available a library of information on the world's religions.

http://virtualreligion.net/vri – an excellent portal on religions, ethics, religious philosophy and psychology.

www.bbc.co.uk/religion – the BBC's excellent site on religion and ethics.

www.beliefnet.com – a wide-ranging and multi-faith approach to spirituality.

www.divinedigest.com – a good overview of the major religions.

www.interfaith.org.uk – promoting good inter-faith relations.

www.religioustolerance.org – an organisation devoted to religions co-operating with each other, it has good information on all major faiths and attempts to explore controversial issues from various viewpoints.

www.unification.net – a comparative anthology of sacred texts organised on a thematic basis.

The Key Religions and Philosophies

Buddhism

http://buddhanet.net – the world-wide Buddhist information and education network. A huge site with, one would guess, everything you need to know.

www.allspirit.co.uk – sacred writings and meditations.

www.ciolek.com/wwwvl-Buddhism.html – the Buddhist studies virtual library.

Christianity

www.anglicancommunion.org – the world-wide Anglican Communion.

www.anglicansonline.org – a huge resource site devoted to Anglicanism with over 10,000 links.

www.biblegateway.com – a searchable bible in 35 languages.

www.catholic.net – a slick site devoted to the Catholic religion; here you'll find everything on the religion, and it seems very comprehensive.

www.cofe.anglican.org – home of the Church of England.

www.crosearch.com – a directory of Christian web sites.

www.methodist.org.uk – the official line in Methodism.

www.newadvent.org/cathen – the Catholic encyclopaedia.

www.pres-outlook.com – a magazine site covering all forms of Presbyterianism; US orientated.

R

www.quaker.org.uk – information on what it is to be a Quaker.
www.russianorthodoxchurch.ws/english – for those outside Russia, with the latest news.
www.salvationarmy.org.uk – excellent site with lots of background information.
www.ship-of-fools.com – excellent radical Christian magazine.
www.thetablet.co.uk – a well-designed Catholic news site.
www.vatican.va – the official site of the Vatican, slow but informative.

Druidism/Paganism

www.druidnetwork.org – an overview of Druid beliefs with links and database.
www.ukpaganlinks.co.uk – web links and other information.

Hinduism

www.hindu.org – a good overview of this complex religion with excellent directory.
www.hindulinks.org – an impressive number of links at this site.

Islam

www.al-islam.org – informative site with good information and links.
www.islamicity.com – a newsy site aimed at explaining Islam and creating more awareness of the religion.
www.islamonline.net – very comprehensive and interesting news and Islamic information site.
www.islamworld.net – a good overview of Islam.
www.salaam.co.uk – wide-ranging site covering all aspects of Islamic culture.
www.ummah.net – an excellent Muslim directory site.
www.usc.edu/dept/msa/reference/glossary.html – a glossary of Islamic terms and concepts.

Judaism

http://shamash.org/trb/judaism.html – a good overview of Judaism plus lots of links.
www.chiefrabbi.org – the official site of the Chief Rabbi.
www.jewfaq.org – an encyclopaedia devoted to Judaism.
www.ritualwell.org – ceremonies for Jewish living.

Scientology

www.scientology.org.uk – comprehensive site on Scientology and what it is.

Sikhism

www.panthkhalsa.org – information on the Sikh nation.
www.singhsabha.com – understanding the religious and philosophical teachings of Sikhism.

Humanism and Secularism

www.freethinker.co.uk – founded in 1881, this magazine has a long history of championing secular humanism.
www.humanism.org – a simple introduction to humanist principles.
www.humanism.org.uk – good introductory site; what humanism is and what they stand for, with information about their campaigns, policies and how to join a group. You can also arrange humanist ceremonies.
www.humanism-scotland.org.uk – the site for Scottish humanists.
www.infidels.org – a serious starting point for sceptics, check out the library for links to sites on atheism and humanism.
www.secularism.org.uk – the National Secular Society campaigns for a secular approach to society. There is a plethora of news features, information about their activities, their parliamentary submissions, the opportunity to join them and buy the T-shirt.

Science

The Internet was originally created by a group of scientists who wanted faster, more efficient communication and today, scientists around the world use the Net to compare data and collaborate. In addition, the layman has access to the wonders of science in a way that's never been possible before, and as for homework – well now it's a doddle.

Pure Science

www.scirus.com   US
> SCIENCE SEARCH
> A straightforward and easy-to-use search engine devoted to
> scientific information only.

www.royalsoc.ac.uk   UK
> THE ROYAL SOCIETY
> An attractive site where you can learn all about the workings of
> the society, how to get grants and what events they are running.
> They've improved the content to include more links and more
> interactivity.

www.scicentral.com   US

> LATEST SCIENCE NEWS
> Apart from being a very good portal, this site offers the latest
> news in the major categories of science, plus a searchable
> database of articles gleaned from papers and magazines around
> the world.

http://scienceworld.wolfram.com   US
> PURE SCIENCE EXPLAINED
> Eric Weisstein's World of Science contains encyclopaedias and
> detailed information written in accessible language on
> astronomy, scientific biography, chemistry, maths and physics.
> The design is easy on the eye and the site is logical to use.

> *See also:*
> **www.firstscience.com** – accessible and colourful, good for older
> children.
> **www.plos.org** – the Public Library of Science provides (free of
> charge) the world's scientific and medical literature online.
> **www.treasure-troves.com** – an eccentric site on various aspects
> of science, quite fun in places too.

Magazines and Blogs

www.newscientist.com   UK
> *NEW SCIENTIST* MAGAZINE
> Much better than the usual online magazines because of its
> creative use of archive material, which is simultaneously fun and
> serious. It's easy to search the site or browse through back

features, however, you have to subscribe to get access to premium content and the online archive of over 60,000 articles. For a more traditional science magazine site go to *Popular Science* at **www.popsci.com** – great for information on the latest gadgets.

www.sciencemag.org   US
SCIENCE MAGAZINE
A serious overview of the current science scene with articles covering everything from global warming to how owls find their prey. The tone isn't so heavy that a layman can't follow it and there are plenty of links too. You need to register to get the best out of it.

See also:
http://vlib.org/Science – the Virtual Library's natural science and maths links page.
www.blacktriangle.org – excellent blog on the latest science news.
www.discover.com – articles from *Discover* magazine.
www.raygirvan.co.uk/apoth/thought.htm – the Apothecary's Drawer, an eclectic blog with news, trivia and information.
www.scitechdaily.com – the latest science news.
www.visions-of-science.co.uk – marvel at the winners of the photographic awards for scientific pictures.

Popular Science

www.sciencemuseum.org.uk   UK
THE SCIENCE MUSEUM
An excellent site detailing the major attractions at the museum with 3-D graphics and features on exhibitions and forthcoming attractions. You can also shop and browse the galleries. You can't help feeling they could do more though. See also **www.exploratorium.edu** a similar but more child friendly site by an American museum.

www.discovery.com   US

THE DISCOVERY CHANNEL
A superb site for science and nature lovers, it's inspiring as well as educational. Order the weekly newsletter, get information on the latest discoveries as well as features on pets, space, travel, lifestyle and school. The 'Discovery Kids' section is very good with lots going on.

www.howstuffworks.com US

HOW STUFF REALLY WORKS
An outstanding and popular site, it's easy to use and truly
fascinating. There are sections ranging from the obvious, like
engines and technology, through to food and the weather. The
current top 10 section features the latest answers to the
questions of the day. It's written in a very concise, clear style with
lots of cross-referencing.

www.si.edu/science_and_technology US
SMITHSONIAN SCIENCE AND TECHNOLOGY
Another excellent set of pages from the outstanding Smithsonian
site, which cover everything from biology to flight and there are
some really well-written and interesting articles and sections too.

www.extremescience.com US

ULTIMATE SCIENCE EXPERIENCE
Not sure that it really lives up to it's billing, but it is a really
entertaining site with lots of useful and useless facts to
bamboozle your brain. Features include a time portal where you
can learn the effects of relativity and other sections on weather,
maps, technology, nature and the earth. It uses the word 'cool' a
lot.

www.dangerouslaboratories.org US
DON'T DO IT YOURSELF
Science with a smile: here you get details of various
'experiments' in a range of scientific fields. It all looks very
amateur and fun as well as educational too.

www.electricmuseum.com US
DON'T TRY THIS AT HOME!
A highly-charged site with sections on lightening and
atmospheric electricity, a high voltage zone, related articles and
some weird and wonderful images. It has the feel of a site under
development.

www.science-frontiers.com US
SCIENTIFIC ANOMALIES
Science Frontiers is a bimonthly newsletter providing digests of
reports that describe scientific anomalies – 'those observations
and facts that challenge prevailing scientific paradigms'. There's
a massive archive of the weird and wonderful; it takes patience
but there are some real gems.

www.world-mysteries.com   US
> WEIRD SCIENCE
> All the mysteries and unexplained phenomena are here,
> rationalised, discussed and illustrated in a fairly unbiased way.
> It makes for an interesting browse.

www.improbable.com   UK
> THE IG NOBLE AWARDS
> These awards are for those inventors whose project initially
> makes others laugh, then makes them think about the science
> behind it. To quote the site, they 'celebrate the unusual and
> honour the imaginative'. The site also offers much in the way of
> unusual scientific gems.

http://whyfiles.org   US
> SCIENCE BEHIND THE NEWS
> If you've ever wondered why things happen and what's the real
> story behind what they tell you in the papers, then a visit here
> will be rewarding. With in-depth studies and brief overviews
> Why Files is easy to follow and you'll get the latest news too.

> *See also:*
> **www.badscience.net** – the very entertaining blog of *Guardian*
> science journalist, Ben Goldacre.
> **www.futuristsnetwork.org.uk** – find out what the future could
> hold for us. Here you'll find essays and discussions on potential
> events.
> **www.scienceagogo.com** – a popular science discussion and
> news site.
> **www.unmuseum.org** – a site devoted to the unexplained and
> natural phenomena. There's some good stuff, but the busy site
> design gets in the way.

Scientists

www.nobelprize.org   NORWAY

> NOBEL PRIZE
> Excellent site on the prize with lots of background information
> and biographies of the winners.

> *See also:*
> **http://galileo.rice.edu** – excellent site on Galileo.
> **www.aip.org/history/curie** – Marie Curie.

www.mos.org/leonardo – the most useful Leonardo Da Vinci site.
www.newton.cam.ac.uk/newton.html#ini – Isaac Newton.
www.rutherford.org.nz – Ernest Rutherford.
www.thomasedison.com – Edison.
www.westegg.com/einstein – Einstein online.

Biology

www.cellsalive.com   US
CELLS UNDER THE MICROSCOPE
The work of one biologist with a fascination for computer-enhanced images of living cells. Fantastic pictures, video and accompanying explanations.

www.innerbody.com   US
INTERACTIVE BODIES
All the body's systems illustrated. Pull your mouse over one of the images to activate labels, which can in turn activate text. The animations are worth checking out.

www.wellcome.ac.uk/en/genome   UK
IN THE GENOME
Excellent site explaining in some detail how the human gene works and its implications for biology, medicine and society. The 'interactive centre' is particularly fascinating.

See also:
www.educationindex.com/biology – for biology links.
www.rbgkew.org.uk/scihort/index.html – look under 'scientific research' for information on most aspects of botany and information about research being undertaken at Kew.

Chemistry

www.webelements.com   US
THE PERIODIC TABLE
So you don't know your halides from your fluorides, with this interactive depiction you can find out. Just click on the element and you get basic details plus an audio description, all in all, a great teaching aid.

www.chemsoc.org   UK
   CHEMICAL SOCIETY
   A really creative site that covers not only industry issues,
   but also educational ones, all in a very entertaining style.
   The timeline is especially well written and there is a very
   useful links page too. For more chemistry links go to
   www.liv.ac.uk/Chemistry/Links/links.html

Physics

www.physicscentral.com   US
   HOW THE WORLD WORKS
   A good place to start when looking for an answer to a physics
   question. It has high-quality information and illustrations,
   physics news, some interesting writing, a good search
   engine and links. For an alternative approach try
   http://particleadventure.org which is both comprehensive
   and well-written.

http://superstringtheory.com   US
   THE OFFICIAL WORD ON STRING THEORY
   If you're curious about theoretical physics, but find it all a bit
   perplexing, or even if you've a good level of understanding, this
   is the site for you. It explains theoretical physics at a basic or
   advanced level with good illustrations, a virtual lecture theatre
   and well-categorised links.

   See also:
   http://physicsweb.org – online edition of the magazine for
   up-to-the-minute publications.
   www.physics.org – a searchable database, plus a few frills.

Practical Science and Science for Children

www.doscience.com   US
   EXPERIMENTS: FUN AND SERIOUS
   A slightly messy but entertaining site that has a number of
   experiments to try both at home and outside. It's informative and
   most of the experiments seem easy to do.

www.planet-science.com   US
   FAST FORWARD TO THE FUTURE
   A visually gratifying site with lots to offer by way of helping

children (and adults for that matter) to learn about science in an interactive and entertaining way.

www.madsci.org   US
THE LAB THAT NEVER SLEEPS
A site that successfully combines science with fun. You can ask a question of a mad scientist, browse the links list or check out the archives in the library.

See also:
http://insideout.rigb.org – a good, if a little dull, educational e-zine from the Royal Institute.
www.amasci.com – for the science hobbyist, an ugly site.
www.cafescientifique.org – Café Scientifique is a forum for those interested in science; find a café near you, or find out how to start one.
www.extremescience.com – a science education site with an emphasis on the biggest, baddest and best in the world of extremes.
www.funsci.com – a serious site with many experiments to try both hard and easy.
www.instructables.com – creativity shared. There's some wacky projects here such as the 3-D chocolate printer made from Lego, but also some serious science projects.
www.practicalphysics.org – over 330 practical physics experiments.
www.scienceboffins.com – a group of children's entertainers who do their stuff using science.
www.spartechsoftware.com/reeko – a quirky site, but a great source of science and chemistry experiments designed to inspire school children; will appeal to kids of all ages.
www.tryscience.org – bright site aimed at children, with a few experiments.

Innovation, Invention and Technology

www.21stcentury.co.uk   UK
YOUR PORTAL TO THE FUTURE
A stylish site that gives an overview of the latest technology put over in an entertaining style. Whether you're using it for homework or just for a browse, it's useful and interesting. They have 12 categories from cars through to humour, people and technology and they even cover fashion.

www.nesta.org.uk   UK
> THE CREATIVE INVENTOR'S HANDBOOK
> The National Endowment for Science Technology not only
> helps inventors get their ideas off the ground with support and
> guidance, but also encourages creativity and innovation. They'll
> also inspire you, as a visit to this well-designed site will show.
> See also the creatively designed **www.inventorlink.co.uk**

www.invent.org   US

> THE INVENTOR HALL OF FAME
> This outstanding and beautifully designed site is sponsored by
> Hewlett Packard. It features advice on how to patent inventions
> and gives details of those who have been inducted into the Hall
> of Fame. If for no other reason, just go to appreciate the web site
> design.

www.gadgets.co.uk   UK
> GAGETS FOR ALL OCCASIONS
> Split into 15 different categories, there are hundreds of things
> here that you didn't now you wanted. More of the same is
> available at **www.paramountzone.com** or **www.firebox.com**

www.robotstoreuk.com   UK
> ROBOSHOP
> A store devoted to selling robot parts and designs, including
> kits and a useful introduction to robotics. See also
> **www.superdroidrobots.com** where you can buy parts
> as well as kits.

Science Fiction and Fantasy

*Science fiction and fantasy deserves its own section given that so many
top movies and books are based on science fiction or fantasy. Here are
a few of the massive number of sites that are around.*

Directories and Reviews

www.thealienonline.net   UK
> THE ALIEN ONLINE
> Great for Sci Fi news, reviews and information, with opinionated
> comments on books, films, television, comics and games from
> some of Sci Fi's biggest names, and links to a host of web sites.

See also:

www.feministsf.org – comprehensive, dour offering on the role of women in Sci Fi.

www.lablit.com – an entertaining site run by scientists rallying against the stereotypical perceptions of scientists in the media and literature.

www.locusmag.com – the online version of US Sci Fi magazine *Locus*. Dull but authoritative.

www.scifisource.com – a directory of all things Sci Fi, not pretty or easy to navigate but it seems comprehensive.

www.sfrt.com – good for reviews, links and forums.

www.sfsite.com – the dated design doesn't detract from the fact that this is one of the most comprehensive review sites you can find; it's quite dense so you need time to digest it.

www.sfx.co.uk – the official site one of the most popular Sci Fi magazines, it offers plenty of content, although is geared to selling the mag.

Awards and Organisations

www.sfwa.org   US
SCI FI WRITERS OF AMERICA
A helpful and informative site from the SFWA including details of their prestigious Nebula awards. If truth were told it's not a great site but the links and writing advice are good.

See also:

www.appomattox.demon.co.uk/acca – home of the UK's Arthur C Clarke Awards.

www.asfa-art.org – the Association of Sci Fi and Fantasy Artists with an index of artists and galleries.

www.bsfa.co.uk – this chatty site represents the British Science Fiction Association.

www.wsfs.org – an amateur-looking site from the World Science Fiction Society home of the Hugo awards and with details of the World Science Fiction Convention.

TV and Movies

www.sciflicks.com   US

SCI FI FILM REVIEW
A comprehensive listing of Sci Fi films with reviews, links, descriptions, cast listing and so on. There's plenty of detail and there is also information on forthcoming movies.

S

www.scifi.com
US

THE SCI FI CHANNEL

An excellent site from the Sci Fi Channel with a very strong emphasis on film and television, although it also includes books, games and other products. It's beautifully designed, easy to navigate, and there is a wealth of extra features, including weekly newsletters.

www.sfon.tv
UK

SCI FI ON TV

A very good site featuring everything Sci Fi on television from the famous and obscure. Dr Sci Fi will even attempt to answer your Sci Fi questions. There's also a good movie review section.

See also:

http://exclamationmark.typepad.com/blog/ – excellent B movie blog.

www.greatlink.org – a UK-oriented site devoted to all things Trek.

www.sadgeezer.com – great for fans of Sci Fi cult TV, though pretty difficult to navigate, it has plenty of other Sci Fi resources too; you should be aware that it is possible to access some adult-oriented content.

www.startrek.com – everything you need to know about Star Trek and its spin off series.

www.starwars.com – outstanding official Star Wars site.

www.superherohype.com – lots of stuff on super heroes plus interviews from those involved in the films and downloads too.

www.timelord.co.uk – Dr Who and much more.

The Writing

http://isfdb.tamu.edu/sfdbase.html
US

INTERNET SPECULATIVE FICTION DATABASE

This excellent resource is an encyclopaedic guide to authors of 'speculative fiction', which includes every Sci Fi, fantasy and horror writer you could think of. The trouble is that it looks more like a library catalogue than a modern web site.

See also:

http://sff.onlinewritingworkshop.com – advice and courses to improve your writing.

www.fantasticmetropolis.com – this good-looking and acclaimed site is dedicated to 'new wave' alternative authors; it includes fiction, essays, interviews, reviews and more. It also has an excellent links section.

www.infinityplus.co.uk – original fiction and non-fiction by many top names.

www.sff.net – somewhere amongst the commercial bits there's a really good website, you just have to be patient and sign up.

www.sfnovelist.com – a writing group who believe in Sci Fi based on hard science; some good short stories, but you need to be a member really.

www.technovelgy.com – a fun site devoted to the inventions of Sci Fi writers and whether they would really work and what they would look like.

The Writers

www.lordoftherings.net   US
LORD OF THE RINGS
Slick on the movie trilogy, including information on the films, interviews, picture galleries, trailers and other downloads. Best accessed on broadband. See also **www.tolkien.co.uk** which is home to the official UK web site from Tolkien's publishers, including a biography, his books, artwork, downloads and other information. Ordering facility through Amazon.

www.discworldmonthly.co.uk   UK
TERRY PRATCHETT
Probably the best of the many sites devoted to this massively popular author and his Discworld creation with lots of links and regular articles and updates.

Other key authors:
Clive Barker – **www.clivebarker.com**
Terry Brooks – **www.terrybrooks.net**
Katherine Kerr – **www.deverry.com**
Stephen King – **www.stephenking.com**
George RR Martin – **www.georgerrmartin.com**
Philip Pullman – **www.philip-pullman.com**
Tad Williams – **www.tadwilliams.com**

Below is a list of key Sci Fi and fantasy publishers:
www.2000adonline.com – home to the venerable British comic, featuring Judge Dredd.
www.marvel.com – great interactive site from *Marvel* Comics with all their major characters suitably involved.

www.orbitbooks.co.uk – home of authors such as Robert Jordan and Iain Banks, it's an attractive, frequently updated site with author pages, new releases, sample chapters, a monthly e-mail newsletter and exclusive offers.

www.titanbooks.com – the UK's largest publisher of graphic novels – also features information on their range of film and TV tie-ins.

www.voyager-books.co.uk – home of HarperCollins' Fantasy and Sci Fi publishing. It's a classy-looking site, with author profiles, news, new titles, sample chapters, interactive features and extras such as downloadable screensavers.

Search Engines

The best way to find what you want from the Internet is to use a search engine. Even the best don't cover anywhere near the number of available web sites, so if you can't find what you want from one, try another. These are the best and most user-friendly. For children's search engines see page 101.

It's Not Just About Google

The Good Web Site Guide's Top 10s of the Internet

1. **www.a9.com** – a search engine that uses many reference resources
2. **www.dmoz.org** – the most comprehensive site directory on the net
3. **www.mirago.co.uk** – great if you want a UK-biased result to your search
4. **www.refdesk.com** – information and links. Very impressive
5. **www.about.com** – fantastic, with expertly written pages on virtually any topic
6. **www.onelook.com** – access to almost 1,000 online dictionaries
7. **www.howstuffworks.com** – if it moves, it's explained
8. **www.nationmaster.com** – information and stats on virtually every country
9. **www.wikipedia.org** – the people's encyclopaedia
10. **www.ehow.com** – instructions on how to do virtually anything

S

www.searchenginewatch.com   US
A GUIDE TO SEARCHING
This site rates and assesses all the search engines and it's a
useful starting point if you're looking for a good or specific search
facility. There's a newsletter and statistical analysis plus
strategies on how to make the perfect search. See also
www.searchengineshowdown.com who do much the same
thing but it's less comprehensive.

General Searching

www.google.co.uk   UK
BRINGING ORDER TO THE WEB
Google is a massive success story and is one of the most useful
sites around. Apart from the simple search facility, it also has a
host of other features which are covered in our Google feature on
page 233. If you want to get the best out of Google then pay a visit
to the non-affiliated but very helpful **www.googleguide.com**

http://search.msn.co.uk   US
MSN SEARCH
A minimal approach, this search engine is supposed to be
Microsoft's answer to Google. It's very fast and it seems to be the
business. You also get access to the Encarta Encyclopedia too.

www.ask.co.uk   UK
ASK
The famous old butler Jeeves has been ditched but, although
less fun, it works very well; it's great for beginners and reliable
for old hands too. See also **www.askforkids.com** which is the
child-oriented version.

http://uk.yahoo.com   US/UK
FOR THE UK AND IRELAND
The UK arm of Yahoo is the biggest and one of the most
established search engines. It's now much more than just a
search facility as it offers a huge array of other services: from
news to finance to shopping to sport to travel to games. You can
restrict your search to just UK or Irish sites too.

www.lii.org   US
THE LIBRARIANS INDEX TO THE INTERNET
This is a search engine with a difference in that all the source
material has been selected and evaluated by librarians

specifically for their use in public libraries. This doesn't stop you using it though, and it is very good for obscure searches and research – like putting together a web site guide, for example.

www.dmoz.org   WORLD-WIDE
THE OPEN DIRECTORY PROJECT
The goal is to produce the most comprehensive directory of the web and relies on an army (some 71,000) of volunteer editors to do so; if you want to get involved it's easy to sign yourself up. If it can't help with your query, it puts you through to one of the mainstream search engines.

Finding the search engine that suits you is a matter of personal requirements and taste. Here are some other very good, tried and trusted ones:
http://uk.altavista.com – limited but very efficient, offers up a list of related options on every search.
www.accoona.com – a good alternative to Google, it allows you to prioritise your searching easily.
www.alltheweb.com – no frills, similar to Google.
www.bbc.co.uk – BBC's search engine is simple to use.
www.copernic.com – download a free search program.
www.dogpile.com – straightforward and no mess . . . US oriented.
www.factbites.com – results come with some context and explanation, which is more helpful than most; strong US bias.
www.infoplease.com – good for homework, one of the best for research.
www.looksmart.com – good, all sites handpicked.
www.pluck.com – a useful little free program that can be used as a search tool, it's also got a useful news feed facility.
www.spurl.net – a search program enhanced with the ability to manage links and bookmarks in a proactive way.
www.yahoo.com – one of the most comprehensive and popular. It's much more than a search facility, which can sometimes get in the way of finding what you want.

Clustering Search Engines

Clustered search engines sort and categorise search results, which is great, but we've yet to find a really good one that isn't US oriented.

www.vivisimo.com
US

CLUSTERING TECHNOLOGY

With Vivisimo instead of the usual list, you get your search results back categorised by subject, or clustered. It makes for easy researching and is one of the three search engines I most use.

www.mamma.com
US

THE MOTHER OF ALL SEARCH ENGINES

Mamma have technology enabling them to search the major search engines thoroughly and get the most pertinent results to your query – it's fast too, your query comes back with the answer and the search engine it came from.

www.A9.com
US

THE WEB AND BEYOND

One to watch this, it uses Google to search the web but enhances that search with information from the Internet Movie Database, Amazon's Search inside the book service and other reference sources. It's a little slow but you get quality results.

See also:

http://turbo10.com – claims to search the bits of the Internet where the major search engines don't go, this is one of the most impressive results-wise.

www.37.com – a bit of a mess but can search 37 other search engines in one go.

www.clusteredhits.com – clutter free, good for technical, scholarly and corporate data although US oriented.

www.metacrawler.com – uses similar technology to Mamma and is a popular choice.

www.profusion.com – an advanced search tool, takes results from several major search engines.

www.search.com – a solid performer from CNet.

www.ungoogle.com – searches many of the major search engines and is good for when 'Google lets you down'.

http://eurekster.com
US

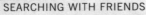

SEARCHING WITH FRIENDS

Here you get the usual search facility with clustered results but you can also sign up with a group of friends, then when one of them does the same search your preferred result will appear higher up their list of results. It's excellent if you share a particular hobby or interest.

UK-Oriented Searching

www.mirago.co.uk   UK
THE UK SEARCH ENGINE
Mirago searches the whole web but prioritises the search for UK
families and businesses. It's very quick, easy to use and offers
many of the services you get from Yahoo. You can tailor your
search very easily to exclude stuff you won't need.

For other UK-oriented search sites try:
http://UK20.co.uk – a good-looking site, it's OK as a search
engine too.
www.4ni.co.uk – a good search engine serving Northern Ireland.
www.britishinformation.com – well designed and
comprehensive.
www.clickclick2.net – odd design and more of a directory.
www.lifestyle.co.uk – a massive directory of specially selected
sites for the UK.
www.lycos.co.uk – easy to use and popular, good for
highlighting offers.
www.scotland.org – small Scotland-oriented site.
www.searchinwales.com – does what it says in the title (i.e.
searches relevant to Wales).
www.searchsaint.com – good looking and easy to use.
www.wotbox.co.uk – excellent for UK-oriented searches, each
site is denoted with its flag of origin.

www.watchthatpage.com   US
CHANGES ON THE WEB
Not strictly a search engine but if you have specific interests you
can download the program, input the URLs and it will let you
know when the site or page has been updated. You can also use
it to search and hunt out specific articles.

Security

*Keeping your computer, its contents and those who use it safe is one of
the biggest priorities for any user; albeit unlikely you'll have any major
problems. Here's a list of sites that will help you keep secure and some
protection software and information that's available for nothing.*

*Visit **www.download.com** for a selection of free and rated programs that
can help with securing your PC, while at **www.microsoft.com/security***

S

you can get updates to ensure your system is working properly. For Apple users try **www.apple.com/macosx/features/security** *for the latest information on keeping your Mac safe. If you're running a business and worried about security, then you might try* **www.cisecurity.org** *which is a non-profit organisation and has plenty of advice as to the best way to look after your system.*

www.getsafeonline.org UK

EXPERT ADVICE

A great place to start to learn about online security. It gives information on personal safety, PC safety and has a businesses section. Much of the advice is suitable for beginners, but old hands can learn something as well. For a site aimed at young people try **www.thinkuknow.co.uk** which is an excellent site dedicated to online safety.

www.firewallguide.com US

HOME PC FIREWALL GUIDE

A firewall is a piece of filtering software that protects your PC and prevents unknown users from sending material to it. But which is the best one? Find out here. For a good and well-regarded firewall program that has a free version available go to **www.zonelabs.com** and if you can't get on with that a good alternative can be found at **www.agnitum.com**

www.software-antivirus.com US

THE INDEPENDENT ANTI-VIRUS RESOURCE

All the anti-virus programs reviewed and rated. This site sets out to blow the myth that once you have virus technology installed you're safe, or that the best-selling products are actually the best at the job. An authoritative site written by several experienced computer experts.

See also:
http://housecall.antivirus.com – a free virus scanner.
www.avast.com – one of the most reliable free anti-virus programs.
www.ccleaner.com – home of an excellent and free little program that you can use to clean your system.
www.clamxav.com – a free virus checker for Macs.
www.free-av.com – another good free-trial-only, anti-virus program.
www.f-secure.com – one of the newer security companies.
www.grisoft.com – for free trial of the AVG anti-virus scanner.

www.kaspersky.com – home of the top-rated anti-virus program, offers free online virus scan and free trials.
www.macafee.com – security specialists.
www.softscan.co.uk – excellent for e-mail security.
www.symanteccom.com – where to go for Norton products (formerly **www.norton.com**).
www.pandasecurity.com – another top-rated program.
www.viruslist.com – if you're really interested in viruses, then go here where you'll find a virus encyclopaedia.

www.anti-trojan-software-reviews.com   US
THE ANTI-TROJAN RESOURCE
OK so you thought you were protected, but not entirely. Trojans are programs that pretend to be other programs and usually hitch a ride into your PC on the back of e-mail attachments. Go here to find the best anti-Trojan programs or just ensure that your anti-virus software does the job on Trojans too.

www.spyware.co.uk   UK
WHO'S WATCHING YOU?
As if viruses and Trojans weren't enough, the chances are that you've got some spyware on your PC sending information on your surfing activities to one of many companies who provide marketing data to retailers for example. Here you can get an overview of the problem plus advice on what to do about it.

See also:
www.lavasoftusa.com – home of the excellent AdAware program.
www.microsoft.com/security/malwareremove – check out whether your system is infected.
www.microsoft.com/athome/security/spyware/software/default.mspx – home of the anti-spyware program Windows Defender.
www.safer-networking.org – home of SpyBot, a useful spyware destroyer.
www.spywarewarrior.com – more information, background and downloads.
www.unwantedlinks.com/macsupport.htm – free download of their spyware program for Macs, plus links to other security programs for Macs.
www.webroot.com – home of the excellent Spy Sweeper program.

S

www.cookiecentral.com   US
COOKIES EXPLAINED
An excellent site dedicated to explaining the workings of that
mysterious animal the 'cookie' and how you can deal with them.

http://nclnet.org/essentials   UK
PRIVACY
An informative site giving an overview of security and privacy
issues on the Internet, it has plenty of helpful advice and links to
related sites.

www.windowsstartup.com   UK
START UP PROBLEMS
A useful little program that helps with cleaning up your PC's
start up.

Ships and Boats

*For shipping and boating enthusiasts here are a few sites that may
interest you. Sailing is listed under Sport, page 471, and water-borne
holidays can be found in the travel section, page 508.*

Boats

www.totallyboaty.co.uk   UK
BOATING DIRECTORY
A very good portal site devoted to all things boating, it's easy to
find what you're looking for and it's developing fast; see also
www.aboard.co.uk which offers a similar service and also
www.boatlinks.com which is a well-categorised, US-oriented
directory.

http://boatbuilding.com   UK
THE BOAT BUILDING COMMUNITY
If you want to repair or build a boat then here's where to go, with
features and discussion forums to help you on your way. There's
also a very good directory of links to suppliers and resource sites.

www.boats-for-sale.com or **www.buyaboat.co.uk**   UK
BUY A BOAT MAGAZINE
Primarily a vehicle to get you to subscribe to the magazine, the
site offers information on brokers and over 20,000 adverts. See
also the well-designed **www.boats.com**

See also:
www.boatingnews.com – news and classifieds.
www.boatingontheweb.com – an American boating directory.
www.boatlaunch.co.uk – a mapping service showing all the places in the UK where you can launch your boat.
www.uscgboating.org – a good site for advice and information on safe boating.

Ships and Navy

www.royal-navy.mod.uk   UK

THE ROYAL NAVY
An excellent site from the Royal Navy giving details of the ships, submarines and aircraft and what it's like to be a part of it all. There's a video gallery featuring highlights from the fleet and details of all the Royal Navy ships. Apart from all the information, you can have a go on the interactive frigate and take part in a strategic game.

www.hazegray.org   US
NAVAL HISTORY AND PHOTOGRAPHY
A well-categorised and comprehensive site featuring naval histories, background on the world's ships and navies and also shipbuilding. It's oriented to the US.

More naval and historical sites:
www.mightyseas.co.uk – a history site on the boats and ships from NW England.
www.naval-history.net – a messy site, but good for the 20th century and links.
www.navsource.org – a thorough unofficial overview of the US navy.
www.nmm.ac.uk – a good site from the National Maritime Museum in Greenwich.
www.skipper.co.uk – nautical publishers and booksellers.
www.tallship.co.uk – a magazine-related site with articles and photo gallery.

www.red-duster.co.uk   UK
RED DUSTER MAGAZINE
Red Duster is a merchant navy enthusiasts' site offering lots in the way of history covering sail, steam and shipping lines.

S

There's also a section on the history of customs. To find out what the current merchant navy are up to go to **www.merchantnavyofficers.com** where you can find information and links.

www.maritimematters.com UK
OCEAN LINERS AND CRUISE SHIPS
An informative site with data on over 100 ships from the earliest liners to the most modern, each has its own page with quality pictures and some virtual tours. It is also good for news and links to related sites.

Other Watercraft

www.hovercraft.org.uk UK
HOVERCRAFT
If you're into hovercraft or are just interested, here's the place to look with three sections – Britain, Europe and the world, which just about covers it all.

www.jetskier.co.uk UK
JET SKI
Home of *Jetskier* magazine and while it's geared to sell the mag, the site does offer much in the way of links and advice. For more tips, forums and chat go to the US-oriented **www.jetskinews.com**

www.rontini.com UK
SUBMARINE WORLD NETWORK
A directory site with over 1,000 links all devoted to the world of submarines. It covers everything from navies to models.

See also:
www.lr.org – Lloyd's register.
www.nao.rl.ac.uk – home of the Nautical Almanac Office.
www.paddling.net – for buying canoes and kayaks.
www.tpl.lib.wa.us/v2/nwroom/ships.htm – the Tacoma public library has a searchable database of some 13,000 ships.

Shopping

*To many people shopping is what the Internet is all about, and it does offer an opportunity to get some tremendous bargains. Watch out for hidden costs such as delivery charges, import duties or finance deals that seem attractive until you compare them with what's available elsewhere. For help on finding comparative prices, see the price comparison sites on page 378, in fact, starting your shopping trip at a site like **www.kelkoo.co.uk** may prove to be a wise move. There is also a section on consumer information on page 109 for the low-down on your rights and what to do when things go wrong. For shopping ethically see the section on page 140.*

Treat Yourself

The Good Web Site Guide's Top 10s
of the Internet

1. **www.which.net** – the consumer's friend
2. **http://froogle.google.co.uk** – looking for something specific? Try here first
3. **www.dooyoo.co.uk** – get an impartial review before you buy
4. **www.amazon.co.uk** – the most popular online retailer
5. **www.kelkoo.co.uk** – a great price checking site
6. **www.ebay.co.uk** – bid for it
7. **www.ukshopsearch.com** – excellent directory of shops
8. **www.johnlewis.co.uk** – the UK's most loved retailer
9. **www.shopperuk.com** – online shopping from over 2,000 stores
10. **www.2020shops.com** – review the shop before you go there

www.tradingstandards.gov.uk   UK

TRADING STANDARDS CENTRAL
Find out where you stand and what to do if you think you're being ripped off or someone is not trading fairly – you can even take a quiz about it. There are advice guides to print off or download and there is help and advice to businesses and schools as well as consumers.

Two other consumer-oriented sites worth checking out are:
www.consumer.gov.uk – rights advice from the Department of Trade and Industry.
www.howtocomplain.com – advice on how to go about airing your grievances and getting a result.

www.which.net   UK

WHICH? MAGAZINE

A good place to start your shopping experience but you have to be a member to get the best out of it. There's a good shopping directory plus their 'product picks' section, which highlights the 'best in class' on a wide variety of products. There are also the useful sections that you associate with the magazine such as legal advice and personal finance.

www.dooyoo.co.uk   UK

MAKE YOUR OPINION COUNT

Media darling Doo Yoo is a site where you the consumer can give your opinion or a review on any product that's available to buy, this way you get unbiased opinions about them – in theory. They cover a wide range of 'products' from books to TV shows and it's easy to contribute. See also **www.ciao.co.uk** where you can actually get paid a small amount of money for your opinion and also **www.epinions.com**

The Virtual High Street

www.marks-and-spencer.co.uk   UK

CLOTHES AND GIFTS

A clear, attractive site that has a good selection of products from clothes to gifts for all, as well as fashion advice and a quick order facility.

www.boots.com   UK

BOOTS

An online shop that reflects what you see when you visit the real store and there are now lots of offers to tempt you. There's lots of choice and it's well categorised, functional too.

www.whsmith.co.uk   UK

WHSMITH

The Smith's site has a clean, easy-to-navigate format, with the emphasis on offers and best-sellers. There is a great deal here including the usual books, music, mags, games, stationery and

DVDs. You can avoid the delivery charge if you collect the goods from your nearest store, which sort of defeats the object of buying online, but you can also claim loyalty points with online purchases.

www.woolworths.co.uk   UK
WELL WORTH IT
A bright and breezy site from Woolworths with all you'd expect in terms of range and prices. They are particularly good on kids' stuff with strong prices on movies, chart music, clothes and games.

www.argos.co.uk   UK
ARGOS CATALOGUE
Argos offers an excellent range of products (some 13,000) across thirteen different categories as per their catalogue. There are some good bargains to be had. You can now reserve an item at your local store, once you've checked that they have it in stock. There's a good search facility and you can find a product via its catalogue number, if you've a catalogue handy that is. Returns can be made to your local store.

www.debenhams.com   UK
AWARD-WINNING FAMILY SERVICE
Not a common sight on the high street but Debenhams have a very good site aimed at their retailing strengths: gifts, weddings and fashion.

www.johnlewis.co.uk   UK
NEVER KNOWINGLY UNDERSOLD
A really attractive and usable site with a wide range of products and some good offers too. Delivery costs start at £3.95, free over £150. Especially good if you haven't got one of their excellent stores near by. For more upmarket gear check out **www.liberty.co.uk** and also **www.selfridges.com** which both have interesting site designs and products to match.

S

www.virgin.net/shopping   UK
LIFESTYLE AND SHOPPING GUIDE
Virgin's shopping guide is comprehensive covering all major categories while allowing retailers to feature some of their best offers. It also attempts to be a complete service for entertainment and leisure needs with excellent sections on music, travel and cinema in particular.

Other high street names . . .

www.bhs.co.uk – no online shopping but they do have a store locator.

www.houseoffraser.co.uk – good store directory but you can only buy vouchers online.

General Retailers, Directories and Online Department Stores

http://froogle.google.co.uk   UK

SHOPPING SEARCH ENGINE

A useful facility from Google: just type in what you want to buy and up pops a list with prices and links to relevant shops. It's quick but the search results don't appear in price order.

www.2020shops.com   UK

THE SHOPPER'S FRIEND

A really likeable site with a great ethic – they don't do cosy deals with other retailers for exposure so the shops they select and rate are there on merit. They are one of the few that give extra information on the shops such as delivery costs, plus some shopping advice and price comparisons. It's fast too. See also **http://uk.bizrate.com** which compares retailers and prices, but it's pretty erratic.

www.shopperuk.com   UK

UK SHOPPING DIRECTORY

An excellent directory of UK shops both specialist and general. It's well categorised by both type and alphabet; a genuinely useful site with each store having a write up and a list of related stores alongside. There is also a product search facility.

www.edirectory.co.uk   UK

IF IT'S OUT THERE, BUY IT HERE

A nice-looking directory of some 700 shops, it has a good reputation for service as well as being topical.

www.catalink.com   UK

CATALOGUES GALORE

If you love shopping via a catalogue then here is the place to start, there are hundreds listed.

See also:

http://theukhighstreet.com – a good UK directory, with the shops rated by you the customer.

www.abound.co.uk – an excellent site offering a wide range of clothes and leisure and electrical products; it's well executed and has some good offers too.

www.buy4now.ie – an Irish shopping portal with a massive selection of goods with prices now quoted in pounds.

www.l-stores.com – a very good store search engine and directory.

www.letsbuyit.com – claiming over a million members and the best prices.

www.mailorderexpress.co.uk – excellent for toys and kids' stuff.

www.shoptour.co.uk – links to hundreds of secure shops in 14 categories, with a price comparison tool.

www.ukshopsearch.com – above average search engine and quality design make this stand out from the crowd.

www.ukshopsnet.com – well-designed and well-categorised store directory site and search engine.

www.worthaglance.com – great-looking shop with some outstanding bargains.

TV Shopping Channels

www.qvcuk.com   UK
TV SHOPPING ONLINE
As a shopping channel on satellite or cable, QVC was already successful; this well-put-together site shows off the breadth of their range and has some good offers. In total they display some 10,000 products.

See also:

www.bestdirect.tv – loads of bargains and celebrity endorsements.

www.idealworld.tv – just details of their channels and presenters, not much to buy.

www.price-drop.tv – the shop with lots of offers, and you can watch it live too.

www.screenshop.co.uk – very limited range on offer.

www.simplyshoppingtv.co.uk – with emphasis on health and home.

S

Value for Money

www.thesimplesaver.com   UK
WHERE TO GET THE BEST DEAL
What started off as a simple e-mail conversation about where to
go for savings has snowballed into a web site. You now have to
register your details and select the category of goods that interest
you and they will send you details of offers on a weekly,
fortnightly or monthly basis.

www.gooddealdirectory.co.uk   UK
THE BARGAIN HUNTER'S BIBLE
Based on the book of the same name, this is basically a
searchable directory of discount shops and sales. It's easy to use
and the information seems comprehensive. The thrifty in London
'should keep an eye on **www.wherearethesales.co.uk** that tracks
sales by category throughout the capital.

British Shopping

www.british-shopping.com   UK
UK SHOPPING LINKS AND DIRECTORY
An excellent comprehensive portal site specialising in British
shops; it also has plenty of related links and information.
www.somucheasier.co.uk also offers a comprehensive
UK-oriented shop listing.

For more quintessentially British shops check out these sites:
www.brooksandbentley.com – classy British gifts.
www.classicengland.co.uk – the best British products on a
fun-looking and easy-to-use site.
www.distinctlybritish.com – a British shop directory with a
wide range of food, clothing, gift and children's retailers on offer.
www.harrods.com – a selection of their products available to
buy from an attractive-looking site.

www.scotsmart.com   UK
SCOTTISH
A Scottish directory of sites, not just for shopping but covering
most areas; you can search by theme or category and the
shopping section is split into books, clothing, food, gifts and
highland wear. See also **www.scotch-corner.co.uk** which is
Scottish through and through.

www.wales-direct.com   UK
   WALES DIRECT
   A well-categorised shop devoted to all things Welsh, it has a
   wide range and some offers too, as well as a good links
   section.

The Good Web Site Guide's Gift Guide

The following sites should help you find the perfect gift!

www.hard2buy4.co.uk   UK
   GIFT IDEAS
   Excellent gift shop with a wide range of unusual products
   including celebrity items, activities and gifts for men, women
   and children in separate sections, some good offers too.

   See also:
   http://shop.christianaid.org.uk – give a gift to help the world's
   poor and needy.
   www.apieceofafrica.co.za – for gifts of an African origin.
   www.boysstuff.co.uk – gifts and products aimed at boys of all
   ages, has a section for girls too.
   www.baby-gifts.co.uk – personalised gifts for the very young.
   www.beautifulthings.co.uk – retail therapy from your desk
   apparently, you can shop by star sign too.
   www.buyagift.co.uk – activities and experiences for those who
   have everything.
   www.cafepress.com – personalised gifts for all, well most
   occasions!
   www.craft-fair.co.uk – a site devoted to bringing UK-made craft
   goods to market.
   www.find-me-a-gift.co.uk – gifts, both products and special
   experiences, can be found here, loyalty scheme and wish lists
   thrown in too.
   www.hawkin.com – odd design but good for range, children and
   the unusual.
   www.indiangiftsportal.com – beautiful and unusual gifts from
   India.
   www.iwantoneofthose.com – for more unusual gifts and stuff
   you don't need but would really like; it has a great gift finder.
   www.jun-gifts.com – Japanese gifts and other products,
   excellent for the unusual.
   www.maleorder.co.uk – presents for the man in your life.

S

www.michaelajdavies.co.uk – a great example of a showcase site with some nice gifts from around the world. If you're a retailer, they'll even make a range especially for you.

www.mumstheword.com – so that mum's-to-be can feel beautiful.

www.needapresent.com – very good site with some out-of-the ordinary gifts.

www.presentcorrect.com – create a gift list for yourself, your friends and family. It's good for suggestions for those difficult-to-buy-for people.

www.presentprovider.com – for all those things that you never knew existed and never really wanted; gifts for people you don't really like.

www.rebirth.co.za – authentic African art and gifts.

www.thedoghouse.co.uk – the gift reminder service, never forget that anniversary again.

www.thesharperedge.co.uk – some good stuff in amongst the tat.

www.voucherexpress.co.uk – the place to buy gift vouchers, including nearly all the major retailers.

So you can't be bothered to shop?

www.anythingforhire.co.uk   UK
> HIRE IT!
> A comprehensive directory of goods and services for hire across the UK, well laid out and easy to use.

Skiing and Snowboarding

These sites tend to include information on both skiing and related travel, so we've moved it from Sports to create a combined section devoted to all things snowy.

www.fis-ski.com   UK

> INTERNATIONAL SKI FEDERATION
> Catch up on the news, the fastest times and the rankings in all forms of skiing at this site. Very good background information and a live online section enabling events to be monitored as they happen.

www.ski.co.uk   UK
> THE PLACE TO START – A SKI DIRECTORY
> Straightforward site, the information in the directory is useful and the recommended sites are rated. The sections include

holidays, travel, weather, resorts, snowboarding, gear, fanatics and specialist services. See also **www.skicentral.com**

www.1ski.com UK

COMPLETE ONLINE SKIING SERVICE
With a huge number of holidays, live snow reports, tips on technique and equipment, and the ultimate guide featuring over 750 resorts, it's difficult to go wrong. The site is well laid out and easy to use. There's a good events calendar too.

Other good ski and snowboarding sites:
www.descent.co.uk – specialists in luxury alpine holidays.
www.flexiski.co.uk – tailor-made skiing holidays.
www.ifyouski.com – comprehensive skiing site that has a very good holiday booking service with lots of deals.
www.iglu.com – holiday specialists with lots of variety and offers.
www.mountainzone.com – great for features, articles and ski adventurers.
www.natives.co.uk – aimed at ski workers, there's info on conditions, ski resorts, a good job section, where to stay and links to other cool sites all wrapped up on a very nicely designed site.
www.skiclub.co.uk – Ski Club of Great Britain with lots of offers and information too.
www.skidream.com – skiing and snowboarding in America and Canada.
www.skireunited.com – a Friends Reunited but for skiing holidays and workers.
www.skisolutions.com – one of the oldest travel companies specialising in skiing holidays, with a huge range of holidays and expertise.
www.snow-forecast.com – weather forecasts for snow areas.
www.snowlife.org.uk – very good directory come advice centre.
www.snowrental.net – online equipment rental, all seems very easy.

www.boardtheworld.com UK

SNOWBOARDING
Masses of information and links covering the world of snowboarding, the site is well designed and doesn't seem to miss out any aspect of the sport.

S

See also:
www.boardz.com/snowboard/snowboardcentral.html – the snowboarding e-zine from Boardz.
www.goneboarding.co.uk – the UK boarding community with lots of information and chat.
www.snowboardinguk.co.uk – forums and snowboarding chat.

Social Networking

Here's how to start up a social network with your friends and consequently with their friends. It's a great way to share experiences, data or photos and particularly good for clubs or if you're fed up with the traditional dating sites. Here are some of the best and most useful sites.

www.friendster.com   US
COMMUNITY
A very easy-to-use set up with clear instructions and design; it's oriented towards dating but it's really adaptable.

See also:
www.bebo.com – social networking for schools and colleges.
www.blackplanet.com – a very popular site for the black community.
www.dudecheckthisout.com – here you can get together online with people who share your interests by sharing the contents of your favourites box.
www.faceparty.com – for teens and those in their early twenties.
www.furl.net – not really a social networking program but its facilities make it useful for sharing internet information in this context.
www.linkedin.com – popular especially in the business community.
www.meetup.com – one of the easiest to use and well designed.
www.profileheaven.com – another popular social site for young people.
www.zorpia.com – photo journals and sharing.

Software, Upgrades, Debugging and Widgets

If you need to upgrade your software, then these are the sites to go to. Shareware is where you get a program to use for a short period of time before you have to buy it, freeware is exactly what you'd think – free. Debugging programs fix problems in established programs that weren't previously identified.

www.softwareparadise.co.uk   UK
THE SMART WAY TO SHOP FOR SOFTWARE
With over 123,000 products and excellent offers, this site should be your the first stop. It's a bit messy but easy to use; there's a good search facility and plenty of products for Mac users.

www.download.com   US
CNET
A superb site covering all types of software and available downloads. There are masses of reviews as well as buying tips and price comparison tools; it also covers handheld PCs, Linux and Macs.

www.softseek.com   US

ZDNET
Another excellent site with a huge amount of resources to download, it's all a little overwhelming at first but the download directory is easy to use and there's lots of free software available.

www.tucows.com   US

TUCOWS
Probably less irritating to use than ZDNet and CNet, the software reviews are also entertaining in their own right, the best thing about it though is that it's quick.

If you feel like shopping around a bit more see also:
http://freshmeat.net – lots of shareware, also good for Linux fans.
http://home.netscape.com/plugins – if you're a Netscape fan then you can improve its performance with 'plug-ins' from this site.
www.annoyances.org – a good site devoted to fixing problems in Microsoft Windows.
www.completelyfreesoftware.com – hundreds of free programs for you to download, from games to useful desktop accessories;

S

if it's available free, then its here. Membership is essential costing around £10 per year.

www.computeractive.co.uk – this good UK-based magazine offers free access to its software reviews and archives.

www.freewarehome.com – a great selection of free programs, well classified and comprehensive.

www.handango.com – a good site specialising in downloads for handheld PCs.

www.kidsfreeware.com – Internet freebies for kids.

www.neatnettricks.com – an archive of useful tips and downloads with regular updates, you need to subscribe though, which costs about £8 per year.

www.versiontracker.com – a massive selection, particularly good for Mac software.

www.vnunet.com – UK-orientated review and download site.

www.winplanet.com – specialises in software downloads and reviews for small businesses.

www.wired.com – popular technology magazine with all the latest news and reviews.

www.winzip.com   US
MANAGE FILES

Winzip allows you to save space on your PC by compressing data, making it easier to e-mail files and unlock zipped files that have been sent to you. It takes a few minutes to download. For Macs go to **www.allume.com** where you'll find Stuffit.

Widgets

Widgets are fun, small but useful programs (mini-applications) that sit on your desktop and quickly impart some piece of specific or useful (sometimes not so useful) information.

Apple has integrated them into the new Dashboard as part of their Tiger operating system; at the blog program Typepad you can integrate them into your blog; and Opera has made them part of the new version of their new browser too. They will become a more common sight, especially as they are so simple to create.

http://widgets.yahoo.com   US
KONFABULATOR

The original widgets program was the Konfabulator: you download the Widget Engine, which comes with several free widgets such as clocks and the weather forecast, then you can explore the widget gallery (**www.widgetgallery.com**); for thousands more, the radio ones are particularly good.

See also:
www.apple.com/downloads/dashboard – for more Mac widgets.
www.dashboardlineup.com – a bit techy but lots of links and you can see how it's all done, Apple only.
http://en.wikipedia.org/wiki/Widget_(computing) – for a more detailed explanation of widget programs.
www.versiontracker.com/macosx/cat/widgets – excellent for Mac owners, they are rated too.
www.widgetopia.net – a site in development but one that has got potential.

Space

The Final Frontier

The Good Web Site Guide's Top 10s of the Internet

1. **www.space.com** – outstanding site on all things spacey
2. **www.nasa.gov** – informative with excellent multimedia
3. **www.heavens-above.com** – track satellites, learn stuff
4. **http://hubblesite.org** – awesome pictures
5. **www.redcolony.com** – what could happen when we colonise Mars
6. **www.solarviews.com** – great collection of views of the planets
7. **www.seds.org/images/** – pay homage to the Space Images Archive
8. **www.bbc.co.uk/science/space** – another outstanding site from the BBC
9. **www.windows.ucar.edu** – windows to the universe
10. **www.astronautix.com** – encyclopaedia astronautica

S

E-zines and Reference Sites

www.space.com
US

MAKING SPACE POPULAR
An education-oriented site dedicated to space; there's news, mission reports, technology, history, personalities, a games section and plenty of pictures. The science section explores the planets and earth.

www.spacedaily.com
US

YOUR PORTAL TO SPACE
A comprehensive newspaper-style site with a huge amount of information and news about space and related subjects. It also has links to similar sister sites covering subjects like Mars, space war and space travel. See also the eccentric **www.astspace.demon.co.uk** – a good portal, once you find it.

www.astronomynow.com
UK

THE UK'S BEST-SELLING ASTRONOMY MAG
Get the news and views from a British angle, plus reviews on the latest books. The store has widened out to include patches, T-shirts and videos as well as the magazine and posters.

www.windows.ucar.edu
US

WINDOWS TO THE UNIVERSE
A well-designed site that provides information about the earth, solar system and universe at three levels of detail, making it suitable for everyone from children to the most serious-minded. There are interesting sections exploring the link between the world's mythology and space, and history and space. There are also sections on geology, space exploration and art.

www.heavens-above.com
US

IT'S ABOVE YOUR HEAD
Type in your location and they'll give you the exact time and precise location of the next visible pass of the International Space Station or space shuttle. They also help you to observe satellites, flares from Iridium satellites and start charts customised to your location. You have to register now, but that means they keep the details of your location for your next visit.

See also:
www.astronautix.com – a comprehensive encyclopaedia of astronomy.

www.astronomy.ac.uk – study astronomy.

www.bbc.co.uk/science/space – superb pages on space from the BBC with interactive features.

www.beagle2.com – a simple presentation on the Beagle 2 mission.

www.deepcold.com – a dark view of the space race, on an interestingly designed site.

www.kidsastronomy.com – astronomy site for kids, simple information, games and sky maps; however, marred by an over-busy site design.

www.skypub.com – a magazine-related site with shop, archive and the latest news.

www.spacescience.org – an American space education site.

www.universetoday.com – a space news-gathering service.

Space Organisations

www.nasa.gov   US

 THE OFFICIAL NASA SITE

This huge site provides comprehensive information on the US National Aeronautical and Space Administration. There are details on each NASA site, launch timings, sections for news, kids, project updates, and links to their specialist sites such as the Hubble Space Telescope, Mars and Earth observation. The site has become more vocal since we last visited and there are a range of multimedia activities including NASA TV.

www.esa.int   FRANCE

EUROPEAN SPACE AGENCY

Learn about the Agency's activities, the specific missions and what's planned to come.

See also:

www.aerospaceguide.net – detailed site with information on the space projects and space craft.

www.arianespace.com – attractive site from the makers of the Ariane rocket.

www.bnsc.gov.uk – Britain's place in space, with links and details of missions and the latest news.

www.iki.rssi.ru/eng – Russian space research.

www.isro.org/space_science – the Indian space programme.

www.jpl.nasa.gov – the goings on at the Jet Propulsion Lab with excellent photography.

www.russianspaceweb.com – a good overview of the Russian space programme with a history and the latest news.
www.sinodefence.com/space/facility/spaceagency.asp – information on China's national space programme.

The Solar System and Beyond

www.seds.org/billa/tnp   UK
THE NINE PLANETS
A multimedia tour of the nine planets, stunning photography; interesting facts combined with good text.

http://hubblesite.org   US
THE HUBBLE TELESCOPE
An action-packed site covering the photographs and discoveries made by the Hubble Telescope, which has been orbiting the earth for several years now. It contains some amazing and staggeringly beautiful pictures, some of which you can download.

www.redcolony.com   US

MARS
A superb site all about the red planet. There is a synopsis of its history, plus details on past and future space missions with a focus on the colonisation of Mars. There's a great deal of information on things like terra forming and biogenesis, it's all taken very seriously too. See also the equally imaginative **www.exploremarsnow.org** where you can find a plausible manifestation of what a Mars mission could look like, backed up with outstanding graphics. At **http://marsrovers.jpl.nasa.gov** you can learn about the latest Mars missions.

For more planetary resources try:
http://chandra.harvard.edu – learn all about space exploration with x-rays here.
http://exoplanets.org – an interesting site on those planets found outside our solar system.
http://moon.google.com – explore the Moon.
http://planetary.org – home of the Planetary Society.
http://seds.lpl.arizona.edu/billa/twn – a site about Nebulae with some beautiful pictures.
www.asi.org – an organisation campaigning for the colonisation of the Moon.
www.fourmilab.ch/earthview – views of the Earth and the Moon from space.

www.solarviews.com – excellent encyclopaedic site on the
planets.
www.spaceweather.com – a detailed site on solar activity with
excellent links pages.
www.the-planet-jupiter.com – excellent site devoted to the solar
system's largest planet. Substitute Jupiter with the names of
any of the other planets and you'll find equally good sites on
those too.
www.the-solar-system.net – great for pictures and links, you
can also test yourself by taking the quiz.

Is There Life Out There?

www.setiathome.ssl.berkeley.edu   US
GET IN TOUCH WITH AN ALIEN
To borrow the official site description 'SETI@home is a scientific
experiment that uses Internet-connected computers in the
Search for Extraterrestrial Intelligence (SETI).' You can
participate by running a free program that downloads and
analyses radio telescope data. Millions have participated
and more than 5 billion potential signals have been located;
they're pointing their scopes at the most promising now.
There's still time for you to be the first! See also NASA's
detailed site relating to the search for life at
http://planetquest.jpl.nasa.gov/SIM/sim_index.cfm

www.ufoevidence.org   US
THEY'RE HERE!
A collection of 'evidence' showing that aliens regularly visit
our planet. There's loads of links and sections on the UK
government cover-up and various other conspiracy
theories. See also **www.ufodigest.com**
Both sites are advert laden.

Miscellaneous and Specialist Sites

www.spaceadventures.com   US
SPACE TOURISM
OK so you want to be an astronaut? Well now you have a golden
opportunity, so long as you have $2 million! Having said that
there are actually some cheaper options including shuttle tours
and a trip to the edge of space. For more extra-terrestrial travel
opportunities see **www.spaceislandgroup.com** – space tourism
is on its way!

S

www.badastronomy.com   US
DEBUNKING THE MYTHS
A site devoted to exploring some of the myths and stories that
surround astronomy and science fiction. It gives the facts in a
straightforward and (because the site owner sometimes gets on
his 'high horse') entertaining way.

www.lpl.arizona.edu/impacteffects   US
WHAT HAPPENS WHEN AN ASTEROID HITS . . .
A cheery little site, you input all the data about the size and
related details of your asteroid or meteor, then the site tells you
what will happen when it hits and whether you'll survive. Some
of it is very technical but it's mostly explained well.

www.telescopeplanet.co.uk   UK
TELESCOPE SHOP
A wide range of telescopes for sale, plus accessories and some
good offers too. See also **www.skyviewoptics.co.uk** and
www.rothervalleyoptics.co.uk

Spectacles is now under Opticians, page 358.

Sport

*One of the best uses of the Internet is to keep up-to-date with how your
team is performing, or if you're a member of a team or association,
keep each other updated.*

General Sport Sites

www.sporting-life.com   UK
THE SPORTING LIFE
A very comprehensive sport site, with plenty of advice, tips,
news and latest scores. It's considered to be one of the best, and
is good for stories, in-depth analysis and overall coverage of the
major sports.

www.bbc.co.uk/sport   UK

BBC SPORT COVERAGE
They may have lost the right to broadcast many sporting events
but their coverage at this level is excellent – much broader than
most and it's always up to date.

With Sport in Mind

The Good Web Site Guide's Top 10s
of the Internet

1. **www.sporting-life.com** – a great overview of the major sports
2. **www.bbc.co.uk/sport** – hard to beat
3. **www.cricinfo.com** – outstanding site on cricket
4. **www.fishing.co.uk** – whether you consider angling a sport or not, this is excellent
5. **www.football365.co.uk** – probably the best football e-zine
6. **www.racingpost.co.uk** – excellent and informative
7. **www.scrum.com** – a great rugby union site
8. **www.mountainzone.com** – if it's outdoors, it's covered here
9. **www.1ski.com** – the best for snow sports
10. **www.kitbag.com** – whatever the sport, get the gear here

www.skysports.com   UK
> THE BEST OF SKY SPORTS
> Excellent for the Premiership and football in general, but also
> covers other sports very well particularly cricket and both
> forms of rugby. Includes a section featuring video and audio
> clips, and there are interviews with stars. You can vote in their
> polls, e-mail programmes or try sports trivia quizzes. Lots of
> adverts spoil it.

www.rivals.net   UK
> THE RIVALS NETWORK
> Independent of any news organisations, Rivals is basically a
> network of specialist sites covering the whole gamut of major
> and some minor sports. Each site has its own editor who is
> passionate about the sport they cover. In general, its promise is
> better than the delivery, but what there is, is excellent with good
> quality content and pictures.

www.sportonair.com   UK

> HEAR ALL ABOUT IT . . .
> If you can't see it then you can always come here to listen to it,
> this site offers up lots of audio content including interviews and
> commentary from most of the major sporting events. There's a
> good archive and most major sports are covered.

S

http://sport.telegraph.co.uk   UK

THE *DAILY TELEGRAPH*

Very comprehensive and well written with lots of archive
material. All the major sports are covered and with contributors
like Mike Atherton, Henry Winter and Sebastian Coe, you know
it has authority.

www.realbuzz.com   UK

GET SPORTY

Aimed at the amateur participant, their stated purpose is to help
everyone to get more out of life by providing an increasing
number of pages on sports, health, fitness, the great outdoors,
charity adventures and travel. There is a buzzing online
community too. Nice site.

Other good all-rounders and sites with good links:
http://dmoz.org/sports – links galore at the Open Directory
project.
http://sport.independent.co.uk – good all-round coverage from
the *Independent* newspaper.
http://sport.scotsman.com – Scottish sport covered.
http://sportscalendar.timesonline.co.uk/times/calendar –
useful sports calendar from *The Times*.
http://sportsillustrated.cnn.com – the latest in American sport
from CNN.
www.EL.com/elinks/sports – list of American-oriented sports
links.
www.eurosport.com – the world of European sport.
www.sikids.com – *Sports Illustrated* for Kids, excellent for
US-based sports.
www.sportsline.com – excellent coverage from CBS.
www.theage.com.au/sport – good coverage of Australian
sport.

Miscellaneous

www.culture.gov.uk/sport   UK

WHAT THE GOVERNMENT IS UP TO

Here's where to go to find the latest policies, what the minister
for sport does and how they are helping sport develop in the
community at large. A fairly dull site though. See also
www.uksport.gov.uk

www.sportengland.org   UK
THE NATIONS BIGGEST SUPPORTER
An attempt to get the English off their backsides and to find
health and happiness through sport. And a very nice site too.

See also:
www.sportsci.org – interesting site covering sports science.
www.sportspubs.co.uk – directory of pubs where you can
watch sport. You can search by sport or by region and there's a
good links section too.
www.streetplay.com – covering the development of sports that
have just sprung up in cities and parks all over America.
www.wada-ama.org/en – home of the World Anti-Doping
Agency.

Sites on Specific Sports

American Football

www.nfl.com   US
NATIONAL FOOTBALL LEAGUE
American football's online bible with a talking homepage, it's a
huge official site with details and statistics bursting from every
page. It's got information on all the teams, players and likely
draft picks; there's also information on NFL Europe and links to
other key sites. All it really lacks is gossip!

See also:
http://football.espn.go.com/nfl/index – ESPN's site is
authoritative and offers links to other sports.
www.hot-iron.co.uk – a very good Scottish e-zine.
www.nfleurope.com – thorough coverage of the European
league.
www.nflplayers.com – for the latest news and background on all
the key people in the game plus nostalgia from ex-players.
www.ukgridiron.co.uk – the UK-oriented view of the game.

Archery

www.archery.org   UK
INTERNATIONAL ARCHERY FEDERATION
Get the official news, events listings, rankings and records
information from this fairly mundane site.

See also:
www.bownet.com – *Bow International Archery* magazine.
www.scottisharchery.org.uk – the Scottish Archery Association.
www.theglade.co.uk – an entertaining and chatty site, basically an e-zine, devoted to all forms of archery.

Athletics and Running

www.iaaf.org   UK
INTERNATIONAL ASSOCIATION OF ATHLETICS FEDERATIONS
The official site of the IAAF is a results-oriented affair with lots of rankings in addition to the latest news. There's also a multimedia section where you can see pictures, listen to commentary or watch videos of the key events. There's a good links page and information on the organisation's activities.

www.ukathletics.net   UK

THE GOVERNING BODY
Many official 'governing body' sites are pretty boring affairs, not so UK Athletics which contains lots of features, is newsy and written with an obvious sense of enthusiasm. There are details on forthcoming events, reports on aspects of the sport, records, biographies of key athletes and advice on keeping fit. Somehow you get the impression the site is sponsored . . .

www.athletix.org   UK
THE ATHLETICS SITE
A statistics and results-led site with coverage of all the major events and some minor ones. It covers international competitions as well as having a good gallery and biographical details of some of the major athletes, it's also good for links.

www.runnersworld.com   US
RUNNER'S WORLD MAGAZINE
A rather dry site with tips from getting started through to advanced-level running. There's lots of information, news and records plus reviews on shoes and gear. See also the comprehensive but ugly **www.runnersweb.com**

See also:
www.athletics-online.co.uk – *Athletics Weekly* magazine.
www.bal.org.uk – results from the British Athletics League.
www.boja.org – a great site for young athletes; there's not much to look at but it contains lots of information.

www.british-athletics.co.uk – a boring site but it has a directory of clubs and regional events. It's good for links to newsgroups though.

www.gbrathletics.com – great for statistics and rankings.

www.marathonguide.com – all you need to know about marathons with news and advice.

www.nuff-respect.co.uk – see what Linford Christie is up to these days.

www.realrunner.com – now part of realbuzz, see under general sports sites above.

www.runnersweb.co.uk – a good site covering all aspects of running including marathon training.

www.runnersworld.ltd.uk – on equipment advice.

www.runtrackdir.com – details of all the UK's running tracks and their facilities.

www.trackandfieldnews.com – all the latest from *Track & Field News*. US bias.

Australian Rules Football

www.afl.com.au   AUSTRALIA
AUSTRALIAN FOOTBALL LEAGUE
A top-quality site covering all aspects of the game including team news, player profiles and statistics as well as the latest gossip and speculation. See also **www.footypedia.com** and **www.allthestats.com**

Baseball

www.mlb.com   US
MAJOR LEAGUE BASEBALL
This now opens with a 'fastcast' bringing you up-to-date with the latest news while you look at information on the top teams and the World Series. It's not the best-designed site but there's good information, statistics on the game and notes about the key players as well as related articles and features.

See also:
www.baseball1.com – very detailed.
www.baseball-links.com – easy to use and has over 11,000 links.
www.gbbaseball.co.uk – all about the game in the UK.

S

Basketball

www.nba.com UK

NATIONAL BASKETBALL ASSOCIATION
A comprehensive official site with features on the teams, players and games; there's also an excellent photo gallery and you can watch some of the most important points if you have the right software.

See also:
www.basketball.com – really extensive coverage including the women's game.
wwwketball365.co.uk – comprehensive overview of the game with news of what's going on both sides of the Atlantic.
www.bbl.org.uk – the official site of the British Basketball League.
www.eurobasket.com – information on the European leagues.

Bowls

www.bowlsengland.com UK

ENGLISH BOWLING ASSOCIATION
A straightforward design making it easy to find out all you need to know about lawn bowls in England, including a good set of links to associated sites.

www.eiba.co.uk UK

ENGLAND INDOOR BOWLING ASSOCIATION
A pretty basic site giving an overview of the game, links and background information on competitions and rules.

See also:
www.bowlsclub.info – a portal site devoted to lawn bowls.
www.bowlsinternational.com – home of a bowls magazine, good for links.
www.esmba.org.uk – informative site from the English Short Mat Bowling Association.
www.short-mat-magazine.com – aimed at selling the mag, but has information on the Irish, English and Welsh games.

Boxing

www.boxinginsider.com US

BOXING INSIDER
An effective site with lots of information on the sport plus chat

and stats. There's a bout-by-bout guide, lots of links and the writing is pretty good too.

See also:
www.bbc.co.uk/boxing – great for the latest news and background information.
www.boxrec.com – a statistician's nirvana here at this Wiki-based site. You'll find virtually any boxing statistic; however it is a little cumbersome to use and it has quite a few adverts.
www.heavyweights.co.uk – who cover the hype around heavyweight boxing.
www.ibhof.com – the International Boxing Hall of Fame has information on the best-ever boxers, it's great but could still do with more photos.
www.secondsout.com – excellent magazine and portal site for fight fans everywhere.

For the different boxing authorities:
www.aiba.net – the official site from the Amateur International Boxing Association.
www.wbaonline.com – the WBA has an OK-looking and functional site.
www.wbcboxing.com – a straightforward site from the World Boxing Council – that is after the sentimental musical introduction!
www.wbu.cc – the World Boxing Union covers the sport well from an unusual site.
www.womenboxing.com – a very comprehensive site devoted to women's boxing.

Clay Shooting

www.clayshooting.co.uk   UK
CLAY SHOOTING MAGAZINE
A good introduction to the sport with a beginner's guide to start you off and a good set of links to key suppliers and associated sites. There's also an online shop where you can buy the odd essential item such as global positioning systems and dog food. Serious shooters can go to the comprehensive
www.hotbarrels.com

Cricket

www.cricinfo.com   UK

THE HOME OF CRICKET ON THE NET

The best all-round cricket site on the Internet, with in-depth analysis, match reports, player profiles, statistics, links to other more specialised sites and live coverage. There's also a shop with lots of cricket goodies.

www.lords.org   UK

THE OFFICIAL LINE ON CRICKET

A pretty measly site these days with basic information, ticket sales details and fixtures, plus a top line history of the place. See also **www.play-cricket.com** which is home to the English Cricket Board and a fine source of information and statistics on the game.

www.webbsoc.demon.co.uk   UK

WOMEN'S CRICKET ON THE WEB

There are not many sites about women's cricket; this is probably the best, with features, news, fixture lists, match reports and player profiles. Nothing fancy, but it works.

www.theprideside.com   UK

CRICKET TO THE ROOTS

A good attempt at encouraging young people to take an interest in cricket with an overview of the game on a really interesting and interactive site.

See also:

http://sport.guardian.co.uk/cricket – good-looking and up-to-the-minute site from the *Guardian* newspaper.

www.334notout.com – a history of the Ashes and the 'bodyline' controversy.

www.cricketonly.com – a comprehensive and news-oriented cricket enthusiasts' site.

www.cricketrecords.com – one for the statistics freaks, lots of pop up adverts too.

www.cricketsupplies.com – a good-looking online store specialising in cricket gear.

www.cricnet.co.uk – the Professional Cricketers' Association official site.

www.windiescricket.com – keep up to date with the West Indies team here, it also covers the game by island too.

S

Cycling

These are sites aimed at the more serious sportsman, for more leisurely cycling see page 113 and for holidays turn to page 506.

www.bcf.uk.com   UK
> BRITISH CYCLING FEDERATION
> The governing body for cycling, their site has become more comprehensive: you can get information on events, rules, clubs and rankings, as well as contact names for coaching and development, plus a news service.

www.bikemagic.com   UK
> IT'S BIKETASTIC!
> Whether you're a beginner or an old hand, the enthusiastic and engaging tone of this site will convert you or enhance your cycling experience. There's plenty of news and features, as well as reviews on bike parts and gadgets, a classified ads section and a selection of links to other biking web sites, all of which are rated.

www.letour.fr   FRANCE
> TOUR DE FRANCE
> Written in English and French this site covers the Tour in some depth with details on the teams, riders and general background information.

www.mtbbritain.co.uk   UK
> MOUNTAIN BIKING
> Routes, tips, advice and gear; it's all here whether you're a real enthusiast or just a weekender. See also **www.dirtworld.com** which also offers news on events and is more sports-oriented.
>
> *See also:*
> **http://uk.sports.yahoo.com/cy/index.html** – keep up-to-date with the latest news.
> **www.cyclesport.co.uk** – home of *Cycle Sport* magazine.
> **www.cyclingnews.com** – race results and more.
> **www.grahamwatson.com** – cycling photography.

S

Darts

www.planetdarts.co.uk   UK
PROFESSIONAL DARTS CORPORATION
A messy site but one that has lots of league information,
statistics, news, articles and rules.

See also:
www.bbc.co.uk/darts – basic information only.
www.cyberdarts.com – a darts e-zine, which contains lots of
information such as articles, chat, forums and rules too.
www.dartbase.com – rules, techniques and equipment advice.

Diving

www.ukdiving.co.uk   UK
DIVING RESOURCE
A very good resource site with the latest news. It seems to cover
all aspects of the sport with some good articles, useful advice
and is good for links too. The wreck of the week is particularly
intriguing.

See also:
www.bsac.com – the British Sub Aqua Club, a basic site with
info on what they do.
www.cmas2000.org – the World Underwater Federation with
an odd but informative site.
www.divegirl.com – a magazine site about women and scuba.
www.padi.com – the place to start when you want to learn to
dive.
www.saa.org.uk – home of the Sub Aqua Association with links
and information.

Dog Racing

For the gambling side of dog racing, see page 202.

www.thedogs.co.uk   UK
BRITISH GREYHOUND RACING BOARD
A well-designed site offering an overview of the sport, the top
dogs and track information, also has help for owners and all the
results. See also **www.retiredgreyhounds.co.uk** where you can
find out how to adopt a retired greyhound.

Equestrian

www.bhs.org.uk   UK
BRITISH HORSE SOCIETY
A charity that looks after the welfare of horses. Here you can get
information on insurance, links, riding schools, competitions,
events and trials.

For more information try:
http://horses.about.com – About.com's excellent suite of pages
devoted to all things equestrian.
www.badminton-horse.co.uk – background and information on
the famous horse trials with lots of extra features and links.
www.britishdressage.co.uk – very good site covering this aspect
of the sport.
www.britisheventing.com – an attractive text-based site with
details on the sport and links.
www.horseandhound.co.uk – excellent magazine site from the
leading authority.
www.horseselect.co.uk – buying and selling competition horses.

Extreme Sports

www.extreme.com   US
EXTREME SPORTS CHANNEL
The official site of the Extreme Sports Channel is hi-tech but
quite slow; however, once downloaded it's got lots to offer in
terms of information, shopping and the latest headlines.

See also:
www.adventuredirectory.com – useful activity-by-sport portal
site.
www.allextremesports.com – good for links and a wide range of
sports.
www.expn.go.com – excellent extreme sports magazine with a
US bias.
www.extremepie.com – good extreme sports gear shop.
www.extreme-sports-world.com – very useful portal site.

Fishing

www.fishing.co.uk   UK

HOME OF UK FISHING ON THE NET
A huge site that offers information on where to fish, how to fish,

where's the best place to stay near fish, even fishing holidays. There's also advice on equipment, a records section and links to shops and shop locations. Shop on-site for fishing books and magazines.

See also:
www.anglersnet.co.uk – good magazine site with lots of information and chat.
www.anglers-world.co.uk – great for fishing holidays.
www.bdaa.co.uk – home of the British Disabled Anglers Association and a comprehensive offering it is too.
www.fishandfly.co.uk – another good magazine site, this one devoted to fly fishing.
www.fisheries.co.uk – excellent for coarse fishing and links.
www.nfsa.org.uk – home of the National Federation of Sea Anglers with lots of links and information.
www.nimpopo.com – basic site with over 3,000 tackle bargains.
www.pacgb.com – the Pike Anglers Club, a bit specialist perhaps, but a good site nonetheless.
www.specialist-tackle.co.uk – excellent store for equipment plus much more in the way of chat and information.
www.tackledirectory.com – a store 'run by anglers for anglers'.
www.thefishfinder.com – yes it's a fish search engine and a pretty good one at that.

Football

www.football365.co.uk   UK

FOOTBALL NEWS
Probably still the best of the football e-zines in terms of the combination of looks, quality writing and features, although it can be a bit dense at times.

http://www.goal.com   UK
GOAL!!
Excellent portal and news site with lots of articles and coverage of the latest gossip; it also covers many of the European leagues as well.

www.teamtalk.com   UK

CHECK OUT THE TEAMS!
The most respected place to go if you want all the latest gossip and transfer information. It's opinionated but not often wrong.

They have many top journalists on their books, so the information is likely to be on the ball.

www.soccerbase.com UK

SOCCER STATISTICS
The site to end all pub rows, it's described as the most comprehensive and up-to-date source of British football data on the Internet.

www.footballgroundguide.co.uk UK
FOOTBALL GROUNDS
Details of all 92 English league football club grounds, locations and facilities, incredibly useful for all away supporters. Excellent for team links too. For information on the new Wembley stadium including a tour, web cams, find your seat in 3-D, events and history check out **www.wembleystadium.com**

It's worth having a look at the sites listed below; just pick the one you like best.
http://pinkfootball.com – a girls guide to football.
http://skysports.planetfootball.com – news, information and OPTA statistics on the world game, now part of the Sky Sports site.
www.4thegame.com – a messy and commercial football news site.
www.conferencefootball.tv – coverage of some of the key conference clubs including replays.
www.e-soccer.com – hundreds of links and the latest news.
www.fansFC.com – gossip and rumours, plus fans' forums for chat and debate.
www.footballchants.org – an advert laden catalogue of football chants, not exactly a riot of wit it has to be said . . .
www.football-rumours.com – the latest transfer gossip and detailed information on the players.
www.footballtransfers.co.uk – very detailed transfer information and likely moves.
www.guardian.co.uk/football – great writing and irreverent articles, uncluttered design.
www.icons.com – site host to many major players, lots of background info plus the latest news.
www.laughfc.co.uk – a humorous look at the game, good for jokes and chants, some adult content.
www.linkupfootball.com – over 3,372 football-related links in 83 categories.

S

www.pureworldcup.com – a fun and informative look at the World Cup.
www.ratetheref.co.uk – where you can get your revenge on the ref if you feel mistreated.
www.soccerbot.com – great for basic information, with interesting interactive league tables.
www.soccerhighway.com – a strange site but good for links.
www.soccernet.com – well-put-together by ESPN, comprehensive but a bit boring.
www.wsc.co.uk – home of the magazine *When Saturday Comes*.

www.footballaid.com   UK
FOOTBALL CHARITY
Football aid is a charity that helps good causes by running football events, you can sign on to play for the team of your choice or just send a cheque.

Football Authorities

www.fifa.com   SWITZERLAND

FIFA
This is FIFA's magazine where you can get information on what they do, the World Cup and other FIFA competitions. For the UEFA go to **www.uefa.com** where you can see how everyone is faring in the Champions League and UEFA cup.

See also:
www.irishfa.com – the Irish Football Association with a pretty standard site.
www.leaguemanagers.com – home of the League Manager's Association.
www.premierleague.com – the FA official site, covering the latest news and information.
www.scotprem.co.uk – a comprehensive offering with links too.
www.welsh-football.net – an independent magazine on the Welsh soccer scene.

Golf

www.golftoday.co.uk   UK

THE PREMIER ONLINE GOLF MAGAZINE
An excellent site for golf news and tournaments with features, statistics and rankings, also a course directory. It's the best

all-round site covering Europe. There are also links to sister sites about the amateur game, shops and where to stay. GolfToday.com also hosts a comprehensive site on the amateur game; you can find it at **www.amateur-golf.com**

www.golfweb.com   US
PGA TOUR
The best site for statistics on the PGA, and keeping up with tournament scores, it also has audio and visual features with RealPlayer. For the official word on the tour go to **www.pga.com** while for the European tour go to **www.europeantour.com** and for a good overview of the Ryder Cup visit **www.rydercup.com**

www.golf.com   US
THE AMERICAN VIEW
Part of NBC's suite of web sites, this offers a massive amount of information and statistics on the game, the major tours and players, both men and women.

www.golfingguides.net   UK
UK GOLF COURSES
Detailed information on selected golf courses classed as 'gems', plus contact information on those lesser courses. A good search facility rounds it off, plus the fact it's pretty well designed.

www.uk-golfguide.com   UK
GOLF TOURISM
A useful directory of courses and hotels with courses, with links to travel agents for the UK and abroad, you can also get information on golf equipment suppliers and insurance. See also **www.whatgolf.co.uk**

www.onlinegolf.co.uk   UK
GOLF EQUIPMENT
A good-looking and comprehensive golf store with lots of offers and a good range, it has a ladies section and a good search facility.

See also:
http://golfbidder.co.uk – store for second-hand clubs and equipment.
www.golflinks.co.uk – a large, UK-oriented site database.
www.grassrootsgolf.com – for summer camps for junior golfers, corporate golf and golf tours.

Gymnastics

www.gymmedia.com   GERMANY
GYMNASTIC NEWS
A bilingual site giving all the latest news, it covers all forms of the
sport and offers lots of links to related sites.

See also:
www.british-gymnastics.org – an official site offering lots of
information and advice.
www.intlgymnast.com – the latest news from *International
Gymnast* magazine.
www.scottishgymnastics.com – comprehensive coverage but
tied to the magazine so it's not all it could be.

Hockey

www.hockeyonline.co.uk   UK
THE ENGLISH HOCKEY ASSOCIATION
A slick site covering the English game with information and
chat on the players, leagues and teams for both the men's
and the women's games. For the Scottish game go to
www.scottish-hockey.org.uk and for the Welsh
www.welsh-hockey.co.uk The latter is not great on design
but both give all the relevant information.

See also:
www.fieldhockey.com – advert-laden with a dull design but has
all the latest news.
www.hockeydirect.co.uk – good equipment store.
www.hockeyweb.co.uk – chat, news and links.

Horse Racing

*For sites that cover the gambling side of horse racing go to
page 202.*

www.racingpost.co.uk   UK
THE *RACING POST*
Superb, informative site from the authority on the sport, every
event covered in depth with tips and advice. To get the best out of
it you have to register, then you have access to the database and
more.

www.bhb.co.uk UK
> BRITISH HORSE RACING BOARD
> A very well-put-together site offering up information and background on the sport including interviews, details of the latest meetings and horse ownership advice.

www.racenews.co.uk UK
> RACING, COURSES AND BETTING
> A slightly different spin from *Racenews*, they have three main sections: their news service, a course guide and a tipsters column. There's also an excellent links section covering racing world-wide.

www.flatstats.co.uk UK
> FLAT RACING STATISTICS
> This site contains masses of detailed and unique statistics – horse, trainer, jockey, sire and race statistics, favourites analysis, systems analysis and much more. You have to be a member to get the best out of it; subscription costs £34.95 per month. See also **www.workrider.com**

www.thejockeyclub.co.uk UK
> THE JOCKEY CLUB
> A campaigning site aimed at promoting confidence in racing. It has news, details on the rules and how stewarding works, as well as links and sporting guidelines. See also **www.jockeysroom.com** which has an A–Z of jockeys with biographies and pictures.
>
> *Other sites worth a visit are . . .*
> **www.attheraces.co.uk** – live action, tips and the latest news plus great design.
> **www.bbc.co.uk/racing** – the BBC's excellent race pages.
> **www.racecall.co.uk** – hear all the action on your phone.
> **www.teletext.co.uk** – the information pages have gone, but under 'mobile services' you can sign up for racing alerts direct to your phone.

Ice Hockey

www.nhl.com US
> NATIONAL HOCKEY LEAGUE
> Catch up on the latest from the NHL including a chance to listen to and watch key moments from past and recent games.

www.icehockeyuk.co.uk
UK

ICE HOCKEY UK

The official site with bags of information and background on the game. It's well designed and great for beginners and those who want to find out more about the sport.

See also:
www.azhockey.com – home of the encyclopaedia of ice hockey.
www.crazykennys.com – ice hockey equipment suppliers.
www.icehockeyhistory.co.uk – a sparse site covering the history of the game in the UK.

Ice Skating

www.frogsonice.com/skateweb
US

LINKS

Not a great design but it offers lots of links to all aspects of skating.

See also:
www.iceskating.org.uk – the official site of the National Ice Skating Association of the UK; good-looking site covering all aspects of ice skating.
www.iceskatingintnl.com – for competitive skating news, US bias.
www.iceskatingworld.com – comprehensive US site with excellent links and the latest news.
www.sisa.org.uk – the Scottish Ice Skating Association.
www.skating-shop.co.uk – for all your skating gear.

Martial Arts

www.martial-arts-network.com
US

PROMOTING MARTIAL ARTS

Possibly qualifies as the loudest introduction sequence, but once you've skipped the intro, the site offers a great deal in terms of resources and information about the martial arts scene, including *Black Belts* magazine and new this year, podcasts. Its layout is a little confusing.

www.britishjudo.org.uk
UK

JUDO

Judo has a proud tradition in the UK, and if you want to follow that you can get all the information you need at the British Judo

Association site. It gives a brief history of judo, a shop and event information. For a broader view go to **www.judoinfo.com**

See also:
http://physical-arts.com – a site in the making, more a way of life than combat.
http://uk.dir.yahoo.com/recreation/sport/martial_arts – a huge number of links.
www.martialinfo.com – slow but comprehensive site with an online magazine.
www.practical-martial-arts.co.uk – useful advice on techniques and an overview of key combat types, there are also forums where you can have your say.
www.ryoku.co.uk – where to go for your gear.
www.kungfuscience.org – wacky site explaining the physics behind chopping blocks with bare hands.

Motor Sport

www.crash.net   UK
MOTOR SPORT PORTAL
An excellent but very commercial news and directory site covering the major motor sports and most of the minor ones too. There's an online shop selling motor sport merchandise amongst other things and there's a good photo library.

www.ukmotorsport.com   UK
INFORMATION OVERLOAD
This site covers every form of motor racing; it's got lots of links to appropriate sites covering all aspects of motor sport. There are also chat sections and forums plus links to product and service suppliers. We're still waiting for that long overdue site overhaul.

www.MSport-UK.com   UK
UK MOTOR SPORT
A good site covering all aspects of motor sport in Britain, highlights include the 'must see' section (I wish more sites had one) and the links page. As they've kept out clutter, it's fast to use.

www.autosport.com   UK
AUTOSPORT MAGAZINE
Excellent for news and features on motor sport plus links and an affiliated online shopping experience for related products such as team gear, books or models.

www.linksheaven.com   US
> THE MOST COMPREHENSIVE LINKS DIRECTORY
> Whatever, whoever, there's an appropriate link. It's biased
> towards Formula 1, CART and Nascar though.

www.worldmotorsport.com   UK
> MOTOR SPORT DEBATE
> Many forums covering all aspects of racing. If you want a say or
> get something off your chest then here's where to go.

Sites Covering Specific Types of Racing

www.itv-f1.com   UK

> F1 ON ITV
> This web site is excellent, it doesn't miss much and there is
> plenty of action. There's all the background information you'd
> expect plus circuit profiles, schedules and a photo gallery.

> *See also:*
> **www.atlasf1.com** – outstanding for information on F1.
> **www.f1-world.co.uk** – more information and background plus
> links too.

www.fota.co.uk   UK
> FORMULA 3
> Formula 3 explained plus info on the teams, drivers and circuits.
> It's the breeding ground for F1 drivers of the future which adds to
> the excitement reflected in the energy of this site.

www.indycar.com   US
> INDY CARS
> A comprehensive offering with coverage of all that goes on in the
> Indy car scene.

www.rallysport.com   UK
> COVERING THE WORLD RALLY CHAMPIONSHIP
> Good for results and news on rallying in the UK and across the
> world.

> *See also:*
> **http://rally.racing-live.com/en** – all the latest news, plus follow
> races stage by stage.
> **www.rallyzone.co.uk** – a comprehensive international e-zine.

www.btccpages.com   UK
>BRITISH TOURING CAR CHAMPIONSHIP
>This site offers a great deal of information and statistics on the
>championship, driver and team profiles, photos and links to
>other related sites. There are also a number of forums you can
>get involved with if you feel like chatting to fellow enthusiasts.

www.karting.co.uk   UK
>GO KARTING
>A well-laid-out portal site to all things karting in the UK, with
>links and directories covering the tracks, manufacturers,
>events and a photo gallery plus the latest news. See also
>**www.gokartingforfun.co.uk**

www.monstertrucks.net   US
>TRUCKS
>All aspects of truck racing, exhibitions and shows, if you like your
>motor sport large, then go here.

Motorcycling

www.motorcyclenews.com   UK

>NEWS AND VIEWS
>A very good magazine-style site giving all the latest news, gossip
>and event information, there are also sections on buying a bike,
>where to get parts and the latest gear, off-road biking and a links
>directory. There's also a chat room and a good classified section.

www.acu.org.uk   UK
>AUTO-CYCLE UNION
>The ACU is the governing body for motorcycle sports in the UK
>and this site gives information on its work and the benefits of
>being a member. There are also links and details of their magazine.

www.motoGP.com   UK
>TRACK AND OFF-ROAD
>A well-laid-out magazine site, covering the world of Moto Grand
>Prix with results, background and biographical details. Available
>in eight languages.

www.british-speedway.co.uk   UK
>SPEEDWAY
>Provides information on the leagues as well as the latest news,
>there's also an events calendar and links to related sites.

www.motocross.com　US
>　MOTOCROSS
>　An authoritative site covering the sport but it's centred on the US,
>　although it has got some information on the European scene.
>　See also **www.motolinks.com**

Have an Adventure

The Good Web Site Guide's Top 10s
of the Internet

1.　**www.adventuredirectory.com** – find an adventure
2.　**www.madadventurer.com** – get inspired by sport
3.　**www.ecovolunteer.com** – do it for nature
4.　**www.africatravelresource.com** – go on a safari
5.　**www.lonelyplanet.com** – choose where to go
6.　**www.ctc.org.uk** – get on yer bike
7.　**www.polartravel.co.uk** – go on a polar expedition
8.　**www.tenrag.com** – charter a yacht
9.　**www.divechannel.co.uk** – take a dive or two
10.　**www.visitbritain.co.uk** – find an adventure at home

Mountaineering and Outside Sports

www.mountainzone.com　US
　FOR THE UPWARDLY MOBILE
>　Thoroughly covers all aspects of climbing, hiking, mountain
>　biking, skiing and snowboarding with a very good photography
>　section featuring galleries from major mountains and climbers.

www.ukclimbing.com　UK
　CLIMBING NEWS
>　Excellent and very informative site covering all aspects of
>　climbing, it has plenty of opportunities for chat along with the
>　latest news. There's also weather information and a very good
>　database of climbs with comments and essential information for
>　each one.

www.rockrun.com　UK
>　ALL THE RIGHT EQUIPMENT
>　Excellent equipment shop covering climbing and walking gear,

which is also pretty comprehensive on the information front too. See also **www.gearzone.co.uk** who have a similar offering.

Other good climbing sites:
www.blacks.co.uk – good camping and equipment store.
www.bouldering.com – revamped site and a good job they've done too, there's a wide range of gear as well.
www.climb-guide.com – the guides are pretty basic but there's a good links page.
www.cruxed.com – nice-looking site with advice on techniques and training, good links.
www.onward-outward.co.uk – a good outdoor clothing store with a wide range and the best brands.
www.outdoorgear.co.uk – everything you need for the outdoors.
www.thebmc.co.uk – good all-round climbing and hill-walking magazine-style site from the British Mountaineering Council with good links pages.
www.ukcrags.com – some good guides to popular climbs, but the site was for sale at time of visiting.
www.upandunder.co.uk – a Welsh mountaineering store with a good links section.

Netball

www.netball.org   UK
INTERNATIONAL FEDERATION OF NETBALL ASSOCIATIONS
Get information on the work of the federation and the rules of the game, plus rankings and the events calendar. See also **www.netballcoaching.com** which is good for advice and links.

Olympics

www.olympics.org/uk   UK
BRITISH OLYMPIC ASSOCIATION
An expanded site featuring highlights of the Torino Winter Games and looking forward to Beijing in 2008 and, of course, London in 2012. You can learn more about 300 Olympic heroes, access an athlete's medal tally and learn more about the sports featured in the games. There's information for collectors and also the doping policy. For a history of the games there's the Olympic museum link and links to sports federations and committees.

www.london2012.org
UK

IT'S OFFICIAL
Find out what's planned and where, download the interactive map, see artists' impressions of the Olympic Park, learn about the business links and you can sign up to be a volunteer or even get a job.

See also:
www.olympianartifacts.com – good site featuring an Olympic memorabilia store.
www.olympics.com – the official site of the Olympic movement.

Rowing

www.ara-rowing.org
UK

AMATEUR ROWING ASSOCIATION
This site offers information on the history of the sport, plus the latest news, coaching tips and links.

See also:
www.steveredgrave.com – Sir Steve's official site offers biographical information, training instruction and tips, links and background on the sport.
www.total.rowing.org.uk – a good rowing portal site.

Rugby

www.scrum.com
UK

RUGBY UNION
An excellent site about rugby union with impressively up-to-the-minute coverage. For a similar but lighter and more fun site go to **www.planet-rugby.com** which has a comprehensive round-up of world rugby with instant reports, lots of detail and information on both union and league. **www.rugbyheaven.com** is also worth checking out. For the history of rugby union go to the **www.rugbyfootballhistory.com** which is also good for links.

www.rfu.com
UK

RUGBY FOOTBALL UNION
Masses of features, articles and news from the official RFU site, it's got team news and information, links and a shop where you can buy gear – delivery starts at £3.

www.rleague.com   UK

WORLD OF RUGBY LEAGUE
Another very comprehensive site, featuring sections on
Australia, New Zealand and the UK, with plenty of chat, articles,
player profiles and enough statistics to keep the most ardent fan
happy. See also the magazine site **www.totalrugbyleague.com**
and also **www.ozleague.com**

www.rugbyrelics.com   UK
RUGBY MEMORABILIA
A good memorabilia store covering most countries and aspects of
the game, everything from autographs to ties and programmes.

Sailing

www.madforsailing.com   UK
THE DAILY SAIL
An informative and well-laid-out site covering all aspects of
sailing both as a sport and as a hobby. There are some really
good and well-written articles, video clips and features such as
a crew search facility and weather information.

www.yachtmonster.com   US
FOR ALL THINGS YACHTING
A combination of search engine and site directory all devoted to
one subject – yachting.

www.ukdinghyracing.com   UK
UK DINGHY RACING
Devoted mainly to this one aspect of sailing, it covers the sport
comprehensively and gives advice on buying, and hosts links to
auctions and specialist shops.

www.ellenmacarthur.com   UK
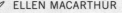
ELLEN MACARTHUR
An interesting and well-put-together site where you can find
out what Ellen is up to as well as biographical details. When
she is sailing, you can follow her progress, access the charts
and weather forecasts while listening to her latest
transmission.

See also:
www.rya.org.uk – a good advice-laden site from the Royal
Yachting Association, very informative at all levels.

www.sailing-411.com – excellent American sailing portal.
www.uksail.com – a sailing portal site offering some 1,000 links.

Skiing and Snowboarding – see page 436.

Skateboarding

www.skateboarding.com   US
Good skateboarding magazine with lots of videos, pictures and
trick tips. For a scientific approach to the subject investigate
www.exploratorium.edu/skateboarding To buy kit online try
www.popcornskate.co.uk who also provide instructions on
making your own board. See also Extreme Sports on page 457.

Snooker

www.worldsnooker.com   UK
THE SITE OF THE PROFESSIONALS
An informative site, which is run by the game's governing body,
World Snooker has all the latest news, tournament up-dates, the
low-down on the players plus photos, videos of highlights and
free live scoring. There's a lot here for everyone, but members get
added extras, and its free.

See also:
www.snooker.net – great for the latest news and gossip.
www.snookersports.co.uk – a snooker equipment shop.

Tennis and Racket Sports

Tennis

www.lta.org.uk   UK
LAWN TENNIS ASSOCIATION
An excellent and attractively designed all-year tennis information
site run by the Lawn Tennis Association, it has information on
the players, rankings and tournament news, as well as details on
clubs and coaching courses. There's also an online tennis shop
where you can buy merchandise and equipment. Check out their
portal **www.totaltennis.net** for chat, news and resources to
download. See also **www.atptour.com** which gives a less
UK-biased view of the game, with excellent sections on the
players, tournaments and rankings.

www.wimbledon.org
UK

THE OFFICIAL WIMBLEDON SITE

Very impressive, there's a great deal here and not just in June, but you need to be patient. Apart from the information you'd expect, you can download screensavers, visit the online museum and eventually see videos of past matches. The shop is expensive.

Other tennis sites worth a look:

www.cliffrichardtennis.org – excellent site aimed at encouraging children to take up the game.

www.itftennis.com/juniors – for the junior game in the UK.

www.juniortennis.com – keep a watch on international young hopefuls.

www.pwp.com – a comprehensive tennis and racket store.

www.racquet-zone.co.uk – a good racket shop.

www.tennis.com – good magazine, with gear guides, tips and hot news.

www.tennisnews.com – the latest news updated daily and e-mailed to you.

Badminton

www.badders.com
UK

BADMINTON COMMUNITY NETWORK

A very good example of a site that pulls together an interest group. It's excellent for news and chat as well as links and information on the sport.

See also:

www.badzone.co.uk – a pretty comprehensive offering, interesting design!

www.baofe.co.uk – the site of the Badminton Association of England with all the latest news.

www.intbadfed.org – home of the International Badminton Federation.

S

Squash

www.squashplayer.co.uk
UK

WORLD OF SQUASH AT YOUR FINGERTIPS

A really comprehensive round-up of the game, with links galore and a great news section; there's also a section for the UK, which has club details and the latest news. See also

www.worldsquash.org for a good site on what's going on world-wide.

Table Tennis

www.ittf.com   UK
INTERNATIONAL TABLE TENNIS FEDERATION
A messy site but one that covers most aspects of the sport around the world. See also **www.ettu.org** for the European view.

Tenpin Bowling

www.btba.org.uk   UK
BRITISH TENPIN BOWLING ASSOCIATION
The home of the game in the UK with rules, information on clubs and background on what the governing body does. See also **www.probowluk.co.uk** – a serious site with useful tips and links.

Water Sports and Swimming

Swimming

www.swimnews.com   US
SWIMMING NEWS
It's up to date and offers a wide coverage of news, with other features such as rankings, events calendar, shopping and competition analysis.

www.pullbuoy.co.uk   UK
UK SWIMMING
A good site that covers the UK scene. You can find unusual features such as a job finder and time converter. It's great for links too.

Other good swimming sites:
www.learn-to-swim.co.uk – learn-to-swim holidays.
www.swiminfo.com – US magazine site with articles, information and results.
www.swimmersworld.com – pretty average site with news and links.
www.webswim.com – forums, articles and help.

Surfing

www.coldswell.co.uk   UK

SURFING THE UK COAST
Includes forecasts for weather and surf, satellite images, live surf
web cams from around the world and a complete directory of
surfing web sites.

www.thesurfingmuseum.co.uk   UK
FOR SURF BUMS
The museum in Brighton is now open and you'll find information
about it here. Online there's also news, exhibitions (including
surfers' stories and videos), campaign issues (e.g. surfers'
against sewage and support the lifeboats) and the history of
surfing. The shop has a disappointing range of goods on offer.
Interesting design too.

See also:
www.britsurf.co.uk – home of the British Surfing Association.
www.coastalwatch.com – great, if you're in Australia.
www.surfline.com – check out weather, sea conditions, the
latest gear – essentially, all you need before you go.
www.surfstation.co.uk – for links, shopping and surf speak.
www.troggs.com – good for surfing gear.

www.2xs.co.uk   UK
WINDSURFING IN THE UK
Where to go windsurfing, plus tips and the latest sports news,
shopping, weather information and advice.

Water-skiing

www.waterski.com   US
WORLD OF WATER SKIING
An American site which features information about the sport,
how to compete, news, tips, equipment and where to ski.
See also **www.bwsf.co.uk** although not an attractive site, it
does have UK-based information on places to ski, clubs,
competitions and a message board. Another good site is
www.planetwaterski.com – an American site with a global
guide to places to ski.

S

Wrestling

www.wwe.com   US

WORLD WRESTLING ENTERTAINMENT

Whether you think it's sport or soap opera, here you can keep up with the twists and turns plus all the action at this exciting site, which has news, clips and of course a merchandise shop.

See also:

www.amateurwrestlingnews.com – amateur wrestling scene with US bias.

www.prowrestling.com – all the latest news and controversy.

www.wrestlingusa.com – a more serious and credible magazine site.

Sports Clothes and Merchandise

www.sweatband.com   UK

SHOP BY SPORT

A wide-ranging shop that supplies equipment for many sports, but it's especially good for tennis, rugby and cricket. Delivery costs depend on the weight of your parcel. See also **www.newitts.com** which is comprehensive.

www.kitbag.com   UK

SPORTS FASHION

Football kits and gear galore from new to retro; it covers cricket and rugby too. Costs on delivery vary according to order. Also offers shopping by brand and a news service.

www.sportsbooksdirect.co.uk   UK

TAKING SPORT SERIOUSLY

Sportspages and Sports Books Direct have joined forces to create an online book store that also stocks video and DVD. Concentrating on sport, they offer a wide range at OK prices, even signed copies. Great for that one thing you've been unable to find.

www.sportsworld.co.uk   UK

SPORT TRAVEL

Specialists in making travel arrangements to sporting events; at this site you can book tickets and find out about future events. It's particularly good for corporate hospitality; they seem to feel the need to talk to you on the phone though!

www.sportingheritage.co.uk   UK
SPORTING GIFTS
A selection of prints, gifts and collectibles available to buy from
this well-laid-out site and they cover all the major sports.

Stationery

www.stationerystore.co.uk   UK
STATIONERY STORE
A well-designed and easy-to-use stationery store supplying
everything from paperclips to office machinery. There are also
sections on green stationery, electronics and lots of offers.

www.staples.co.uk   UK
NOT JUST STAPLES
A good all-rounder with a wide range and some good offers; next
day delivery is available, in the past this site was reserved for
business use, however, now all it takes is a basic registration and
anyone can order online.

For other stationery stores try:
www.cardcorp.co.uk – good place to go for your business cards
and other printing needs.
www.katespaperie.com – to some it's just 'paper with bits in'
but for those who pay regular homage to the New York stores,
Kate's Paperie represents the best in hand-made stationery.
Delivery is expensive.
www.paperchase.co.uk – you can't buy online but it looks great
and you can order by phone – how archaic.
www.papershed.com – delicious hand-made paper, creative
supplies and wedding stationery.
www.penhome.co.uk for pens and pen repairs.
www.theperfectcardcompany.co.uk – handmade cards, photo
albums, guest books and keepsake boxes.
www.viking-direct.co.uk – excellent range, now serving
everyone, not just business customers.
www.whsmith.co.uk/stationery – part of the WH Smith site with
some offers and multi-buys but a limited range, which does
include some of their fashion stationery.

http://rps.gn.apc.org   UK
TOTALLY RECYCLED
For all your stationery needs from computer paper to art

supplies, all recycled and several ranges to choose from. They will also print your letterheads and customise promotional goods. There's lots of information on paper making and recycling too. For more, try **www.greenstat.co.uk**

See also:
www.paper-caper.co.uk – nice range of notebooks and gift stationery – all fair trade.
www.remarkable.co.uk – for pencils made from recycled plastic cups.

Student Sites

There's masses of information for students on the Internet. Here are some sites worth checking out. The links are generally very good, so if the topic isn't covered here, it should be easy to track down.

Universities and Colleges

www.ucas.co.uk   UK
THE UNIVERSITY STARTING BLOCK
A comprehensive site listing all the courses at British universities with entry profiles. You can view the directory online and order your UCAS handbook and application form. If you've already applied, you can view your application online. There are links to all the universities plus really good links to related sites. There is good advice too. If you want to learn a language you can try finding a course through **www.edunet.com**

www.nusonline.co.uk   UK

STUDENTS UNITE
Lots of relevant news and views for students on this really good-looking site. You need to register to get access to their discounts directory and special offers. Once in, you can send e-cards and use their mail and storage facilities too.

See also these other useful sites:
www.braintrack.com – a comprehensive directory of links to universities world-wide.
www.britishcouncil.org/education – the student section is full of options for further education and training.

www.careers-portal.co.uk – tasters of their comprehensive selection of books on surviving university and finding a career. You can buy the books too.

www.findaphd.com – find a PhD, Masters or Post Doc course.

www.hotcourses.com – a very good database of courses for students at all levels, with careers and money advice thrown in.

www.slc.co.uk – home of the Student Loan Company.

Working Abroad and Job Finding

www.gapyear.com   UK

COMPLETE GUIDE TO TAKING A YEAR OUT

Whether you fancy helping out in the forests of Brazil or teaching in Europe you'll find information and opportunities here. There's loads of advice, past experiences to get you tempted, chat, a message board, competitions and you can subscribe to their magazine (an old-fashioned paper one).

www.payaway.co.uk   UK

FIND A JOB ABROAD OR A WORKING HOLIDAY

A great starting place for anyone who wants to work abroad. There is an e-zine with reports from travellers, and you can register with their online jobs service. They've missed nothing out in their links section from embassies to travel health.

www.anyworkanywhere.com   UK

JOBS IN THE UK AND WORLD-WIDE

A bright and breezy site with jobs and all the right advice, plus links.

See also:

www.bunac.co.uk – combine work and travel with these programmes from an experienced specialist.

www.world-challenge.co.uk – take part in any one of a number of expeditions. They're age ranged and vary greatly in scope, so there should be something for everyone.

www.yearoutgroup.org – a mass of information and help for both those taking a gap year and their parents too.

Careers

www.prospects.ac.uk   UK
> CAREER OPTIONS
> Home of the official graduates' careers guide offering a huge
> amount of information, which is all packed into a pretty
> dense site.

Discount Cards

www.istc.org   UK
> INTERNATIONAL STUDENT TRAVEL CONFEDERATION
> Get your student and youth discount card as well as info on
> working and studying abroad. Also help with such things as
> railpasses, phonecards, ISTC registered travel agents world-
> wide, plus e-mail, voice mail and fax messaging. For a wide
> range of discounts sign up for a card at **www.isiccard.com** and
> be sure to get a European youth card for discounts within the EU
> at the cool **www.euro26.org**

Student Life

www.studentuk.com   UK
> STUDENT LIFE
> A good-looking, useful and generally well-written student's
> e-zine featuring news, music and film reviews, going out, chat,
> even articles on science and politics. There's also some excellent
> advice on subjects such as gap years, accommodation and
> finance. For an alternative look at the same information, and
> learn how to survive boring lectures, see **www.funky.co.uk**

www.good2bsecure.gov.uk   UK
> FIGHT CRIME AGAINST STUDENTS
> Students are more likely to be victims of crime than any part of
> society, here you can get advice on security and keeping safe.

www.studenthealth.co.uk   UK
> CLICK IT BETTER
> Written by doctors for students, this site offers printable advice
> leaflets on hundreds of topics along with a health problem page.
> They're not publishing more recent estimates, but in 2004 they
> provided over 2 million leaflets – that's over 6,000 a day, so I
> guess everyone already knows about this site. Sadly, the jokes

and competitions have gone this year; let's hope they're not having problems themselves.

www.accommodationforstudents.com UK
ACCOMODATION SEARCH ENGINE
A searchable database for students in need of accommodation. As well as providing information about accommodation available, you can find/rent out a room or advertise for housemates via their noticeboard.

www.capitalstudents.com – from clubbing to jobs for students in London with e-mail and chat.
www.studenttimes.org – online version of the free, independent student newspaper written for students by students.
www.wrecked.co.uk – the perils of drinking (not just for students).

Links and information

www.lazystudent.co.uk UK
SITE LISTING
The perfect site for those who can't be arsed to look things up properly. It's well categorised and has listed virtually any site that a student might need.

www.whatnow.co.uk UK
INFORMATION AND ADVICE
Excellent, well-constructed site giving information for young people on everything from sex to careers. You can make an enquiry directly to them or chat with people who have similar issues. There's also a good links section.

Teenagers

*Here's a small selection of the best sites aimed at teenagers. Many of the most hyped sites are just heavily disguised marketing and sales operations, treat these with scepticism and enjoy the best, which are generally done for the love of it, or through a genuine desire to help. We've also indicated the sort of age group that the magazines are aimed at. We should add our thanks to all those who keep writing in to us suggesting sites for this section. Don't forget your personal safety if you chat online, see page 86 for details or go to **www.thinkuknow.co.uk** for a look at the issues and **www.whatnow.co.uk** for information and advice.*

T

Teenage Magazines

www.globalgang.org.uk   UK
WORLD NEWS, GAMES, GOSSIP AND FUN
See what the rest of the world gets up to at Global Gang. You
can find out what kids in other countries like to eat, what
toys they play with, chat to them or play games. Lastly you get to
find out how you can help those kids less fortunate than yourself.
10 plus

www.girland.com   UK
GIRL AND . . .
An excellent, really attractive and well-put-together site aimed at
teenage girls. It has chat forums, news and lots of features, but
you do have to register. It has won loads of awards and the
environment is safe. *11 plus*

www.mykindaplace.com   UK
IT'S MY KINDA PLACE
Excellent site for teens, with the latest news, gossip and celebrity
features. Aimed squarely at girls it seems to have everything,
including lots of adverts! *11 plus*

www.dubit.co.uk   UK
GAMES, ARTICLES – THE LOT
Dubit combines 3-D graphics with chat, games, video, music
and animations in a fun and interactive way. It's a completely
different approach to the normal teen magazine. It needs a little
patience but it's worth it in the end. Registration is required,
which is a pity as it is a pain and very slow. *12 plus*

www.teentoday.co.uk   UK
FOR TEENAGERS BY TEENAGERS
Get your free e-zine mailed to you daily or just visit the site:
which has much more games, chat, news, entertainment, free
downloads, ringtones and message boards. It's well designed
and genuinely good with not too much advertising. *13 plus*

www.bbc.co.uk/teens   UK
E-ZINES FOR BOTH SEXES
The BBC's teen magazine site addresses the loves and concerns
of the two sexes. Boys get plenty of games, quizzes, cartoons
and useless facts while the girls get a dose of celebs, beauty,
horoscopes plus some fun and games too. There are excellent

advice and information sections for both sexes and both are treated to some brilliant competitions, prizes and fun articles too. *13 plus*

www.alloy.com   US
ALLOY MAGAZINE
On the face of it, this is great; it's got loads of sections on everything from personal advice to shopping albeit a bit American. But with too many adverts, it all seems to be geared to getting your name for marketing purposes and selling stuff. *13 plus*

www.cheekfreak.com   US
FOR THE FREAK IN ALL OF US
Best for stories, blogging and reviews. It's got chat sections, forums and a search engine. Some of the forums are devoted to serious topics such as suicide, sexual hang-ups and family break-up, as such they may prove helpful in dealing with teenage angst. *13 plus*

www.cyberteens.com   UK
CONNECT TO CYBERTEENS
One of the most hyped sites aimed at teenagers, it contains a very good selection of games, news, links and a creativity section where you can send your art and poems. Don't bother with the shop, which was still being re-designed at the time of writing, but on previous visits it was expensive, as is the credit card they offer. *13 plus*

www.4degreez.com   US
INTERACTIVE COMMUNITY
A friendly and entertaining site with reviews, poetry, jokes, polls and links to other related sites. You have to become a member to get the best out of it though. *15 plus*

www.myspace.com   US
A PLACE FOR FRIENDS
Something of a phenomenon, My Space is credited with launching several new bands via its music section and it has a great deal to offer including blogs, chatrooms, the latest gossip and lots to entertain. Parents may just want to check out the terms and conditions before signing up. *14 plus*

www.teentoday.co.uk   UK
  TEEN TODAY
  A UK-oriented magazine site aimed at teenagers. It covers all the
  things you'd expect: quizzes, music, films, plus chat and free
  SMS. Not bad. *13 plus*

Directories

www.teensites.org   US
  WEB DIRECTORY FOR TEENS
  A huge directory of sites covering loads of subjects of interest to
  teenagers. It's biased to the US, but if you don't mind that, then it
  should have everything you need.

www.ipl.org/div/teen   US
  TEEN SPACE
  Part of the Internet Public Library, these pages offer a directory
  of links for help and information on everything from careers,
  homework, issues, technology and entertainment.

  See also:
  http://directory.google.com/Top/Kids_and_Teens – good
  directory from Google.
  http://teensites.student.com – a directory of sites aimed at
  teenagers, the same site offers a free blog service.
  www.echoica.net/glitter – a site that lists and acts as a directory
  for blogs created by teenagers.
  www.kidgrid.com – well laid out and easy to use, with a US
  bias.
  www.kidsclick.org – massive database of sites put together by a
  group of librarians.
  www.surfnetkids.com – a comprehensive directory put together
  by an American journalist.

Advice

www.worriedneed2talk.org.uk   UK
  CRUELTY TO CHILDREN MUST STOP!
  A site from the NSPCC aimed at helping teenagers and children
  cope and deal with violence, family problems and drug advice.
  Also available in Welsh.

www.mindbodysoul.gov.uk   UK
GET THE LOW-DOWN ON HEALTH
A health site for teenagers. It covers all you'd expect, all wrapped
up in good-looking graphics; it's also not too densely written or
too patronising.

www.trashed.co.uk   UK
R U THINKING ABOUT IT?
Excellent site on sex and sexuality. There is well-balanced
information on contraception, sexually transmitted infections,
the law and about where to go for help and advice. Sections
devoted to girls and lads give a gender-based perspective too.
See also the US-based **www.teenwire.com** and also
www.thehormonefactory.com

www.thesite.org.uk   UK
THE SITE
This site offers advice on a range of subjects: careers,
relationships, drugs, sex, money, legal issues and so on.
Aimed largely at 15 to 24 year olds, it's well laid out and very
informative.

www.no-ur-rites.com   UK
KNOW YOUR RIGHTS
A basic but useful information site providing legal information on
everything from drugs to online shopping. As it's put together by
a local trading standards authority, the information should be
current. See also **www.youthinformation.com** which aims to
serve as an 'information toolkit' for young people.

http://teenadvice.about.com   US
QUESTIONS AND ANSWERS
An agony aunt service of sorts, it's a bit of a jumble but
the quizzes are entertaining. Parents should check out
http://parentingteens.about.com

Telecommunications

*In this ever-changing section there's information on ADSL and
computer-related communications, where to go to buy mobiles, get the
best out of them and even have a little fun with them. For phone
numbers see the section entitled Finding Someone on page 168. For
broadband/ADSL see page 64.*

www.ofcom.org.uk   UK
    THE REGULATOR
    Ofcom is the regulator for the UK communications industries,
    with responsibilities across television, radio,
    telecommunications and wireless communications services.
    Theirs is a useful site with the latest news and consumer
    information surrounding this complex world. If you have a
    complaint, here's where to seek redress. See also
    www.icstis.org.uk for the Independent Committee for the
    Supervision of Standards of Telephone Information Services, and
    the Telecommunications Ombudsman at **www.otelo.org.uk**

www.magsys.co.uk/telecom   UK
    COMPARE TARIFFS
    A potentially useful site if you want to see how your tariff
    compares with those of other phone companies; it's not exactly
    user friendly though. For a site that is campaigning against
    expensive telephone lines have a look at **www.saynoto0870.com**

Mobile Phones

www.carphonewarehouse.com   UK
    CHOOSING THE RIGHT MOBILE
    You need to take your time to find the best tariff, then take
    advantage of the numerous offers. Excellent pictures, details of
    the phones and the information is unbiased. There's a shop that
    also sells handheld PCs and delivery is free too. You can
    download a wide range of new phone ring tones, from classical
    to the latest pop tunes.

www.mobileedge.co.uk   UK
    MOBILE INFORMATION
    A quirkily designed site with help on buying the right mobile, it
    also offers information on health and mobiles, links and contact
    numbers, pre-pay deals, global networks, ring tones, shop and
    much more.

    See also:
    www.b3k.net – excellent site with a wide range of phones and
    accessories, good for the hard to get bits too.
    www.dialaphone.co.uk – another phone shop. They'll match
    anyone else's prices though; let's hope they continue to survive.
    www.expansys.com – dense site with masses of information
    and competitive prices.

www.mobilefun.co.uk – a huge range of phones and accessories.
www.mobileshop.com – nice design and lots of offers.
www.onestopphoneshop.com – nicely designed site with a deal finder. Also promise to match competitors' prices.

Here's where to find the major phone operators:
www.motorola.co.uk
www.o2.co.uk
www.orange.co.uk
www.three.co.uk
www.t-mobile.co.uk
www.virginmobile.com
www.vodafone.co.UK

Recycling

www.oxfam.org.uk/what_you_can_do/recycle/phones   UK
SEND YOUR OLD MOBILES HERE
If you have all your old mobiles hanging around the house then go here to find out how you can put them to good use.
www.helptheaged.org.uk and **www.actionaidrecycling.org.uk** have similar schemes.

Ring Tones and Text Messaging

www.ukyourmobile.com   UK
NEW RING TUNES FOR YOUR PHONE
There are several hundred tunes, icons and logos that you can download on to your mobile using text messaging and most are free.

www.treasuremytext.com   UK
SAVING YOUR TEXTS
Here you can store your text messages online, even create a mobile blog and share your text conversations with your friends.

See also:
www.onmymob.com – offering hundreds of free ring tones and logos.
www.ringtones2go.co.uk – massive selection, all the latest tunes.

www.chatlist.com/faces.html UK
TEXT MESSAGING
Confused about your emoticons? %-) Here's a list of several
thousand for you to choose from.

Accessorising Your Phone

www.theaccessoryphoneshop.com UK
FOR COMPLETE MOBILE COVERAGE
Covers, body pouches, chargers, batteries, cables, memory
cards – all the kit for all the phones. Sat nav, Bluetooth, PSP and
iPod accessories too. Clear and well organised.

Services

www.buzzme.com UK
NEVER MISS A CALL
An online answering machine that gives you the option of
accepting, ignoring or sending voice messages, very useful if you
only have the one line.

www.mapminder.co.uk UK
MOBILE PHONE TRACKING
Map Minder' phone tracking service is excellent if, for example,
you're Big Brother or a parent wanting to keep track of your kids
or you're a business wanting to co-ordinate sales teams. It
combines their mapping which is pretty clear with mobile
technology. See also **www.mapaphone.co.uk** and also
www.verilocation.com

www.jiwire.com US
WIFI
A very useful site if you travel with a laptop and need to know
where the nearest WiFi spots are. There is also a great deal of
advice on how to get the best out of it and keep secure too.

Faxing

www.efax.com UK
FAX USING E-MAIL
A paid-for service that makes it easy for you to send faxes via
your e-mail service. See also **www.j2.com** who offer a similar
service. For more information go to **www.tpc.int** and it's also
worth checking out **www.download.com** for fax programmes.

Lowering the Costs

*Broadband users can take advantage of Voice over IP (or VoIP), the technology that allows the transfer of conversations over the Internet at vastly lower prices than we're used to paying over the normal land lines. Wikipedia has a thorough overview of the subject, which can be found at **http://en.wikipedia.org/wiki/Voip***

*A full listing of sites that sell or use VoIP can be found at **www.dmoz.org/Business/Telecommunications/Services/VoIP/***

www.skype.com   US
   FREE CALLS
   Now owned by eBay, this one allows you to make free calls using
   the Internet to other Skype users, quality is pretty good but you
   have to pay to call someone not using Skype.

   See also:
   www.18866.co.uk – cheaper international calls plus VoIP too.
   www.bt.com – with details of its own VoIP system, which is
   charged for but you get good quality lines.
   www.freeworlddialup.com – one of the best for features.
   www.gossiptel.com – lots of options here too.
   www.voiponline.com – a directory and VoIP news service.
   www.vonage.co.uk – a subscription service, which, on the face
   of it, looks good value.

Technology

www.bluetooth.com   US
   OFFICIAL BLUETOOTH
   A superb official Microsoft site devoted to Bluetooth technology;
   it's amazing how fast it's become so widespread and so old hat.

www.3g.co.uk   UK
   3G
   Excellent site devoted to bringing you the latest information and
   developments in this technology.

   See also:
   www.gprshelp.co.uk – helpful site covering GPRS.
   www.mobiledevelopers.com – the latest information on what's
   happening in the world of mobile telecommunications.

T

Television

TV channels, listings and your favourite soap operas are all here, some have great sites, others are pretty naff, especially when you consider they're in the entertainment business. Television now shares a regulator with telecommunications in general. See Ofcom below.

www.ofcom.org.uk   UK
OFCOM
Ofcom is the regulator for the UK communications industries including television, radio, telecommunications and wireless communications services. If you've a complaint, here's the place to go – they've made it quite easy.

www.tvlicensing.co.uk   UK
TELEVISION LICENCE
All you need to know about your TV licence, how to pay and how to deal with problems.

Channels and Digital

www.bbc.co.uk   UK

THE UK'S MOST POPULAR WEB SITE
The BBC site deserves a special feature, it is huge with more than 2 million pages and it can be quite daunting. It has sections covering everything from business to the weather and there are also regional sections, a web guide, as well as tips on how to use the Internet and you can subscribe to a newsletter. There are feature sites on all their major programmes and most of the minor ones too, it's a fantastic site and more than a useful resource.

www.itv.co.uk   UK
ITV NETWORK
ITV has a pretty straightforward site with links to all the major programmes, soaps, topics and categories, their related web sites and a 'what's on' guide, plus a few extras such as quizzes. For a history of Independent Television go to **www.itw.org.uk**

www.citv.co.uk   UK
CHILDREN'S ITV
A bright and breezy site that features competitions, safe surfing, features on the programmes including all the favourite characters and much more. You need to join to get the best out of

it though, and because there's so much on the site, it can be a
little slow.

www.channel4.co.uk   UK
CHANNEL 4
A cool design with details of programmes and links to specific
web pages on the best-known ones. There are also links to other
initiatives such as Filmfour and the 4learning programme.

www.channel5.co.uk   UK
CHANNEL 5
The usual programme information, scheduling details, news and
competitions. There are also some useful programme related
factsheets and a bright and breezy children's section featuring
the *Milkshake* magazine.

www.sky.com   UK
SKY TV
Links to the main Sky sites – news, sport etc, plus information on
their digital packages.

www.nick.com   US
NICKELODEON
Bright doesn't do this site justice – you need sunglasses! It's got
info on all the top programmes plus games and quizzes.

www.freeview.co.uk   UK
FREEVIEW
Details of the Freeview service and where it's available in
the UK.

www.wwitv.com   US
WORLD-WIDE INTERNET TV
Watch several international channels, the BBC and listen to
radio too. Probably best for broadband users. See also the
excellent **www.liketelevision.com** which is very much geared to
broadband.

www.broadband-television.com   US
STREAMING TV
A huge range of channels available to view including music as
well as TV. You have to download the free software but the
results are generally worth the effort. It's making a selection
that's the difficult part.

TV Fans and Nostalgia

www.sausagenet.co.uk   UK
    CULT AND CLASSIC TV
    An outstanding nostalgia site devoted to popular children's TV
    programmes from the past 40 years. You can download theme
    tunes or buy related merchandise via the excellent links
    directory. See also **www.sadgeezr.com** which is Sci Fi-oriented.

www.uktvadverts.com   UK
    TV ADVERTS
    A collection of TV adverts and background information, now you
    can find out who did that voiceover. See also **www.adwatch.tv**
    who offer a similar collection. And about that piece of music you
    can't remember . . . **www.commercialbreaksandbeats.co.uk**
    is the place to go.

See also:
http://epguides.com – a massive database of episode guides
covering a wide variety of US and some UK TV shows and series.
http://tv.cream.org – great for nostalgia from the 70s and 80s.
www.625.uk.com – a personal celebration and overview of the
rights and wrongs of British telly, with downloads of logos and
even public information films.
www.advertsongs.co.uk – find music used in adverts, pretty out
of date though.
www.animus-web.demon.co.uk – eclectic look back on several
shows from the 70s; the Blue Peter section is very good.
www.apts.org.uk – history of Alexander Palace where it all began.
www.beonscreen.com/uk/index.asp – the chance to appear on
your favourite show.
www.bigglethwaite.com – great for TV-related links.
www.british-tv-history.co.uk – fact-oriented site with a timeline
of sorts, great for checking information.
www.clappers-tickets.co.uk – be part of the TV show audience,
free tickets for selected shows.
www.geocities.com/TelevisionCity/1011 – home of 'Watched
it', a look back on Children's TV.
www.kaleidoscope.org.uk – an organisation devoted to
preserving classic TV; it puts on events and shows too.
www.offthetelly.co.uk – a good e-zine about telly.
www.petford.net/kaleidoscope – the site of a voluntary
organisation devoted to the appreciation of classic TV, lots of
links and information to be found here.

www.saturdaymornings.co.uk – great site about those programmes that used to be shown on Saturday mornings.
www.sitcomsonline.com – a huge amount of information on US sitcoms.
www.thetvroom.com – if you want to know anything about TV presenting go here.
www.transdiffusion.org/emc – selection of articles, sites and links which look back at television history, diverse and not easy to navigate but there's some excellent stuff here especially in the Halcyon Days section.
www.tv-ark.org.uk – another excellent archive site.
www.tvfetish.net – a good site if you can navigate it; poorly designed but there's a lot here for those looking to reminisce.
www.tvradiobits.co.uk – an excellent excerpt and clips site.
www.ukgameshows.com – an encyclopaedic site about games shows.
www.waveguide.co.uk – keep up to date with what's going on in the world of TV.
www.whirligig-tv.co.uk – a great site for 50s TV nostalgia.

TV Review and Listings Sites

www.digiguide.co.uk   UK
THE DOWNLOADABLE GUIDE
If you have Sky digital, you'll be familiar with this guide. It follows a similar format, although you can customise it. Simply download the program and you get 14 days, forward programming for up to 200 channels, masses of links and background information. It costs £8.99 per annum.

www.radiotimes.com   UK
THE *RADIO TIMES*
Excellent listings e-zine with a good search facility for looking up programme details, plus competitions, links and a cinema guide. There are also sections on the best-loved TV genres – children's, sci-fi, soaps and so on.

See also:
www.onthebox.com – a simple and effective daily TV guide. Lots of pop-up ads.
www.thecustard.tv – a personal, fun and well-put-together TV and listings guide, which deserves to succeed.

Theatre

Here's a great selection of sites that will appeal to theatre goers everywhere. Be aware that some online ticket services charge large processing fees for the privilege plus postage as well. Check the invoice carefully before you commit yourself.

www.whatsonstage.com   UK
HOME OF BRITISH THEATRE
A really strong site with masses of news and reviews to browse through plus a very good search facility and booking service (through a third party), a real theatre buff's delight. For more information try out the British Theatre Guide at **www.britishtheatreguide.info**

www.aloud.com   UK
ONLINE TICKET SEARCH
You can search by venue, location or by artist, it's fast and pretty comprehensive and there's a hot events section – it mainly covers music and festivals nowadays though it's good for comedy. The review section is good and you can buy tickets.

www.theatrenet.com   UK
THE ENTERTAINMENT CENTRE
Get the latest news, catch the new shows and, if you join the club, there are discounts on tickets for theatre, concerts, sporting events and holidays. You can also search their archives for information on past productions and learn how to become a theatre angel.

www.uktheatre.net   UK
PASSIONATE ABOUT THEATRE
Whether you're a fan or an actor this site has much to offer both as a useful source of information and as a good site directory. You need to be a member which costs one pound per week.

www.uktw.co.uk   UK
UK THEATRE WEB
A cheerful site offering all the usual information on theatre plus amateur dramatics, jobs, chat, competitions and just gossip. For a search engine devoted to the subject check out **http://utse.list-team.com/index.php** it's a little erratic though.

www.rsc.org.uk UK
THE ROYAL SHAKESPEARE COMPANY
Get all the news as well as information on performances and tours. You can book tickets online although it's via a third party site. There is also loads of information about the life and times of the Bard and synopses of his plays.

www.reallyuseful.com UK
ANDREW LLOYD WEBBER
At this attractive, hi-tech site you can watch video clips and listen to top audio clips, download screen savers and wallpaper, take part in competitions and chat. There's also a good kids' section plus details on the shows.

www.nt-online.org UK
THE NATIONAL
Excellent for details of their shows and forthcoming plays with tour information added. You can't buy tickets online, but you can e-mail or fax for them.

www.officiallondontheatre.co.uk UK
SOCIETY OF LONDON THEATRES
The latest news, a show finder service and hot tickets are just a few of the services available at this great site. You can also get a Theatreland map, half price tickets and they'll even fax you a seating plan. See also **www.thisislondon.co.uk** who have a good theatre section and also **www.thisistheatre.com** which lists all the London shows.

www.dresscircle.co.uk UK
THEATRE SHOP
A long-established supplier of music, books and products related to the theatre, with links and the latest news.

www.uktheatrebreak.co.uk UK
THEATRE BREAKS
A useful site and booking service that allows you to combine your trip to the theatre with a short holiday or overnight stay.

To book online also try the following sites:
www.lastminute.com
www.londontheatretickets.com
www.ticketmaster.co.uk
www.uktickets.co.uk

T

Travel and Holidays

Travel is one of the biggest growth areas on the Internet, from holidays to insurance to local guides. If you're buying, then it definitely pays to shop around and try several sites, but be careful, it's amazing how fast the best deals are being snapped up. You may find that you still spend time on the phone, but the sites are constantly improving. The amount of information available is staggering and it's no wonder this is the biggest section in the book.

When checking out travel sites, you should be aware that the same company may own many sites, for example Lastminute.com (owned by Expedia) has interests in sites covering everything from skiing holidays to general travel and even ferry bookings. These sites will be listed under their specialist area.

*If you are concerned about a particular company and want to check, nearly all sites have company information hidden away, usually at the bottom of the page, or you can quickly check them out at Companies House **www.companies-house.gov.uk***

Information for disabled travellers can be found on page 121.

Starting Out

www.ukpa.gov.uk   UK
> UK PASSPORTS
> Pre-apply for your passport online and get tips on how to get the best passport photo amongst other very useful information.

www.visaservice.co.uk   UK
> QUICK VISA
> This service will get you your visa in double quick time, for a price.

www.hmce.gov.uk   UK
> HM CUSTOMS AND EXCISE
> All you need to know about visiting the UK, exporting and importing and the regulations surrounding what you can bring back with you from your holidays.

Travel Sites that Make You Want to Go There

The Good Web Site Guide's Top 10s of the Internet

1. **www.africatravelresource.com** – covers East Africa. Excellent design
2. **www.travelCanada.ca** – attractive and informative
3. **www.franceway.com** – culture, history and travel
4. **www.jnto.go.jp** – great site from the Japanese Tourist Association
5. **www.nepal.com** – making the most of what nature has given them
6. **www.tourspain.es** – colourful and a great overview
7. **www.visitbritain.com** – comprehensive or what!
8. **www.seeamerica.org** – great for links and information
9. **www.ecuadorexplorer.com** – awesome, and covers the Galapagos Islands too
10. **www.sg** – at least you'll remember the URL. A great portal on Singapore

www.abtanet.com   UK
ABTA
Make sure that the travel agent you choose is a member of the Association of British Travel Agents as then you're covered if they go bust halfway through your holiday. All members are listed and there's a great search facility with links for you to start the ball rolling. See also the Air Travellers Licensing home page **www.atol.org.uk** which is part of the Civil Aviation site.

www.brochurebank.co.uk   UK
BROCHURES DELIVERED TO YOUR HOME
Holiday brochures from the major and specialist travel companies can be selected then delivered to your home, free of charge. The selection process is easy and the site is fast. Delivery is by second class post.

Health, Safety and Tips

www.fco.gov.uk/travel   UK
ADVICE FROM THE FOREIGN OFFICE
Before you go, get general advice or safety or visa information.
Just select a country and you get a run-down of all the issues
that are likely to affect you when you go there, from terrorism to
health.

www.travelhealth.co.uk   UK
STAY HEALTHY
An authoritative site with sections on general health advice
and disease prevention, a shop and links.

For more health and safety travel information and tips . . .
www.1000traveltips.org – tips from the very well-travelled
Koen De Boeck and friends.
www.bloodcare.org.uk – the Blood Care Foundation offers a
wide range of advice and tips for many illnesses and
situations.
www.cdc.gov/travel – official American site giving sensible
health information world-wide.
www.cyborlink.com – international etiquette and facts covering
120 countries. Designed for business users but useful for the
traveller too.
www.first48.com/guide/features/muslimcode.php – clothing
advice for women travelling to Muslim countries.
www.flyana.com – good advice from an experienced
traveller.
www.masta.org – authoritative health advice and an online
shop to get your medicines.
www.medicalert.org.uk – buy a bracelet that contains all your
essential medical details.
www.travelhealthresources.com – data on over 250 countries,
though US oriented.
www.tripprep.com – country-by-country risk assessment
covering health, safety and politics; it can be a little out of date so
check with the foreign office as well.
www.who.int/en – statistics and health information country by
country.

Family Travel

www.family-travel.co.uk   UK
PRACTICAL INFORMATION
A wide-ranging site covering every aspect of travelling with
children, including health, hotels, culture, products and just
getting to your destination.

See also:
www.familytravelforum.com – an American site offering lots of
information and advice.
www.flyingwithkids.com – sensible air travel advice for those
travelling with babies and small children.
www.kidstravel.co.uk – bright and breezy design but it could
have more content, still some good ideas and travelling tips for
parents though biased to England.
www.opfh.org.uk – good information for single-parent families,
but turn the sound off . . .
www.smallfamilies.co.uk – a wide range of holiday options for
single-parent families.
www.thefamilytravelfiles.com – a US-oriented e-zine with lots
of advice and links.
www.themeparkinsider.com – reviews theme and amusement
parks world-wide.
www.tinytravelers.net – a well-designed and attractive site
offering tips, product reviews and travel advice.
www.travellingwithchildren.co.uk – good for ideas and advice,
if you can put up with the adverts.

Travel Services

www.whatsonwhen.com   UK
WORLD-WIDE EVENTS GUIDE
An easy-to-use site with information on every type of event you
can think of from major festivals to village fêtes.

www.worldtimezone.com   US
TIME ZONE MAP
Useful time zone mapping, although it's heavily advert laden.
See also **www.timeanddate.com**

T

www.kropla.com   US
    PHONE HELP
    Here you can find out about where to plug in your modem, if
    your mobile will work, international dialling codes, even TV
    standards.

    Also worth checking out for more information:
    http://cybercaptive.com – a directory of world cyber cafés.
    http://mytravelrights.com – an American site devoted to
    travellers rights abroad.
    www.cybercafes.com – over 4,000 cyber cafés listed
    throughout the world.
    www.jiwire.com – locate wireless hotspots worldwide.
    www.tipping.org – good advice on how much to tip around the
    world.

While you're away

*All these companies offer similar services looking after your home,
pets or plants while you're away – so there's no need to worry.*

    www.home-and-pets.co.uk – wide-ranging service.
    www.homesitters.co.uk – for a premium service.
    www.minders-keepers.co.uk – pet-oriented service.

www.holiday-companions.com   UK
    TO KEEP YOU COMPANY
    If you need a companion to go away with you, then start
    here. See also **www.people-connection.co.uk** and
    http://travelmatesonline.com

Luggage and Travel Gear

www.bags123.com   UK
    BUYING LUGGAGE
    A wide range and with some good offers, this store is worth a
    visit if you have to replace that tatty old case.

www.excessluggage.co.uk   UK
    EXCESS LUGGAGE
    For problems concerning excess baggage, here's the place to go.
    There are lots of options and it's best to discuss your
    requirements with them.

www.holidayadditions.co.uk   UK
ESSENTIAL ITEMS
A bright and breezy shop that offers a small range of
'essential' travel-oriented products from padlocks to mosquito
repellents.

Travel Money and Insurance

www.xe.net/ucc   UK
ONLINE CURRENCY CONVERTER
The Universal Currency Converter could not be easier to use, just
select the currency you have, then the one you want to convert it
to, press the button and you have your answer in seconds. See
also **www.oanda.com**

www.onlinefx.co.uk   UK
FOREIGN CURRENCY DELIVERED
A pretty straightforward and potentially hassle-free way of getting
your currency, just order with your card and it gets delivered the
next working day. They charge a flat rate £4.95 handling fee, but
no other commission or service fee. They also offer financial
services such as international transfers.

www.travelinsuranceclub.co.uk   UK
AWARD-WINNING TRAVEL INSURANCE CLUB
Unfortunately there isn't one site for collating travel insurance
yet, it's a question of shopping around. These sites make a good
starting point offering a range of policies for backpackers, family
and business travel.

All these companies offer flexibility and good value:
www.costout.co.uk – well-rated insurance and good value.
www.direct-travel.co.uk – nice design and some good offers
too, online quotes.
www.moneysupermarket.com/travelinsurance – compare
policies and pick the best one for you.
www.saga.co.uk/finance/travelinsurance – if you're of a certain
age, travel insurance is often difficult to get. Check out Saga's
policies for over 50s.
www.underthesun.co.uk – good for annual and six-monthly
policies.

T

Travel Shops and Agents

www.travel-lists.co.uk   UK
TRAVEL OPERATORS DIRECTORY
A largely subscription-based service but with free access to their
database of travel specialists and agents. Each entry has a link,
contact number and a short overview of what they do.

www.expedia.co.uk   US/UK
THE COMPLETE SERVICE
This is the UK arm of Microsoft's very successful online travel
agency. It offers a huge array of holidays, flights and associated
services, for personal or business use, nearly all bookable online.
Its easy and quicker than most, and there are some excellent
offers too. Not the trendiest, but it's a good first stop. As with all
the big operators, you have to register. They've also got sections
on travel insurance, mapping, guides, ferries and hotels.

www.lastminute.com   UK
DO SOMETHING LAST MINUTE
Last Minute has an excellent reputation not just as a travel agent,
but as a good shopping site too. For travellers there are
comprehensive sections on hotels, holidays and flights, all with
really good prices. There is also a superb London restaurant
guide and a general entertainment section. Mostly, you can book
online, but a hotline is available.

www.thomascook.com   UK
THE WIDEST RANGE OF PACKAGE HOLIDAYS
This site is easy to use and well laid out and, with over 2 million
package holidays to chose from, you should be able to find
something to your liking. You can also browse the online guide
for ideas or search for cheap flights or holiday deals. Again you
have to call the hotline to book.

www.e-bookers.com   UK
FLIGHT BOOKERS
Acclaimed travel agents specialising in getting good flight deals,
but also good for holidays, special offers and insurance.

www.travel.world.co.uk   UK
FOR ALL YOUR TRAVEL REQUIREMENTS
A massive, comprehensive site, it basically includes most
available travel brochures with links to the relevant travel agent.

It concentrates on Europe, so there are very few American sites, but provides links to hotels, specialist holidays, cruises, self-catering and airlines.

www.uk.mytravel.com UK
SEARCH FOR THE RIGHT DEAL

This site has got an excellent search engine that enables you to find a bargain or just the right holiday. There are also good offers and the late escapes holiday auction site.

www.priceline.co.uk UK
LET SOMEONE ELSE DO THE WORK

Although they now offer a discounted travel service, Priceline still offer the facility to let someone else do the travel searching for you. You provide details of the trip/flight/hotel you want and how much you're willing to pay, then they try to find a deal that will match your requirements. If you're flexible about timing then there are some great offers. Priceline want your credit card details before you agree to any transaction so you may feel more comfortable using the more traditional route.

www.budgettravel.com UK
BUDGET TRAVEL

Rubbish design but masses of links and information for the budget traveller plus advice on how to travel on the cheap. It can be difficult to navigate but the information is very good.

See also:
www.aito.co.uk – offers and information from the Association of Independent Tour Operators, excellent for the unusual.
www.bargainholidays.com – probably the best for quick breaks, excellent for late availability offers.
www.dreamticket.com – the usual holiday offers, but the site also offers much in the way of information too.
www.firstchoice.co.uk – bargains from First Choice holidays.
www.holiday.co.uk – a portal offering a massive number of package holidays and a wide range of other options from all the major operators.
www.opodo.co.uk – slick site from some of the major airlines, worth checking out for flight offers and discounts on hotels.
www.packageholidays.co.uk – late bargain holidays and flights from a wide range of tour operators including Airtours, Cosmos, and Thomson.

T

www.teletext.co.uk/holidays – much better than browsing the TV, you can now get all those offers on one easy-to-use site. There is also lots of useful travel information and online video brochures.

www.thefirstresort.com – a good general site with some good deals and a price promise, owned by Tui UK, formally Thomsons.

www.thisistravel.co.uk – in association with the newspaper group that publishes the *Daily Mail*, this is a comprehensive offering with some good offers. Lots of pop-up ads too.

www.thomson.co.uk – for a wide range of package holidays as well as low-cost flights on their airline.

www.travelagents.co.uk – another all-rounder, nothing special but competent.

www.travelbag.co.uk – straightforward and easy-to-use long haul flight and holiday finder. Part of same group as ebookers.

www.travelcareonline.com – loads of deals and honest information from the UK's largest independent. Winner of the British Travel Awards 2004 'Best Online Travel Agent'.

www.travelmood.com – individual design and long haul destinations.

www.travelocity.com – one of the oldest online travel agents; it's similar to Expedia, comprehensive with plenty of advice and background information.

Short and City Breaks

www.eurobreak.com – click on the map for your destination and you get presented with lots of options including hotel details and online booking.

www.shortbreaks.com – hotel breaks in the UK, Europe and US; arranges theatre breaks too.

www.shortbreaksbyair.com – a good selection of city breaks from this specialist operator.

www.webweekends.co.uk – specialists in weekend breaks both in the UK and abroad.

Luxury and Tailor-made Holidays

Here's a list of the best known luxury holiday specialists and a few we've had recommended to us . . .

www.abercrombiekent.com – one of the most experienced luxury travel operators with a very competent site.

www.amanresorts.com – exclusive hotels and villas in gorgeous locations.

www.audleytravel.com – tailor-made itineraries for escorted groups.

www.balesworldwide.com – for something special, tailor-made holidays to the exotic parts of the world. This hi-tech site is excellent especially now you can book online.

www.carrier.co.uk – luxury holiday specialists, nice looking site too.

www.caz-loyd.com – specialists in the more exotic destinations.

www.coxandkings.co.uk – a slightly disappointing site from one of the oldest travel companies.

www.essentialescapes.com – exclusive luxury spa holidays.

www.exsus.com – tailor-made luxury adventures.

www.hayesandjarvis.co.uk – long-haul holiday specialists, lots to choose from.

www.itcclassics.co.uk – luxury everything basically.

www.jeffersons.com – taking a holiday with your own private jet . . .

www.jewelholidays.com – India, Turkey, Red Sea and Asia.

www.journeysbydesign.co.uk – tailor-made African specialists.

www.luxurylink.com – luxury holiday auctions.

www.originaltravel.co.uk – holidays for activity and well-being, outstanding site design too.

www.pura-aventura.com – active holidays in comfort, mainly Latin America and Spain.

www.rbrww.com – opulence and fishing.

www.seasonsinstyle.co.uk – world-wide luxury in the world's finest hotels.

www.tailor-made.co.uk – basic site but the holiday options look good.

www.tripsworldwide.co.uk – despite the name, it specialises in Latin America and the Caribbean. Some beautiful photography enhances the site.

www.vjv.co.uk – Voyages Jules Verne with an excellent selection of luxury activity holidays.

Cruises

www.discover-cruises.co.uk   UK
    CRUISE INFO
    A clear, new site put together to encourage people to take cruise holidays featuring 35 cruise lines. Factsheets are provided to enable you to find the perfect trip, whoever you are and whatever

you want from your cruise. If you can't find information here, there's a good collection of links. Formally
www.cruiseinformationservice.co.uk

See also:
www.cruisedeals.co.uk – easy to use, a little sparse on info but some good offers.
www.cruisedirect.com – information, advice and good prices.
www.cruiseline.co.uk – a great site from one of the UK's leading specialist cruise companies.
www.cruisesandvoyages.com – a cruise specialist with a basic site and some good deals.
www.psa-psara.org – useful information from the Passenger Shipping Association.

Activity and Sporting Holidays

Cycling Holidays

www.ctc.org.uk   UK
WORKING FOR CYCLING
The CTC have a great travel section with routes, tours, offers, links and directories. It's a great place to start your search for the perfect cycling holiday.

Also check out:
www.backroads.com – a US-based specialist with a wide range of options.
www.bicycle-beano.co.uk – Bicycle Beano have a good site covering cycling holidays in Wales and the borders.
www.bikemagic.com – go to the travel pages for an excellent section on where Bike Magic have got partners who'll supply flight deals for cyclists or rail travel and holidays.
www.byways-breaks.co.uk – a nice-looking site, Byways Breaks arrange cycling and walking holidays in the Peaks, Shropshire and Cheshire countryside.
www.cycleactive.co.uk – excellent for action-packed cycle holidays.
www.cyclebreaks.co.uk – cycling holidays in Suffolk and Norfolk.
www.cycle-rides.co.uk – a very good selection of biking tours through Europe and further afield.
www.discoveradventure.com – a great selection of biking holidays for the more adventurous.

www.rough-tracks.co.uk – a wide range of active adventure holidays for beginners and experts.

www.scotcycle.co.uk – Scottish Cycling Holidays are specialists in cycling holidays in Scotland obviously. Nice site too.

www.skedaddle.co.uk – one of the best for variety, everything for the beginner or expert. It covers most of the world too.

www.sustrans.co.uk – the National Cycle Network is featured as part of this campaigning charity site.

Diving Holidays

www.aquatours.com – the site isn't up to much but they offer a world-wide service.

www.divechannel.co.uk – excellent site specialising in diving holidays and travel.

www.divequest.co.uk – lots of detail, prices and choice make this a good site to visit.

www.ifyoudive.com – this portal is a good place to start.

www.regaldive.co.uk – learn to dive in the best diving locations.

Golfing Holidays

www.golfbreaks.com – a travel agent specialising in holidays for golfing nuts.

www.lorringolf.com – high level golfing holidays, an academy and corporate events. (Formerly **www.grassrootsgolf.co.uk**)

www.prosolgolf.com – holidays on the Costa del Sol, the laboured English is somewhat endearing.

Hobby and Culinary Holidays

www.shawguides.com   US

LOOKING FOR SOMETHING TO DO?
A massive database of cultural, hobby and learning holidays, mostly American but you can find UK-based ones if you search hard enough.

See also cookery courses on page 182 and . . .
www.arblasterandclarke.com – wine tours world-wide.
www.chiangmai-online.com – includes buying produce from local markets as well as learning to cook Thai-style.
www.epiculinary.com – culinary holidays.
www.theinternationalkitchen.com – cookery vacations in France, Italy, Spain and Morocco.

www.martinrandall.com – cultural travel with expert lecturers.
www.holidayonthemenu.com – as well the usual European offerings, you can learn to cook in Australia, Indonesia, Jordan, Vietnam . . . Part of **www.onthegotours.com** holidays for the semi-independent who want to mix culture and fun.

Language Learning

See the languages section on page 301.

Riding Holidays

www.equineadventures.co.uk – a good agent for riding holidays.
www.equitour.co.uk – a wide range of riding holidays available for all levels of rider.
www.horsebackholidays.com – a similarly broad selection of places and types of holiday for the enthusiastic rider.
www.inthesaddle.com – a good-looking site covering a variety of holiday options.
www.ranchweb.com – excellent site on all forms of ranch holidays mainly in the US.

Sailing

www.sunsail.com   US
SAILING AND WATERSPORT HOLIDAYS
A wide-ranging and informative site with lots to offer whether you're an enthusiast or a beginner, plenty of special offers too.

See also:
www.allafloat.com – lots of choice and online booking.
www.bootoo.co.uk – the luxury yacht Bootoo takes you around the Caribbean.
www.compass24.com – a good shop for sailing enthusiasts, over 14,000 products.
www.elitesailing.co.uk – learn to sail.
www.neilson.com – award-winning operator, they run a sailing training school and a wide variety of other water-based holidays too.
www.sailingholidays.com – specialists in Greece and Croatia.
www.sea-trek.co.uk – specialist in Greece, learn-to-sail holidays too.
www.tenrag.com – charter your own yacht.

Backpacking and Adventure

www.adventuredirectory.com   UK
THE ADVENTURE DIRECTORY
A huge directory of sites devoted to adventure, just click on the world map or search and away you go . . .

See also:
www.backpackeurope.com – aimed at Americans but useful for Europeans too.
www.footprint-adventures.co.uk – birding, trekking and wildlife all over the world.
www.highplaces.co.uk – treks in high places in some 20 countries.
www.iexplore.com – a high-quality offering with a huge amount of information for the adventure traveller.
www.igougo.com – more of an information exchange for global travellers, but you can book trips through them. There are plenty of features and the IgoUgo awards too.
www.madadventurer.com – excellent site design with loads of mad adventures to choose from while helping community development in 23 countries.
www.spicemcr.com – vibrant activity and social club with holidays to match.
www.theleap.co.uk – similar approach to Mad Adventurer but based in Africa.
www.trailsource.com – excellent resource covering the world's great trails, categorised by mode of transport.
www.transitionsabroad.com – excellent for long-term travelling and working holidays.

Eco-tourism and Nature

www.responsibletravel.com   UK
GIVE THE WORLD A BREAK
Endorsed by Anita Roddick, this site provides a huge range of travel experiences all selected for their sensitivity to the local environment and its people. You can search by destination, activity or accommodation type. If you become a member, you can receive their monthly magazine. There are a several campaigns to join too ranging from protecting wildlife to outlawing child sex tourism.

www.tourismconcern.org.uk   UK
ETHICAL TOURISM
If you're concerned about the impact of your trip, then come here for advice or help with one of their campaigns. It all goes to ensuring that the poorest holiday workers are not exploited.

See also:
www.btcv.org – conservation holidays.
www.changingworlds.co.uk – worthwhile working holidays.
www.coralcay.org – 'providing resources to help sustain livelihoods and alleviate poverty through the protection, restoration and management of coral reefs and tropical forests'.
www.csv.org.uk – information for volunteers.
www.discoveryinitiatives.co.uk – responsible wildlife holidays.
www.ecoclub.com – a network providing a wealth of information about all aspects of ecotourism.
www.eco-res.com – make a reservation at an eco-friendly lodge, camp or reserve.
www.ecotourism.org – the International Ecotourism Society.
www.ecotravel.com – a US-based site with a magazine and an excellent search facility.
www.ecovolunteer.com – if you want to give your services to a specific animal benefit project.
www.exodus.co.uk – specialist agents and winners of the 'Best Tour Operator' in the Responsible Travel Awards 2004.
www.inntravel.co.uk – specialists in walking and cycling holidays, excellent, informative site.
www.naturetrek.co.uk – excellent nature holiday specialists.
www.northsouthtravel.co.uk – a small travel agent which channels much of the profit into aid projects in Africa.
www.sacredearth.com – ethnobiology and eco-travel to South America, for those seriously interested in nature.
www.thetravelfoundation.org.uk – information on the effect of tourism and how you can help.
www.traveltree.co.uk – for eco-sensitive volunteer work overseas.
www.wildshots.co.uk – wildlife photography holidays.

Healthy Holidays

If you want to lie back and relax then try one of these . . .

www.bodyandsoulholidays.com   UK
SPA BREAKS AND HOTELS
A cool site where you can pick out your treatments or activities

and they will select the resort or holiday to suit your needs. There's quite a bit of choice and some of the locations are stunning.

See also:
http://spas.about.com – a useful directory with tips and information on taking a spa holiday.
www.inspa-retreats.com – a combination of luxury and health.
www.nealsyardagency.com – healthy holidays.
www.thermalia.co.uk – one of the leading specialists in spa holidays.

Air Travel

With climate change in mind, you may wish to visit
www.carbonneutral.com *to calculate your emissions and buy trees to compensate for the carbon emissions your flight has generated.*

Airline and Flight Sites

www.cheapflights.co.uk   UK
NOTHING BUT CHEAP FLIGHTS
You don't need to register here to explore the great offers available from this site; you still need to phone some of the travel agents or airlines listed to get your deal although an increasing number have web links. If you're after a last-minute deal, they have a handy calendar that will search for deals from your local airport.

www.netflights.com   UK
THE AIRLINE NETWORK
Discount deals on over 100 airlines world-wide make The Airline Network worth checking out for their flight offers page alone. It's good for flights from regional airports. They also do all the traditional travel agent things and there are some good holiday bargains too.

www.openjet.com   UK
NO FRILLS MADE EASY
This site searches the low-cost carriers to find you the best prices to European destinations and gives you the results for adjacent days to enable you to fly at the lowest possible price. See also **www.whichbudget.com**

T

www.traveljungle.co.uk   UK
> FARE COMPARISONS
> Travel Jungle have become very popular and it's easy to see why:
> here you can compare offers from 23 airlines and 7 travel agents
> so you should be able to get a great deal.
>
> *For more cheap flight deals try these sites:*
> **www.attitudetravel.com/lowcostairlines** – now covering the
> world's low cost airlines and where they fly to.
> **www.bargainflights.com** – good search facility and plenty of
> offers, but you need to be patient.
> **www.bmibaby.com** – the low-cost arm of British Midland.
> **www.deckchair.com** – a strong site where you can get some
> good flight bargains as well as plan the rest of your holiday. Now
> part of the Lastminute.com empire.
> **www.easyjet.co.uk** – great for an ever increasing number of
> destinations, particularly good for UK flights.
> **www.flightcentre.com** – they guarantee to beat any genuine
> current quoted airfare!
> **www.ryanair.com** – very good for Ireland, northern Europe,
> Italy and France. Clear and easy-to-use web site, massive
> discounts.
> **www.skyscanner.net** – excellent for Europe and comparing the
> budget airline offers.
> **www.travelselect.com** – good flight selection and lots of
> different options available at this very flexible site.

Airport and Airline Information

www.worldairportguide.com   GERMANY
> WHAT ARE THE WORLD'S AIRPORTS REALLY LIKE?
> It seems that no matter how out of the way, this guide has details
> on every airport – how to get there, where to park, facilities, key
> phone numbers and a map. There are also guides on cities,
> resorts and even world weather. See also
> **www.airportcitycodes.com**

www.baa.co.uk   UK
> BRITISH AIRPORT AUTHORITY
> Details on all the major UK airports that are run by the BAA, you
> get all the essential information plus flight data, weather and
> shopping information.

www.a2bairports.com   UK
UK AND IRISH AIRPORTS
These pages from A2B Travel offer all the relevant information on all the major airports and lots of the smaller ones too. Another site with information on UK airports is **www.airport-maps.co.uk** which also has flight route information along with maps, facility details and related links.

www.airlinequality.com   UK
RANKING THE AIRLINES
An independent ranking of all the world's airlines and their services, see who's the best and the worst and why. Each airline is rated using a number of stars (up to five) on criteria such as seat quality, catering and staff.

www.sleepinginairports.net   UK
GUIDE TO SLEEPING IN AIRPORTS
Rated 'Good' 'Tolerable' or just 'Hell' here is a sleeper's guide for budget travellers on many of the world's airports. It's actually pretty funny too.

www.airfraid.com   US
CONQUER YOUR FEAR OF FLYING
A good place to go if you're of the opinion that getting on a plane is the last thing you'll ever do. There's advice gleaned from various reputable sources and details on how you can go on courses to help you overcome your fears. See also **www.aviatours.co.uk** which is a course backed by British Airways and also **www.freedomtofly.biz**

THE KEY AIRLINES

www.aa.com – American Airlines, standard airline site.
www.aerlingus.ie – good, easy-to-use site.
www.airfrance.co.uk – plenty of offers.
www.airindia.com – good offers and travel information and destination guide.
www.alitalia.it – a no-nonsense site.
www.ba.com or **www.britishairways.co.uk** – easy-to-use, efficient site.
www.cathaypacific.com – comprehensive flight service and guide.
www.emirates.com – no-frills design and flight booking facilities.

www.flybmi.com – British Midland, good offers for European destinations.

www.klm.com – good design with lots of offers.

www.lufthansa.co.uk – masses of information and express booking.

www.quantas.com – straightforward booking facility.

www.singaporeair.com – follows the formula but with the added extra of a multi-city flight planner.

www.united.com – United Airlines offers a good all-round service at this site.

www.virgin-atlantic.com – good online booking facility with some offers.

UK Regional Airlines

It's worth trying out regional airlines, not only because they may be cheaper, but also they might fly to your destination from a more convenient local airport. Here are the best of them.

www.air-scotland.com – owned by Greek Airlines and billed as Scotland's low-cost airline, they fly out of Glasgow and Edinburgh to Spanish and Greek resorts. The site follows the usual design and at the time of writing, there were lots of offers.

www.airsouthwest.com – small airline offering great-value flights from the South West of England to London.

www.airwales.co.uk – Awyr Cymru offer a wide variety of flights throughout the UK and Ireland from Swansea and Cardiff, again it looks good value. Better than average site too.

www.excelairways.com – an ambitious and service-oriented charter airline, they offer luxuries, such as leather seating, and fly to a wide range of European and Middle Eastern destinations.

www.flyglobespan.com – a Scottish low-cost airline flying to European holiday destinations on a no frills site.

www.jet2.com – flying from Leeds-Bradford, Manchester and Belfast to a select number of European destinations, Jet2 is offering seats at very low prices.

Airport Parking

www.uk-airport-car-parking.co.uk   UK
BOOK YOUR SPACE
Probably the best of the sites dedicated to helping you find somewhere to park your car while you're away. It offers more options and information than the others listed but it's

always worth shopping around, so you should try these alternatives.

See also:
www.bcponline.co.uk – easy to use and with some good savings on airport car park rates.
www.holidayextras.co.uk – who are also good for parking, airport hotels, airport lounges and also have information on getting to airports by public transport.
www.ncp.co.uk – airport parking and more.
www.parking4less.co.uk – high-quality secured parking assured.
www.securedcarparks.com – as the title suggests, a useful guide to car parks nationwide with decent security.

Rail, Taxi and Coach Travel Abroad

www.seat61.com   UK
THE MAN IN SEAT 61
You can get timetables and book on many routes whether by train, ship or coach. You can compare costs and there's plenty of information and links too.

See also:
www.busabout.com – create your own trip through Europe by bus. Island explorer tickets available too.
www.busaustralia.com – for some really long road trips.
www.busstation.net – great links for bus info worldwide.
www.eurail.com – details of the Eurail ticket, information and prices, and you can now buy online.
www.eurolines.com – Europe's coach network, covering 500 destinations, 15- or 30-day passes available.
www.eurostar.com – through the Channel Tunnel . . . online booking plus timetables and offers.
www.eurotunnel.com – online passenger bookings.
www.greyhound.com – the famous American coach company.
www.greyhound.com.au – Greyhound buses Australia.
www.holidaytaxis.com – book a taxi in a limited number of destinations, mainly in Europe but also USA.
www.railaustralia.com.au – for some of the world's great train holidays.
www.raileurope.co.uk – booking European rail travel.
www.trainseurope.co.uk – European and North American trains with online booking.

www.taxisabroad.com – book taxis in a selection of European countries.

Places to Stay

Hotels

www.hotelguide.com   UK
COMPREHENSIVE
With services available in nine languages and specialist sections such as golfing breaks, this site ranks amongst the best for finding the right hotel. It lists around 120,000 at time of writing.

www.hiphotels.net   UK
FOR THE HIPPEST HOTELS
Excellent for the unusual, it's a directory of the unique and offbeat with good illustrations of each hotel, not much in the way of deals, but then they are very special.

www.from-a-z.com   UK
A–Z OF HOTELS
A well-designed British site with over 20,000 hotels to choose from in the UK, Eire and France and a further 40,000 world-wide; it's quick and easy to use and there's online booking available plus plenty of special discounts.

Other good hotel directory and booking sites:
www.all-hotels.com – 100,000 hotels listed with lots of options, American bias.
www.ase.net – some 150,000 listed properties here with many reviews.
www.best-inn.co.uk – another hotel/motel directory containing thousands of entries, very good for London and links to specialist accommodation.
www.discount25.com – great for hotel discounts, primarily in Spain but also the major European cities.
www.octopustravel.com – a huge number of rooms and deals available, one of the most used sites for hotel booking.
www.openworld.co.uk – a collection of links to hotel sites, just use the interactive world map.
www.placestostay.com – simple to use and provides a list of hotels, descriptions, prices, maps and an online reservation service.

Hostels

www.hostels.com   US
INTERNATIONAL HOSTELLING
An excellent resource for anyone looking for budget accommodation. Many of the hostels are reviewed and it's easy to find one using the click-through maps.

See also:
www.hihostels.com – a hostelling booking service with lots of information too.
www.hostellingworld.com – a hostelling club with online booking.
www.yha.org.uk – very good site from the Youth Hostels Association.

Villas and cottages

http://ownersdirect.co.uk – some 8,000 cottages and villas to be rented direct from their owners.
www.cheznous.com – holiday cottages in France.
www.cvtravel.net – passionate about villas, mainly in Europe.
www.jamesvillas.co.uk – over 500 villas in the Med.
www.ownerssyndicate.com – a wide choice with some good offers.
www.villa-rentals.com – from Abercrombie & Kent, villas world-wide, some look outstanding.

Travel Guides and Information

www.johnnyjet.com   US
TRAVEL PORTAL
A very detailed and comprehensive portal site devoted to all things travel. It's well categorised but has an American bias.

www.lonelyplanet.com   UK
LONELY PLANET GUIDES
A superb travel site, aimed at the independent traveller, but with great information for everyone. Get a review on most world destinations or pick a theme and go with that; leave a message on the Thorn Tree; find out the latest news by country; get health reports; read about the travel experiences of others – what's the real story?

T

Travel Abroad

The Good Web Site Guide's Top 10s
of the Internet

1. **www.expedia.co.uk** – not always the cheapest but the best
2. **www.fco.gov.uk/travel** – essential advice from the Foreign Office
3. **www.xe.net/ucc** – the online currency converter
4. **www.e-bookers.com** – reliable and good value, especially for flights
5. **www.baa.co.uk** – information on the major UK airports and flights
6. **www.uk-airport-car-parking.co.uk** – book your parking in advance
7. **www.lonelyplanet.com** – superb for independent travellers
8. **www.mappy.co.uk** – get to where you're going
9. **www.brochurebank.co.uk** – order your brochures and get them delivered to you
10. **www.johnnyjet.com** – great travel portal

---

www.bugbog.com   UK
   TRAVEL INFORMATION
   An outstanding and well-organised site offering information and
   advice on all aspects of travel, with guides and a good directory
   too.

www.tripadvisor.com   US
   UNBIASED REVIEWS
   An excellent site offering guidance on almost any destination
   with reviews and links. It includes magazine articles as well as
   guide book reviews and opinions from members.

http://travel.roughguides.com   UK
   ROUGH GUIDES
   Lively reviews on a huge number of places. In addition, there's
   general travel information, a place to share your travel thoughts
   with other travellers, or you can buy a guide. Excellent for links
   and you can get some good deals via the site. You can now order
   interactive city maps for your PDA or listen to world music on
   rough guides radio.

www.fodors.com   US
> FODOR'S GUIDES
> These guides give an American perspective, but there is a
> huge amount of information on each destination. The site is
> well laid out and easy to use. See also the comprehensive
> **www.mytravelguide.com**

http://kasbah.com   UK
> THE WORLD'S LARGEST TRAVEL GUIDE
> A site facelift for the worse. Ignore the travel agency stuff and
> head for the 'travel guide' section. Unfortunately, the search
> engine has also gone but if you find the alphabetical index at the
> bottom of the page you'll be able to access good quality
> information. The highlights on each destination are useful and
> the 'Global Travel Toolbox' provides info, telecommunications,
> maps, currency and more. What a pity they've made it all so
> difficult now.

www.packback.com   UK
> PACKBACK TRAVEL GUIDE
> A good-looking and useful site with an independent travel guide,
> a growing membership and a reputation for quality reviews. It
> includes a discussion forum, travel tools and flight booking.

www.guardian.co.uk/travel   UK
> FROM THE *GUARDIAN* NEWSPAPER
> A good reflection of the excellent *Guardian* weekly travel section
> with guides, information and inspiration throughout. There's
> also the latest news and links to sites with offers plus extra
> features such as audio guides and articles on parts of the UK.
> See also **www.ivebeenthere.co.uk** which is their very useful
> collection of traveller's tips, there are several hundred across lots
> of categories, nearly enough for a book!

www.gorp.com   US
> FOR THE GREAT OUTDOORS
> A great title, Gorp is dedicated to adventure, whether it be hiking,
> mountaineering, fishing, snow sports or riding the rapids. It has
> an American bias, but is full of relevant good advice, links and
> information.

www.timeout.com   UK
> *TIME OUT* GUIDE
> A slick site with destination guides covering many European
> cities and an increasing number further afield such as New York

T

and Sydney. Not surprisingly, it's outstanding for London. You can also book tickets and buy books via other retailers.

www.bradmans.com   UK
BRADMAN'S FOR BUSINESS TRAVELLERS
A really excellent city guide with none of your fancy graphics, just a straightforward listing of countries and sensible information on each one, includes restaurant reviews and tips on orienting yourself in the city.

www.vtourist.com   UK
THE VIRTUAL TOURIST
Explore destinations in a unique and fun way. Travellers describe their experiences, share photos, make recommendations and give tips so others benefit from their experience.

Other guides and sites worth checking out are:
http://away.com – lots of links and information hidden away amongst the offers.
http://picturesofplaces.com – here you can find a huge number of photos from around the world.
www.about.com/travel – a comprehensive travel directory from About.com.
www.bootsnall.com – aimed at the independent traveller, it has several guides and is packed with information, looks good too.
www.citypopulation.de – lots of information about cities and regions throughout the world.
www.citysearch.com – a listing for mainly US cities with entertainment and orientation guides.
www.officialtravelinfo.com – a directory covering the world's official tourism sites.
www.nytimes.com/pages/travel/index.html – travel news and information from the *New York Times*.
www.roadnews.com – help and information for those of us who travel with a laptop computer.
www.thetravelportal.com – hotel reviews and an excellent set of links from a bigger web directory.
www.travelintelligence.net – the opinions of more than 100 travel writers.
www.travel-library.com – less entertaining than some but combines recommendation with hard facts very well.
www.world-heritage-tour.org – a list and tour of World Heritage sites around the globe with panoramic views.

www.worldinformation.com – not specifically a travel guide but there is a mountain of information on the world's countries, their culture and advice about how to deal with issues like corruption.

Maps and Route Finders

www.multimap.com   UK
GREAT BRITAIN
Outstanding design, easy to use, excellent for the UK, you can search using postcodes, London street names, place names or Ordnance Survey grid references. Once you've found what you're looking for, you can also see an aerial view of the area.

www.mappy.co.uk   UK
START HERE
Mappy has a great-looking site which is easy to use and has lots of added features such as a personal mapping service where you can store the maps you use most. The route finder is OK, and business users can fill in their mileage allowance and Mappy will calculate how much they should claim.

See also:
http://maps.msn.com – excellent mapping and route-finding service from MSN.
www.expedia.co.uk – select 'maps'; limited to the US, Canada, France, Germany and UK. Modest route planner.
www.mapquest.com – find out the best way to get from A to B in Europe or America, not always as detailed as you'd like, but easy to use and you can customise your map or route plan.
www.mapsonus.com – it's notoriously difficult to find your way around America, but using the route planner you should minimise your risk of getting lost.
www.memory-map.co.uk – a useful range of downloadable maps based on Ordnance Survey mapping.
www.ordnancesurvey.co.uk – a good site with mapping for sale; links to the GPR service **www.gps.gov.uk**
www.stanfords.co.uk – travel book and map specialists.
www.uk.map24.com – excellent interactive and static mapping but the directions are a little difficult to follow at times.
www.viamichelin.com – a good all-round travel site with an improved route-finder service, which is OK.

www.theaa.co.uk UK

AUTOMOBILE ASSOCIATION

A superb site that offers route-planning and traffic information, a hotel and restaurant guide with a booking service, and help with buying a car or even a GPS. There is also information on insurance and other financial help.

www.rac.co.uk UK

GET AHEAD WITH THE RAC

Great for UK traffic reports, this site has a very reliable route planner, which seems to be very busy and slow at peak times. There's also a good section on finding the right place to stay, and lots of help if you want to buy a car.

Destinations

www.antor.com UK

ASSOCIATION OF NATIONAL TOURIST OFFICES

A useful starting point for information about the 90 or so countries that are members of the association. It also has very good links to key tourism sites. See also **www.towd.com** who list every official government tourist office and some unofficial ones too.

www.embassyworld.com US

EMBASSIES AROUND THE GLOBE

Pick two countries, one for 'whose embassy' and one for 'in what location', press go and up pops the details on the embassy with contact and essential information.

Here's an alphabetical list of countries and regions to help you research your chosen destination and plan your holiday.

A

www.africatravelresource.com UK

EAST AFRICA

An exceptional site that specifically covers Burundi, Kenya, Rwanda, Uganda and Tanzania plus the resorts of Lamu and Zanzibar. The level of detail is great but because the site is packaged so well, it doesn't overwhelm. A lesson in how a travel site should be set up.

See also:
http://i-cias.com – an excellent information site covering North Africa and the Middle East.

www.africaguide.com – detailed country-by-country guides, discussion forums, shopping, culture and a travelogue feature make this site a good first stop.

www.africa-nature-photography.com – how to take the best shots while on safari.

www.africanodyssey.co.uk – African and Arabian specialist agents.

www.africansafariclub.com – cruises and safaris a speciality.

www.backpackafrica.com – excellent site for backpackers with over 400 links and advice on where to go and what to see.

www.ecoafrica.com – tailor-made safaris with the emphasis on eco-tourism.

www.onsafari.com – good advice on what sort of safari is right for you.

www.phakawe.demon.co.uk – safaris in Botswana.

www.sahara-overland.com – the trans-Sahara experience with information and travellers' reports.

www.vintageafrica.com – awesome safaris and destinations from this specialist travel agent, who will tailor-make holidays if requested.

www.wilderness-safaris.com – specialises in providing safaris that go to pristine wilderness.

www.wildnetafrica.net – an excellent travel and information portal for safaris to south and south-east Africa.

www.turisme.ad   ANDORRA
ANDORRA
A nice little site extolling the many virtues of this tiny country.

www.polartravel.co.uk   UK
ARCTIC AND ANTARTICA
How to get to the Poles in safety and even enjoy yourself when you get there!

See also:
www.arctic-experience.co.uk – spectacular holidays in the Arctic.

www.arcticseakayakingadventures.com – experience the Arctic waterways in kayaks.

www.iaato.org – International Association of Antarctic Travel Operators, has links to all the major agents.

www.nunavik-tourism.com – the wild frontier of the Quebec Arctic with a list of tour operators.

T

www.argentour.com   ARGENTINA
     ARGENTINA
     Outstanding (but very slow-loading) travel site with video clips,
     regional information, history and slide shows of the major cities.
     There's even a section on how to tango. See also
     www.argentinatravelnet.com/indexE.htm

www.asiatravel.com   SINGAPORE
     ASIA
     A horribly designed site packed with travel information about all
     the Asian countries and beyond. Fortunately, the quality of the
     information is much better than the site design would suggest
     and covers accommodation, travel and background facts on the
     countries and what to buy while you're there.

www.austria-tourism.at   AUSTRIA
     AUSTRIA
     An excellent site covering all you need to know about the
     country, with information on skiing and summer holidays too.
     See also **www.tiscover.at**

www.australia.com   AUSTRALIA
     DISCOVER AUSTRALIA
     The Australian Tourist Commission offer a good and informative
     site that gives lots of facts about the country, the people, the
     lifestyle and what you can expect when you visit.

     See also:
     www.acn.net.au – a directory of Australian cultural and
     recreational resources.
     www.australianexplorer.com – excellent and well-illustrated site
     with some 14,000 pages of information.
     www.travelaustralia.com.au – informative site, good for
     regional information.
     www.travelmate.com.au – a comprehensive site with masses of
     information, which is especially good if you're driving.
     www.voyages.com.au – stay in luxury at Ayers Rock, or Uluru
     as it's officially known now.
     www.wilmap.com.au – excellent for Australian maps and links.

B

www.indo.com   INDONESIA
     BALI ONLINE
     This site covers Bali and its top hotels, but there's also plenty of
     information on the rest of Indonesia and links to other Asian sites.

www.virtualbangladesh.com   US
BANGLADESH
A colourful and atmospheric travel site that contains all the
practical information you need to start planning a trip written in
an informal, welcoming style. You can find out about the people,
customs, flora and fauna, and there is an interesting section on
the politics. For another general tourist site go to
www.discoverybangladesh.com

www.trabel.com   BELGIUM
BELGIUM
The Belgium Travel Network offers a site packed with
information about the country and its key towns and cities.
You can get information on hotels, travelling, an airport
guide, flight information and there's also a good links page.
See also the well-designed **www.belgium-tourism.net**
and **www.visitflanders.co.uk**

www.belize.com   US
BELIZE
A good general site covering the country. It's not just aimed at
tourists but it's incredibly useful for the visitor.

www.boliviaweb.com   US
BOLIVIA
A useful and well-put-together portal site.

www.botswana.com   SOUTH AFRICA
BOTSWANA
A well-illustrated site covering Botswana's exciting collection of
game lodges. It also offers links to hotel and services directories
too. See also **www.okavango.com**

www.brazil.com   BRAZIL
BRAZIL
A straightforward, no-nonsense guide, travelogue and listing site
for Brazil that also contains information on hotels and resorts.

See also:
www.brazil.org.uk – very informative site from the Brazilian
Embassy.
www.carnaval.com – you have to hunt for the information but
there's a very helpful site in there.
www.helisight.com.br – book your helicopter tour over Rio.

www.ipanema.com – outstanding site by people who really know Rio, with masses of links and detailed cross referencing.
www.varig.co.uk – the national airline, good site with online booking.

www.travel-bulgaria.com   BULGARIA
EXPLORE BULGARIA
A well-put-together portal site with all the information you should need, Bulgaria is the hottest place for cheap property at the moment. See also the slow **www.bulgaria.com** and the UK-based specialist **www.balkanholidays.com**

C
www.cambodia-travel.com   CAMBODIA
HOME OF THE KHMER
A wide-ranging site with some interesting spelling! There are sections on Angkor Wat, the Khmer and the usual accommodation details. See also **www.eyeoncambodia.com**

www.travelcanada.ca   CANADA
EXPLORE CANADA
Did you know that the glass floor at the top of the world's tallest free-standing structure could support the weight of 14 large hippos? Find out much more at this wide-ranging and attractive site, from touring to city guides. See also **www.canadianaffair.com** who offer some excellent low-cost flights and tours, and for an outdoor experience of the country go to **www.playday.com** Canada's recreation website. For cheap flights check out Zoom at **www.zoomairlines.co.uk**

www.turq.com   US
CARIBBEAN
All you need to organise a great holiday in the Caribbean. There's information on flights, hotels, cruises, a travel guide and trip reports to the islands, all on a well-presented and easy-to-use site.

See also:
www.antigua-barbuda.com – competent site from the Antiguan High Commission.
www.barbados.org – great overview of the island with excellent links.
www.caribbeandreams.co.uk – UK travel agent specialising in the Caribbean.

www.doitcaribbean.com – information, booking and an interactive map.

www.jamaicatravel.com – a pretty comprehensive site devoted to the island with regional guides and help in planning your trip.

www.visittnt.com – basic information site on Trinidad and Tobago.

www.gochile.cl   CHILE
CHILE

A great overview of the country with all the holiday information you'll need including details on Easter Island. See also **www.chile-hotels.com**

www.chinatour.com   CHINA
INFORMATION CHINA

A comprehensive site stuffed with data on China: where to go and stay, how to get there and what to see, maps and visa application information. See also the China Travel System at **www.chinats.com** who have a good-looking and very polite site where you can book hotels and tours, get travel information and chat to others who've experienced China.

See also:

www.chinapage.com/china.html – information on everything from calligraphy to language to tattoos. Some historical background information on major sites.

www.discoverhongkong.com – for Hong Kong.

www.haiweitrails.com – organised treks in SW China and Tibet.

www.croatia.hr   CROATIA
CROATIA

An excellent site covering the country and its virtues with sections on events, attractions, background, accommodation and an all-round travel guide. For villas and general info check out **www.croatianaffair.com**

www.cubanculture.com   US
CUBA

A fast, easy-to-use site with the basic information about Cuba and its heritage. There are lots of useful links too.

www.cyprustourism.org   CYPRUS
CYPRUS

A pretty basic site about the country, well the Greek-run bit anyway.

T

www.czech-tourism.com   CZECH REPUBLIC
CZECH REPUBLIC
A good directory site providing information and links in 15
categories from business to the weather including tour operators
and a country guide. See also Czech It Out at **www.goaway.co.uk**

D
www.visitdenmark.com   DENMARK
DENMARK
The official Danish tourist board site where you can get links to
book a holiday and all the advice and information you'd expect
from a well-run and efficient-looking site. See also
www.woco.dk for an excellent site on Copenhagen.

E
www.ecuadorexplorer.com   US
ECUADOR
A very well-put-together directory site covering all you need for a
visit to one of the most beautiful countries on the planet. For
specific sites on the Galapagos go to the thorough
www.galapagos-travel.com and also the Galapagos
Conservation Trust at **www.gct.org** which is full of information
and good for links.

http://touregypt.net   EGYPT
EGYPT
A pretty ugly but very comprehensive site covering the country
and in particular its history. It's really a very good portal site as
well as a travel guide.

See also:
www.ancient.co.uk – archaeological tours with this specialist
operator.
www.discoveregypt.co.uk – a well-illustrated site from a
UK-based specialist.
www.peltours.com – great site from an agent specialising in
Egypt.

www.visitestonia.com   ESTONIA
ESTONIA
Gushing with enthusiasm for the charms of this small Baltic
state, this site gives you information on travel, accommodation,
history, climate and money. For another view try the
no-nonsense **www.estoniantravel.com**

www.eurotrip.com   UK
BACKPACKING EUROPE
Student and independent European travel with in-depth
information, facts, reviews, articles, discussion, live reports,
links and travel advice on a good-looking and well-designed site.
Also connects to a no-frills airline booking service and a section
with information on finding low-cost air fares.

www.eurocamp.co.uk   UK
SELF-CATERING EUROPE
The leading self-catering company with over 150 holiday parks
in 12 countries. Here you can find details of the accommodation
and book a holiday; there are some bargains too. See also
www.eurocampindependent.co.uk who offer a European
campsite reservation service.

www.visiteurope.com   US
EUROPEAN TRAVEL COMMISSION
A site aimed at Americans to encourage them to visit Europe. It's
informative and there's a section for each country.

F
www.visitfinland.com   FINLAND
FINLAND
Look under the 'Individual holiday planner' for good-quality
information on travelling around, accommodation and outdoor
activities. There are also organised tours available for the British
traveller. Don't miss out on Santa's homepage and arrange a
Christmas visit. See also **www.wildnorth.net** – a visual treat
with fishing and hunting tours.

www.franceway.com   FRANCE
VOILA LA FRANCE!
Excellent site giving an overview of French culture, history, facts
and figures, and of course, how to book a holiday. You can also
sign up for the newsletter.

See also:
www.brittanytourism.com – a good site on all that Brittany has
to offer.
www.cdt-nord.fr – useful site on northern France.
www.cheznous.com – holiday cottages in France.
www.corsica.co.uk – good site from a Corsican specialist.

www.franceguide.com – official French Government Tourist Office portal site or **www.francetourism.com** the sister site aimed at US tourists.

www.francemag.com – really informative and useful e-zine devoted to France.

www.frenchconnections.co.uk – French holiday specialist.

www.gites-de-france.fr/eng – a wide variety of gite accommodation with online booking.

www.justparis.co.uk – details on how to get there and hotels for when you've arrived.

www.le-guide.com – a messy but informative guide to the South of France.

www.logis-de-france.fr – reliable guide to 3,000 hotels and restaurants throughout France.

www.magicparis.com – revamped, stylish guide to Paris with comprehensive information and beautiful pictures.

www.manchetourisme.com – what to do in La Manche, Normandy.

www.normandy-tourism.org – excellent and informative site on Normandy.

www.northernfrance-tourism.com – a scrappy site on northern France.

www.parishotels.com – a fast booking service for Paris hotels.

www.rhonealpes-tourism.co.uk – information and holidays.

www.vive-la-france.org – very comprehensive and good fun.

G

www.visitthegambia.gm   GAMBIA
GAMBIA
A good tourist site which promotes Gambia's wildlife and ecological sites with particular emphasis on the bird-life and waterways. See also **www.gambia.co.uk**

www.germany-tourism.de   GERMANY
GERMANY – WUNDERBAR
As much information as you can handle with good features on the key destinations, excellent interactive mapping and links to related sites. For further information try **www.germany-info.org**

www.gibraltar.gi/tourism   GIBRALTAR
GIBRALTAR – THE ROCK
A good site devoted to the area with sections on the sights plus travel information.

www.gnto.gr   GREECE
GREEK NATIONAL TOURIST ORGANISATION
An attractive site with the official word on travelling in Greece,
also a good travel guide and information for business travellers
plus accommodation, advice and details on what you can do.

See also:
www.culture.gr – excellent site covering Greek culture and its
legends.
www.filoxenia.co.uk – a specialist, good for unusual
accommodation in Greece.
www.gogreece.com – a search engine devoted to all things Greek.
www.greekisland.co.uk – an entertaining and personal view of
the Greek islands with over 200 links.
www.gtpnet.com – the Greek Travel Pages with the latest ferry
schedules for island hoppers.
www.islands-of-greece.com – another specialist operator with a
good site and features on the better islands.
www.travelalacarte.co.uk – specialists in holidays in the best of
the Greek islands.

H
www.holland.com   HOLLAND
HOLLAND IS FULL OF SURPRISES
A very professional site offering a mass of tourist information and
advice on how to have a great time when you visit. There are
sections on how to get there, what type of holiday will suit you
and city guides.

www.gotohungary.com   HUNGARY
HUNGARY
All the information is here to enable you to plan your trip to
Hungary including information on the wide range of cultural
events taking place in Budapest. If it's restoration you're after,
there's an interesting section on Hungary's curative spas. See
also **www.budapest.com** and **www.hungarytourism.hu**

I
www.iceland.is   ICELAND
ICELAND
The official site of the Icelandic Ministry of Foreign Affairs with
a wealth of information about the country, the people and its
history. It's easy to navigate and there are good links to related
sites. See also **www.iceland.com** which is more tourism

oriented and also **www.icelandexpress.com** which is good for low-cost fares.

www.incredibleindia.org   UK
INDIAN TOURIST OFFICE UK
Essential tourist information and advice as well as cultural and historical background on the country and its diverse regions. It has a massive hotel database as well.

www.indiamart.com   UK
INDIA TRAVEL PROMOTION NETWORK
Basically a shopping site with diverse information including travel, hotels, timetables, wildlife, worship, trekking, heritage and general tourism. It's well organised and easy to use.

See also:
www.greavesindia.com – luxury holidays in India and Nepal.
www.hindustantimes.com – full of useful information, news and gossip.
www.indianrail.gov.in – passenger information and timetables for the largest rail network in the world.
www.india-travel.com – a really strong travel site with lots of information and guidance as well as essential links.
www.indiatraveltimes.com – great for links and the latest news.
www.mapsofindia.com – an excellent site with maps of the country and a rail timetable and route planner.
www.partnershiptravel.co.uk – specialist Indian travel agent.
www.rrindia.com – another good information site offering tour itineraries and hotel booking.
www.taj-mahal.net – explore the Taj Mahal.

www.tourismindonesia.com   INDONESIA
INDONESIA
A very good overview of the country and its people, with lots of useful information about travelling there and a good links section. See also **www.indo.com** and for trips to see the Komodo Dragon go to **www.komodotours.com**

www.shamrock.org   IRELAND
IRELAND
A wide-ranging site giving you the best of Ireland. Aimed at the American market, it really sells the country well with good links to other related sites. See also **www.ireland.ie** – the very good, official Irish Tourist Board site.

See also:
www.12travel.co.uk – Irish holiday specialists with lots of holiday options.
www.camping-ireland.ie – over 100 parks listed for caravanning and camping.
www.heritageireland.ie – exploring the history of Ireland.
www.iol.ie/~discover – a good travel guide plus lots of links.
www.irelandhotels.com – a good accommodation directory.
www.visitdublin.com – very comprehensive official guide to Dublin.

www.goisrael.com   ISRAEL
ISRAEL
Excellent site with information on the country, its sights and sites, how to get there and how to organise a tour. See also **www.infotour.co.il** and **www.e-israel.com**

www.italytour.com   ITALY
VIRTUAL TOUR OF ITALY
Good looking, stylish and cool, this site is essentially a search engine and directory but a very good one.

See also:
www.doge.it – a basic but informative site on Venice.
www.emmeti.it – slightly eccentric site with bags of good information, although it takes a while to find it. Very good for hotels, regional info and museums.
www.initaly.com – another 'Italian' site but generally well organised, informative and useful.
www.itwg.com – Italian hotel reservations with online booking.
www.travel.it – a messy information site but you can book online.
www.tuscanynow.com – villas for rent in Tuscany.

J
www.jnto.go.jp   JAPAN
JAPAN
This excellent site is the work of the Japanese Tourist Association. There's a guide to each region, the food, shopping and travel info with advice on how to get the best out of your visit.

See also:
www.jaltour.co.uk – travel agents specialising in Japan.
www.japan-guide.com – comprehensive information site about Japan with links, culture notes, shopping and a hotel finder.

www.uk.emb-japan.go.jp – a new site for the Japanese Embassy with details on how to study or work in Japan, plus visa, tourist and background information.

www.see-jordan.com   JORDAN
JORDAN
An attractive and interesting site from the Jordanian tourist board. It is very cultural and informative with good links and a photo gallery. See also **www.jtehome.com** where you'll find the attractive site of the Jordan Travel Exchange.

K
www.visit-kenya.com   KENYA
KENYA
A slightly amateurish site with links and information on travelling in Kenya. There are sections on Nairobi and the coast as well as the expected safari information.

See also:
www.bwsafaris.com – a stunning site from this Kenyan safari specialist.
www.kenya.com – good-looking site with a safari deal finder and information on the country too.
www.kenyaweb.com – a good portal site on all things Kenyan.

L
www.lata.org   UK
LATIN AMERICA
The Latin American Trade Association's text-based site has a good country-by-country guide to the region plus links and general information.

www.southamericanexperience.co.uk   UK
SOUTH AMERICA
Specialists on South America are hard to come by, but at this site you can get tailor-made tours to suit you plus some scant information on the countries and special offers. See also **www.adventure-life.com** and **www.gosouthamerica.about.com** both are very informative and are good for links.

See the sites below, most of which also cover South America:
www.journeylatinamerica.co.uk – lots of tour and country options from this specialist agent.

www.lastfrontiers.com – tailor-made itineraries for holidays across the continent.
www.latinamericatraveler.com – great for links and information.
www.steppeslatinamerica.co.uk – from the Steppes group offering tailor-made packages.

www.nexteurope.com/tourism   LATVIA
LATVIA
A valiant effort with information on what to do when you get there and a good selection of links. They will also arrange for a translator/guide to show you around. For a second opinion go to **www.latviatravel.info**

www.destinationlebanon.com   LEBANON
THE LEBANON
The Lebanon is going through a resurgence and is successfully rebuilding itself. Written with the help of US-aid money to encourage tourism, this site successfully provides all the resources you need to organise a visit and see its many attractions.

www.tourism.lt   LITHUANIA
LITHUANIA
A straightforward offering from the State Department with basic tourist information.

www.luxembourg.co.uk   LUXEMBOURG
LUXEMBOURG
Comprehensive information on the Grand Duchy with good links to other sites. It could do with a few pictures to whet the appetite though.

M
www.malaysianet.net   MALAYSIA
MALAYSIA
Great for hotels in particular but you'll also find flight information and hidden away is a pretty good travel guide to the country. For air travel info see also **www.malaysiaair.com**

www.visitmaldives.com   MALDIVES
MALDIVES
A good overview of the islands and all the options available to tourists with links and a section on the capital Male.

www.visitmalta.com   UK
MALTA

A text-heavy but informative site about this beautiful island,
with good details on accommodation and interactive
mapping.

www.tourbymexico.com   UK
MEXICO

A basic site, but there is a travel guide to Mexico plus information
on tours, hotels, health, tips, links and sights. See also the bright
and breezy European gateway into Mexico
www.mexicanwave.com/travel

http://i-cias.com   NORWAY
THE MIDDLE EAST

Probably the best site for information on the Middle East, just
click on the interactive map. There's really extensive information
on selected countries including maps, statistics, history, plus the
religious, economic and political state of each nation. See also
www.ancient.co.uk

www.arab.net   SAUDIA ARABIA
RESOURCE FOR THE ARAB WORLD

A wide-ranging site covering North Africa and the Middle East
with excellent country guides. See also
www.arabianodyssey.co.uk

www.tourism-in-morocco.com   MOROCCO
MOROCCO

Take the guided tour and visit the major tourist sites in Morocco.
There are also sections covering museums, tourist events,
Moroccan culture and you can try out a recipe at home. The site
provides links, but for more see **www.morocco.com** and
www.morocco-travel.com

N

www.namibweb.com   NAMIBIA
NAMIBIA

Comprehensive as a description doesn't quite do this site justice,
it seems to have covered everything. The result is a little messy
but it's easy to find what you need, and it is a stunning country to
visit.

www.nepal.com   US
NEPAL AND THE HIMALAYAS

A beautifully presented site showing Nepal in its best light.
Business, sport, culture and travel all have sections and it's a
good browse too. The travel section is not that comprehensive, it
has a basic guide.

Specialist tour companies and information sites. Also check out
entries under China and India in this section.
www.himalayankingdoms.com
www.nepaltravelinfo.com
www.rrindia.com/nepal.html
www.trans-himalaya.com

www.purenz.com   NEW ZEALAND
NEW ZEALAND

A good-looking and informative site about the country with a
section devoted to recollections and recommendations from
people who've visited. See also the comprehensive but
www.nz.com and **www.newzealand.com**

www.nicaragua.com   US
NICARAGUA

On the face of it a comprehensive portal devoted to all things
Nicaraguan, it's not what it seems, however, and only the guide
book information seems useful.

www.visitnorway.com   NORWAY
NORWAY

The official site of the Norwegian Tourist Board offers a good
overview of what you can get up-to-when you're there, from
adventure holidays to lounging around in the midnight sun to
cruising the coast. You need an up-to-date browser to get the
best out of the site. See also **www.norway.org** which is the
Norwegian Embassy's site and also **www.norwayshop.com**
great for dodgy patterned jumpers

P
www.tourism.gov.pk   PAKISTAN
PAKISTAN

A pretty lightweight site but it has all the basic information and a
good set of links with a travel guide built in. See also
www.pak.org which is a very comprehensive portal site.

www.enjoyperu.com   US
PERU
It's amazing how much there is to see in Peru and this site does a
good job of reflecting the country's assets. It has plenty of tourist
information and deals. See also the basic but useful site of the
Peruvian embassy **www.peruembassy-uk.com**

www.polandtour.org   US
POLAND
A basic overview of the country, tourist facilities and travel
information. For a portal site go to **http://poland.pl**

www.portugal-web.com   PORTUGAL
PORTUGAL
A complete overview of the country including business as well as
tourism with good regional information, news and links to other
related sites.

See also:
www.madeiratourism.org – all about Madeira although you
have to hunt for the English site, we found the link in the top right
of the Portuguese page.
www.portugal.com – a news and shopping site with a good
travel section.
www.portugal.org – well-designed information site with good
travel information.
www.portugalregional.pt – a shop devoted to Portuguese wine
and arts.
www.thealgarve.net – all you need to know about the Algarve.

R
www.rotravel.com   ROMANIA
ROMANIA
Good historical information, maps and regional guides backed
up with tourist services for both the independent traveller and
those wanting a ready-made tour, make this site a good starting
point for the exploration of this central European gem. The
Romanian National Tourist Office has a good web site at
www.romaniatourism.com

www.russia-travel.com   RUSSIA
RUSSIA
The official guide to travel in Russia with good information on
excursions, accommodation, flights and trains; there's even a

slide show, plus historical facts and travel tips. See also
www.themoscowtimes.com/travel which offers a more
traditional approach. For links go to **www.russia.com**

www.rwandatourism.com   RWANDA
　　RWANDA
　　It's good to see Rwanda back on the tourist map and here at the
　　Tourist Board site you can find out what the country has to offer
　　including interactive mapping on the gorilla treks.

S
www.sey.net   US
　　SEYCHELLES, PARADISE – PERIOD
　　A good all-round overview of the Seychelles with background
　　information on the major islands and activities. There are also
　　links to travel agents.

　　See also:
　　www.seychelleselite.co.uk – specialists in the Seychelles.
　　www.seychelles-travel.co.uk – excellent site from another
　　specialist agent.
　　www.seychelles.uk.com – informative and geared to a British
　　audience.

www.sg   SINGAPORE
　　SINGAPORE
　　The shortest URL in the book brings up one of the most detailed
　　and comprehensive sites – all you need to know about the
　　country and its people. See also **www.satours.com** and the
　　official uniquely Singaporean site **www.visitsingapore.com**

www.slovenia-tourism.si   SLOVENIA
　　SLOVENIA
　　A good introduction to the country, which is trying to establish a
　　tourist industry.

www.sacr.sk   SLOVAKIA
　　SLOVAKIA
　　The official word of the Slovak Republic on their tourist
　　attractions. For similar but more wordy information go to
　　www.slovakia.org/tourism who also have an audio guide to
　　common phrases in Slovak.

T

www.southafrica.net   SOUTH AFRICA
SOUTH AFRICA
Official tourist site with masses of information about the country
and how you can set yourself up for the perfect visit with
suggested itineraries.

See also:
www.gardenroute.org.za – excellent site covering the Garden
Route and south coast.
www.southafrica.com/travel – very good portal site with a
comprehensive travel section.
www.southafricanaffair.com – tailor-made itineraries, basic site
though.

South America see Latin America on page 534.

www.tourspain.es   SPAIN
TOURIST OFFICE OF SPAIN
A colourful and award-winning web site that really makes you
want to visit Spain. Very good for an overview.

You could also try any of these listed below:
www.costablancaworld.com – Costa Blanca revealed.
www.iberia.com – the Iberian airlines site, with helpful advice
and offers.
www.majorca.com – great site about the island.
www.munimadrid.es – comprehensive site on Madrid.
www.okspain.org – nice all-round information and travel site.
www.red2000.com – a colourful travel guide, with a good
search instrument!

www.lanka.net   SRI LANKA
SRI LANKA
An exhaustive site, which isn't easy to navigate, but it has loads
of information and news on the country.

See also:
www.bouncebacksrilanka.org – a great site on how Sri Lanka is
getting back on its feet since the tsunami.
www.slmts.slt.lk for the Ministry of Tourism.

www.sverigeturism.se/smorgasbord   SWEDEN
SWEDEN

The largest source of information in English on Sweden. It's essentially a directory site but there are sections on culture, history and a tourist guide. For more details of Sweden's cities see the very good **http://cityguide.se** and **www.visit-sweden.com** and also **www.sweden.com**

www.switzerlandtourism.ch   SWITZERLAND
SWITZERLAND

An excellent overview of the country with the latest news, travel information, snow reports and links. See also **www.myswitzerland.com**

T

www.tanzania-web.com   TANZANIA
TANZANIA

Find your way around Tanzania with its wonderful scenery, Mount Kilimanjaro, safaris and resorts with this very good and comprehensive online guide from the official tourist board. For a range of safaris and personalised tours try **bush2beachsafaris.com**

www.thailand.com/travel   THAILAND
THAILAND

Another excellent portal site, which acts as a gateway to a mass of travel and tourism resources. It covers some of South East Asia too and it has a good search facility. The helpful **www.tourismthailand.org** is the official tourist board site and is very informative, as is **www.thaismile.co.uk** which is the official tourist site.

www.tourismtunisia.com   TUNISIA
TUNISIA

A welcoming and easy-to-use site with lots of interactive links that gives you a good introduction to the country, its tourist sites and its people. There's information on hotels and restaurants – plus what to eat when you get there and links to travel agencies.

www.allaboutturkey.com   TURKEY
TURKEY

The best-looking and most informative site on the country and its people, though some sections are pretty odd. It's the work of one professional tour guide.

See also:

www.exploreturkey.com – pretty boring but comprehensive.
www.tourismturkey.org – great for links and basic information
from the Ministry of Culture and Tourism.
www.turkey.org – informative site from the Turkish Embassy in
Washington DC.
www.turkeycentral.com – a huge number of Turkish links.

U

www.uae.org.ae   UAE
  UNITED ARAB EMIRATES
  A useful guide to the seven states that make up the UAE, it
  carries historical and social information as well as the usual
  travel guide stuff – turn down your sound, though. See also
  www.godubai.com

www.visituganda.com   UGANDA
  UGANDA
  A great site and directory from the Ugandan Tourist Board with
  excellent-quality pictures.

www.ukraine.co.uk   UK
  UKRAINE
  A basic site with information on flights, the cities, mapping and
  links.

www.usatourism.com   US
  US
  A state-by-state guide to the US, just click on the interactive map
  and you get put through to the relevant state site. See also
  www.areaguides.net which is very detailed.

www.usembassy.org.uk   US
  VISA INFO
  This site gives a dull look at the latest tourist entry requirements
  plus information on gripping topics such as driving. It also
  provides some limited but useful links. For tourist information
  they send you to **www.visitusa.org.uk**

See also:

www.americanadventures.com – great site devoted to budget
adventure tours. Now merged with **www.trekamerica.com** to
offer an even broader range of holidays.
www.americanroundup.com – ranch holidays for wannabe
cowboys.

www.amtrak.com – rail schedules and fares across America.
www.cruiseamerica.com – rent an RV for your fly-drive holiday.
www.disneyworld.com – all you need to know about the world's number-one theme park.
www.eosairlines.com – travel to New York in style.
www.gocitykids.com – a family-friendly guide to some of the major cities in the US.
www.gohawaii.com – great site for checking out Hawaii and its many attractions.
www.greyhound.com – coach and bus schedules; for selected cities you can now buy tickets online using the 'will call' option and pick them up before boarding the bus.
www.hawaii-tourism.co.uk – the official site of Hawaii's tourist board, excellent information on all the islands.
www.kidscamps.com – a massive directory of kids' camps, mainly in the US.
www.seeamerica.org – an excellent portal to American travel sites.
www.themeparksonline.org – over 200 of them, apparently.
www.usa-by-rail.com – the definitive guide book for touring the US by rail.
www.usahotelguide.com – reserve your room in any one of 55,000 hotels across the US.
www.us-national-parks.net – the fabulous US National Parks Service with plenty of info; use the online Reservation Centre to book accommodation.

V

www.vietnamtourism.com   US
VIETNAM
Vietnam is the hot destination, apparently. Here's the official tourism site, which is informative and good for links.

Z

www.zambiatourism.com   ZAMBIA
ZAMBIA
Comprehensive tourist site with loads of information about places to visit, where to stay and what to do when you get there.

www.allaboutzanzibar.com   TANZANIA
ZANZIBAR
An outstanding tourist site with concise (then very detailed if you need it) descriptions covering all the information you need, including accommodation and cultural stuff. Other tourism sites could learn a lot from this. See also **www.zanzibar.net**

There are sections on the animals and birds you might see, plus maps and a good travel directory.

Travel UK

The Good Web Site Guide's Top 10s
of the Internet

1. **www.visitbritain.com** – all you need to know about us
2. **www.timeout.com/london** – probably the best guide to the capital
3. **www.sightseeing.co.uk** – information on what to see and how to get there
4. **www.nationaltrust.org.uk** – over 200 homes and gardens
5. **www.ctc.org.uk** – the perfect site for cyclists
6. **www.traveline.org.uk** – all you need on public transport
7. **www.walkingworld.com** – great for the UK and abroad
8. **www.goodbeachguide.co.uk** – where best to put up your windbreaker
9. **www.hebrides.com** – beautiful
10. **www.knowhere.co.uk** – a warts and all overview of our islands

Travel in Britain

www.visitbritain.com   UK
HOME OF THE BRITISH TOURIST AUTHORITY
Selling Britain using a holiday-ideas-led site with lots of help for the visitor, maps, background stories, images, entertainment, culture, activities and a planner. There's also a very helpful set of links.

www.informationbritain.co.uk   UK
HOLIDAY INFORMATION
Where to stay and where to go with an overview of all the UK's main tourist attractions, counties and regions; it has good cross-referencing and links to the major destinations.

www.ukholidaybreaks.co.uk UK
FIND YOUR PERFECT HOTEL
A directory of hotels in the UK, you find the one you want by drilling down through a series of maps or selecting by category. It's easy, although results are a bit hit and miss, but it claims to use the latest technology to find just the right break for you.

www.thetravelplanner.co.uk UK
UK TRAVEL PLANNER
A good resource if you're planning a journey anywhere in Britain. There are good links and it makes a useful addition to your favourites list.

See also:
www.aboutbritain.com – attractive, well-laid-out and comprehensive UK guide.
www.anothertravel.com – a good-looking site, a bit light on information though.
www.atuk.co.uk – billed as the UK travel search engine, unattractive design.
www.enjoybritain.com – useful links directory.
www.i-uk.com – useful information on the UK, mainly aimed at visitors.
www.touristnetuk.com – a good regional guide.
www.ukguide.org – well-organised directory with a UK and a London guide plus mapping.
www.ukvillages.co.uk – not a great design but has good information on over 30,000 places.

www.knowhere.co.uk UK
THE USER'S GUIDE TO BRITAIN
An unconventional 'tourist guide', which gives a warts-and-all account of over 1,000 places in Britain; it's very irreverent and if you are squeamish or a bit sensitive, then they have a good list of links to proper tourist sites.

For the separate countries and regions:

England

http://themeparksofengland.com – reviews and information on all of England's major theme parks.
www.enjoyengland.com – official tourist site with lots of information and features.

www.travelengland.org.uk – nice online guide to everything English, places to visit and accommodation.

English Holiday Regions

www.blackcountrytourism.co.uk – visiting the Midlands and the Black Country.
www.cumbria-the-lake-district.co.uk – a good guide to the Lake District.
www.dorset-newforest.com – Dorset and the New Forest.
www.ntb.org.uk – visit North East England.
www.peakdistrict.org – home of the Peak District Park Authority.
www.the-cotswolds.org – all about the honey-stoned world of the Cotswolds.
www.visiteastofengland.com – for East Anglia and the Broads.
www.visitenc.com – visit England's North Country.
www.visitenglandsnorthwest.com – the official tourist site of the North West.
www.visitnorthumbria.com – Northumbrian countryside.
www.visitnorthwest.com – what to do in the towns and cities of the North West.
www.visitpeakdistrict.com – good site on tourism in our oldest National Park.
www.visitsoutheastengland – for history, gardens and more.
www.westcountrynow.com – official guide to England's West Country.
www.yorkshirevisitor.com – get to know Yorkshire.

London

http://london.flavourpill.net – an excellent and entertaining London city guide which is updated weekly.
www.londonhotelreservations.com – some good deals on London hotels.
www.londontown.com – very comprehensive survival and holiday guide rolled into one, with sections on restaurants, hotels, attractions and offers. It is quite slow.
www.timeout.com/london – *Time Out* mag's excellent guide to the capital.

Northern Ireland

www.discovernorthernireland.com – Northern Ireland Tourist Board has an attractive site showing the best that the region has

to offer. It has a virtual-tour holiday planner.
www.gotobelfast.com – excellent site on Belfast.
www.guide-to-nireland.com – a good directory site and guide.

Scotland

www.aboutscotland.com – excellent site with information on a broad range of accommodation and sights to see, it's fast too.
www.agtb.org – pour yourself a whiskey it's Aberdeen and the Grampians!
www.edinburgh.org – comprehensive offering on Edinburgh.
www.scotac.com – accommodation by region.
www.scot-borders.co.uk – what to do on the Scottish/English Borders.
www.scotland.com – nicely illustrated site with a good overview of the country.
www.scotland-info.co.uk – very good online guidebook covering Scotland by area; it's quite slow but the information is very good.
www.seeglasgow.com – excellent site on Glasgow.
www.visithebrides.com – a light and airy site with links and information relating to the islands. See also **www.hebrides.com** which offers beautiful photography.
www.visithighlands.com – all you need to know about the Scottish Highlands and more.
www.visitorkney.com – from the Orkney Tourist Board a very informative and appealing site. See also **www.orknet.com**
www.visitscottishheartlands.com – Argyll, the Isles, Loch Lomond, Stirling and the Trossachs.
www.visitshetland.com – a definite green theme to this site devoted to Shetland, highlighting its outdoor life and spirit of adventure.

Wales

www.cadw.wales.gov.uk – historic monuments in Wales.
www.cardiganshirecoastandcountry.co.uk – great guide to West Wales.
www.data-wales.co.uk – not so much a tourist site, but excellent for history and culture and quite funny too.
www.nwt.co.uk – North Wales tourism.
www.southernwales.com – Cardiff and the south.
www.stayinwales.co.uk – for hotels, cottages, B&Bs, campsites, even bunkhouses.

www.valleyconnection.co.uk – a useful directory devoted to all things Welsh.
www.visitmidwales.co.uk – Wales' best kept secret.

The UK's Islands

www.alderney.net – a good-looking site devoted to the third largest Channel Island.
www.islandbreaks.co.uk – official site on the Isle of Wight.
www.isle-of-man.com – learn all about this unique island with help on where to stay and, of course, background on the famous TT races.
www.jersey.com – very slick site on Jersey.
www.jerseyhols.com – good-looking site with lots of information on where to stay and what to do.
www.sark.info – a lively site with all the information you need plus online booking for ferries.
www.simplyscilly.co.uk – specialists in travel to the Isles of Scilly with info on how to get there and what to do.
www.visitguernsey.com – all the information you need on Guernsey.
www.wightlink.co.uk – Isle of Wight ferries and holiday information.

Things to do in Britain and Ireland

www.sightseeing.co.uk   UK
SIGHT-SEEING MADE EASY
A good-looking and very useful site if you're looking for something to do. Just type in what you want to see and where you are, then up pops a list giving basic information on each attraction, how far away it is, the entrance fee and a map. However, it would be better if there was more background information on each attraction or at least a link.

www.daysoutuk.com   UK
TAKE A DAY OFF
An excellent directory of venues and events with lots of search options. It's easy to use and you can get discounts to many attractions too. For a similar but more colourful site go to **www.daysout.co.uk** which includes a useful section for the disabled too.

www.gardenvisit.com   UK
GO TO A GARDEN
A basic text-based site, which lists some 2,000 gardens in the
UK and abroad, giving details of each, how to get there and how
they rate. There's also an excellent overview of garden history.
See also the section on Gardening page 227.

www.nationaltrust.org.uk   UK
PLACES OF HISTORIC INTEREST AND BEAUTY
The National Trust's site has an excellent overview of their
activities and the properties they own. There is a very good
search facility and up-to-date information to help with your visit.
See also **www.nts.org.uk** for the National Trust for Scotland.

See also:
www.castles-of-britain.com – informative and lively site on
Britain's castles.
www.english-heritage.org.uk – excellent, high-quality site with
information on their properties and an events calendar.
www.hrp.org.uk – pretty boring site devoted to five historic royal
palaces – the Tower, Hampton Court, Kensington, Kew and the
Banqueting House.
www.statelyhomes.com – comprehensive site devoted to our
stately homes, with links and an e-zine to keep you updated.

www.goodbeachguide.co.uk   UK
THE BEST BEACHES
From the Marine Conservation Society you can find out which
are Britain's worst and best beaches. It's set out regionally and
the site is updated regularly.

What to do With the Kids

www.babygoes2.com   UK
ESSENTIAL TRAVEL GUIDE FOR PARENTS
An excellent resource for parents who have children under five, it
covers a wide range of holiday options, plus plenty of advice,
guides and information.

For more ideas try:
www.barracudas.co.uk – activity camp holidays.
www.butlins.co.uk – bright and breezy site from this popular
family-oriented company.

www.campbeaumont.com – a summer camp covering southeast England.

www.centerparcs.com – attractive site from this holiday village specialist, covering the UK and parts of Europe.

www.kidscamps.com – a massive directory of kids' camps, mainly in the US.

www.kidsdaysout.co.uk – a directory of things to do by county, covering England, Scotland and Wales.

www.kidstravel.co.uk – up-beat design but it could have more content, still some good ideas and travelling tips for parents though biased to England.

www.pgl.co.uk/holidays – activity holidays for children with lots of options.

www.xkeys.co.uk – specialist in residential camps for children of all ages, excellent web site with lots of information and references.

Holiday Cottages and B&B

www.bedandbreakfast-directory.co.uk   UK
B&B

A regional directory of B&Bs with a good search facility. Each entry has contact details, a description and information such as whether online booking is available.

See also:

www.cottagesdirect.com – click on the interactive map and away you go, plenty of cottages to choose from.

www.goodcottageguide.com – a good selection from this established specialist.

www.nationaltrust.org.uk – look under holidays for cottages and b&b with a difference.

www.oas.co.uk/ukcottages – over 1,000 cottages available throughout the UK.

www.preferredplaces.co.uk – good site with a wide range of options.

www.pub-explorer.com – find a pub with rooms and a good pint.

www.pub-rooms.co.uk – stay in a pub, unfortunately most don't have websites, but you can e-mail.

www.seasidecottages.co.uk – all within 10 miles of the sea.

www.selfcatering-directory.co.uk – a very useful directory site listing hundreds of cottages with information and contact details.

Camping and Caravanning

Many of the sites listed specialise in Britain but some have information on camp sites abroad too.

www.camp-sites.co.uk   UK
FIND A SITE
Excellent regional listing of the UK's campsites with comprehensive details on each site and links to other related directories.

See also:
www.eurocampindependent.co.uk – excellent site if you want to go camping in Europe, some special offers and you can chat about your experiences too.
www.keycamp.co.uk – European specialist with sites in seven countries.
www.ukparks.com – directory site covering caravan and camping sites.

www.caravan.co.uk   UK
THE CARAVAN CLUB
This site offers help and advice, and has a huge listing of over 200 sites and some 2,600 other certified locations where you can park up. There's also a European service. You can join the club online and request any of the 50 or so leaflets they publish.

See also:
http://camping.uk-directory.com – a good regional sites directory, with retailing links, caravans for sale and forums. Camping in New Zealand is covered too.
www.campingandcaravanningclub.co.uk – an OK offering with information on sites and technical help and advice too.
www.campinguk.com – a basic regional campsite directory for campers and caravanners.
www.caravannersreunited.co.uk – forums, chat, information and meeting up with old friends.
www.caravan-sitefinder.co.uk – listing of over 3,500 caravan sites, with background information on a wide range of topics.
www.clicreports.co.uk – the Chat Line for Internet Campers offers loads of advice in a fun and informative way.

Waterways

www.britishwaterways.co.uk   UK
BRITISH WATERWAYS
This organisation is responsible for maintaining a large part of
Britain's waterways and this excellent site details their work. On
two sites (also **www.waterscape.com**) it features interactive
mapping of the routes with a great deal of background
information, events, holidays, listings and history.

See also:
www.blakes.co.uk – a boating holiday specialist.
www.broads-authority.gov.uk – excellent overview of the
Norfolk Broads.
www.canalholidays.com – an easy way to book your
narrowboat holiday.
www.gobarging.com – luxury barging in Europe.
www.hoseasons.co.uk – great site from the specialists in
boating holidays, you can book online too.
www.waterways.org.uk – Inland Waterways Association site,
dedicated to keeping canals open and you can find out about
their organised activities too.

Adventure and Activity

*Listed below are UK-oriented sites, see also page 509 for international
adventure specialists.*

www.sportbreak.co.uk   UK
THE SPORTS BREAK DIRECTORY
A good directory, apart from sports it covers all activity holidays
including leisure breaks, health clubs, even stag and hen
parties. They specialise in corporate entertaining too. It's easy to
use and the information is well put over.

Other adventure holiday sites:
www.activityholsni.co.uk – Activity Holidays in Northern
Ireland have a great site and lots to do.
www.adventuredirectory.com – for an excellent portal site.
www.adventureholiday.com – ProAdventure specialise in
activity holidays in North Wales.
www.hightrek.co.uk – strenuous activities in the mountains of
North Wales.

www.mountainandwater.co.uk – wide range of activities for adults and children in Wales.

www.sportstoursinternational.co.uk – sports holidays (mainly running, cycling and swimming) in the UK and abroad, but many to international events.

www.trailplus.com – the ultimate adventure, offering lifestyle experiences, adventure camps and much more.

www.uksurvivalschool.co.uk – learn new skills; learn how to survive in many different situations on the courses.

Walking and Rambling

www.ramblers.org.uk   UK
THE RAMBLERS' ASSOCIATION
News, strong views and plenty of advice on offer here, where you can find out about the Association's activities and even join a campaign. There are features on events and details of *The Rambler* magazine, shopping and holidays.

www.walkingbritain.co.uk   UK
BRITISH WALKS
Some 3,300 pages of information about walking in Britain, it mainly covers the National Parks but it is expanding to include less well-known areas. They provide decent route maps and photos to guide you. There's also a list of handy links and a good photo gallery.

www.onedayhikes.com   US
WHERE DO YOU WANT TO HIKE TODAY?
A great site, which is basically a directory of hikes that you can complete in a day; it's not just for the UK either, it covers the whole world. There's excellent information on each hike plus pictures and you get the chance to win a digital camera if you send in a report of a hike you've done and it gets accepted.

www.walkingworld.com   UK
OVER 3,000 WALKS
Each walk has a detailed description and map, and it's easy to find a good one. In addition, there's advice on difficulty and what you can expect to see. The walks cost £1.50 or you can become a member for £17.45 per annum, then they're free.

For more sites for hikers try:

www.gelert.com – equipment for sale, a good-looking site, well worth a visit.

www.georgefisher.co.uk – another excellent equipment store.

www.hfholidays.co.uk – excellent specialist travel agent with walking holidays for all levels and all around the world.

www.ramblersholidays.co.uk – Ramblers Holidays specialise in escorted rambling holidays.

www.trailsource.com – the hiking section of this big site has some great walks and detailed mapping.

Train, Coach and Ferry Journeys

www.transportdirect.info   UK

PUBLIC TRANSPORT INFORMATION

Excellent travel resource for public transport or the car driver. You opt for a quick journey plan or a more detailed door to door plan. If you just need to find a train, bus or coach or even a car route, this information is available too. There is information for travellers with disabilities, maps, live travel info and you can also link to your mobile or PDA. An alternative is **www.traveline.org.uk** although this site only finds journeys between major towns and cities. They do, however, provide timetables and links and details for all the major transport providers.

See also

http://journeyplanner.tfl.gov.uk is very useful for travelling around London.

www.internet.xephos.com – a subscription service which offers a high degree of accuracy on train and bus timetables.

www.seat61.com – the UK pages give extensive rail information.

Railway Travel

www.rail.co.uk   UK

RAILWAY LINKS

A directory of useful links including timetables, operators and associated businesses.

www.nationalrail.co.uk   UK

NATIONAL RAIL

National Rail's site has all the latest information, timetables and links you need to plan a rail journey. It's very comprehensive with up-to-the-minute information on what's going on. The TrainTracker facility enables you to get departure/arrival board information via your mobile and enquiries are now enabled on PDA. They are trying . . .

www.thetrainline.com UK

BUY TRAIN TICKETS

You have to log in first but you can book a ticket for train travel, whether business or leisure (except sleeper, Motorail, and ferry services). They have an up-to-date timetable and the tickets will be sent or you can collect. You can now buy European rail tickets and other travel services from the site. See also the fast-working **www.qjump.co.uk** which is similar. At both these sites there are a bewildering number of options and prices, a little help regarding ticket type and relative costs wouldn't go amiss.

See also:

www.gensheet.co.uk – information on unusual rail journeys in the UK.

www.greatrail.com – escorted railway holidays world-wide. Well-illustrated site.

www.networkrail.co.uk – what was Railtrack, some useful information.

www.orient-express.com – details of their holidays and routes.

www.traintaxi.co.uk – useful site if you need a taxi once you're off the train, with taxi company contact details and advice on whether there are usually taxis waiting.

www.trainweb.com – a huge train portal site, particularly good for Amtrak in the US and Via Rail in Canada.

www.youngpersons-railcard.co.uk – how to save as much as a third on your rail travel.

www.tfl.gov.uk UK

LONDON TRANSPORT

Transport for London is an excellent and informative site featuring the London Underground, DLR, buses, taxis and river transport plus advice for travellers who come by car, use a bike or just walk. At **www.thetube.com** you'll find lots of features, articles on visiting London and links to related sites. There's a good journey planner and tube maps too. See also the Tube Planner at **www.tubeplanner.com** which is a straightforward journey planner and a tube guide and history at **http://owen.massey.net/tubemaps.html**

Coaches and Buses

www.nationalexpress.com   UK
BOOK COACH TICKETS
Organise your journey with this easy-to-use web site from
National Express, and then book the tickets. Also offers an
airport service, transport to events and tours. See also
www.stagecoachbus.com where you can find information about
Stagecoach services and buy tickets, and **www.citylink.co.uk**
for their Scottish Services.

www.megabus.com   UK
NO FRILLS
The coach equivalent of low-cost planes, Megabus is expanding
rapidly, currently they serve over 30 towns and cities. Tickets
can only be purchased online and all you need is your booking
reference to present to the driver on the bus. Tickets start from
£1 if you book soon enough, with only a 50p booking charge.

See also:
www.busabout.com – for independent travellers, mainly covers
Europe and North Africa.
www.wallacearnold.co.uk – coaching holiday specialist with
online booking.

Ferries

www.ferrysavers.com   UK
BOOK YOUR CROSSING
Low-cost ferry crossings and plenty of special offers on a number
of routes, you can book online but the price promise seems to
have disappeared.

See also:
www.boozecruise.com – for ferry tickets, guides to the French
ports and maps for locating the hypermarkets and shopping areas.
www.brittany-ferries.co.uk – crossings to France and Spain
with online booking and special offers, also cruises and holidays.
www.dfdsseaways.co.uk – details and offers on Scandinavian
routes.
www.directferries.co.uk – claims to offer the widest choice of
routes and crossings.
www.drive-alive.com – motoring holiday specialists who get
good rates on channel crossings as part of their package.

www.eurotunnel.com – we know its not a ferry; also have hotel and holiday deals.

www.ferry.co.uk – great offers on selected crossings.

www.ferrycrossings-uk.co.uk – a helpful site with offers and links, a shopping guide too.

www.hoverspeed.com – online booking and all the information you need to make the fastest channel and Irish Sea crossings.

www.irishferries.ie – excellent magazine-style site where amongst all the features you can find timetables and book tickets.

www.poferries.com – P&O Stena Line with online booking, details of sailings and offers.

www.seafrance.com – bookings and information on their Calais–Dover service plus some special offers.

www.speedferries.com – a low-cost operator offering crossings on the Dover–Boulogne fast-ferry service. Book online to save admin fee.

www.steam-packet.com – get Sea Cat to destinations on the Irish sea.

www.stenaline.co.uk – details of their routes and offers.

www.transmancheferries.com – the new boys on the south coast offering Newport to Dieppe at competitive prices.

Car Hire

*It's probably best to go to a price-comparison site before going to one of the car hire companies, that way you should get the best prices. One of the best is to be found at **www.priceline.co.uk***

www.holidaycars.co.uk   UK
WORLD-WIDE CAR HIRE
Over 4,000 car hire locations throughout the world means that this site is well worth a visit on your quest, you can get an instant online quote and you can book too. Very good for the US.

See also:
www.easycar.com – low-cost, online car hire specialist, part of the Easyjet group.

www.holidayautos.co.uk – excellent prices and a wide choice too.

www.insurance4carhire.com – who have a number of options to suit.

www.pelicancarhire.co.uk – competitive rates from this specialist in Europe.

T

Road Travel

For mapping see page 521. Here are some sites that may help your journey to go smoother still.

www.5minutesaway.com   UK
> JUST OFF THE MOTORWAY
> An excellent site which lists by motorway junction the facilities that exist within a five minute's drive of the exit. It's excellent for those who hate motorway services. See also **www.offthemotorway.com** which is still in development but has potential.
>
> *See also*
> **www.gloveboxloo.co.uk** – yes, it really exists.
> **www.moto-way.com** – the company that runs most of the services.
> **www.motorwayservices.info** – a feedback site where people give their views on motorway service stations.
> **www.welcomebreak.co.uk** – book a hotel room and find out about their services.
> **www.westmorland.com** – home of the Tebay services who show everyone how a motorway service station should be run.

Travel Writing

> *Here are some sites covering the work of our favourite travel writers . . .*
> **http://worldhum.com** – a descriptive site derived from the rush people get from travelling. Some excellent writing.
> **www.gridskipper.com** – described as an 'urban travel guide', here you'll find a wide variety of personal views of the major cities around the world.
> **www.palinstravels.co.uk** – an outstanding site from Michael Palin with his recommendations, excerpts from the books and video clips as well as competitions and links.
> **www.paultheroux.com** – a biography and details on all his books.
> **www.randomhouse.com/features/billbryson** – an official site from Bill Bryson's publisher, it has a short biography, his book lists and a forum. Given the breadth of material available it could be so much better . . .

www.timseverin.net – details about his life and his remarkable voyages.

www.travelwriters.com – the place to go if you want to become a travel writer, the place to go if you are one already.

Utilities

Get the best prices on your gas, electricity and water and find out what the big suppliers are up to as well.

www.ofgem.gov.uk   UK

GAS AND ELECTRICITY SUPPLIER WATCHDOG

Data on the suppliers and companies. The comparison information makes for interesting reading. There's also background on how bills are made up, complaints, government policy and how energy reaches your home. For more impartial advice see also the independent watchdog Energywatch at **www.energywatch.org.uk**

www.uswitch.com   UK

CUT YOUR BILLS – COMPARE PRICES

Take a few minutes to check the prices of the key utilities and see whether you can save on your current bills, its easy and quick. It also gives you the option to change to a green energy tariff. In addition you can check out phones, broadband access, digital TV and loans.

See also:

www.energylinx.co.uk – one of the best switch sites with a wide range of options, particularly good on renewable energy.

www.greenelectricity.org – switch to green energy.

www.switchandgive.com – switch energy suppliers and give to charity at the same time.

www.switchwithwhich.co.uk – *Which* Magazine's impartial switching site.

www.theenergyshop.com – very easy to use and fast results.

www.unravelit.com – savings on gas and electricity plus numerous other services.

www.utilitydeal.com – helps business users as well as home owners.

U

Electricity and Gas

Here are the main energy sites, who owns them at the time of writing and the highlights of the site:

www.british-energy.com – one of the largest electricity providers with a good-looking but not very useful site.

www.centrica.co.uk – owners of British Gas, this site aims to give information about the group, could be a lot more helpful.

www.esb.ie – messy site from an Irish supplier with online sign-up available.

www.house.co.uk – a comprehensive service from British gas with account viewing and offers.

www.hydro.co.uk – Scottish Hydro Electric has one of the sites most oriented to its customers.

www.edfenergy.com – a stylish site for London Energy, SWEB Energy, Seeboard Energy and Virgin Home.

www.nationalgrid.com/uk – the National Grid, the Railtrack of power.

www.nie.co.uk – Northern Ireland Electricity with customer information on their service, the rest is fairly corporate.

www.npower.com – nicely designed site with online application and the usual incentives to switch to their service.

www.powergen.co.uk – Powergen has a neat site with calculators and a switching service.

www.scottish-southern.co.uk – owner of Swalec, their site is aimed at shareholders and provides company information.

www.scottish-power.co.uk – a messy site from one of the cheaper suppliers.

www.swalec.co.uk – Swalec, useful information, special site for kids and renewable energy.

www.nationalgrid.com/uk   UK
FORMALLY TRANSCO, FOR GAS LEAKS
Transco doesn't sell gas, but maintains the 24-hour emergency service for stopping gas leaks – call 0800 111 999 to report one.

www.corgi-gas-safety.com   UK
COUNCIL OF REGISTERED GAS INSTALLERS
CORGI is the gas industry watchdog; the site has advice on gas installation and where to find a fitter or repairman.

www.calorgas.co.uk   UK
CALOR GAS
Information on your nearest stockists, how best to use Calor Gas

and Autogas; there's also corporate background and customer services too. You can also order it online with payment collected on delivery.

Solid Fuel

www.solidfuel.co.uk   UK
SOLID FUEL ASSOCIATION
Information about solid fuels, about which is right for you and what appliances to buy; also covers suppliers and has a wealth of information and links. See also **www.coal.gov.uk**

Saving Energy

www.natenergy.org.uk   UK
NATIONAL ENERGY FOUNDATION
Devoted to saving energy in order to benefit the environment. There's lots of advice and information to help save money too.

See also:
www.banthebulb.org – campaign site aimed at promoting the use of energy efficient light bulbs.
www.battery-force.co.uk – buying batteries at discounted prices including good prices on rechargeable ones.
www.clear-skies.org – information about grants for those installing renewable energy systems such as solar panels.
www.ukace.org – Association for the Conservation of Energy.

Alternative energy

www.cat.org.uk   UK
CENTRE FOR ALTERNATIVE TECHNOLOGY
Get information on how to help save the planet and ease your conscience including strategies on how to be more energy efficient.

See also:
www.eaga.co.uk – the Energy Action Grants Agency.
www.energysaving.me.uk – energy saving products.
www.energywatch.org.uk – independent energy watchdog.
www.est.org.uk – home of the Energy Saving Trust.
www.greenelectricity.org – sign up for a greener tariff.
www.greenenergy.org.uk – home of the Solar Trade Association.

U

www.nef.org.uk – energy-saving advice from the UK charity for energy efficiency, the National Energy Foundation.

Water

www.ofwat.gov.uk   UK
OFFICE OF WATER SERVICES
A relatively poor effort, especially when compared with the Ofgem counterpart's site; however, you can find out about what they do and you can contact them for advice. There's a search facility to help you navigate the site.

The following are the main water company sites:
www.nwl.co.uk – Northumbrian Water with information and bill-paying info.
www.stwater.co.uk – the consumer site of Severn Trent Water, it's good looking, useful and easy to use.
www.swwater.co.uk – lots of information and good advice, bill paying online.
www.thameswater.co.uk – good information and advice.
www.unitedutilities.co.uk – United Utilities has a well-designed site with help, information and good advice for consumers, with online access to your account.
www.wessexwater.co.uk – good site with bill-paying facilities and information, even which reservoirs you can fish in.

www.wateraid.org   US
WATER FOR LIFE
A charity devoted to helping people for whom getting water is very difficult or almost impossible, you can find out about their work and how to help. See also **www.actionaid.org**

The Weather

www.met-office.gov.uk   UK

EXCELLING IN WEATHER SERVICES
Comprehensive information on our favourite topic of conversation: easy to use with interactive maps. Includes details on world weather and world weather news, UK weather headlines and flash-weather warnings, weather for aviators and sailors and you can see what the weather is like on their webcams. There's also a good selection of links and a mobile phone service.

www.bbc.co.uk/weather   UK

ANOTHER WINNER FROM THE BBC

Another page from the BBC site, it gives up-to-the-minute forecasts, and is very clear and concise. It features: 5-day forecasts by town, city or postcode; specialist reports such as ski resorts, pollution, sun index; world weather and the shipping forecast. There are also audio and video forecasts and links.

See also:

www.intellicast.com – a general weather guide from the US.
www.weather.com – geared to the US but has some really good articles and features.
www.weather.org.uk – informative UK weather information site.
www.weatherunderground.com – an entertaining site with colourful, interactive mapping.

www.weatherimages.org   US

SEE THE WORLD'S WEATHER – LIVE

Weatherimages is compiled by a true weather fan. Split into twenty or so areas of interest, there is plenty of information and loads to see. The best feature is the network of weather cams from which you can see the best and worst of the world's weather. See also the excellent **www.weather-photography.com**

Other interesting and useful weather sites worth checking out:
www.chasingstorms.com – home of the Storm Chasers and Spotters Association.
www.climateark.org – all the links you'll ever need on climate change.
www.cloudappreciationsociety.org – all you need to know about clouds and how to appreciate them; stunning photography too.
www.everythingweather.com – information and links.
www.hurricaneadvisories.com – American hurricane information.
www.hurricanes.net – information on tropical storms and their effects.
www.risingslowly.com – an entertaining blog devoted to weather in the UK, with lots of links and other related blogs.
www.spaceweather.com – for daily updates on solar winds and flares plus information on solar weather patterns in general.
www.stormstock.com – the world's premier storm footage library with some stunning clips.

W

www.stormtrack.org – another US storm-tracking site, very comprehensive though.
www.torro.org.uk – the Tornado and Storm Research Organisation, an interesting UK-oriented site.
www.weatherbase.com – statistics on world weather, data on over 16,000 cities.
www.worldclimate.com – weather data, averages and statistics.

Web Cameras

One of the most fascinating aspects of the Internet is the ability to tap into some CCTV or specially set-up web cameras from all around the world. Some sites will contain adult material though.

www.camcentral.com   US

WEB CAM CENTRAL
An excellent selection of cameras, chosen for quality rather than quantity; the wildlife ones are very good in particular but there's a good search facility too.

See also:
www.bbc.co.uk/webcams – the BBC has a great selection of regional and world webcams.
www.camvista.com – web cam shots of the UK and the US from a web cam manufacturer, annoying pop-ups.
www.webcam-index.com – lists over 1,900 sites from around the world.
www.webcamworld.com – a big directory of web cams.
www.webcamsearch.com – excellent search engine and directory of web cams from around the world.

Web Site Guides and Directories

If you can't find the site you're looking for in this book, then rather than using a search engine such as Yahoo or Google (both of which have superb directories), you might want to check out one of these web sites.

www.uk250.co.uk   UK

1000S OF QUALITY SITES IN 250 CATEGORIES
Heavily advertised and hyped though this site has been, many people seem to think that it consists of just the top 250 sites, but it's actually a very comprehensive database of Britain's most

important and useful .co.uks and .coms. The sites listed are not reviewed but a one-liner gives a brief description of what they are about.

www.ukdirectory.co.uk UK
DEFINITIVE GUIDES TO BRITISH SITES
A massive database of web sites conveniently categorised into fifteen sections, they don't review, but there are brief explanations provided by the site owners.

www.bored.com US
IF YOU'RE BORED
Basically a directory of unusual and humorous sites to occupy you when you've nothing better to do; it's quite entertaining really.

www.thebrickwall.com UK
PICK A BRICK
An entertaining route to categorised directories. Each brick represents a category, clicking on a general category brick brings up more bricks and the sites you're looking for.

Weddings

www.confetti.co.uk UK

YOUR INTERACTIVE WEDDING GUIDE
A good-looking and busy site designed to help you through every stage of your wedding with information for all participants. There are gift guides, planning tools, advice, a supplier directory and a shop. They don't miss much.

www.theknot.com UK
PREPARATION
All (well nearly all) your wedding needs catered for, excellent and attractive design too. You even get your own web pages and a useful countdown to the day.

www.wedding-service.co.uk UK
UK'S LARGEST WEDDING AND BRIDE DIRECTORY
A huge list of suppliers, service providers and information by region, everything from balloons to speechwriters are listed. The site is not that easy on the eye and it takes a little while to find what you want.

W

Other good sites for weddings:

http://bridesandgrooms.com – a comprehensive guide and community site.

www.bipp.com – the home of the British Institute of Professional Photographers and a good place to find one for your wedding pics.

www.bridesuk.net – excellent site from *Brides* magazine; get all the latest in bridal fashion and a guide to where to go on honeymoon.

www.hitched.co.uk – another good all-rounder with the added feature of a discussion forum where you can swap wedding stories.

www.lastnightoffreedom.co.uk – everything you need to organise your stag or hen night.

www.limoshop.co.uk – reserve your stretch limo.

www.partydomain.co.uk – if you want to organise your own party, then this is the site for you with some fairly naff offerings for hen and stag nights.

www.printed4u.co.uk – invitation printing.

www.pronuptia.co.uk – illustrated details of the range and stores, not much else.

www.thebridalconsultant.co.uk – organise an overseas wedding.

www.trading-direct.co.uk – your wedding presents taken care of with an online wedding list service.

www.webwedding.co.uk – lots of expert advice and inspiration, you need to join up to get the best out of it.

www.weddingguide.co.uk – clean-looking site with shop, directory, forums and advice plus a good search facility.

www.weddings-abroad.com – overseas wedding and honeymoon packages.

www.whitesandweddings.co.uk – for more overseas options.

Women

The following are a few sites of particular interest to women.

Equality Issues and Politics

www.womenandequalityunit.gov.uk   UK
THE WOMEN AND EQUALITY UNIT
Dedicated to promoting a 'vision of equality and opportunity for all'. Politics aside, the site provides useful information on how government policies impact on women's lives, covering hot

Aimed at Women

The Good Web Site Guide's Top 10s
of the Internet

1. **www.handbag.com** – apparently the most useful place for women on the internet
2. **www.bbc.co.uk/radio4/womanshour** – excellent magazine spin off
3. **www.healthywomen.org** – get healthy, get informed
4. **www.journeywoman.com** – safe travel resource
5. **www.womengamers.com** – for a great selection of games
6. **www.ivillage.co.uk** – a great magazine site
7. **www.bintmagazine.com** – irreverent e-zine that takes no prisoners
8. **www.fashionangel.com** – all the fashion links you'll ever need
9. **www.womanmotorist.com** – proving that cars aren't just for men to enjoy
10. **http://shinyshiny.tv** – a girl's guide to gadgets

topics such as encouraging women to become more involved in public life, balancing work and family, domestic violence, money, health and equal opportunities. Worth visiting for the useful links. For information on what the UN is doing to promote gender equality go to **www.un.org/womenwatch** where there is information on all their initiatives and international treaties. A dry but informative read.

www.eoc.org.uk   UK
EQUAL OPPORTUNITIES COMMISSION
Know your rights by checking here about sex discrimination in the workplace, sexual stereotyping in education or work, the legalities of part-time work, maternity leave, etc. A useful resource although not very user-friendly.

www.womensaid.org.uk   UK
UNTIL WOMEN AND CHILDREN ARE SAFE
Excellent site aimed at helping women (and children) cope with

W

domestic violence. As you'd expect, there are plenty of links and help for anyone in distress.

See also:
www.onlinewomeninpolitics.org – aimed at Asian Pacific women, but interesting global perspective on women.
www.now.org – The National Organisation for Women.
www.poptel.org.uk/women-ww – dedicated to supporting the rights of women workers world-wide.
www.wen.org.uk – the Women's Environmental Network campaigns and educates on environmental matters.

Working Women

www.everywoman.co.uk   UK
NOT JUST FOR BUSINESS WOMEN
A really useful site aimed at women business owners, but the 'home' channel provides sound information on personal finance, family and well-being for all women.

www.womenatwork.co.uk   UK
DIRECTORY OF WOMEN IN BUSINESS
If you want to support local women in business, search the site for self-employed freelancers, consultants, home workers, tradeswomen or women running small businesses in your area. If you're one of those women, join here for networking and support.

See also:
www.busygirl.co.uk – a more serious site than the name suggests, their aim is to advance women by supporting the business and career needs of women.
www.ivillage.co.uk/workcareer – useful advice and information on a range of employment issues for women.
www.scottishbusinesswomen.com – a good community site aimed at business women in Scotland.
www.the-bag-lady.co.uk – international women's trading portal with plenty of information and links for those in business.

Women and Their Families

Information on divorce, separation and family relationships is found on page 380.

www.fulltimemothers.org   UK
FOR FULL-TIME MUMS
This organisation aims to promote the status of stay-at-home
mums and campaign for changes in taxation, the benefit system
and employment policy to give women more choice. There is
also information on how to join a local group, or set one up. See
also **www.netmums.com** while for the working mother's
perspective see **www.workingmother.com** a campaigning
e-zine for working mothers from the US and
www.motheratwork.co.uk a very useful e-zine for British
mothers.

See also:
www.matchmothers.org – self-help support site for mothers
separated from their children for whatever reason. There is
useful information for all, but you need to join to get the most out
of it.
www.mothers35plus.co.uk – support and information for older
mothers.
www.mumsnet.com – a rather advert-laden site devoted to
product reviews with advice and tips thrown in. You have to
subscribe to get the best of it.
www.thebritishsecondwivesclub.co.uk – support for second
wives and the problems they face.
www.womensaid.org.uk – national charity working to end
domestic violence against women and children.

Women Students

www.womanstudent.co.uk   UK
FOR WOMEN IN HIGHER EDUCATION
Loads of information for UK and international students with
sections on money and careers, travel, health, leisure and
universities. There is a helpful section for overseas women
planning to come to British Universities.

Magazines

www.handbag.com   UK
THE ISP FOR WOMEN
Described as the most useful place on the Internet for British
women, Handbag lives up to that with a mass of information
written in an informal style and aimed at helping you get through

W

life. There's shopping and competitions too. For some it's a little too commercial though.

www.ivillage.co.uk UK

WHERE WOMEN FIND ANSWERS

All the sections you'd expect in a women's magazine, the difference here is that they are trying, and succeeding, to create a community with a range of message boards, advice, a good section on work, even a dating service. Alternatively, visit MSN's Women's Channel at **www.msn.co.uk/womens**

www.bintmagazine.com UK
ALWAYS A PLEASURE

An irreverent weekly that strives to turn the word bint into something better than its regular usage. It's fun, controversial and no prisoners are taken.

www.blackwomen.co.uk UK
THE VOICE OF BLACK WOMEN

A serious magazine-style site which in addition provides a list of services targeted at Black women living in the UK. For the 'interactive magazine aimed at women of colour' visit **www.preciousonline.co.uk**

www.asianamag.com
ASIANA

All the usual features of a women's magazine written for Asian women. There are a number of forums, a wedding directory and an online shop, which serves mainly to sell back issues of the magazine. For a more tabloid magazine go to **www.asianimage.co.uk** which, although aimed at the Northwest, has some interesting and useful articles.

www.mookychick.co.uk UK
THE ALTERNATIVE VOICE

A light-hearted, spirited e-zine for younger women with many of the usual features but written with a distinctive voice. In addition there's a section on 'tek stuff', action and travel, spirit, blogs, forums, quizzes and more.

www.bbc.co.uk/radio4/womanshour UK
WOMAN'S HOUR

An excellent magazine spin-off from the popular Radio 4 programme, you can listen to programmes, have your say and go

www.womenwelcomewomen.org.uk   UK

CIRCLE OF FRIENDSHIP

With 2,500 members in 70 countries, the aim is to foster international friendship and understanding by enabling women from different countries to visit one another. Members range in age from teens to over eighties and visit each other's homes as individuals or as part of organised gatherings.

See also:

www.christinecolumbus.com – travel tips for women plus the opportunity to share the experiences of other women.

www.goodadventure.com – opportunities for adventurous travel with other active women.

www.wildroseholidays.co.uk – holidays for single women in the UK and overseas.

Leisure and the Arts

www.wsf.org.uk   UK

WOMEN'S SPORT FOUNDATION

The voice of women's sport is committed to improving and promoting opportunities for women and girls in sport at every level. It does this by lobbying and raising the awareness of the importance of women in sport to the organisers and governing bodies. Here you can find out how to get involved or get help.

www.womengamers.com   US

BECAUSE WOMEN DO PLAY

The aim is to provide a selection of reviews and games geared specifically to a female audience (although it doesn't stop this being an enjoyable site for men to visit). It has up-to-the-minute reviews, really well-written articles, lots of content and high-quality design.

www.womeninmusic.org.uk   US

WOMEN IN MUSIC

If you're a musician be it classical, jazz, folk or hip hop, then you'll find support and encouragement here. It seems particularly good for women composers. There's a very good 'what's on' section, one on competitions, links and a forum.

W

www.pinknoises.com   UK
PROMOTING WOMEN'S MUSIC
Giving women a voice in the male-dominated international
electronic music scene by providing music, profiles of artists,
review, essays, a message board and comprehensive links. Truly
international in the artists it features and an invaluable resource
for women DJs and electronic music freaks.

www.nmwa.org   US
NATIONAL MUSEUM FOR WOMEN IN THE ARTS
Take a tour of this New York-based museum dedicated to women
artists. They have paintings and artefacts dating from the 16th
century up to the present day with a reasonable collection
available to view online. The shop is tempting, but remember
delivery from the US is expensive.

http://digital.library.upenn.edu/women   US
A CELEBRATION OF WOMEN WRITERS
A site with a passion for the work of women writers; the quality
and quantity of information on this site is tremendous with
links to biographical and bibliographical information about
women writers as well as providing complete books written by
women.

For other sites on women's arts see:
http://web.ukonline.co.uk/n.paradoxa – feminist art journal
with good links to artists and women's art associations.
http://womenwriters.net/links.htm – a guide to Internet
resources as well as book reviews and features.
www.blackwomenart.org.uk – dedicated to black women in
fashion, design, crafts and the performing arts.
www.society-women-artists.org.uk – join the Society of Women
Artists, learn about their annual exhibition and see some of the
exhibits.
www.the-womens-press.com – publishers of incisive feminist
writing.

History

*We haven't found a brilliant, comprehensive site, but the following are
interesting on women in history:*

http://womenshistory.about.com – About.com's pages, good on
suffrage and has a good women's history picture gallery.

www.bbc.co.uk/history/society_culture/women – once again, the BBC offers one of the best online resources including some good interactive material.

www.distinguishedwomen.com – biographies and information on women's impact on history.

www.greatwomen.org – the US National Women's Hall of Fame, biographies of women who have made a difference.

www.lothene.demon.co.uk – Scottish women warriors from the 9th to the 18th century (with a lot of information about porridge!).

www.thewomenslibrary.ac.uk – an extensive collection of archives on women's history with some now available electronically. You can also see the catalogue and book a visit to the reading room.

www.womeninworldhistory.com – an limited educational site, but some good information.

Miscellaneous

http://shinyshiny.tv   UK
A GIRL'S GUIDE TO GADGETS
A fun blog which catalogues, gadgets and gifts that have particular appeal to women. The authors have great taste and the stuff featured is mostly gorgeous and desirable whoever you are.

www.hintsandthings.co.uk   UK
PEARLS OF WISDOM
Not strictly for women, but it features serious hints and tips on such things as not losing your children, bank statements and computer viruses, but also some tongue-in-cheek information on the rules of cricket and what to do with unwanted CDs. It's a good place to visit for a coffee break.

www.girlsstuff.co.uk   UK
GIFTS GALORE
Loads of silly gifts that you didn't know you wanted and certainly don't need.

W

Stop Press

Due to it's topicality, we've decided to devote our Stop Press section to some of the great sites and programs you can find on Web 2.0. This new aspect of the Internet allows you to use common programs online rather than as an application based on one computer. Using Web 2.0, you can access your work from anywhere and share it, rather than send attachments via e-mail.

Here are some of the most useful programs and sites . . .

www.writely.com – probably the most high profile site on Web 2.0. It offers a fully functioning word processor, which is a good blogging tool. We also found the flexibility of **www.ajaxwrite.com** very impressive.
www.box.net – is an excellent place to store your digital photos safely and a good alternative to the leading site **www.flickr.com**

*There are some great programs designed to keep yourself up to date and well organised, the best being the comprehensive **www.backpackit.com** For listings try **www.tadalist.com** while **www.kiko.com** is an excellent calendar application. **http://voo2do.com** appears to be a great combination of all these things.*

*If it's online data storage you want, then Web 2.0 is the place for you; our particular favourite is **http://openomy.com** which is currently free. See also **http://xdrive.com** and **http://allmydata.com***

*One aspect of Web 2.0 to keep an eye on is gaming and gambling, check out **www.millionsofgames.com** which is under development (in the beta phase) and you can see the potential.*

*One of my favourites of the new sites is **www.protopage.com** which basically allows you to create new feeds, notes and permanent links to your home pages. An advantage of this is that you don't have to be limited by what your ISP wants you to see.*

This is just the start of a revolution in 'live' programs and systems available through Web 2.0. Next year I can see a large section of the book devoted to applications such as these.

Index